SOUTH
PACIFIC

FODOR'S TRAVEL PUBLICATIONS

are complied, researched, and edited by an international team of travel writer, field correspondents, and editors. The series, which now almost covers the globe, was founded by Eugene Fodor in 1936.

OFFICES
New York & London

Fodor's South Pacific

Editor: Kathleen McHugh
Area Editors: Lois Brett, John Campbell, Kathleen Hancock, Marael Johnson, Graeme Kennedy, Sandy MacDonald, Jan Prince, Jennifer Pringle-Jones
Drawings: Sandra Lang
Maps: Pictograph
Cover Photograph: Stephen Frink/The WaterHouse Inc.

Cover Design: Vignelli Associates

Fodor's 89

SOUTH PACIFIC

Reprinted from *Fodor's Australia, New Zealand, The South Pacific 1989*

FODOR'S TRAVEL PUBLICATIONS, INC.
New York & London

ISBN 0–679–01698–8

MANUFACTURED IN THE UNITED STATES OF AMERICA
10 9 8 7 6 5 4 3 2

CONTENTS

FOREWORD

For hundreds of years people have dreamed of the South Seas—the white-sand beaches, blue waters, glorious flowers, warm people. *Fodor's South Pacific* is designed to help you plan your own trip to Paradise, based on your time, your interests, your budget, your idea of what this trip should be. Perhaps having read this guide you'll have some new ideas. We have, therefore, tried to offer you the widest range of activities and within that range selections that will be safe, worthwhile, and of good value. The descriptions we provide are designed to help you make your own intelligent choices from among our selections.

The first section of this book Facts at Your Fingertips, consists of material designed to help you plan your trip, providing you with general information on what sorts of activities and amenities are available as well as useful facts such as necessary travel documents, time zones, and the like.

Next is an introduction to help you with the background of the area: some history, the people and their way of like, and so on.

Following the introduction comes the detailed descriptions of the islands. All islands are first broadly described; following is the Practical Information to help you explore each place: how to get to the islands, hotels, restaurants, tours, and more.

While every care has been taken to ensure the accuracy of the information contained in this guide, the publishers cannot accept responsibility for any errors which may appear.

All prices quoted in this guide are based on those available to us at the time of writing. In a world of rapid change, however, the possibility of inaccurate or out-of-date information can never be totally eliminated. We trust, therefore, that you will take prices quoted as indicators only, and will double-check to be sure of the latest figures.

Similarly, be sure to check all opening times of museums and galleries. We have found that such times are liable to change without notice, and you could easily make a trip only to find a locked door.

When a hotel closes or a restaurant produces a disappointing meal, let us know, and we will investigate the establishment and the complaint. We are always ready to revise our entries for the following year's edition should the facts warrant it.

Send your letters to the editors of Fodor's Travel Publications, 201 E. 50th Street, New York, NY 10022. European readers may prefer to write to Fodor's Travel Publications, 30–32 Bedford Square, London WC1B 3SG.

PLANNING YOUR TRIP

DEFINING THE AREA. This book covers many of the islands of Oceania, which are divided into three main groups: Melanesia in the southwest, Micronesia in the northwest, and Polynesia—all islands east of the International Date Line and a few islands west of it. We have selected for this guide the most tourist-oriented of the South Pacific islands. Polynesia, the largest group in this book, made up of: Cook Islands, French Polynesia (popularly called *Tahiti*), the Samoas, Tonga, and Niue. Melanesia is Fiji, New Caledonia, Papua New Guinea, Solomon Islands, and Vanuatu (formerly the New Hebrides). The islands of Kiribati and Tuvalu (former-ly Gilbert and Ellice Islands) and Wallis and Futuna are in the Micronesian group. All but French Polynesia and American Samoa exist as independent countries.

Many of the islands are lush in plant life, and coconut palm flourishes most every-where. Rainfall varies from a few inches to several hundred inches a year.

Historians believe that most of the people of the South Pacific crossed land brid-ges from Asia to Indonesia, and then skilled navigators sailed their canoes to the islands of the Pacific. The sea skills of the South Pacific islanders are as dramatic today as they were when their ancestors roamed the Pacific.

There are no big cities in the South Pacific islands and though life isn't exactly as it was in the stories of Melville or Michener—or even in the Rodgers and Ham-merstein musical *South Pacific*—the idyllic setting is the same and the people are just as friendly and hospitable. The South Pacific islanders are people in the world who are most comfortable with their environment. It's not a matter of going native when you are there, but learning to come to grips with the islands' nature. There is no sense of urgency in the South Pacific; it is a place in which one learns to relax. The seasoned traveler should take less than five minutes to settle down on arrival; this is the advice offered to the first timer.

VISITORS' INFORMATION. All of the islands in this book maintain official information bureaus. However, the South Pacific is shy of tourist offices in the Unit-ed States and most of them are either on the West Coast or in Hawaii. Many do have offices in either New Zealand or Australia. The fastest way to get information is to cable or telex. They will respond as soon as mail is received but service is slow. When requesting information, be sure to ask about special holidays and events in the country you plan on visiting—some are worth scheduling a whole holiday around if you plan well in advance. Also, if you have a special interest, it is worth making an inquiry.

Addresses of the official tourist information bureaus in the South Pacific Islands are listed below, as well as some other offices where you may obtain further details. All addresses, telephones and telexes subject to change.

American Samoa. *Economic Development Tourism Office American Samoa Govt.*, Box 1147, Pago Pago, American Samoa 96799; telephone: (684) 633–5181; telex: 782501. *Government of American Samoa Office of Tourism,* 300 Ala Moana Blvd., Suite 1106–A, Honolulu, HI; telephone: (808) 545–7451. 1071 Victoria Rd., West Ryde, NSW, Australia; telephone: (02) 85–2040.

Cook Islands. *Cook Islands Tourist Authority,* Box 14, Rarotonga, Cook Islands; telephone: 29435; cable: Cooktour. Box 3647, Auckland, New Zealand; telephone: (09) 79–4314; telex: NZ21419. Box R177, Sydney, NSW 2000, Australia; telephone: (02) 32–7226; telex: 70655. Elsewhere: Information from any office of *Air New Zea-land* or *Polynesian Airlines.*

Fiji. *Fiji Visitors Bureau,* GPO Box 92, Thomson Street, Suva; telephone: 22867; cable: Tourist Fiji; telex: FJ2180. Box 9217, Nadi Airport, Nadi; telephone 232–3277; cable: Fiji Tour. 38 Martin Pl., Sydney, NSW, 2000; telephone: 231–4251; telex: 72585; 7/F 100 William St., Suite 6, Sydney, NSW 2011; tele-phone: 358–405; telex 75548. 6151 W. Century Blvd., Suite 524, Los Angeles, CA 90045; telephone: (213) 417–2234 and (800) 621–9604; telex: 759972.

Kiribati. *Kiribati Visitors Bureau, Ministry of Natural Resources Development,* Box 64, Bairiki, Tarawa, Republic of Kiribati, Central Pacific; telephone: 21075; cable: Resources Tarawa; telex: 77039.

New Caledonia. *Office Territorial du Tourisme de Nouvelle Caledonia,* BP 688 25 Avenue du Marechal Foch, Noumea, New Caledonia; telephone: 272632; telex: 3063. 8th floor, BNP Bldg., 12 Castlereagh St., Sydney, NSW 2000, Australia; telephone: (02) 231–5244. *UTA French Airlines,* 11 Commerce St., Auckland, New Zealand; telephone: (09) 31–229; telex: NZ2447.

Niue. *Niue Tourist Board,* Box 69, Alofi and *Niue Consular Office,* Samoa House, Karangahape Rd., Newton, Auckland, New Zealand.

Papua New Guinea. *Papua New Guinea National Tourist Office,* Box 7144, Boroko, Papua New Guinea; telephone: 25–1269; telex: 23472. *Air Niuguini–National Airline Papua New Guinea,* 5000 Birch, West Tower, Suite 3000, Newport Beach, CA 92660; telephone: (714) 752–5440; telex: 910–596–1501 NW PT BCH NPB.

Solomon Islands. Solomon Islands Tourist Authority, Box 321, Honiara, Solomon Islands; telephone: 22442; telex: 66436; cable: Tourists, Honiara.

Tahiti (French Polynesia). *Tahiti Tourist Board,* Box 65, Papeete, Tahiti; telephone: 689–429626; telex: 254. 12233 W. Olympic Blvd., Suite 110, Los Angeles, CA 90064; telephone: (213) 207–1919; telex: 4971603 JMB. B.N.P. Bldg., 12 Castlereagh St., Sydney, NSW 2000, Australia; telephone: (02) 235–0703; telephone: 235–0703; telex: 176246AA.

Tonga. *Tonga Visitors Bureau,* Box 37, Nuku'alofa, Kingdom of Tonga; telephone: 21733; telex: 66269; cable: Tourbureau. Vava'u Island: *Tonga Visitors Bureau,* Branch Vava'u Island, Box 18, Neiafu, Vava'u; telephone: 115. *Pacific Asia Auckland,* 15 Flavia Place, Lynfield, Auckland, New Zealand; telephone: (09) 31–149. *Tonga Visitors Bureau,* 35 Clarence, Sydney, NSW, Australia; telephone: (02) 29–8841.

Vanuatu. *Tourist Information Bureau,* Box 209, Port Vila. *Air Melanesiae,* Box 72, Port Vila, Vanuatu; telephone: 292753. *National Tourist Office of Vanuatu,* 14252 Culver Dr., Suite A316, Irvine, CA 92714; telephone: (714) 733–1744.

Western Samoa. *Western Samoa Department of Tourism,* Box 862, Apia, Western Samoa; telephone: 20471; cable: MALO; telex: 21SX. *Polynesian Airlines,* 9841 Airport Blvd., Suite 418, Los Angeles, CA 90045; telephone: (213) 642–7487.

The *Pacific Asia Travel Association (PATA)* is a non–profit corporation to promote and facilitate travel and tourism to and among Pacific destinations: PATA, 1 Montgomery St., Telesis Tower, Suite 1750, San Francisco, CA 94104; telephone: (415) 986–4646. Write for information on any of the Pacific Islands.

ENTRY REQUIREMENTS. A valid passport is required for all destinations in this book. For other requirements see Practical Information for the specific islands.

Health Certificates. In 1986, the *International Association for Medical Assistance to Travelers (IAMAT)* issued a release warning tourists of the malaria increase throughout the world, including many destinations in the South Pacific. This warning is still in effect. Chloroquine has been the usual treatment; however, in Papua New Guinea and the Solomon Islands, there is a resistance problem and visitors should consult their doctors for alternative medications. Malaria medication *must be continued for six weeks after leaving infected areas.* For IAMAT's free folder *How to Protect against Malaria,* which gives complete details about the disease, its control, and high-risk areas, write: IAMAT, 417 Center St., Lewiston, NY 14092. In Australia: 575 Bourke St., 12th Floor, Melbourne 3000. In Canada: 188 Nicklin Road, Guelph, Ontario N1H 7L5.

Other Medical Assistance Associations: *Worldcare Travel Assistance Association, Inc.* is staffed worldwide 24 hours a day by American physicians, nurses, and paramedics as well as a team of multilingual assistance coordinators. Worldcare provides immunizations, visa requirement information, medical assistance, evacuation, and hospitalization coverage, as well as immediate advances of funds for medical costs incurred abroad. If a member is hospitalized for more than 10 days, round-trip airfare and up to $1,000 living expenses is provided for minors if left unattended as a result of member's hospitalization. Individual and family memberships are available for any length of trip. For information write: 2000 Pennsylvania Ave. NW, Suite 7600, Washington, DC 20006, or call (202) 293–0335 or (800) 521–4822.

I.T.C. Travellers Assistance Ltd. This international group offers assistance service with coordination centers in 174 countries. Trained, local, multilingual personnel provide free medical aid 24 hours a day. Worldwide membership includes: free telephone access to any of eight ITC emergency control centers, all required medical assistance (ambulatory, hospitalization, prescribed medication, transportation); repatriation, free return tickets for children left unattended because of the member's hospitalization. Individual or family membership is available for any length of trip up to 180 days. Write the above: Box G-759, Station G, Calgary, Alberta, Canada T3A 2G6. Or call (403) 228–4685. Telex 03–825754.

The U.S. Department of Health and Human Services, Public Health Service Centers for Disease Control, Atlanta, GA 30333, makes the following suggestions for visitors to South Pacific destinations: gamma globulin, typhoid-tetanus: Two shots 30 days apart, if you've had no immunization before, or typhoid-tetanus booster and polio booster if it has been ten years since your last. *These are not requirements to enter these countries, but they are strongly recommended.* Please consult your physician. You may also wish to check with your doctor about the gamma globulin shot; because of the AIDS scare, some people have preferred not to take this shot. This is totally your decision, but it would be wise to have professional advice.

The health requirements of each island are in their Practical Information sections.

WHEN TO GO. There are only a few months during the year when the South Pacific islands are not balmy with cooling tradewinds. Usually May through October is best but because of the distances across the Pacific, each country has its own pattern. See individual chapters for details.

WHAT TO PACK. Women's clothing: Casual summer clothing—drip dry cotton or wash-and-wear are ideal. Light-weight skirts and blouses are practical. Shorts and bathing suits are worn on beaches, around pools, at private clubs, or homes, but never in public. South Pacific Islanders are very modest and appreciate your respecting their customs. In Tahiti and some of the other islands, the *pareau* (a single cloth worn as a wrap-around) can take the place of a dress and is worn from breakfast to dinner. At most, all you'll need are two dinner dresses, two pairs of shorts, blouses, a skirt, and a couple of bathing suits, sandals (for the beach), one pair of dress shoes, and a good pair of walking shoes. At international hotels, such as the Hyatt or Regent, women usually dress up for dinner. Consider saving some of your travel wardrobe money for a shopping spree in Tahiti or New Caledonia where you can buy items from France, Italy and London at the local boutiques.

Men's clothing: Casual clothing will be the most comfortable—lightweight slacks and an open neck, short-sleeve sport shirt. Neckties and very lightweight jackets may be worn in the evening. Two pairs of shorts, shirts, a couple of bathing suits, and a sweater are about all you'll need, plus walking shoes, sandals for the beach, and one pair of street shoes. Many men wear Bermuda shorts with long socks in the day.

Extras: Bring a tape recorder to bring back the sounds of the country and to enjoy while you are there. Don't forget medication for diarrhea (Lomotil), insect repellent, and your camera. Converter and adapter plugs for electric razor or hair dryer. Bring extra tapes, batteries for your tape recorder and camera, and lots of film—they're very expensive there. Remember you'll be in the tropics, so bring film that will adapt to the glare.

WHAT WILL IT COST? There is such a variety of hotels in the South Pacific that you can meet almost any budget. A few of the islands are very tourist oriented and have very sophisticated, international-class resorts—such as the Hyatt, Fijian, or Regent in Fiji, and the Tahara'a, Bali Hai, and Tahiti Beachcomber hotels in Tahiti. These hotels offer every possible amenity for from US $130 and up. For a little less (US $110–$130) you stay in an expensive property and have nearly as many extras as the deluxe hotels. However, there are many other hotels in the inexpensive (US $40–$75) and moderate (US $75–$110) ranges.

All other islands have hotels in the above ranges, but service and standards are a bit different. The Fiji and the Cook Islands perhaps offer the best bargains in the South Pacific, in the international class, not only due to the exchange rate, but because they offer many small hotel/motel units, complete with small kitchens at very reasonable prices—US $24–$40.

Where once it was expensive to stay in New Caledonia or Vanuatu because of the French influence, you can now stay at some of the nicest resorts in these countries for under US $50. The Samoas and Tonga are always bargains, perhaps because it takes a little planning to get there—but once you arrive, accommodations are so reasonable it's possible to stay a month for what it costs to stay a week at similar hotels elsewhere in the world.

Perhaps the most expensive island on which to stay is Papua New Guinea—but that is due to logistics. There, wherever you go, you usually have to fly in—as do the food and all the other amenities.

Typical Expenses for Two People

Room at moderate hotel or motel	US$50
Continental breakfast at hotel	7
Lunch at an inexpensive restaurant	10
Dinner at a moderately priced restaurant	30
Sightseeing tour*	35
	US$132

*This is a one time sightseeing charge. Most island communities can be seen in one organized tour, thereby cutting your average daily cost for two to under $100, especially if your accommodations are in the moderate range.

CRUISES: In 1989, as in preceding years, a large number of cruises will be offered to the South Pacific, so that you can sail from the West Coast, take segments of cruises, or take a cruise around a country's islands such as Fiji or Tahiti. Some examples:

Royal Viking Line, 750 Battery St., San Francisco, CA 94111, (800) 422–8000.

Princess Cruises, 2029 Century Park East, Los Angeles, CA 90067; outside California: (800) 421–0522; or call collect from within California (213) 553–1770.

Cunard Line Ltd., 555 Fifth Ave., New York, NY 10017; (800) 221–4770.

Society Expeditions Cruises, 3131 Elliott Ave., Suite 700, Seattle, WA 98121; (800) 426–7794.

The following offer weekly cruises around and to a number of islands within French Polynesia: *Windstar Sail Cruises,* 7205 NW 19th St., Suite 410, Miami, FL 33126; (305) 592–8008; toll-free in the U.S. (800) 258–SAIL, in Florida (800) 341–SAIL. *Exploration Holidays and Cruises,* 1500 Metropolitan Park Bldg., Olive Way at Boren Ave., Seattle, WA 98101; (206) 624–8551; (800) 426–0600. Cruises around Fiji: *Blue Lagoon Cruises Ltd.,* 6 Nuga Place, Marine Drive., Box 54, Lautoka, Viti Levu, Fiji; telephone: 63938; telex: FJ5282; cable: KAYCO. *South Seas Cruises Ltd.,* Box 718, Nadi, Fiji; telephone: 70144; telex: FJ5180.

INTER-ISLAND SHIPS. You may be able to schedule a number of unusual and different trips by checking out the ships that travel from port to port from the list below. Many ships travel between small islands carrying everything from chickens to light freight, mail and hearty, adventurous passengers. Write: *Bank Line,* 51 Pitt St., Sydney, NSW 2000, Australia; *Burns Philp and Company,* also at 51 Pitt St., Sydney, NSW 2000, Australia; *Nauru Pacific Line,* 80 Collins St., Melbourne, Victoria 3000, Australia. This type of travel is not for those in a hurry as much of the shipping schedule depends on the loading and unloading of cargo. One hazard is that you could be stranded on an idyllic South Sea island for an indefinite time! Contact the addresses below for additional inter-island boat trips.

American Samoa: *Government of American Samoa,* Office of Tourism, Pago Pago, American Samoa 96799.

Cook Islands: *Silk and Boyd Ltd.,* Box 131, Rarotonga.

Fiji: See "Cruises," above.

Kiribati: *The Gilbert Islands Shipping Corp.,* offers occasional service according to cargo requirements. For details write to *Kiribati Tourist Bureau,* Box 77, Bairiki, Tarawa, Republic of Kiribati (Central Pacific).

New Caledonia: Cruises to the coral reef and nearby islands; scheduled passenger service between Noumea and the Isle of Pines and Ile Ouen. Write: *Office Territorial du Tourisme de Nouvelle Caledonie,* BP 688, 25 Avenue du Marechal Foch, Noumea, New Caledonia.

Papua New Guinea: Cargo/passenger service between Madang and Lae is offered by *Lutheran Shipping M.V. Totol,* Box 789, Madang, Papua New Guinea. *Melanesian Tourist Services Pty. Ltd.,* Box 707, Madang, Papua New Guinea, or UNIREP through your travel agent, offers cruises on the *Melanesian Explorer.* (*Note:* It is not as easy to get passage on these small ships as it used to be but, if you are determined, your best bet would be to try to find passage on those ships leaving Rabaul rather than Port Moresby.)

Solomon Islands: The *Government Marine Department* runs scheduled and non-scheduled services and, like the commercial operators, carries a limited number of passengers. Write: *Solomon Islands Government,* Ministry of Transport & Communications, Marine Division, Box G22, Honiara, Solomon Islands, for information. *Solomon Islands Government,* Central Co-Operative Association, Commonwealth St., Box 151, Honiara, Solomon Islands, also offers transportation, as do *Ysabel Development Company,* Commonwealth St., Box 92, Honiara; *Melan-Chine Shipping Co.,* Box 71, Honiara; *Coral Seas Ltd.,* Commonwealth Street, Box 9, Honiara; *Saratoga Shipping Company,* off Commonwealth St., Box 611, Honiara, Solomon Islands.

Tuvalu Government (Ellice Islands): *Ministry of Communication & Transport,* Vaiaku, Funafuti, Tuvalu, Central Pacific. (There are no cabins—accommodations available on deck only. Be sure to have your own food and soft drinks; inflatable cushion and sleeping mat. This trip is for the very adventurous.)

Tahiti: See also "Cruises," above. There is scheduled ferry service from Papeete on the *Raromatai Ferry* which sails from Papeete to Huahine, Raiatea, Tahaa, Bora Bora, and returns via Raiatea, Huahine, Papeete. Rates vary according to destination and accommodation. Reservations through: *Immeuble Cowan,* Rue des Remparts Prolongee, Fare-Ute, Papeete, Tahiti; telephone: 43.90.42. There is also daily scheduled ferry service from Papeete to Moorea. For further information write the *Tahiti Tourist Promotion Board,* 12233 W. Olympic Blvd., Suite 110, Los Angeles, CA 90064.

Compagnie Francaise Maritime de Tahiti, BP 368, Papeete, Tahiti, Society Islands, offers inter-island service through the Society and Marquesas Islands. *Tahiti Yachting Arue Nautical Center,* BP 363, Papeete, offers 28- to 65-foot sailboats for rental on daily or weekly basis. Write for information and rates. Eight- and 14-day cruises aboard a 52-foot trimaran (*Espirit*) and a 46-foot ketch (*Roscop*) are offered by *Ocean Voyages,* 1709 Bridgeway, Sausalito, CA 94965; telephone: (415) 332–4681.

Tonga: The *Pacific Navigation Company* operates a local shipping service. Write: *Tonga Visitors Bureau.* Box 37, Nuku'alofa, Tonga; telephone: 21733; telex: 66269; cable: Tourbureau.

Western Samoa: Passenger/vehicle ferry service between Upolu and Savaii islands daily. The *Apia/Pago Pago Ferry* (passenger/car) leaves Apia (Western Samoa) Sundays, Tuesdays, and Thursdays at 10 P.M., and returns from Pago Pago (American Samoa) on Mondays, Wednesdays, and Fridays at 4 P.M. Takes approximately 6 hours. WS $12 per person. Bookings through *Western Samoa Shipping,* Matafele, Apia. Make your arrangements only after arrival in Samoa, and confirm well in advance. Prices and itineraries are subject to change.

HINTS TO MOTORISTS. Cars, *minimokes* (small jeep-type cars), motor scooters, and bicycles are available most everywhere and most are reasonably priced. Car rentals from *Budget* (800–527–0700), *Avis* (800–331–2112), or *Hertz* (800–654–3131), are usually available and reservations can be made by their international bureaus. It is sometimes possible to save money by renting your car on arrival through local companies, which do not have the overhead of the international firms. However, on some of the smaller islands, there are only a certain number of rental cars available, so you might consider making advance reservations.

There are several safety factors to consider when driving in the South Pacific. Slick surfaces during the rainy season and potholes can cause problems. Drivers should be aware of this situation, especially at night and when driving motorbikes.

Also, since there are no sidewalks in many of the island communities, drivers should be aware that local islanders use the roads as sidewalks day and night; there are few street lights.

HOTELS. Variety is the spice of life in the South Pacific. There's a place for every pocketbook, but you may discover a fine distinction between the sophisticated hotels of the major cities of the world and those in these island communities. Some of the islands, namely Fiji and Tahiti, have world-class hotels and resorts. The large resorts are plush and offer almost every amenity possible—usually golf, swimming, tennis courts, lawn bowling, fishing boats, snorkling, scuba diving, glass bottom boats, and water skiing equipment. Naturally, the larger the hotel, the more facilities offered. The best way to take advantage of these resorts is to look into trips offered by large tour operators. Try *Ted Cook's Islands in the Sun, Tahiti Nui's Island Dreams,* or air carriers such as *Air New Zealand* and *Qantas.* Check with your travel agent for savings offered through their air/hotel/drive packages. The advantage of the tour operators is that they usually have contracts with the larger resorts and, consequently, offer you quite a bargain.

The other islands have a cross between world class resorts and mom-and-pop-type hotels. Many of these smaller hotels/motels are usually run by retired couples who take special pride in their operation. Their hotels are comfortable and quite frequently offer all the comforts of home—a small kitchenette and utensils, a bed/sitting room, and private bath. Many have swimming pools, or are close to or on the beach. What they all have is amazingly low prices compared to the resort hotels.

Many of the small island hotels, while not considered resorts, will have some sport activities or access to nearby clubs. Large hotels frequently have travel tour desks. At the smaller establishments, proprietors are usually quite willing to assist in helping you discover the community.

On many of the small islands, you can rent self-contained cottages by the week or month—allowing you to do as you please and to find out just what getting away from it all really means. Just so you are not completely out of touch, there are usually other facilities nearby—restaurants, small grocery stores, swimming pools, and the ever-present white, sandy beach and palm trees.

Whichever island you're on, the atmosphere of most hotels will be enhanced by magnificent scenery. Your selection of hotel will depend upon how you want to discover these islands. The smaller islands, such as the Samoas, Tonga, or the Cooks, are unsophisticated and delightful, offering a chance to really meet the people and discover what Polynesia is all about.

One important point to remember is that service will vary with the climate. Learn to relax and don't expect the same rapid service you might receive in the United States. Enjoy the slow pace—whether at the dining table or awaiting room service. The climate and humidity will slowly catch up with you, and it will become easy to understand why service, regardless of how plush the hotel, takes just a little longer than in cooler destinations.

ROUGHING IT. There are some youth hostel type facilities in the South Pacific and a few of the islands have actual campsites. But very few! It is best to check with the tourist bureaus on arrival for details. There are no real campsites like those in the U. S. or Canada. And while it is quite possible to camp on your own, on some of the islands it is not encouraged. If you plan on staying in or near any of the small village communities, you must ask permission of the local chief.

HOME STAYS. It is possible to stay with local families on some of the islands. One of the easiest ways to get to know the people is to stay in some of the local boarding or guest houses. Names of these can usually be obtained from the tourist office and are generally quite inexpensive.

If you are determined to stay awhile (more than two or three days), and with a family, write to the tourist office and state your case. In most instances, they will respond but it is possible that some bureaus will not. Finding a family to stay with is less difficult once you are in the country, but it is more difficult to make arrangements by mail.

You should also be aware of certain customs concerning hospitality. On many of the islands, when you stay with a family, you are more than an honored guest, you become part of the family. You share everything they have and in return, you share everything you have. Usually something for the larder, or something that can be used by the whole family. Each island, each village, and each community has a different set of protocols. It is important you learn the customs of the country in order to avoid embarrassment on either side.

DINING OUT. All of the resort hotels in the South Pacific have good-to-excellent restaurants offering continental cuisine. The better the resort, the better your chances of finding an excellent internationally trained chef. In the smaller hotels, you will usually have to settle for less—but quite frequently you will be pleasantly surprised at the high quality. There is such a variety of food it would be impossible to describe specialties for all the countries in this book in a paragraph or two. Listed below, however, are some of the kinds of food that can be expected and the types of restaurant facilities available. Check each country's *Practical Information* section for particular ideas of where to dine.

American Samoa: Don't expect gourmet food here, although there are plenty of different types of dining establishments: from pizza parlors to Chinese restaurants. Try a *fia fia*—a Samoan feast that consists of suckling pig, chicken, fish, *pulusami* (young taro leaves cooked in coconut sauce), breadfruit, coconut, bananas, lime and mango. Guests sit cross-legged on straw mats and are entertained by Samoan singers and dancers.

Cook Islands: Restaurants and dining facilities on Rarotonga are limited. Most tourists eat at the hotels where they are staying although there are a few small restaurants and cafes around the town.

Fiji: It used to be that good food was available only at the few major hotels. Today, however, Fiji is opening up more quality resorts where you can dine alfresco—on international cuisine, complete with entertainment and a live band for dancing. In Suva there are a number of excellent restaurants serving everything from Chinese to Indian delicacies at reasonable prices. A few Fijian and Indian foods worth trying are: *kokoda*—a marinated local fish steeped in coconut cream and lime; *rourou*—special taro leaf dish; *kassava* (tapioca) is used in a variety of dishes and is boiled, baked, or grated and cooked in coconut cream with sugar and mashed bananas. An unusual vegetable is the asparagus-like *daruka,* (in season only during April and May).

Kiribati and Tuvalu: You will have to depend on your hotel for all meals unless you are adventurous and wish to sample the local food. There are no tourist restaurants. On Christmas Island, you can have a huge juicy lobster, or the fish you've just caught that day.

New Caledonia: You might suspect you are in France when you taste some of the outstanding French food throughout the country. But there is a great variety of other foods, too: Indonesian, Chinese, Indian, Spanish, Vietnamese. Take your pick. The *bougna,* a native feast, consists of roast pig, fish, or chicken wrapped in banana leaves and cooked on white-hot stones covered with sand.

Papua New Guinea: Beef and poultry from the Highlands, plus fresh vegetables and fruit are the choices you have in hotels and restaurants around the country. Seafood is delicious and you can dine on crab, prawns, crayfish, and barramundi. Papua New Guineans claim their local fruit—strawberries, pineapples, pawpaws, mangoes, passionfruit, bananas—are best buys.

Solomons: Except for those in the *Mendana Hotel* and the *Honiara Hotel,* there are few restaurants worth writing home about. However, 28 miles west of Honiara is the *Tambea Village Resort* that serves both Western and Chinese food. While you are exploring the country, it will be worth a stop off here for lunch or dinner, and do try the fresh fruits, vegetables, and seafood available.

Tahiti: You can dine on gourmet foods in the most elegant atmosphere. Or dine on the foods of Normandy and Brittany—such as frog legs or smoked salmon—for much less. Cheaper still, just for a few francs, you can buy the long, slender, delicious, crusty French bread—as fresh as the loaves you buy in Paris. Add a little cheese and some wine, then sit along the waterfront and watch the life of French Polynesia pass by. One reminder—your food budget here can go out of sight if you don't plan carefully.

Tonga: In addition to the dining rooms at the various hotels, the main street of Nuku'alofa has several small restaurants featuring Tongan food such as *'ufi* (a large white yam), taro, or *lu pulu* (meat and onions, marinated in coconut milk and baked in taro leaves in an underground oven). If you want to enjoy an evening out with music, dancing, and special entertainment, try a Tongan feast of roast suckling pigs, crayfish, chicken, with local fruits and vegetables, all cooked in an underground oven. For something special, try some of Tonga's huge avocados—with some cheese and bread you can make yourself a marvelous picnic lunch.

Vanuatu: The best restaurants are French and located in the hotels (mostly in Vila) or on the island resorts. All hotels in Santo have restaurants. Many cafes in Vila have French, Chinese, Vietnamese, and European menus. You can also find pizza and spaghetti.

Wallis and Futuna: Don't count on anything fancy here, not even in your hotel—which probably will be the only place where you will eat.

Western Samoa: *Aggie Grey's Hotel,* the *Hideaway Beach Resort,* and the *Hotel Tusitala* serve the best of Samoan and Western meals. The *fia fia* in Western Samoa is the same feast as in American Samoa (see above).

DRINKING WATER. Generally speaking, the water in most of the South Pacific islands is safe to drink in the major areas and capital cities. If there is a question about the local water, you will usually find bottled water in your hotel room and in the dining room. However, in the outlying areas on *all* the islands only drink bottled water.

In Tahiti most tourists seem to have problems with the water, so take a local tip, and drink bottled mineral water wherever you are.

If you are heading for remote areas, you might take a supply of water purification tablets, available in most drug stores. They may make water taste peculiar, but at least render it potable.

If you plan on driving long distances, it is wise to take bottled water with you.

LIQUOR LAWS. Except for Tahiti, which follows French custom, you will not find many bars in the South Pacific. Tourists usually do their drinking at their hotels or resorts. Only a few of the small hotels have liquor licenses, so if you are planning to stay in one of them you may want to have your own liquor supply. Where there are pubs, hours will vary from island to island; all close on Sunday, when most of the towns shut down. Tourist hotels are exempt from this and visitors can usually get drinks at their own hotels as long as the bars are open. Restaurants must have licenses to serve alcohol. You do not take your own bottle to restaurants like in Australia or New Zealand. Alcohol is sold in licensed bottle shops and frequently in food shops.

TIPPING. Tipping is a very touchy subject in the South Pacific. It is one place in the world where you can usually keep your hand in your pocket—except for very exceptional services. It is important you consider the feelings of the islanders and honor their custom of no tipping.

Tahiti has made this a big issue. When you arrive at the airport, you'll find signs advising you of the no tipping policy—as it is "contrary to the Tahitian tradition and idea of hospitality." This custom follows throughout the islands in this book.

BUSINESS HOURS AND LOCAL TIME. Business hours vary quite a bit from island to island. One thing they have in common, however, is that most stores will close for the noon hour—which can actually be several hours. Most village markets open quite early and close early in the afternoon.

Throughout the South Pacific, Sunday or the Sabbath is taken very seriously. *Nothing*—that is, next to nothing—will be open. This frequently means restaurants, bars, and theaters. So, plan on enjoying your hotel, or taking a picnic lunch to some scenic spot on that day. However, all resort hotels and some of the smaller hotels are open. The town areas will be deserted and the streets will just about be empty. Islanders take advantage of the Sabbath and spend the day in church and with their families.

SPORTS. It is obvious with all the water and beach in the South Pacific, that any sport remotely connected with the two is extremely popular—and there are many experts to help you to swim, water ski, sail, fish, surf, snorkel, skin and scuba dive.

However, sports activities are by no means limited to water. Golf, yachting, tennis, fishing, horseback riding, lawn bowling are all available. The climate is most conducive to play, and in the South Pacific islands you'll find a lot of action—whether participant or spectator.

American Samoa. Fishing, snorkeling, surfing, swimming, tennis, golf, skin diving, scuba diving, yachting, cricket. Deep sea fishing is very popular and the surrounding waters provide a variety of game. Marlin is one of the most exciting catches.

Cook Islands. Fishing, golf, horseback riding, lawn bowling, sailing, skin diving.

Fiji. Fishing, lawn bowling, scuba and skin diving, and golf—two good 18-hole courses: one in Suva and the other in Pacific Harbor.

Kiribati. Lobster and big-game fishing. Many people from Hawaii and elsewhere fish and fast-freeze their catch to take home. Hawaii is only a 3-hour flight away.

New Caledonia. Cricket, horseback riding, snorkeling, spear fishing, squash, swimming, tennis, water skiing. Cricket is played by both men and women. Women wear bright colored Mother Hubbards (*muumus*) and men wear lava-lava wraparounds. Some championship tennis courts available. Try the French-style *petanque* game of bowls, similar to that played in the South of France.

Papua New Guinea. Bush walking, game fishing, golf, horseback riding, sailing, scuba diving, squash. The Youth Hostels Association organizes monthly walks, and has bi-monthly meetings. Papua Yacht Club welcomes visitors. Sailing season begins late April. Excellent scuba diving in the area around Madang.

Tahiti. Fishing, golf, horse racing and riding, scuba diving, swimming, tennis, yachting. Horse racing at Hippodrome in Pirae. This is considered a great social event—betting is pari-mutuel, but payoffs are small. *Club Mou-Tahiti,* Papeete, provides information and assistance for climbs of Mt. Acrai, with a shelter at 5900 feet, and of Mts. Orohena and Diademe. For boaters there are a number of yacht clubs in Tahiti, and visitors are welcome.

Tonga. Boating, fishing, horseback riding, skin diving, swimming.

Vanuatu. Fishing, golf, skin diving, squash. Perhaps most unusual are the Pentecost land divers. Arrangements to see the world-famous divers can be made through the Tourist Information Bureau. Men dive from a 70-foot tower with vines attached to their ankles to break their fall just before touching the ground.

Western Samoa. Boating, cricket, fishing, golf, horse racing, lawn bowling, skin diving, swimming, tennis. Boxing matches are held weekly, July–December.

MAIL. Mail to and from the island communities varies a great deal, so prepare well in advance if you are planning to use the mail for any reason. The main post office may also serve as the cable office and the telephone exchange. In many instances you may want or need to make your overseas calls from there. Usual post office hours are from 8 A.M. to 4:30 P.M., but hours vary from island to island. A few are open on Saturday from 8 to 11 A.M. Mail boxes are few, except in the main cities. Aerograms and post cards from the South Pacific average about 50 U.S. cents mailed to North America.

ELECTRIC CURRENT. The current is different than in North America. In fact it varies to such a degree that it is wise to carry a mini-converter. This device converts 220V foreign current into 110V domestic. The wall outlet is different from North American and European outlets. Most South Pacific outlets take a 3-prong flat plug: the 2 prongs at the top are set at an angle. (The set of adapter plugs you have at home may not work here.) Most hotels have 110V outlets for razors.

While American appliances work on 60 cycles and most foreign systems use 50 cycles, there may be a slight slowdown but no harm to your equipment. (Exceptions are hi-fi equipment and clocks.) If you're staying in a large international hotel, they will probably be able to supply you with an electrical converter and adapter plug for all your small appliances. Otherwise, get them before you leave home—they are not available on the islands.

The Franzus Co. (Murtha Industrial Park, Railroad Ave., Beacon Falls, CT 06403) sells a travel pack that has a converter and all the plugs needed for foreign travel. Write for information and a list of the type of equipment you may need.

TELEPHONES. All hotels catering to the international tourist have telephone service. And, in many instances, costly surcharges can be added on international calls placed from a guest's room. These fees can vary from country to country, and from hotel to hotel within a country. In most instances, rates are not published, so be sure to ask before you place your call. Many of the smaller hotels may have only the owner's personal telephone. In that case, go to the Overseas Telephone Office, usually located in the local post office.

There are coin-operated phone booths in some of the larger cities. Once you are away from the major tourist spots, telephone service in the outlying areas is almost non-existent; don't count on phone booths along the roadway.

Phone service to North America can take awhile in some communities, so be prepared. Below are the international country codes for the islands and some notes on service.

American Samoa. Country code: 684. Coin-operated booths in Pago Pago. Telephone service available at major hotels. Limited service elsewhere.

Cook Islands. Country code: 682. Major hotels have room telephone service. Limited service elsewhere.

Fiji. Country code: 679. Coin-operated booths in Suva. All major tourist hotels have room telephone service. Limited service elsewhere.

Kiribati. Country code: 686. Limited service throughout country.

New Caledonia. Country code: 687. Coin-operated phones in major areas. Telephone room service at major hotels.

Papua New Guinea: Country code: 675. Public telephones in Port Moresby. Telephone service in major hotels. Limited in outlying areas.

Solomon Islands. Country code: 677. Available at international hotel but very limited elsewhere.

Tahiti. Country code: 689. Most tourist hotels have room telephone service. Limited service elsewhere.

Tonga. Country code: 676. Limited service throughout the country. Telephone room service available at some tourist hotels.

Vanuatu. Country code: 678. Some public phones available. Major hotels have room telephone service.

Western Samoa. Country code: 685. Tourist hotels have telephone service but there is limited service elsewhere in the country.

To dial direct to the Pacific Area from the United States, on the AT&T system, dial: 011 (International Access Code) plus the country code (see above), plus the city code, if any, plus the local number. After dialing the entire number, please allow at least 45 seconds for the ring to start. Many islands, such as Kiribati, Wallis, and Futuna, do not have direct dialing and you may have to place your call through an operator in Sydney, Australia—in which case your call can take anywhere from ten minutes to three hours.

MEDICAL TREATMENT. You will never be far from medical attention, but it will vary a great deal from island to island. There are no large medical centers.

THE
SOUTH PACIFIC

THE PACIFIC WAY

An Introduction to the South Pacific

by
GRAEME KENNEDY

Graeme Kennedy is a feature writer for the Auckland Star *specializing in aviation and travel—especially the South Pacific Islands.*

Let's get one thing straight, right from the start. The South Pacific is not Paradise.

Those who believe the South Pacific is heaven on earth—and there are millions who do—are excused, for this is totally understandable. For almost five centuries, Europeans have returned from the Pacific with tales of friendly and handsome men and women inhabiting enchanted islands with warm blue lagoons, miles of white powdery sand, palm trees whispering in the trade winds, mystical green-jungled peaks, rainbowed waterfalls, brilliant birdlife, and flowers with perfumes that overwhelm the senses.

All this is, of course, perfectly true. There is barely an island which does not fulfill the promise. Whether a towering volcanic peak or a gemlike coral atoll only feet above sea-level, the South Pacific isles are unique in their warmth, their vivid color, and their slower, gentler pace.

For close to a century writers have seduced us with stories from these islands, stories of adventure, mystery, and romance to send the mind wandering through dreams of, yes, Paradise. Rupert Brooke wrote lovingly and poetically of the South Pacific; Robert Louis Stevenson continues to enchant millions of youngsters with his classic *Treasure Island* (although

13

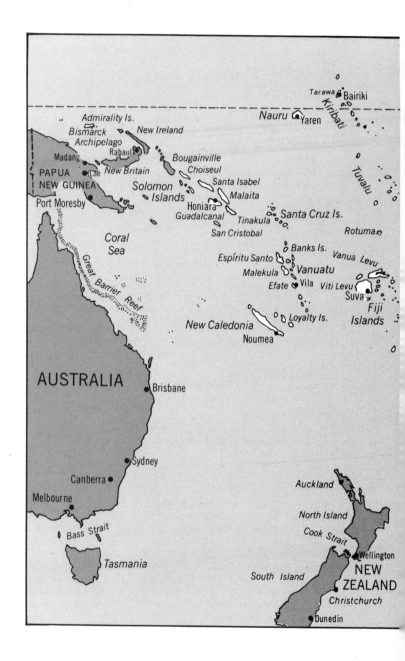

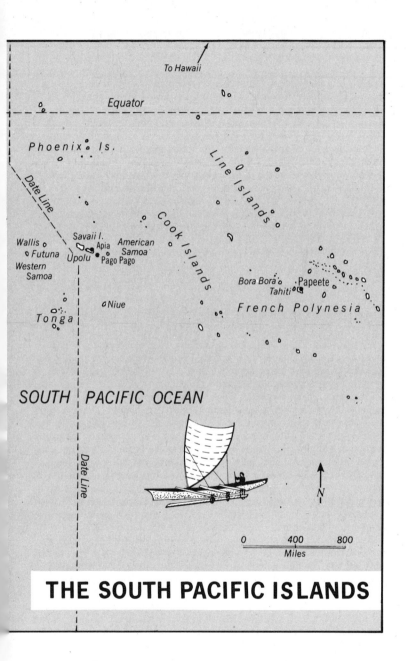

To Hawaii

Equator

Phoenix Is.

Date Line

Line Islands

Cook Islands

Wallis
Futuna
Western
Samoa

Savaii I.
Apia
Upolu
American
Samoa
Pago Pago

Bora Bora
Tahiti
Papeete

French Polynesia

Niue

Tonga

SOUTH PACIFIC OCEAN

Date Line

N

0   400   800
Miles

THE SOUTH PACIFIC ISLANDS

he wrote it in misty Scotland, years before he ever set eyes on a coconut palm); Herman Melville's *Typee, Omoo,* and the classic *Moby Dick* will be read as long as there are books; Frisbee is known for his sensitive prose about the Pacific; and Louis Becke's dozens of short stories present a harsher, sometimes savage, reality of island life. Who has not read James A. Michener's *Tales of the South Pacific* or *Return to Paradise?* Who has been able to ignore those anonymous men and women of Pacific literature—the writers of tourist brochures which decorate every travel agency? These are the people who invite us to travel to these magic lands, to sun, swim, surf, dive, sail, canoe, scuba, snorkel, eat, drink, dance, laugh, love, and enjoy, enjoy, enjoy the South Pacific.

And how easy that is today. For the price of an air ticket and a hotel room, anyone can have a lagoon at the doorstep, surf thundering on the reef a mile out, the trades in the palms overhead, warm sand sifting between the toes, the heady smell of flowers, and the warmth of a tropical sun.

After World War II the military's great advances in aviation technology spilled over to the airline industry and long-range commercial air travel for the first time carried leisure-seeking affluents on holidays abroad. The South Pacific did not miss out on the travel boom. DC4s and DC6s, Constellations, then jets created a huge new industry for the islands—first in Hawaii, then Tahiti and on to Fiji to gradually spread throughout almost all of the quiet, untouched South Pacific.

And with the jets came the hotels, first on the main islands, then on the smaller groups—the Beachcomber and Tahara's on Tahiti, the Grand Pacific in Suva, Tanoa and Gateway at Nadi, Pago's Rainmaker, Aggie Grey's in Apia. Club Meds, Ibises, Sofitels, Regents, Sheratons, Hyatts, and dozens of local enterprises sprang from the beaches, the mountaintops, and beside the fabled lagoons. They all employed native people, the tourist infrastructure went deep into the economy, and the smiling faces of Tahitians, Fijians, Samoans, Cook Islanders, Tongans, and Nieuans became synonymous with the ultimate holiday experience.

Restaurants, bars, nightclubs, and car, yacht, motorcycle, and boat rental companies proliferated. Sightseeing and tour companies channeled visitors to the best the islands have to offer—and usually it was the local people who managed and ran these exciting new enterprises. In doing so they discovered an important fact. They themselves were just as important an attraction as the lagoons and reefs and sand and palms—a reason visitors came to the islands. Europeans and North Americans alike wanted to share a time, if only brief, with these laughing, gentle, and hospitable people they had read so much about.

Ferdinand Magellan, of course, knew nothing of this when he became the first European to enter the great ocean in 1520. He took six months to cross the Pacific—which he named for its serenity—and was killed when he reached the Philippines, failing to become the first man to sail around the world.

In those days of the great Spanish and Portuguese navigators, brave adventurers followed the ill-fated Magellan across the Atlantic, around Cape Horn, and into the Pacific in the hope of finding a western route to the fabulous Spice Islands of the East Indies. The Pacific was simply somewhere on the way to somewhere else and, therefore, of little importance. Just four years after Magellan's death, Andres de Urdaneta of Spain sailed into the great ocean and went all the way to Indonesia without seeing a single island.

This is hardly surprising, as the Pacific's 64 million square miles cover one-third the earth's surface and its hundreds of islands are relatively tiny indeed.

Pedro de Quiros of Portugal had better luck in 1565. He was the first European to sight the atolls of the Tuamoto Archipelago and went on to discover the New Hebrides, now Vanuatu. He didn't bother to stop at either, as they were obviously not the Spice Islands, and it is presumed that he died without knowing what he missed.

Alvaro de Mendana de Nevra of Spain had his turn in 1567, discovering the Marquesas, the Santa Cruz Islands, and the Solomons—which he named for King Solomon's fabulously rich gold and diamond mines he thought were there.

Exploration of the South Pacific in the 17th century was notable for Dutch explorer Abel Janzoon Tasman's 1640s discovery of Tasmania, New Zealand, Tonga, and Fiji. But he didn't make a lot of fuss about it, as he was really searching for the mythical Great Southern Continent—which all men of science at the time were convinced had to exist to balance the land masses of the Northern Hemisphere.

Fellow Dutchman Jacob Roggeveen sailed into the South Pacific in 1722 to discover the Samoas and Easter Island and was followed 42 years later by Englishman Samuel Wallis, who was to find Tahiti and the island group northwest of Samoa which now bears his name. Many explorers and navigators left their wakes across the trackless Pacific in the 18th century, but none made such stunning advances as Captain James Cook, the British naval officer who—in three voyages from 1768 until he was killed by natives in Hawaii on February 14, 1799—took his ships the *Endeavour* and *Resolution* on voyages that filled in vast unknown areas of the great ocean.

Cook and his notable contemporaries Bougainville and La Perouse and their crews must have believed they had arrived in paradise when, after months of fighting storms, disease, and incredible hardship they sailed into clear lagoons teeming with fish, surrounded by trees loaded with fruit for the taking, on islands populated by proud races of strong, handsome men and beautiful women, many of whom shared their charms with these rugged and lonely sailors from Portsmouth and Marseilles. They returned home with tales of warmth and love in the South Seas, of unbelievable beauty, and a way of life their shipmates in the dingy waterfront taverns could barely imagine.

The navigator-captains of these expeditions were lauded by London and Paris society somewhat like the first lunar astronauts were in the 1960s. Like them, the 18th-century explorers had been into the unknown and returned with reports, pictures, and specimens so vastly different from anything before seen that the South Pacific seemed on another planet.

Nothing promoted the image of paradise more strongly than the infamous mutiny on the *Bounty* in 1788. Captain William Bligh, who had sailed as a junior officer with Cook on his final voyage, led an expedition to Tahiti to gather breadfruit plants for the West Indies, where British plantation owners hoped to use the fruit as a bread substitute to feed their slaves. After savoring the delights of Tahiti and the friendly wahines, Bligh's crew could not face a return to impoverished, cold England and, led by Fletcher Christian, set him adrift in an open longboat with a handful of officers who sailed to Timor in one of the epic sea voyages of all time.

Stories of adventure, romance, and easy living in the South Seas, of the new paradise, sparked the rush to the Pacific islands—a rush which continues today, driven by the same factors.

They came as rogues and rascals, traders in copra and pearlshell, hunters of whale, seal, and fleshly pleasures. They jumped ship or stowed away, worked their passage or joined the navy and deserted to gamble on a future unheard of in the crowded cities and mill towns of the Northern Hemisphere.

Meager settlements began to grow around the deepwater ports on the islands—Nuku'alofa in Tongatapu, Levuka on Ovalau in Fiji, Apia on Upolo, Western Samoa, Pago Pago on Tutuila (now American Samoa), and Papeete on Tahiti. The South Pacific ports of the early 1800s were wild, lawless towns. The masts and rigging of sailing ships stood like forests in the harbors as sealers, whalers, traders, and naval vessels flocked to the islands. Hard-drinking men caroused ashore with exotic native women only too eager to join in whatever frolicking might ensure. They were sometimes brutal days, when pirates, thieves, and rogues, like Bully Hayes, always wore a cutlass or carried a gun.

Hayes was the most infamous of the "blackbirders" who forced thousands of fit young men from islands throughout the Pacific into their sailing ships and, in appalling conditions, took them to be sold to the highest bidder to work plantations of copra, sugar, coffee, and cocoa for their new European owners. After the practice was outlawed, workers came from farther afield—Indians to Fiji's sugar-cane, Chinese to Tahiti, Japanese and Indonesians to the fields and nickel mines of New Caledonia, Taiwanese and Japanese to American Samoa's fishing industry—all imparting a colorful social and ethnic mix to the region that remains today.

The port towns flourished, more affluent and larger outlying villages became satellites as the island people gradually accepted a kind of civilization, with its rum, revelry and, inevitably, religion.

The first men and women of God to preach fire and brimstone in the South Seas began arriving in the last decade of the 1700s. They are depicted as severe, black-suited, top-hatted, Bible-clutching men and equally severe, bonnetted women of the London Missionary Society threatening all manner of hell and damnation if the heathens did not change their happy ways.

The French Catholics were close behind—one of their flock, Father Louis Beauchemin, is still bringing the Gospel to the Samoan people, more than 50 years after he was sent to the islands as a missionary. He says he will preach there until he dies.

But the best-known Pacific missionary was a Methodist, John Williams, who brought Christianity to much of Polynesian from 1830 until he was killed by natives at Erromanga nine years later. Most of the islands he touched have a monument erected to commemorate his landing.

The Pacific was fertile ground for missionaries seeking converts. Here lived people with their own cultures developed over many thousands of years since they migrated to these beautiful islands, probably from Southeast Asia. Different sub-races developed—the Melanesians remained in the west, settling from Papua New Guinea through the Solomons and Hebrides to Fiji; the Micronesians went north, to the Marianas, the Marshalls, and the Carolines; while the Polynesians set out on great migratory canoe voyages from their legendary Havaiki. Some say this was Savai'i, others the Manu'a group, but almost everyone agrees it was from Samoa—the cradle of Polynesia—from which they spread to Tahiti, Tonga, Hawaii, and New Zealand.

They took their gods, myths, and legends with them—and cannibalism, sacrifice, and an open attitude to sex, which were parts of their culture.

The missionaries attacked these "vices" with zeal in the name of their western God. They stopped the eating of human flesh, taught the islanders modesty, banished their centuries-old gods of the sea, sky, wind, and forest—and made them wear dress more befitting a Londoner than a South Seas islander.

The islanders embraced Christianity, with its promise of everlasting life in another kind of paradise, and they've never let go.

Even the poorest South Pacific village has a church—sometimes even two or three—of cathedral proportions. The faithful congregate several times on Sundays to pray, sing in wonderful choirs, and to pay the local minister or preacher. Sundays are truly sacred in the South Pacific and travelers need to appreciate their importance. On many islands, particularly Tonga and Samoa, it is considered almost blasphemous to drive through a village, create a disturbance, or make a noise during church services. In Tonga, even swimming was banned on Sundays until recently and tourists dancing in hotels on the Lord's Day is still only tolerated. There are no air services into Tonga on Sundays—the aircraft noise interferes with the church choirs.

Modesty, though, must remain the visitor's byword in the South Pacific. It's a missionary-days' hangover that will never go away, but bikinis and minishorts away from the beach and the hotel pool are seen as insults, even in the most tourist-oriented islands like the Cooks. Male tourists appearing bare-chested in downtown Nuku'alofa risk arrest, and police squads have swooped on unthinking nude-bathing tourists in Samoa.

The Methodists, Catholics, and London Missionary Society factions remain the main religions in the South Pacific, but others, like the Mormons and Adventists, are gaining ground quickly.

But accepting Christianity had its price. Unaccustomed to wearing tight, Western-style clothing, thousands of islanders died from pneumonia, influenza, and tuberculosis while clinging to their new Bibles. Disease swept the Pacific on a wave of previously unknown viruses—venereal disease, cholera, typhoid, malaria, measles, and small pox took a terrible toll, decimating the populations of some islands. The Marquesas and Fiji were particularly hard-hit, but all the islands suffered. Within only a few years, paradise became a hell of sickness, suffering, and death, of guns and rum and exploitation of a once-proud people.

In the mid-1800s the colonial powers moved in to establish administrations on islands they claimed by right of discovery. It didn't always work that way, though—the French took over Tahiti, discovered by Englishman Wallis. The Germans—after a gunboat standoff with the Americans and British—got Western Samoa. America settled for Tutuila, the British took Fiji, the Germans got great slices of Melanesia, and the New Hebrides were ruled by a British and French "condominium" until independence nine years ago. The medieval fiefdom of Tonga was peacefully bypassed and remains the only Pacific island never colonized. The new rulers generally handled things well, particularly the Germans who established vast, ordered plantations and tidy towns on their possessions. Their presence vanished with World War I, their places taken first by the British and then by regional authorities like Australia and New Zealand which, as young nations themselves, were unimpressive colonists; their inexperience at ruling exploded into violent bloodshed on several infamous occasions. They had not learned how to handle their own indigenous people—how could they cope with other cultures?

The South Pacific grew up with World War II, as almost every island was touched by the conflict.

Some islands became bloody battlegrounds, like Papua New Guinea, the Hebrides, and the Solomons, while others were forward bases for the mighty Allied war machine as it rolled across the Pacific toward Japan.

One such base was near Apia, Western Samoa, where a plucky young widow named Aggie Grey desperately eked out a living from her run-down Samoan drinking club. She was adopted by thousands of U.S. servicemen who passed through on their way to the front and began the legend that persists today. Rusting, battered relics of the bloody conflict still litter beaches and lagoons throughout the Western Pacific, reminders of that tragic period when thousands of islanders from the bigger Pacific towns and remote atolls fought and died alongside Americans, Australians, and New Zealanders.

But peace returned and with it came the tourists, seeking another paradise after the dark years. Wartime runways were rebuilt and extended to become international airports. Little clubs and bars became guest-houses, then hotels. New accommodations mushroomed, a tourist infrastructure developed, and suddenly the South Pacific was again the dream. Tourism meant, above all, employment and money.

Since those post-war days, the South Pacific islands have been the world's biggest recipients of foreign aid and, with their tiny, fragile economies, are likely to remain so. But independence has been the cry most heard throughout the area since Western Samoa became the first self-governing South Pacific nation in 1962. Fiji followed in 1970, then Papua New Guinea and the smaller states of Nauru, the Solomons, Tuvalu, Vanuatu, and Kiribati. Only the French have clung to their colonial past and resisted native aspirations for autonomy; they will not relinquish their nuclear testing facility in French Polynesia nor the strategic importance of New Caledonia.

Bitter battles, shootings, violence, and bloodshed have not gained the native Kanaks independence from their colonial rulers in Noumea, yet the Club Med, Ile de Pines, beaches, and French-influenced hotels still attract tourists. Visitors were still lured to Moorea and Bora Bora after separatists in 1987 rioted and burned buildings in downtown Papeete in their claim to determine their own future. Tourism figures have plummeted, though, in Fiji, where army colonel Sitiveni Rabuka twice staged armed coups in 1987 to prevent the Fiji-Indian majority from gaining democratically won political power.

Meanwhile, the international community is paying more attention to the South Pacific. Its global strategic importance is complicated by an increasing Soviet naval presence and the 1987 signing in Rarotonga of a regional accord to prohibit the passage of nuclear weapons through the Pacific. The measure followed the New Zealand Labor government's ban on U.S. Navy warships, underscoring fears that such policies might be attractive to other newly independent nations. Also worrying is the Kiribati-Soviet fishing agreement, which signaled a possible USSR economic expansion, as well as military influence in the Pacific. Add to all this the growing concern at French nuclear testing on Mururoa atoll and the ripple effect of the French terrorist bombing of the Greenpeace protest vessel *Rainbow Warrior* in Auckland Harbor, and the sum is anything but political stability.

But life goes on in the South Pacific, as it always has. The sun rises over the brilliant lagoon every morning, the thunder of the surf on the reef a mile out continues, the coconut palms sway in the trades as we know they will, and the islanders are still friendly and courteous.

Visitors should always be aware, though, that the smiling islanders they meet are not the cardboard cut-outs of tourist brochures and promotional videos. They, too, have their own families, interests, hopes and dreams, failures and triumphs, their own lives to be lived. Keep in mind that the South Pacific islands have produced many who have won international acclaim—writers, painters, lawyers, doctors, scientists, statesmen, and, yes, even kings. Each Pacific Islander is as individual as his island.

Fiji, with its racist dictator in the shadows, pushes its majority Indians to political purgatory while presenting an image of "The Way the World Should Be" to the world. Yet it is a splendid group of islands with the essence of the Pacific—white sands, coral reefs, blue lagoons, mountains, jungle, and a lifestyle that is pure South Seas. Backstreet Suva still reeks of more bawdy times, for those who choose to seek them.

Tahiti has survived the nuclear testing protests and cries for independence and remains, perhaps more than any other island, "the dream." Moorea, Bora Bora, Raiatea, Tetiaroa, Huahine, and Rangiroa burn into our consciousness with all that is magic about the South Pacific, and we are not disappointed.

Tonga, its depressed people paying outrageous obeisance to their king and scratching out an existence from their pitifully small plots of land, has a jewel in Vava'u—its northernmost splendor of reef, jungle, lagoon, beach, and lake, a true respite after experiencing the dust and dirt of Nuku'alofa on Tongatapu.

Tiny Niue, poor and struggling for its very life as two-thirds of its population drift south to the jobs and bright lights of New Zealand, has fabulous wealth in its grottoes, caves, and subterranean lakes, yet exists almost totally on foreign aid.

The Cook Islands, far-flung and often ravaged by cyclones and nepotistic political intrigue, are everything New Zealand and Australian tourists seek: good accommodation at reasonable prices, palm trees, tropical sun, smiling natives, and a round-island drinking tour. But despite the plastic, the loudness, the tourism-as-culture, it all seems to work. The beach at Arorangi and the lagoon at Aitutaki are as bright and clear and fresh in the trades as they might have been centuries ago.

Then there are tiny Wallis and Futuna, with a lagoon that cries out with color and drama. Another French territory with a long strategic runway for maritime surveillance operations, Wallis is a Polynesian sanctuary kept alive with aid.

Aid, of course, is what the Pacific is all about, and nowhere is that more evident than in American Samoa, with its towering island of Tutuila and its stunning harbor capital of Pago Pago, reaching out to the gems of the Manu'a group. Downtown Fagatogo remains decadent, with raunchy backstreet bars and the South Seas characters to match. Very American and very Pacific.

But to know the real Polynesia—the Polynesia sophisticated enough to have become the first Pacific nation and claim to have been the birthplace of the race, the mythical Havaiki—turn to Western Samoa and its twin islands of Savai'i and Upolu. Here is Polynesia at its purest. While adapting to and accepting the Eighties, Western Samoans retain a social structure they have maintained for centuries—Fa'a Samoa, the old way based on a society of respect, compassion, and community-as-family.

These communities have inevitably inherited the worst, as well as the best, of the societies of their discoverers, colonists, and settlers. They know crime, poverty, greed, violence, and corruption as well as we do in our cities.

Think about this when you stand in the bar at Lucky Eddie's or the Golden Dragon in Suva, Joe's Tropicana in Nuku'alofa, the Banana Court in Rarotonga, the Pago Bar or the Bamboo Room in Pago, the Lautoka Hotel's front bar, the Mt. Vaea Disco or Lafayette in Apia, Le Junk on the Papeete waterfront or any one of the dozens of sweating, dark, and loud establishments I like to frequent around the Pacific and you will know there is more to the South Pacific than sand, reefs, palms, and smiling faces on tourist brochures. Think about it when you drive through villages on Tongatapu and see kids with their bulging bellies, when outside your hotel, you brush away five-year-olds pleading with you to spend 50 cents on a frangipani lei they've spent hours making—probably from stolen flowers—when you walk past an old crippled woman begging on the pavement outside the village market, when the drunk young island girl threatens to make a scene if you don't buy her another drink, and another, and another.

Ah, paradise.

But you will come here for the same reason those adventurers, mutineers, wanderers, pirates, and hunters came. For the dream. Put your toes in the water of the clear, warm lagoon, listen to the reef's thunder, and gaze into the middle-distance as the sun blazes down through the breeze-shuffled coconut palms. It's not paradise, it only seems that way.

FRENCH POLYNESIA

The Bustling Paradise

by
JAN PRINCE

Flowers! The heady, sweet scent of tropical blossoms permeates the air you breathe as you enter Tahiti. Whether you come by airplane or ship, you are greeted by leis of Tiare Tahiti gardenias or the fragrant frangipani. Smiling Tahitian beauties welcome you to their island in their high musical voices as they place the flowers around your neck and you are happy to have arrived in Paradise. After clearing immigration and customs and learning that there is "No Tipping!" in Tahiti, you cheerfully proceed to your hotel by taxi or escorted tour bus. If it should be in the daylight hours when you arrive, you will be sitting back in the car when you suddenly become aware of something—what is that noise?

Welcome to modern day Tahiti! That's just what it is—noise. Hundreds of motorcycles, motorbikes, Vespas, trail bikes, automobiles and trucks all zoom along, zigzagging in and out of the traffic, trying to get there first. There is even a small section of freeway cut through the mountains now, giving two lanes that are usually made into five lanes by the speed happy motorists.

Look out into the lagoon and there is more noise. Even the traditional outrigger canoes have engines on them, as well as the power boats and, the most annoying of all, the racing boats that whine round and round the once calm (oh, how long ago!) lagoon.

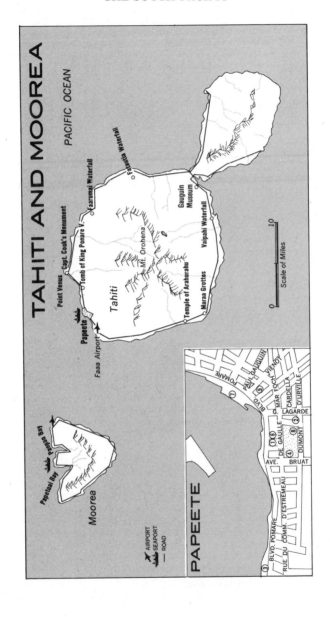

TAHITI AND MOOREA

PACIFIC OCEAN

Faaurumai Waterfall

Fautaua Waterfall

Point Venus
Capt. Cook's Monument
Tomb of King Pomare V.

Gauguin
Museum

Papeete

Tahiti

Mt. Orohena

Vaipahi Waterfall

Faaa Airport

Temple of Arahurahu

Maraa Grottos

0   10
Scale of Miles

Papetoai Bay   Papao Bay

Perpetual Bay

Moorea

✈ AIRPORT
⚓ SEAPORT
— ROAD

PAPEETE

POMARE

BLVD. GAUGUIN
AVE. GAUGUIN
VIENOT
MAR FOCH
CARDELLA
D'URVILLE
LAGARDE
G. LAGARDE
DE GAULLE
DUMONT
AVE.   BRUAT
BLVD. POMARE
RUE DU COMM. D'ESTREMEAU

Points of Interest

1) Bougainville Park
2) Cathedral
3) Cultural Center and
   Auditorium
4) High Commissioner's
   Residence
5) Market
6) Post Office
7) Sea Passenger
   Terminal
8) Territorial Assembly
   and Convention
   Auditorium

The other noise that tourists once complained about is still here also—that of the roosters crowing at all hours of the night and the mynah birds fussing outside the hotel windows in the early morning hours. Compared to the machines, though, these natural noises are like music to the ears.

Take a stroll downtown. What has happened to dear old "Papeete town"? It has almost vanished forever. Gone are the old landmarks, many of the centuries old trees, and whole blocks of once familiar Chinese stores, replaced by modern shopping centers or buildings under construction.

When the most famous bar in the South Pacific, Quinn's, was torn down in 1973, "Papeete town," as it was known to hundreds of seamen, voyagers, adventurers and South Seas characters, ceased to exist. The urge to build shopping centers and apartment buildings seemed to affect everyone with money to invest, and a rash of fires on the waterfront speeded up the process of changing the face of Papeete. And that's what it is now; Papeete, a true city, bustling and noisily busy. The town that was once the land of "*aita pea pea*" (who cares?) and "*haere maru*" (take it easy) has become the city of "*depêchez-vous*" and "*ha'a viti viti*" (hurry up).

Paradise Found

But don't despair. Take heart, for the good old days do still exist and can easily be found outside of Papeete. There are some 130 islands in the vast area known as French Polynesia. To some people all this is collectively known as Tahiti, meaning more a state of mind than any geographic location. However, it is not necessary to leave the island of Tahiti to seek your ideal of a tropical setting. Just get away from the downtown area, take a tour around the island and you will find all the beauty, tranquility and color you could wish for.

Go to Point Venus and see where the first known Europeans set foot on the island that later came to be known to the world as "paradise." This famous spot is today a lovely park with a lighthouse, monuments, permanent artisan exhibits and a *fare pote'e,* a traditional Polynesian style meeting house. The wonderful swimming here and the large black-sand beach with mountain views make it a favored location for many, including topless female sunbathers. It was here, on June 23, 1767, that Captain Samuel Wallis of the British Royal Navy, and his crew of 150 men aboard HMS *Dolphin,* anchored in Matavai Bay, five days after first sighting the tall mountains of Tahiti and following the coastline to seek a safe anchorage. The exhausted and scurvy-ridden men aboard the 32-gun frigate had left England eight months before in search of Terra Australis Incognita, the great land mass that King George III and his geographers were convinced lay somewhere between Cape Horn and New Zealand, in balance with the northern hemisphere. Imagine their surprise and joy the following morning when they found their ship surrounded by "upwards of five hundred canoes" containing four thousand athletic paddlers and loaded with fruit, coconuts, fowl and young pigs. But the most astonishing sight to their sea-weary eyes was that of the fair young girls, standing in the middle of each canoe, nude to the waist, "who played a great many droll, wanton tricks." While the hungry sailors were enjoying the free strip-tease, the Tahitians began to hurl fist-sized stones at the men on board the "Dolphin." The sailors retaliated by firing the ship's cannons at the canoes, killing forty or fifty of the Tahitians and sinking a great number of the canoes. After a second attack that the men of the ship easily won, the Tahitians decided to be friendly and peaceful.

As Wallis was too weak from scurvy to claim the new land in the name of the King, the second lieutenant, Tobias Furneaux, hoisted a pennant on a long pole and took possession of the island, calling it "King George's Island." The remainder of the five-week visit was spent trading earrings, nails and beads for foodstuffs. However, the men of the *Dolphin* began to wholeheartedly engage in "a new sort of trade . . . it might properly be called the old trade," according to George Robertson, master, whose journal is the best account given. When the men had emptied their sea chests to exchange their possessions for the ladies, they began to pull out the iron nails and cleats from the ship. The initial cost of such carnal exchange was a 20 or 30 penny nail. This rose to a 40 penny as demand outgrew the supply, and some women demanded as much as a seven- or nine-inch spike. Very soon two-thirds of the men had no nails to hang their hammocks on. The *Dolphin* sailed back to England soon afterward, without looking further for the southern continent.

Here at Point Venus is a marker for Captain Wallis and another one for the French explorer Louis Antoine de Bougainville, who was the second visitor from Europe to claim Tahiti for his country. Bougainville, captain of the French ships *Boudeuse* and the *Etoile,* had been searching also for the mythical Terra Australis Incognita and sought refuge on the windward side of the island off the district called Hitiaa, arriving nine months after Wallis' departure. His short visit, lasting only from April 6–14, 1768, was very much a repetition of the reception Wallis had received. One unusual incident marked this landing, when the Tahitians spotted among the 314 officers and men of the two ships a woman who had made the voyage disguised as a man. When one big Tahitian man grabbed her up to run off to the hills, her secret became known. Her name was Jeanne Baret and she had sailed as the personal valet of Bougainville's botanist, amongst all those French sailors, without any of them knowing there was a woman on board. She became the first white woman to visit Tahiti and to circumnavigate the world.

Bougainville, not knowing that his new island had already been "discovered" by Wallis and claimed for England, proclaimed French sovereignty over the island he called New Cythere or the New Island of Love. He found many similarities between the ancient worship of Aphrodite-Venus, whose birthplace was the Greek island of Cythere, and the Tahitian love rites.

Before Bougainville sailed away, his botanist named the scarlet and violet paper-like flowers they saw growing in such profusion Bougainvillea, after his captain. And when the *Bodeuse* left, there was a young Tahitian man from Hitiaa named Ahutoru, who sailed with her. He became the first Tahitian to discover Europe.

The following year Tahiti had her third visitor. Lieutenant James Cook, who later came to be known as England's most famous explorer, anchored in Matavai Bay in HMS *Endeavour* on April 13, 1769. After 25 years at sea, half in the merchant marine, Cook had so impressed his superiors in the Royal Navy (he is credited with originating the art of making charts) that they took the almost unprecedented step of transferring him to the command of a very important mission, promoting him from the ranks to lieutenant.

This expedition assigned to Cook was to take an astronomer either to the Marquesas Islands or to New Zealand for the purpose of observing the transit of the planet Venus across the disc of the sun. This event was to take place on June 3, 1769, and there would be no further opportunity to witness such a phenomenon again until 1874. Astronomers were anxious to take advantage of this rare occurrence as it would enable them to ascertain the distance of the earth from the sun, the fundamental base line in all astronomical measurements, and which was imperfectly known. Expeditions organized by the Royal Society had been sent to various parts of the world, but Cook's was the only one to the southern hemisphere and was therefore of special importance.

Two months before Cook left for the South Seas, Wallis returned to England with the disappointing news that he had not found the great southern continent. When he learned of the imminent voyage Cook was to command, Wallis suggested King George III's Island as the ideal spot to establish an observatory. There Cook and his men would find hospitable natives and an abundance of food and water.

Cook's expedition consisted of eighty-four officers and seamen and eight civilians. The civilians included Joseph Banks, a young botanist who later became president of the Royal Society; Dr. Daniel Solander, an eminent Swedish botanist and zoologist who had studied with the great Linnaeus; and astronomer Charles Green, who, in addition to supervising the observation of Venus, provided Cook with precise estimates of longitude, indispensable on such a discovery voyage.

When Cook and his noteworthy assistants anchored in Matavai Bay, seven weeks before the transit of Venus was expected, the "Endeavour" was given an enthusiastic welcome by the Tahitians. Crowds of natives greeted the ship with the now customary friendliness and immediately recognized four of the officers who had visited the island with Wallis.

The first thing Cook did upon arrival in what was then known to the English as King George III's Island was to erect a fort to protect the astronomer and his instruments. He chose the same site that Wallis had selected, the strip of land between the beach and the river. In less than three weeks' time the 150 foot long and 80 foot wide fort was finished, complete with five foot high walls and two four-pounder cannons.

These precautions proved superfluous, however, for the Tahitians, especially the women, were so friendly and hospitable that the British sailors forgot their duties. Cook had posted regulations concerning trade with the natives to prevent a repetition of Wallis's nail-removing fiasco. It was ordered that no iron be exchanged except for provisions. He also asked his men to treat the natives with "all imaginable humanity" and to use every fair means of cultivating their friendship. The natives appreciated this treatment and came to know the Englishmen affectionately by their "Tahitianized" surnames—Tute (Cook), Opane (Banks), Tolano (Solander), and so forth.

The major problem Cook encountered was constant pilfering. From time to time he was obliged to take one or more of the chiefs hostage against the return of pilfered objects. The most important item taken was the quadrant, an essential instrument for astronomical observation. Although the instrument was eventually returned, the culprit had removed it from its box and taken it apart to see what made it tick and it proved of no use in the operation.

On the day of the observation, there was not a cloud in the sky and the scientists were able to witness every phase of the transit from the fort at the place named Point Venus in honor of the occasion. However, it was subsequently found that the readings taken in Tahiti and other places were of little value because of unforeseen optical distortion caused by the irradiation of the sun.

Cook's expedition stayed in Tahiti for three months, during which time he learned much about the Tahitian way of life. He made precise observations of native customs, manners, religion and law. He described the people's appearance (explaining their tattoos), cooking methods, foodstuffs and apparent social and political order. He also made a trip around the island and drew a complete and accurate map of the whole coastal region of Tahiti.

By this time Cook had learned what the natives called their island and began using the name he understood it to be—Otaheite. When he asked them the name, they replied, "This is Tahiti," and in their language it sounded like Otaheite. Actually, the full name is *Tahiti-nui-i-te-vai-uri-rau,* "Great Tahiti of the many-colored waters."

Several of the things Cook learned about the Tahitian way of life shocked the 41-year-old seaman. "It is this," he said in his Journal, "that more than half of the better sort . . . have enter'd into a resolution of injoying free liberty in Love, without being Troubled . . . by its consequences. These mix and Cohabit together with the utmost freedom, and the Children who are so unfortunate as to be thus begot are smothered at the Moment of their Birth." He noted that couples lived together for years, destroying all children. His reference was to the Arioi Society that was in existence at that time, and their meetings during which "the Women in dancing . . . give full Liberty to their desires." He was also aghast that "both sexes express the most indecent ideas in conversation without the least emotion" and that "chastity . . . is but little valued. The Men will very readily offer the Young Women to Strangers, even their own daughters, and think it very strange if you refuse them; but this is merely done for the sake of gain."

However, the Tahitian people were suffering consequences of having enjoyed free liberty in love. Cook found, to his distress, that many of them, as well as his own men, were suffering from venereal disease. How they had caught it is a toss-up between the men on Cook's ships or the former discoverers. The English blame the French and vice-versa.

In years to come, the ravages of venereal disease, as well as other illnesses the Europeans introduced to the islands such as tuberculosis, small pox, measles and alcoholism, as well as the guns they brought to the natives, helped to reduce the population at an alarming rate. Cook gave the estimate of the population at over 200,000. Just 36 years later it was determined to be 8,000.

Cook and his men sailed away from Tahiti on July 13, 1769. Heading westward, he discovered the islands of Huahine, Raiatea, Tahaa and Bora Bora. He named them the Society Islands "because they lay contiguous to one another." He then sailed on to New Zealand and Australia, discovering many islands in the process. He was to return to Matavai Bay again, as Captain Cook, on three separate occasions in 1773, 1774 and 1777, during his second and third voyages of exploration. Today there is a monument to this great discoverer at Point Venus.

"Breadfruit Bligh" and the Bounty

In the following years many ships called at Tahiti, some anchoring in Matavai Bay and others stopping at Tahiti-iti, the peninsula which means "little Tahiti." One of the most famous ever to drop anchor in these waters was the HMS *Bounty,* commanded by Lieutenant William Bligh. The *Mutiny on the Bounty* saga is well known as it was imaginatively told by co-authors James Norman Hall and Charles Nordhoff, two Americans who moved to Tahiti after fighting in World War I. The *Bounty* story, starring Marlon Brando, Trevor Howard, and the Tahitian beauty, Tarita, was filmed at Point Venus in 1961, and a 1980's version, with English and Australian actors, was filmed on Moorea.

Bligh, who had been to Tahiti previously with Cook on his third voyage, aboard the *Resolution,* was married to a lady whose uncle had a number of large plantations in Jamaica, was well connected in government circles and was the owner of several ships. A petition was made to King George III by English merchants in the West Indies, asking that the breadfruit tree be transplanted from Tahiti to their islands. Cook and others had spoken highly of the breadfruit as a substitute for bread and had told of how healthy and strong the Tahitians were, who ate it as their staple diet. The merchants believed it would be a cheap and nourishing means of feeding their slaves. The petition was approved and Bligh was appointed to command the voyage. There was no problem in signing on a crew as the reputation of the friendly and voluptuous Tahitian ladies was well known in Europe by that time.

By the time the *Bounty* arrived in Matavai Bay, October 26, 1788, there had already been problems aboard between captain and crew. For five months they stayed in Tahiti, waiting for the breadfruit to reach the right stage for transplanting. During this lengthy stay the discipline slackened while the sailors lived among the happy Tahitians, who were not accustomed to let work interfere seriously with their many pleasures and amusements.

As the time drew nearer for their departure, Bligh became excessively severe with his men. And on April 4, 1789, when the *Bounty* weighed anchor and steered towards the leeward islands of the Society group, he carried a reluctant crew.

The magic of Tahiti proved too strong a magnet and Bligh's insults to his officers, especially to acting Lieutenant Fletcher Christian, too harsh to endure. Thus, on the early morning of April 28, Bligh was awakened by four of his men, hauled out of bed, tied up and dragged on deck. There he learned that a mutiny was being staged, under the leadership of Christian, and he was put into a launch, along with eighteen of his officers and men, a 28-gallon cask of water, 150 pounds of bread, some wine and rum, a compass, a quadrant, some canvas, lines and sails. Then the mutineers cast the boat adrift in the open ocean, a few miles from Tofua in the Tongan Islands. Bligh made one of the most notable open boat voyages in history, sailing 3,600 miles to Timor and Batavia in the Dutch Indies, losing only one man during this grueling voyage. Six others died after reaching safety.

The mutineers first tried to settle at Tubuai, in the Austral Islands, but the natives were so hostile that the *Bounty* turned back to Tahiti three days later to resupply and reconsider what to do next. The twenty-five men who remained in the *Bounty* consisted of two parties: those who had taken an active part in the mutiny and those who had not. On June 6 the ship once again anchored in Matavai Bay, where she remained for ten days, loading pigs, goats, a cow and a bull, dogs, cats and fowl. When she sailed for Tubuai again, the mutineers were accompanied by nine Tahitian men, eight Tahitian women and nine children, many of whom were stowaways.

Life with the aggressive Tubuaians proved impossible (about 100 natives were killed in skirmishes), so the mutineers finally decided to retreat to Tahiti. Some of the men remained there and Fletcher Christian led eight of his fellow mutineers, with six Tahitian men, one little girl and twelve Tahitian women, aboard the *Bounty* and they sailed away to eventually settle on the uninhabited island of Pitcairn. There they burned the ship and were not heard of again for 18 years.

Meantime 16 of the original *Bounty* crew lived in Tahiti, some taking wives and having families. Here they were discovered in March, 1791, when HMS *Pandora* sailed into Matavai Bay, in search of the mutineers. Two of the *Bounty* men had died by the time the *Pandora* reached Tahiti, but Captain Edward Edwards arrested the remaining 14. On their way to England for their trial, the *Pandora* was shipwrecked and four were drowned. A court martial inquiry was held in England and three men were condemned to death and hanged, while the remaining seven were allowed to live as free men. During his confinement, one of the men, Peter Heywood, wrote the first Tahitian dictionary while awaiting trial.

Even after all the troubles he had been through on the *Bounty,* old "Breadfruit" Bligh didn't give up on his mission. He appeared again in Matavai Bay on April 10, 1792, as Captain Bligh and commander of HMS *Providence* and her armed tender, the *Assistance.*

When he arrived there was a native war going on and he was afraid it would make it hard for him to collect the breadfruit. Finally he went ashore to supervise the building of storage sheds for his plants.

During the three months he was in Tahiti on this visit, Bligh had ample time to note the changes that had occurred. He was disappointed to learn that "little of the ancient customs of the Otaheitans remains . . . It is difficult to get them to speak their own language without mixing a jargon of English with it, and they are so altered that I believe in future no Europeans will ever know what their ancient customs of receiving strangers were." He also felt that their method of dress had degenerated and they were "no longer clean Otaheitans, but in appearance a set of ragamuffins with whom it is necessary to observe great caution."

By July 18, Bligh had collected 2,126 breadfruit plants and about 500 others and set sail for the West Indies with no major problems. There, in St. Vincent and in Port Royal, Jamaica, the breadfruit seedlings were planted. But when the trees grew and bore fruit, the Negro slaves, for whom the breadfruit was intended, disliked the taste and refused to eat it.

Heathen and Missionary

Thirty years after Captain Wallis discovered Tahiti, a shipload of an entirely different type of conquerors arrived in Matavai Bay. These were the missionaries. Composed of Presbyterians, Methodists, Episcopalians and Independents, the newly formed London Missionary Society left England in 1797, bound for Tahiti. This island was chosen as their first foreign country because they felt the society should begin its work in some place where "the difficulties were least."

By the time their ship, the *Duff,* anchored in Matavai Bay, on March 5, 1797, a Sunday morning, more than a hundred natives were dancing and capering on the decks, crying *"tayo, tayo"* (friend). Even though they were unarmed, the captain ordered the ship's guns to be hoisted. The Tahitians cheerfully assisted in placing them in their carriages.

As the 18 missionaries settled into their new quarters on Point Venus, formerly the house of Lieutenant Bligh, they began to realize the immensity of their task in imposing bleak, puritanical ideas on the uninhibited, idolatrous islanders. They soon became aware that there was "more to apprehend from being caressed and exalted, than from being insulted and oppressed."

There were only four ordained ministers in the group, while the rest were carpenters, weavers, tailors, shoemakers, bricklayers, and a harness maker. Most of them were in their early twenties and only five of them were married and had their families with them. Therefore, it is not surprising that the first problem to face the new settlers was how to deal with the beautiful and alluring Tahitian women. Even though they agreed that it would be sinful to marry a heathen woman, some of the men succumbed to the weakness of the flesh and committed the unforgivable sin of fornication.

The missionaries' life was not an easy one, in that they never learned the Tahitian language well enough to preach the gospel in an intelligible manner. The natives would scoff and ridicule them and laugh when they tried to convince the Tahitians that Jehovah was the only true God and their pagan rites and human sacrifices should be abolished. It took the missionaries more than 15 years to make their first convert, even though they had some 2,300 natives attending their meetings and instructions. Some of the Tahitians felt that the missionaries should pay them to attend the mission schools. The missionaries also quarreled among themselves and many of their number left for other islands or back to England. They made the mistake of taking sides in the local power struggles and usually supported the wrong chief for the wrong reasons.

After baptizing the powerful chief, Pomare II, whom the missionaries thought of as king of Tahiti, the other people followed suit and their idols and temples were destroyed in favor of the Christian religion.

For almost forty years the Protestant missionaries enjoyed tremendous success in Tahiti before any competition arrived. They had gained strong political control and some had lined their pockets well.

Therefore, when a small band of Catholic missionaries arrived in Tahiti with the intent of opening a new mission, the Protestants used all their influence to prevent this from happening. The first Catholic group landed on the island of Mangareva, 900 miles away, in 1835. One of them was sent to Tahiti disguised as a carpenter. The Protestants protested when they learned his true mission and they were even more incensed when two French Catholic priests arrived on the scene the following year.

The priests were asked to leave the island but refused. Queen Pomare IV, the illegitimate daughter of Tahiti's first Christian convert, who was now in power, wrote a letter to the French priests, ordering them to leave on a ship that was in port. When they again refused, the two men were forcibly removed from the island and placed aboard the ship.

The Brink of War

This action began a series of events that almost brought England and France to the brink of war. When the French government learned of this affair, it was decided that the "scandalous treatment" of the two priests could not go unpunished. Thus the frigate *Venus,* under the command of Captain Abel Du Petit-Thouars, was ordered to proceed to Tahiti to demand "a full reparation" from the Queen for "the insult done to France in the person of our compatriots." The punishment called for the Queen to write a letter to the King of France, apologizing; an indemnity of 2,000 Spanish dollars was to be paid for losses suffered by the two priests and the French flag was to be hoisted and saluted with twenty-one guns. The Queen wrote the letter but had neither the money nor the flag nor the powder. Du Petit-Thouars provided the flag and the gunpowder for the salute and George Pritchard, the most prominent missionary, and two other English residents gave the money.

The French Commander also proposed that a treaty of perpetual peace be drawn up between Tahiti and France and that Frenchmen of every profession would be allowed the right to come and go and to trade in all the islands composing the government of Tahiti. He also proposed that Frenchmen should be "received and protected as the most favoured foreigners."

As soon as the *Venus* had sailed, Queen Pomare and four of her principal chiefs wrote to Queen Victoria asking for British protection. This was not the first time the Queen of Tahiti, persuaded by George Pritchard, had asked the Queen of England to make Tahiti a British protectorate. But England was having her own troubles with France and Queen Victoria "expressed deep concern at the difficulties under which Queen Pomare appeared to labour," but decided it would be impossible for her to "fulfill, with proper punctuality, any defensive obligations towards the government and inhabitants of Tahiti." For that reason, she was unable to make Tahiti a protectorate of Great Britain, but she would always be glad to "give the protection of her good offices to Queen Pomare in any differences which might arise" with any foreign power.

Queen Pomare began having serious problems with a foreign power very soon after this letter was received from the Queen of England. A Frenchman who was also a Catholic, M. Moerenhout, had been appointed as the French Consul. While the queen was visiting in Raiatea and while the former missionary, George Pritchard—who was now the British Consul—was away in England, Moerenhout took advantage of the opportunity to trick four of the chiefs into signing a document he had composed, asking that Tahiti be made a French protectorate.

When the French government received this request, they found it suited their needs at the time, since they were looking for a base in the Pacific for the warships, whalers and merchant vessels sent out from France. They had already decided to take possession of the Marquesas Islands. So Rear Admiral Du Petit-Thouars, aboard the flagship "La Reine Blanche," was chosen to establish the French protectorate in Tahiti as well.

Despite the protests of Queen Pomare and her chiefs, who admitted they didn't understand what the document was about that they had signed, the French began to install themselves very firmly on the island. With threats and troops, Du Petit-Thouars obtained the signature of the Queen on a letter accepting "the proposal to place the government of Queen Pomare under the protection of His Majesty Louis Philippe, King of the French." He then set up a provisional government of three—the Commissioner Royal, a military governor and a captain of the port of Papeete.

When news of the French protectorate reached England six months later, the matter was brought up in Parliament, and the decision was made to accept the French protectorate as long as the Protestant missionaries would be allowed to carry on with their work.

However, when it was learned in England and in France that Du Petit-Thouars had not merely established a protectorate in Tahiti but had actually taken full possession in the name of the French king, this far-away island became the main topic of conversation on both sides of the Channel. The issue was debated even more heatedly when it was learned that the Tahitian flag had been replaced by the French flag after 500 French troops surrounded the palace, and Queen Pomare had been dispossessed and forced to flee to the safety of an English ship in the Papeete harbor. But all of England was outraged when Pritchard arrived on July 26, 1844, in H.M.S. *Vindictive* with the news that he had been arrested and deported.

The matter was heatedly discussed in all circles and given much publicity in the newspapers of both countries. Both the French and English governments found it difficult to avoid war as both sides felt they had been humiliated. Finally King Louis Philippe offered to pay Pritchard 25,000 francs out of his own pocket, hoping that he could maintain the "entente cordiale" with Great Britain. This offer was rejected and accord was maintained between the two governments when France apologized to England for the treatment given Pritchard and an "equitable indemnity" was paid for his loss and sufferings.

This affair was kept alive in the French parliament for three more years and contributed to the eventual overthrow of the government and monarchy in the famous revolution of February 24, 1848.

While England and France were carefully avoiding war back in Europe, the Tahitians were staging a lot of skirmishes with the French troops in Tahiti, and sometimes getting the upper hand. Their queen sought refuge in Raiatea, where she wrote to Queen Victoria, pleading for help in regaining her sovereignty. The letters were never answered and she realized that she would have to fight alone. The natives, however, never gave up hope that Britain would come to their aid. They could not believe that England had deserted them and they refused to submit to the French protectorate.

The protectorate had been re-established and the Queen's sovereignty restored in early 1845, after France and England had come to terms over the George Pritchard affair. But Queen Pomare refused to return to Tahiti under French rule. Finally, in February, 1847, she gave up the useless struggle when she heeded the advice of a Tahitian chieftainess and agreed to accept the French protectorate. Thus she was brought back to Tahiti, where she was little more than a figurehead until her death on September 17, 1877.

King Pomare V, the last of the dynasty to carry this title, was totally unfit for even the most nominal duties of kingship. He preferred drinking and gambling and had none of his mother's pride in the Tahitian heritage. Therefore, it was easy to get him to abdicate, with the promise of an annual pension for himself, his wife and two brothers.

The century-old rule of the Pomares formally came to an end on December 30, 1880, and Tahiti became a full-fledged French colony, when the French government accepted Tahiti and her dependencies as forming one and the same country with France.

In 1903 the whole of the French establishment in the Eastern Pacific was declared one colony and was called French Oceania. In 1957 the status was changed from a colony to a Territory and the name was changed to the present, French Polynesia.

Modern Polynesia

Before you leave Point Venus and the site where white man first stepped ashore to change the lives of these 'noble savages,' take a moment to look up at the green peaks of Mt. Orohena, Tahiti's tallest mountain of 7,353 feet. Follow the line of the mountains around to where the hotel Tahara'a is situated on top of the famous "One Tree Hill," so named by Captain Cook. Here you have the continuity of the magic of Tahiti, bridging the unknown past with the uncertainty of the future. Eight million years have passed since these mountains first rose from the blue waters. Radio-carbon dates indicate that human history began in what we now know as the Society Islands around A.D. 850. As there was no written language until the missionaries devised an alphabet for the natives, very little is known about their origins. Scientists have learned some interesting things about their ancient culture by studying their language and by excavations that have revealed their temples, called "maraes," and their stone adze heads, fishhooks and artifacts.

In modern times, after more than 200 years of white man's influence, the Tahitian and Polynesian culture is very much alive. A leisurely drive around the island of Tahiti reveals many of the same attractions that brought romanticists to these shores—writers and artists such as Robert Louis Stevenson, Jack London, Somerset Maugham, Rupert Brooke, Paul Gauguin, Henry Adams—who were, each in his own way, trying to capture the "same charm of light and air." There are the several rivers and waterfalls; the fern-covered mountains; coconut plantations and taro fields; the simple Tahitian *fares* painted in rainbow colors; the soft featured and golden skinned women, clad in their bright *pareos* and with flowers behind their ears, holding a baby on their hips and gossiping alongside the road; and there are the friendly and athletic men who still fish on the reefs at night and play their guitars and drums. The *tamure* and other traditional dances are still performed with skill and enthusiasm even though the modern French Polynesian eagerly adopts the latest dances from Europe or America and performs them with vigor and an abandon seen nowhere else.

It is true that the faces of Tahiti have changed from the days when Wallis and de Bougainville and Cook first came ashore. With the arrival of the Europeans in 1767 and the Chinese—who were first introduced to these islands during the American Civil War to work in the cotton plantation where the golf course is today—there has been more racial intermingling than in any other part of the Pacific except Hawaii. With the exception of the Chinese community, who are the merchants of these islands and who still try to maintain their tradition of marrying within their own race (although it is increasingly difficult to control), there are no financial, racial or social barriers.

Even though many of the couples who live together are not legally married, the population continues to grow, so that more than half the population of 175,000 in French Polynesia is under the age of 20. There is no stigma for an unmarried girl to have a baby and there are few unwanted babies. Tahitians love any tiny infant, cat, or dog, as long as they are very young. Life is not so easy for the growing youngster or animal, however, in many cases. And the growing rate of juvenile delinquency in downtown Papeete is equivalent to the population explosion.

As you end your tour of Tahiti you find that you have stepped back into modern day Papeete, just in time for the evening rush hour to begin as the workers go home from their offices. The euphoria that surrounded you around the island as you walked through the botanical gardens, picked a flower, watched the surf breaking on the reef, listened to the wind whistling through the casuarina trees at the edge of a black sand beach, drank the cool liquid of a coconut, or viewed the mountains of Tahiti from the plateau at Taravao on the isthmus, begins to dissipate as you enter the downtown area with its high rise shopping centers and parking meters.

But if you can keep that magic around you and get to the waterfront area undisturbed by the noise and the incredibly undisciplined traffic, then you will be amply rewarded as the sun begins to set behind the peaks and spires of Moorea, that land of "Bali H'ai," just 12 miles across the bay. As you sip a tall cool one at one of the sidewalk cafés and watch the sky turn all shades of red, pink and orange, the last of the traffic disappears and you can see the outrigger canoes in the harbor, where their vigorous paddlers are practicing for their next race. When you finish your drink and before you return to your air conditioned hotel room, walk down the waterfront to the corner across the street from the Tahiti Tourist Board. Here, in a thatched-roof *fare,* you will find a tradition that has existed ever since there have been Tahitians. The old women are sitting on the floor, making crowns of flowers for the merrymakers to wear when they go out that evening, dining and dancing. This scene is one of the last remnants of "Papeete town."

For the curious traveler who doesn't adhere to the belief that "if you've seen one island, you've seen them all," French Polynesia is a veritable treasurehouse. Because it covers such a large area of the eastern Pacific and the five archipelagoes are at different latitudes, choices can be made from the high volcanic islands of the Society group, the low coral atolls of the Tuamotus, the remote and mysterious islands of the Marquesas, or the temperate climate of the distant Australs.

Many a visitor has made the mistake of allowing too little time for visiting the outer islands of French Polynesia and quite often the complaint is heard, "Oh, how I wish I had come here first."

At the Tahiti-Faaa airport in Tahiti there are lockers where it is possible to store luggage while visits are made to the other islands. Also the hotels are very good about keeping your bags while you are away from Tahiti.

The islands most frequently visited are those with first class hotels. They are: *Tahiti, Moorea, Bora Bora, Huahine,* and *Raiatea* in the Society Islands; and *Rangiroa* and *Manihi* in the Tuamotus. The following information will enable you to determine which ones suit your desires most, and includes some of the lesser known islands.

Moorea

This sister island just 12 miles from Tahiti is the most frequently visited one after Tahiti. Many tourists say it is worth the airfare to Tahiti just to see Moorea's spectacular bays. There are several launches that leave daily from the Papeete harbor for the 45-minute crossing, returning to Tahiti in the afternoon. Also there is an air taxi service that will land you on Moorea in just seven minutes flying time. Once there, you can choose from several hotels, most of which are located on white sand beaches.

In Moorea, as on the other islands, most of the activities are centered around the clear waters of the lagoon. A coral reef several yards offshore protects the lagoons from the pounding surf and, as a result, the lagoons are usually as calm as a giant swimming pool.

If you're not a swimmer, snorkeler or diver, then you can ride a bike around the island or take a tour arranged by the hotels. It is also well worth the money to rent a car and drive the 37 miles around the island and up into the valley of Opunohu, passing coffee plantations and pineapple fields. Be sure to drive up to Le Belvedere, a lookout spot where you will be well rewarded with a magnificent view of Moorea's jagged mountains and Cook's Bay, also called PaoPao and of Opunohu Bay, also known as Papetoai Bay. On all the tours the mountain called "Bali H'ai" by the tourists will be pointed out. This is a needle shaped mountain named Mou'aroa that appeared in the movie *South Pacific* as the mythical Bali H'ai.

Most of the nighttime activities take place in the hotels, where there are regular Tahitian feasts, called *tamaaraas,* dance shows or singing to the accompaniment of guitars and ukuleles. For those with rental cars it is fun to dine out at one of Moorea's excellent restaurants, and then to hotel hop, checking out the evening's action at each hotel bar.

Bora Bora

More "purple prose" has been written about this little island than any other in the South Pacific and justly so. Situated 143 miles northwest of Tahiti, it can be reached in 55 minutes by Air Tahiti, plus another 45 minutes by launch from the airport to the main village of Vaitape. Or you can go by an air-conditioned ferry that leaves Tahiti twice weekly, stopping at Huahine, Raiatea, and Tahaa enroute, and arriving in Bora Bora the following day.

The island is fringed by small islets, called "motus," and boasts one of the clearest and most colorful lagoons anywhere, with a variety of coral gardens that can be viewed through glass-bottom boats or while snorkeling and diving. The two highest mountains, Mt. Otemanu at 2,379 feet and Mt. Pahia at 2,165 feet, can be seen from many vantage points as one travels the 17 miles around the island on a partially paved road.

There are three rental car locations that have bicycles and motorbikes, as well as jeeps and cars. Bicycles are a popular method of transportation in Bora Bora and can facilitate the many stops you will need to make to visit the villages, the old barracks and seaplane base built by the Seabees, the ancient temples, called "maraes," or to inspect the curios at the many souvenir stands around the island. You will want to stop for a drink at the Bloody Mary Restaurant and make reservations to return for a seafood dinner, cooked and served in a setting right out of a South Seas movie.

The largest hotel, the Hotel Bora Bora, offers all types of water sports, and frequent Tahitian dance shows or slide shows. The Club Mediterranée, with over-water bungalows, also has a full range of activities, including picnics and swimming on a nearby *motu*. The Hotel Marara was built to house a movie crew while filming a Dino DiLaurentiis movie, *The Hurricane*. The Marara is now operated by Sofitel, owned by the group ACCOR. It faces toward Tahaa and Raiatea. Next door is the Hotel Ibis, built as Climat de France, but taken over in July 1986 by the ACCOR group. Hotel Sofitel Matira Beach opened in June 1987, with over-water bungalows. The Hotel Oa Oa has eight bungalows near the principal village and the Revatua Club is on the opposite side of the island from all the other hotels. You can rent a luxurious bungalow at the Bora Bora Condos; the Hotel Matira has housekeeping bungalows, complete with individual outrigger canoes, built beside the island's prettiest beach.

If you just want to lie back and take life easy, this island is an ideal place to do just that. There is no hustle and bustle unless you want to create it yourself. Serenity is the password on Bora Bora, which means "firstborn-of-silent-paddle."

Huahine

Quickly becoming one of French Polynesia's most popular tourist islands, Huahine is only 40 minutes by air from Tahiti, or just an overnight trip by inter-island schooner.

This quiet and peaceful island, which is actually two islands, called Huahine-Nui (big Huahine) and Huahine-Iti (little Huahine) is only 20 miles in circumference. There are mountains over 2,000 feet high and two lakes, where it is easy to dig for clams and crabs. Most of the island's population of 4,000 fish and farm for a living and produce watermelons and cantaloupes for the market in Tahiti.

The principal village, called Fare, is reminiscent of an old western town from some cowboy country. There are a handful of Chinese stores lining the tree-shaded waterfront, plus a billiards parlor, two banks, the Air Tahiti office, and a couple of small boutiques, one with lovely pottery made by an American man and his Tahitian wife. The 2-story Hotel Huahine overlooks the harbor and beach and Lovina's small hotel sits next door to a photo shop. Pension Enite serves great meals behind the Snack Te Marara, which also is popular for its hamburgers and Hinano beer and is a good place to hang out and talk with yachting people.

When the Raromatai Ferry and copra/cargo/passenger boats *Temehani II* and *Taporo IV* arrive from Tahiti or return from Bora Bora and Raiatea, there is much excitement in the village, with truckloads of Tahitians coming to town for market day. The rest of the week the village takes on a somnolent air with only a few people strolling under the big almond trees.

The first class Hotel Bali H'ai Huahine can be reached in just five minutes from the village by walking on a path alongside the strip of white sand beach that stretches from the village past the hotel.

Rental cars or mopeds can be ordered at the Hotel Bali H'ai, Hotel Huahine, or with Lovina. Budget Rentals has Mehari jeeps. Also there are guided tours from each place around the island, or visits to the village of Maeva, a Polynesian village that is a sort of "open-air" museum. Many interesting Tahitian temples or "maraes" are located in or near this village.

Five miles from Fare is the Hotel BelleVue, with 15 colonial-style bungalows and eight double rooms, a swimming pool, and a restaurant that features locally caught seafood prepared Chinese-Tahitian style.

At the south end of Huahine-Iti two hotels were opened in mid-1985 near the pretty village of Parea. The Huahine Beach Hotel and the Relais Mahana are built beside long white sand beaches and offer attractive bungalows each, plus restaurant, boutique, all water sports, and other activities. Parea has a few "pensions" where guests share the Polynesian lifestyle, including children and dogs.

Raiatea

This second largest island in the Society group is only a 45-minute flight from Tahiti or an overnight passage aboard the "Raromatai Ferry," an air-conditioned passenger and car ferryboat that departs Tahiti twice weekly. The inter-island schooners *Temehani II* and *Taporo IV* also service the Leeward Society Islands, with a true Polynesian atmosphere.

Although there are not many white sand beaches to be found on this island, many visitors favor Raiatea because of the friendly people and the historic landmarks. It was from the river called *"Faaroa"* located here that the original Maoris set off for New Zealand. This was also the former educational and religious center for the ancient Tahitians, and the most famous temple or *marae* called *Taputapuatea,* is located on the southeast point of the island.

The Hotel Bali H'ai chain offers first class accommodations with many over-water bungalows, all water sports, bicycles, a swimming pool and games area, as well as being the center for the nightly social events and dancing.

The Raiatea Village, with 12 bungalows complete with kitchenettes, opened in late 1983 by the Faaroa River. Although this small hotel is not close to the village it does offer a peaceful beauty. In the center of Uturoa is the Hotel Motu, with clean rooms for the budget traveler, and a very good French restaurant upstairs.

There are various tours available with the hotels, including speedboat trips to the nearby island of Tahaa, where time seems to have stopped a hundred years ago.

A lot of fun can be had just by walking or biking into the principal town of Uturoa. There are Chinese shops to explore and the public market, in the center of town, is interesting to visit during the early morning hours of market days. Even though Raiatea has a population of 7,400 and Uturoa is the second-largest town in French Polynesia, there is little nighttime activity except on weekends, when the young Raiateans head for the disco or local nightclub to dance the night away.

Another kind of dancing is performed on special occasions at the Hotel Bali H'ai, when the firewalking ceremonies recreate the ancient rites of walking barefoot across white-hot stones.

Tahaa

Tahaa is the sister island of Raiatea, sharing the same lagoon. It is nearly circular in shape and is only 15 miles in circumference, half the size of the main island of Raiatea. From Tahaa you can easily see Huahine, Raiatea and Bora Bora. It is necessary to go to Raiatea first if flying and take the *Ramanui* or one of the other small ferry boats that arrive in Raiatea early each morning and return to Tahaa before noon.

Most tourists visit Tahaa for the day only, but it is now easier to find a room for the night. The Tahaa Iti Village is an old hotel recently taken over by a French couple, offering excellent cuisine, marvelous views of Bora Bora and the sunset. Tahaa Lagon, across the mountains or around the bay, is a small and new French bungalow/restaurant complex. Marinaiti is a good stopover place for those chartering yachts. And a few rooms are still available with local families in some villages. The *Raromatai Ferry* and the copra ships *Temehani II* and *Taporo IV* call at Tahaa.

Maupiti

This small and beautiful island lies 37 kilometers (22 miles) west of Bora Bora and is surrounded by a protective barrier reef with off-shore *motus* lying between the main island and the coral reef, Air Tahiti has an airstrip on one of these islets, with flights from Tahiti and Raiatea to Maupiti each Monday and Thursday morning and from Bora Bora to Maupiti and return to Raiatea and Papeete on Monday and Thursday afternoons. The cargo/passenger boat *Taporo I* leaves Raiatea for Maupiti each Tuesday at midnight, arriving through the dangerous pass into the tranquil harbor the following morning at 6 A.M. and departing for Raiatea by way of Bora Bora three hours later. Maupiti's 800 residents are mostly watermelon farmers and fishermen, or they produce copra, pandanus, taro, yams, tapioca, and bananas. This tranquil island has mostly been kept a secret; there are no big hotels. White-sand beaches and excellent snorkeling are found around the motus, where a few tourist bungalows have been built. Accommodations are also available in the main village, in small pensions. Activities, besides water sports, include walking or biking around the island, which is only 5.7 miles in circumference, and visiting the archeological ruins and *marae* temples that are remnants of a former powerful civilization. There are nursery and primary schools, a city hall, infirmary, post office, and a few general stores.

Tetiaroa

Tetiaroa is the atoll that belongs to Marlon Brando, just a 17-minute flight from Tahiti. Accommodations include 14 bungalows and 5 A-frame rooms built of coconut trees. Beautiful beaches and an interior lagoon are the natural attractions here, with trips to the surrounding "motu" islets.

Tuamotus

The Tuamotu archipelago, also called the Low or Dangerous archipelago and comprising 78 low islands called coral atolls, is scattered over several hundreds of miles of the eastern Pacific that is part of French Polynesia.

Thirty of these atolls are uninhabited, while the rest are very sparsely populated. The islands rise only some six to twenty feet above the water and are surrounded by coral reefs with rarely a pass or break in the reef;

when there is a pass it is usually navigable only at certain tide levels. The reefs are graveyards for the many boats that didn't make it through the passes. Life on these remote atolls is simple and often lonely, because of the lack of people or visiting boats. The diet of the people consists mostly of fish, coconuts and canned food.

There is airplane service to several of the atolls—Rangiroa, Manihi, Arutua, Hao, Tatakoto, Pukarua, Reao, Nukutavake, Fangatau, Fakahina, Tureia, Puka Puka, Kaukura, Mataiva, Apataki, Napuka, Fakarava, Takapoto, Anaa, Makemo and Tikehau—but there are no first class hotels on any except at Rangiroa and Manihi. There are facilities available with Tahitian families on the other atolls, for those travelers who don't require too many comforts and services.

Rangiroa is a perfect example of a coral atoll. The reef encloses a lagoon 42 miles long and 14 miles wide at its extreme width. Air Tahiti has flights six days a week from Tahiti to Rangiroa and in only one hour you are there, in a completely different world, surrounded by blindingly white sand beaches, with the multi-colored lagoon on one side and the pounding surf of the Pacific on the other side of this narrow strip of land.

The atoll life can be observed in the villages of Tiputa and Avatoru on Rangiroa, where there are the churches, schools, the usual Chinese stores and ancient bakery still producing long loaves of French bread daily. Tiputa can be reached by speedboat from the Kia Ora Hotel in a few minutes. Avatoru is located on the same atoll as the airport and the hotel can be reached by car. There is a pass into the lagoon at both Avatoru and Tiputa. Many visitors and locals enjoy swimming through the passes as the extremely powerful tide rushes through. You can see hundreds of tropical fishes, as well as sharks, who are swept along with the current.

The hotels Kia Ora Village, Rangiroa Village, and La Bouteille a la Mer are located on the main atoll, and the small hotel Sans Souci is across the lagoon on a private islet.

These atolls of the Tuamotus are often ravaged by hurricanes or cyclones. Their limpid lagoons have been found to be the perfect place to farm the famous South Seas black pearl, which is sold in Tahiti.

For the diver, a trip to these waters is a dream come true, for it offers some of the finest diving in the world.

Marquesas

The twelve islands that comprise *Les Îles Marquises* are little known to the world and are considered to be strange and mysterious by the outsider. The first white man to discover any of these high volcanic islands was Alvaro Mendana de Neira of Spain, who arrived in 1595 and discovered four of the southernmost islands. He named the group in honor of the Viceroy of Peru's wife, the Marquesa de Mendoza.

Before the missionaries converted the people to Christianity, the Marquesans fought many wars among themselves and were noted cannibals, but the diseases and vices introduced by white man had a more devastating effect on the population than earlier practices had. The population was once more than 100,000 but numbers 6,500 today.

For 40 years prior to the French government taking over, the Marquesas group was ravaged by whalers, traders, blackbirders (slave traders) and others. Finally the Marquesan chiefs asked France to help, and a treaty was signed between the chiefs and Admiral du Petit-Thouars in May 1842.

Today, the Marquesans are noted for their native handicrafts, especially for their wood carvings. They also earn money from copra and the sale of shells.

The island of Nuku Hiva can be reached by airplane from Tahiti. This 5-hour flight normally runs each Saturday with a stopover in Rangiroa. There are additional flights often added during high season, operating on Thursdays. It is advisable to make reservations well in advance. There are internal flights within the Marquesas islands, connecting Nuku Hiva with the islands of Hiva Oa, Ua Pou and Ua Huka. The Aranui, a 264-foot long cargo/copra/passenger ship departs Tahiti each month for 16-day round trips to the Marquesas, with two brief stops in the Tuamotus enroute. This is the best way to visit the Marquesas; the ship is comfortable, clean, and air-conditioned, with a French chef, and the Aranui calls at each principal Marquesan island and at isolated valleys.

There are a few small hotels on some of the islands, as well as a room or two in village homes. For those adventurous enough to visit these still-peaceful islands where wild horses, cattle, goats, sheep, and pigs roam through the mountains, the trip will be an experience.

Australs

For those who want to see French Polynesia but prefer their climate a bit cooler than is usually found in the Society Islands, then perhaps the Austral group will be just what you're seeking.

The five inhabited and two uninhabited islands form a chain that extends from the southwest to northwest over a distance of about 800 miles. The nearest island to Tahiti is Rurutu, which is 300 miles south, placing it in a temperate zone where potatoes and strawberries grow in addition to mangoes and papayas.

Rurutu, as well as Tubuai, can be reached by plane from Tahiti in less than 2 hours. The flights leave on Mondays and Thursdays, returning the same day. A passenger-cargo schooner, the *Tuhaa Pae II,* makes regular trips between Tahiti, Rurutu, Tubuai, Raivavae and Rimatara. The round trip takes 6–7 days. A 15–17 day round trip is made between Tahiti, the above islands and Rapa about once a month.

On the island of Tubuai there are a few accommodations in Tahitian-style bungalows close to the beach. There are bicycles, horses and outrigger canoes to rent for exploring this oval-shaped small island that is only six miles long by three miles wide. This is the island where the *Bounty* mutineers attempted to make a settlement but were forced to leave when the natives became violent. Today, the people of the Australs are very friendly and love to include the visitor in their daily events.

On Rurutu there is a hotel that opened in February, 1982. Each of the 16 bungalows includes a sunken bathtub, lush carpets, bedding and towels. A freshwater swimming pool and excellent food are part of the hotel's offerings for the visitor who wishes to explore Rurutu in comfort and style. Chez Catherine in Moerai village has 10 double rooms, restaurant, and bar. There are also lodgings available with the local people in the three villages of Moerai, Avera and Hauti. The handsome Rurutuans grow taro, arrowroot, sweet potatoes, pumpkins, and vanilla. The woven hats from Rurutu are very well made and bring a high price in the stores of Papeete.

Anyone planning to visit these islands of the Austral group that Captain Cook discovered should bring a heavy cardigan and warm clothes during the months of May through October.

PRACTICAL INFORMATION FOR
FRENCH POLYNESIA

FACTS AND FIGURES. French Polynesia covers an area as big as Europe without Russia (1,545,000 sq. miles) and consists of some 130 islands with a land area of only 1,544 sq. miles. These islands, many of which are uninhabited, are divided into five archipelagoes: the Society Islands (Windward and Leeward Islands), the Austral Islands, the Tuamotu-Gambier Islands and the Marquesas Islands. Total population is 175,000.

Tahiti, the largest island, is the seat of government and the capital, with Papeete (pronounced Pah-pay-ay-tay, meaning 'water (from a) basket') the major city and harbor. Population for Tahiti is 123,000, consisting of Polynesians of Maori origin representing 69%, Polynesians mixed 14%, Asians 4% and Europeans (including Americans) 13%.

French Polynesia is administered as an overseas Territory of the French Republic. The High Commissioner is appointed by France to serve for three years. A 1984 revision to the constitution allows more internal autonomy, with a local president and council of 10 ministers elected by the 41 Territorial Assembly members for 5 years. The Territory is represented in France by a senator and two deputies to the National Assembly.

WHEN TO COME. There are only two real seasons in French Polynesia—the warm and rainy season from November to April and the cooler and drier season from May through October. The daytime temperature in the hotter time of the year averages 82°F. and during the cooler months the average is 76°F. The flowers and fruits are at their best during the warmer months but the tropical winds are usually blowing during the months of April through August.

Average Temperature (°Fahrenheit) and Humidity

Papeete	Jan	Feb	Mar	Apr	May	June	July	Aug	Sept	Oct	Nov	Dec
Average max. day temperature	86°	86°	86°	85°	83°	82°	82°	82°	82°	83°	84°	85°
Days of rain	14	11	9	8	7	7	6	5	6	8	9	13
Humidity, percent	79	79	79	79	80	79	78	76	77	77	79	79

WHAT WILL IT COST? Due to the fluctuation of the American dollar the exchange rates vary daily. At time of publication the average rate of US $1–105 CFP (French Pacific Francs).

LANGUAGE. The official language is French, although Tahitian is usually spoken by the Polynesian population, especially away from Papeete. English is spoken in many of the shops and in all the hotels. Keep in mind, however, that this is French Polynesia, and the English you hear will not always be perfect. Try to learn a few words of French and Tahitian and you'll have more fun as well as a warm response to your efforts.

TIPPING. Signs are posted at the airport in Tahiti in three languages, "No Tipping." In other places, such as hotels and travel brochures, you will read that tipping is contrary to Tahitian hospitality. This is true and it is not the custom to tip; however, the employees of the larger hotels in Tahiti, as well as tour escorts and drivers, do graciously accept occasional tips.

PASSPORTS AND CUSTOMS. All passengers entering French Polynesia must be in possession of a valid passport and outbound ticket. Visas, issued by the French

Consulates and Embassies, are required by all visitors except citizens of the Europe-an Economic Community, Switzerland, Liechtenstein, Andorra, and Monaco. Citi-zens of the U.S.A., Canada, and Japan can receive a temporary visa upon arrival in Tahiti. This is not an immigration country and foreigners looking for work are discouraged from applying for long-term visas. A few retired or independently wealthy Americans have moved to these islands and bought property, with the ap-proval of the local government. A work visa is necessary before non-French citizens can be employed in French Polynesia. Professionals such as teachers, nurses, archi-tects, etc. need French diplomas and licenses before working here.

No shots required.

Cruising Yachts

Special formalities apply to those visitors arriving in yachts. Official ports of entry into French Polynesia are: Tahiti and Moorea in the Windward Islands; Raia-tea, Huahine, and Bora Bora in the Leeward Islands; Nuku-Hiva, Ua-Pou, and Hiva-Oa in the Marquesas Islands; Tubuai, Rurutu, and Raivavae in the Austral Islands; and Rangiroa in the Tuamotu-Gambier Islands. A special passport is neces-sary from the Customs Officer or Gendarmerie in the arriving seaport or bay, nor-mally valid for three months, with extensions usually available following applica-tion in Tahiti. Return airplane tickets are required for everyone or an equivalent sum of money can be deposited into an account.

WHAT TO TAKE. Pack lightweight summer clothes, which are used all year round in the tropical weather of Polynesia. A light sweater or jacket feels good in the evenings during the cooler months of June through October. Rarely is a man seen wearing a jacket and tie in Tahiti. The standard attire for men even at dinner parties is simply slacks and shirt. The women usually wear pretty, long dresses in the evenings and normal resort wear around the hotels. *Pareos* or *pareus* (brightly colored and versatile) are worn in most of the outer islands around the hotels, but Tahiti is more cosmopolitan. Tennis shoes or plastic beach sandals for walking on the coral reefs and in the lagoons. If you're going to some of the more remote is-lands, such as the Marquesas or Tuamotus or Australs, take your own supply of tobacco, cigarettes, and booze. Suntan lotion, dark glasses, and mosquito repellent come in handy, also.

TIME ZONE. Tahiti is Greenwich Mean Time minus 10 hours; 2 hours behind U.S. Pacific Standard Time.

ELECTRICITY. Most of the hotels use 220 volts, 60 cycle, with 110 volt outlets for razors only. Some of the older hotels still use 110 volts. Converters can some-times be borrowed from reception desks in the hotels. A small, portable voltage converter with input holes for American appliances and round output plugs for standard French outlets can be purchased at hardware stores in the States and in Tahiti. Most outlets in Tahiti have two round holes.

WATER. Some tourists seem to have problems with the water, so drink bottled mineral water wherever you are.

HOW TO GET THERE. By air: The airport of Tahiti-Faaa is served by seven international airlines and one charter flight operation. *UTA French Airlines* has three weekly flights from Los Angeles to Tahiti and two weekly flights from Paris via San Francisco to Tahiti. UTA also flies to Tahiti from Noumea via Sydney or Auckland twice weekly. *Air France* flies a B747 from Paris to Los Angeles to Papee-te once a week, arriving in Tahiti each Friday. *Air New Zealand* flies to Tahiti from Auckland, Los Angeles, Dallas-Fort Worth, Fiji, and the Cook Islands. *Qantas Air-ways* flies B747M's from Los Angeles to Tahiti three times weekly, and three weekly flights arrive from Melbourne and Sydney. *Continental Airlines* operates two weekly flights from Los Angeles to Tahiti, on to Sydney, Auckland and return, using DC-10 aircraft. *Lan Chile* arrives each Wednesday and Sunday from Honolulu and Easter Island. *Hawaiian Air* flies in twice a week, from Honolulu and the Cook Islands.

By sea: Several international ships call at Tahiti but on an infrequent basis, offer-ing connections from Europe, South Africa, Panama or Australia. These ships are from the lines of Sitmar, Cunard, Holland America, Norwegian America and Bank Line. A few cruise ships leave from San Francisco or other California ports, as well as New York and Florida, and stop in Tahiti.

Charters and excursions. Royal Viking Lines, Princess Cruises, Queen Elizabeth II, Sagafjord, Vistafjord, Alexandre Pushkin, Rotterdam and other large passenger ships cruise to Tahiti and beyond. The Society Explorer (formerly Lindblad) and World Discoverer call at Tahiti en route to Marquesas, Pitcairn and other Pacific islands.

Bali Hai Holidays, 3636 4th Ave., Suite 310, San Diego, CA 92103 (800–854–1513; in California 800–542–6251), Telex 910–3351156. Package programs arranged for honeymooners, independent travelers or groups, featuring Tahiti and Her Islands for Americans.

Continental Airlines has included the island of Moorea in its Los Angeles-Papeete-Moorea flight for $598, with no seasonal adjustment. A weekend excursion package (depart Thursday, return Sunday) is $698. Roundtrip rates for connecting flights within the U.S.A. range from $50 on the West Coast to $200 on the East Coast.

Minerve, a French charter company operated by Compagnie Française de Transports Aeriens, 4, Rue Cambon, 75001 Paris (42–96–16–86), offers reduced roundtrip rates from Paris to Tahiti via San Francisco.

Ted Cook's Islands in the Sun, 760 W. 16th St., Suite L, Costa Mesa, CA 92627 (Nationwide 800–854–3413, California 432–7080, Orange County 714–645–8300) is a wholesale tour operator with a variety of package plans, tours, and excursions to the South Pacific. Owned by French company ACCOR.

Ron Armstrong, *World Adventure Tours,* 2183 Fairview, Suite 106, PO Box 3009, Costa Mesa, CA 92627 (Nationwide 800–222–8687; California 800–221–8687; from area codes 213 and 818, 800–492–2828; and Orange County 714–645–8873), is a wholesale tour operator specializing in the South Pacific, with many programs featuring French Polynesia.

Tahiti Nui Holidays, 6033 W. Century Blvd., Los Angeles, CA 90045 (800–824–4976; in California 800–922–6851), a branch of Tahiti Nui Travel in Papeete, is Tahitian-owned, with special programs and rates for all the tourist islands in French Polynesia.

ACCOMMODATIONS. Accommodations in French Polynesia range from the air-conditioned, carpeted deluxe rooms with telephones and room service, similar to what you can find throughout most of the world, down through thatched-roofed bungalow "fares" and Tahitian pensions, where you share a room and the bathroom may be outdoors with cold water showers or a barrel of water that you splash on with half a coconut shell. The Hotel Sofitel Maeva Beach and the Ibis Hotels in Tahiti and Moorea, and several other hotels in Tahiti, have television sets in the rooms, as well as in-house video programs. Some of the hotels in Tahiti and the outer islands now have a big-screen video for evenings and rainy-day entertainment.

In Tahiti, most of the hotel rooms are conventional in that they are in buildings easily identified as hotels. In the outer islands, the resort hotels normally have individual gardens and overwater bungalows and rooms, many of which are built of bamboo with pandanus roofs and a porch or veranda. These all have large bathrooms with showers. Bathtubs are found only in the deluxe hotels in Papeete and one or two others of the expensive category. Swimming pools are becoming more popular, even in some of the outer islands, although they are still not standard amenities. However, there is usually a lagoon nearby where one can swim in clear water.

The listings below are ranged according to price categories. The rates for the island of Tahiti are based on double occupancy, without meals and the ranges are *Deluxe,* $130 and up; *Expensive,* $110–$130; *Moderate,* $75–$109; *Inexpensive,* $40–$74. The rates for all accommodations in the outer islands vary widely and are often more expensive than deluxe-rated hotels in Tahiti. The classification given is based on double occupancy, without meals, although in some remote islands meals are included. *Deluxe Overwater Bungalow,* $270–$400; *Expensive,* $125–$269; *Moderate,* $65–$124; *Inexpensive,* $25–$64. Hotel Tax is 7%.

Listings begin with Tahiti; other islands and (island groups) follow alphabetically.

TAHITI

Hotel Sofitel Maeva Beach. *Deluxe.* Box 6008, Faaa Airport, Tahiti; 42.80.42, Telex 214FP. On the west coast of Tahiti, on a man-made white sand beach, 4.5 miles from Papeete. One 7-story building, 230 rooms and suites, totally air conditioned with elevators, 2 restaurants (one of them gourmet class), 2 bars, meeting room, beauty parlor, boutiques, 5 acres of gardens, swimming pool, tennis, all water sports, TV sets in all rooms with in-house video and direct distance dialing telephone system. Tahitian dance shows several times weekly.

Tahara'a. *Deluxe.* Box 1015, Papeete, Tahiti; 48.11.22, Telex 225FP. Five miles northeast of Papeete, 8 miles from airport, this hotel is built on the famous "One Tree Hill," commanding one of the finest views in Tahiti. 200 air-conditioned rooms and suites, all with terraces overlooking Matavai Bay and the island of Moorea. Elevators, coffee shop, gourmet restaurant, bar, banquet-and-bar facility, meeting room, beauty parlor, boutiques, 10 acres of gardens, swimming pool, tennis, skeet shooting, jogging trail, beach club and lovely cove with black-sand beach at bottom of cliff reached by stairs built into the cliff or by beach buggy from hotel entrance. Varied water sports including sunset cruises. Tahitian dance shows several times weekly. Hotel is American owned and operated.

Tahiti Beachcomber. *Deluxe.* Box 6014, Faaa, Tahiti; 42.51.10, Telex 276FP. On the west coast of Tahiti, 4.3 miles from Papeete with good view of Moorea. 200 rooms, including overwater bungalows and suites, air conditioned, elevator in 3-story building, pool, tennis, 9-hole golf course, all water sports, conference room, boutique, beauty parlor, 2 bars, coffee shop, gourmet restaurant, refrigerators and coffee maker in rooms, free slide shows and video movies, Tahitian dance shows, Friday night gastronomic seafood buffet and show on white sand beach beside lagoon. Very pretty location.

Te Anuanua. *Expensive.* Box 1553; 42.68.02. In the Pueu district, 7.5 miles from Papeete. Twelve bungalows on the beach, with double beds, private bathrooms, and verandas.

Belle-Fleur Punaauia. *Expensive.* Box 576, Papeete, Tahiti; 42.60.40, Telex 428FP. Located at PK. 7,800 on hill between Hotels Te Puna Bel Air and Sofitel Maeva Beach, overlooking lagoon and Moorea. 40 rooms with TV and video, swimming pool, two tennis courts, restaurant and bar.

Le Mandarin. *Expensive.* Box 302; 42.16.33. Opened in 1988 in conjunction with the famous central Papeete restaurant of the same name. Thirty-seven air-conditioned rooms with TV, video, minibar.

Royal Tahitian. *Expensive.* Box 5001, Pirae, Tahiti; 42.81.13. 2.5 miles east of Papeete, with 45 motel-style rooms and beach bungalows with TV and video, situated in large tropical garden, air conditioned, beach restaurant and bar. A normally very quiet hotel, except on weekends when locals come to enjoy the good swimming in the gentle swells of open ocean that sweep onto the long, curving black-sand beach.

Ibis Papeete. *Moderate.* Box 4545, Papeete, Tahiti, Telephone 42.32.77, Telex 319FP. Located at intersection of Blvd. Pomare and Ave. Prince Hinoi in the middle of downtown Papeete, across street from Moorea boat dock. 72 sound-proofed air-conditioned rooms have color TV, in-house video, and include 4 rooms for handicapped. 90-seat Le Restaurant serves continental cuisine and "Ibisburgers" on second floor, and bar is on street level.

Matavai. *Moderate.* B.P. 32, Papeete, Tahiti; 42.61.29 or 42.67.67, Telex 222FP. Located 1.2 miles from center of Papeete at Tipaerui, 3 blocks inland from lagoon. 146 rooms, some with kitchenettes, air-conditioning, elevators, pool, squash courts, meeting room, game room and boutique, restaurants, bars, night club with special balls and dance shows on occasion. Tahitian dance show each Sunday noon.

Pacific. *Moderate.* Box 111, Papeete, Tahiti; 43.72.82. Medium-sized highrise across street from pier for Moorea boats, located on Blvd. Pomare in downtown Papeete. 44 air-conditioned rooms with private balconies facing harbor or mountains, with La Bellevue Restaurant on top floor and Bar Lea nightclub at street level.

Puunui. *Moderate.* Box 7016, Taravao, Tahiti; 57.19.20, Telex 410FP. This hotel, with 54 rooms and 23 fully equipped 2-bedroom villas, located on the peninsula of Tahiti-iti (little Tahiti) in the district of Vairao, is built on a mountain 1,353 feet high, overlooking Tahiti's southwest coast. It is run as a family-style hotel with junior suites, which include kitchenettes, TV, and video. A swimming pool, restaurant, bar, boutique, and meeting room are included in the mountain portion of the hotel, with a beach bar, restaurant, marina, and sports area bordered by a white-sand beach and lovely lagoon on the sea level. Water activities includes motorboat trips to Tahiti-iti's beautifully unspoiled rugged coast where there are no roads and nature reigns supreme.

Royal Papeete. *Moderate.* Box 919, Papeete, Tahiti; 42.01.29. On Blvd. Pomare in downtown Papeete, across from Moorea boat dock. An old hotel with a new wing and soundproof walls, has 85 rooms and is popular with business people and those who want to be in the midst of the city without the noise. Owned and operated by local Chinese family. Totally air conditioned, with popular restaurant, bar, disco and night club "La Cave," where Tahitian dance band performs on weekends. Favorite night spot for most of Tahiti's young social set.

Tahiti. *Moderate.* Box 416, Papeete, Tahiti; 42.95.50 or 42.61.55. On the lagoonside, at Auae, 1.2 miles from Papeete. This was once the most popular hotel in Tahiti, before the 3 deluxe hotels were built. Renovations have upgraded the quality and rates during the past few years. Very Polynesian style, with immense thatch roof covering reception, boutique, restaurant, bar, and huge dance floor, where balls are held every weekend. Overwater restaurant, swimming pool, swimming dock (no beach), lovely gardens, and lacy woodwork-trimmed buildings in South Seas colonial style. The 92 rooms and 18 bungalows are spacious with verandahs or terraces, air conditioners, refrigerators, and TV. Live Paumotu music several nights a week.

Te Puna Bel Air. *Moderate.* Box 354, Papeete, Tahiti; 42.82.24 or 42.09.00. On west coast of Tahiti, between Hotels Tahiti Beachcomber and Sofitel Maeva Beach, sharing same white-sand beach and reef-protected lagoon. 48 rooms are in motel-style buildings with 28 Tahitian style thatched-roof bungalows, many air conditioned or kitchen equipped. Natural spring-fed swimming pool, restaurant, bar, tennis court, beach snack bar, and swimming pool.

Chez Coco. *Inexpensive.* C/o Coco Dexter, Box 8039, Puurai, Faaa, Tahiti; 42.83.60. Coco, who speaks American and drives a taxi, shares his 3-bedroom hillside home at No. 39 Lotissement Puurai, with 8 guests maximum. Kitchen, bath and swimming pool, and excursions on request. Located on public "Le Truck" route.

Chez Solange. *Inexpensive.* C/o Solange Vandeputte, Box 4230, Papeete, Tahiti; 58.21.07. Lagoon-side pension at PK 15,800 in Punaauia has 2 rooms; mountainside house at No. 123 Punavai Plaine in Punaauia has room for 5, with access to beach. Share facilities. Half-board. Free airport transfers. Located on "Le Truck" route.

Mahina Tea. *Inexpensive.* Box 17, Papeete, Tahiti; 42.00.97. A 10-minute walk from center of Papeete, behind Gendarmerie on Rue St. Amelie. A simple and clean pension with 16 rooms and 6 studios, private baths or shared, with hot water, TV downstairs, and reduced rates for longer visits.

Le Petit Mousse. *Inexpensive.* Box 12085, Papara, Tahiti; 57.42.07. A very popular restaurant with 12 bungalows alongside the lagoon in the district of Papara on Tahiti's west coast, almost 20 miles from downtown Papeete. Food is French, Italian, and "Pied Noir", or North African. Nautical activities include outrigger canoes, sailboards, pedal boats. Tennis courts and golf course nearby. At 4200 CFP a night for two persons, bungalows are said to be the cheapest in French Polynesia; the smiles are free of charge.

Shogun. *Inexpensive.* 10 Rue du Commandant Destremeau, Papeete, Tahiti; 43.13.93, night phone 48.08.75. Located above the Boutique Keiko one block from the waterfront in Papeete, between Ave. Bruat and Rue de la Canonniere Zelée. 11 rooms and 2 suites can be rented by day, week, or month. Complete with air conditioning and bathrooms, these conveniently located rooms are only a couple of blocks from the principal shopping district of Papeete.

Territorial Hostel Center. *Inexpensive.* Box 1709, Papeete, Tahiti; 42.68.02. Located a few blocks from downtown on Blvd. Pomare across from Olympic pool. 18 triples and 3 doubles, sharing bath facilities. Student ID or valid youth hostel card required.

AUSTRAL ISLANDS

Rurutu

Hotel Rurutu Village. *Moderate.* Box 16, Rurutu, Austral Islands, French Polynesia; telephone 42.93.85 (Tahiti) or 392 Rurutu, Telex 311 FP. 16 bungalows outside village of Moerai, with carpets, sunken bathtubs, luxurious bedding and draperies, freshwater swimming pool, tennis court, bar and excellent restaurant, small library, shallow lagoon, and white-sand beach in front of hotel, island excursions, horse rentals.

Chez Catherine. *Inexpensive.* C/o Mme. Catherine Ariiotima, Moerai Village, Rurutu, Austral Islands, French Polynesia; telephone 377 Rurutu. This pension, with 10 double rooms and private baths, is located in the center of the village, between Protestant temple and seaport. Restaurant and bar with seafood specialties and meals for the health-conscious. Catherine's daughter, Bébé, who helps run the pension, speaks English and involves guests in local activities, including jogging, diving in the waves from white sand beach, horse rides, and picnics.

Chez Maurice. *Inexpensive.* C/o Maurice Lenoir, Avera, Rurutu, Austral Islands, French Polynesia; telephone 426 or 448 Rurutu or 43.60.19 (Tahiti). In Avera village, behind the Protestant temple, a few steps from a white-sand beach and lagoon. One huge house that can sleep a group of 13 people maximum, with equipped kitchen, electricity, a communal bathroom, and furnished linens. No meals included.

Chez Metu Teinaore. *Inexpensive.* Village of Moerai, Rurutu, Austral Islands, French Polynesia; telephone 315 or 434 Rurutu. Big furnished house in village center for 10–12 people.

Chez Patrice. *Inexpensive.* C/o Patrice Teinauri, Moerai Village, Rurutu, Austral Islands; telephone Rurutu 443, or 42.88.50 (Tahiti). A one-bedroom house with bathroom and equipped kitchen, with or without meals. Located in Moerai Village with lagoon swimming from white-sand beach.

Tubuai

Chez Taro Tanepau. *Inexpensive.* C/o Tahimata Tanepau, Mataura Village, Tubuai, French Polynesia; telephone 382 Tubuai or 43.87.32 (Tahiti). House with double bed, bathroom, and kitchen. Available by day, week, or month, and located in Tubuai's principal village, with excursions and lagoon swimming principal activities.

Chez Turina Victor. *Inexpensive.* Box 7, Mataura, Tubuai, French Polynesia; telephone 327 Tubuai. Small A-frame house for 2, with kitchen and bathroom. Located in Taahuaia village, 3 km from Mataura. White sand beach and lagoon across road. Rental bicycles and boat with chauffeur to explore offshore "motu" islets. Meals included upon request.

Ermitage Sainte Helene. *Inexpensive.* C/o Mme. Tehinarii Ilari, Village de Mahu, Box 79, Tubuai, French Polynesia; telephone 479 Tubuai. 3 houses for 4 persons maximum each, with bathrooms, hot water and equipped kitchens, in Mahu Village. White-sand beaches and lagoon swimming, boats, bicycles, picnics, excursions arranged.

BORA BORA

Moana Beach. *Deluxe.* Box 156, Bora Bora. 67.73.73. Opened in December 1987, beautifully situated on Nutiva Point and, with rates up to $395 a night, this is the most expensive hotel in the South Pacific. Thirty suites overlooking the ocean, 10 beach bungalows, outdoor gourmet restaurant, beachfront bar, all water sports.

Bora Bora *Expensive.* Nunae, Bora Bora; 67.70.28 or 67.71.28. For reservations, Box 1015, Papeete, Tahiti; 48.12.06, Telex 225FP. 15 acres of tropical gardens are bordered by a very long, sugar-white beach with some of the best snorkeling anywhere among colorful fish and coral formations. 80 large, attractively decorated thatched-roofed Polynesian-style bungalows are nestled among tropical flowers and palm trees or built over the water on stilts. Overhead fans, hair dryers, coffee makers, and refrigerators in rooms. 2 bars, 2 restaurants (one serving gourmet cuisine), beach snack bar for light lunches, boutique, conference and lounge room, village-type store for supplies. Hotel supplies lots of complimentary equipment for activities: bicycles, outrigger canoes, snorkel equipment, games, tennis, basketball, volleyball, rides on outrigger sailing canoe, video movies, slide shows, billiards, table tennis, garden tours, *pareu* demonstrations, lessons in dancing the *tamuré*, or making *poisson cru*. Also available are glass-bottom boat tours, sunset catamaran cruises, reef trips, island picnics, speedboat excursions, scuba diving and sailing or fishing expeditions.

Hotel Sofitel Marara. *Expensive.* Box 6, Vaitape, Bora Bora; 67.70.46, Telex 326FP. This 64-bungalow hotel was built in 1978 to house crew for film *Hurricane*. Thatched-roof bungalows, with overhead fans and refrigerators, are located in gardens, along white-sand beach and on stilts over water near village of Anau. Tennis courts, swimming pool, nightly shows and disco, European food and ambiance. Emphasis is on water activities—there's a special speedboat excursion around island, with visits to reef and very popular shark-feeding show, where you can actually go into water with sharks.

Ibis Bora Bora. *Expensive.* Box 252, Vaitape, Bora Bora; 67.71.16, Telex 302FP. Located next to Hotel Sofitel Marara on beautiful white-sand beach in Amanahune community, this hotel, formerly Climat de France, has 9 blocks of 4 rooms each on the beach side and across the road in several acres of gardens. Restaurant, bar, boutique, nightly giant screen video programs, boat dock and all water activities in marvelous lagoon.

Sofitel Matira Beach. *Expensive.* Box 6008, Faaa, Tahiti; (689) 42.80.42 ext. 905, Telex 214FP. Opened in 1987, this 40-bungalow hotel is built over the lagoon on the famous Matira Beach, 30 minutes by boat from airport.

Bora Bora Bungalows. *Moderate.* Box 98, Vaitape, Bora Bora; 67.71.33. Luxury condos, built as Polynesian-style bungalows on stilts over lagoon and on hillside, facing airport and offering fantastic sunset views. Two bedrooms with sleeping capacity for 4–5 persons, completely equipped for cooking, with laundry facilities, maid service, and taxi available on premises.

Bora Bora Yacht Club. *Moderate.* Box 17, Vaitape, Bora Bora; 67.71.50 or 67.70.69. Less than 2 miles from Vaitape village, at Pointe Fare Piti is the Fare Iati, as the yacht club is known in Tahitian. Three overwater bungalows provide a double bed in each, with bathroom, attractive furnishings and terraces overlooking the deep lagoon, where yachts anchor. 6 floating bungalows are available for those who want complete privacy; these are built in the thatched-roof Polynesian style, and are equipped with a kitchen, shower and toilet, bar, loggia, and sleeping accommodations for 4, plus a small boat to travel back and forth to shore.

Club Mediterranée. *Moderate.* Box 575, Papeete, Tahiti; 42.96.99, Telex 256FP. On lagoon less than a mile from Vaitape village, 45 minutes by boat from Bora Bora airport. The 41 twin units are built as Polynesian style thatched-room bungalows on stilts over the lagoon. Large restaurant, bar, nightclub, and boutique. Disco dancing nightly, sailing, picnics, glass-bottom boat, excursions on lagoon and to mountains, private swimming dock. No beach, but there are several shuttle boat trips made daily to the beautiful Motu Tapu, where there are blinding white-sand beaches and good swimming.

Fare Toopua. *Moderate.* C/o Madame Annie Muraz, Box 87, Vaitape, Bora Bora; 67.70.62 (leave message). Situated on Motu Toopua, a small island 5 minutes by speedboat from Vaitape village. 4 bungalows with mezzanine and a bedroom, bathroom, equipped kitchen in each bungalow. White-sand beach and lovely lagoon at your doorstep, with aluminum dinghy available upon deposit. Minimum stay 3 days, with monthly rentals available.

Hotel Matira. *Moderate.* Box 31, Vaitape, Bora Bora; 67.70.51. Some of the 28 bungalows are kitchen equipped and are located on Matira Plage, Bora Bora's most beautiful white-sand beach. Others are built across the street from the beach in the gardens or on the hillside, 5 miles from Vaitape village and 45 minutes by boat from airport. Restaurant Matira, Bora Bora's only Chinese restaurant, serves 3 daily meals to the hotel guests, if desired, and the offices for the hotel are also located here.

Hotel Oa Oa. *Moderate.* Box 10, Vaitape, Bora Bora; 67.70.84. Next door to Club Med, less than a mile from Vaitape and 45 minutes by boat from Bora Bora airport. 8 bungalows situated on lagoon with restaurant, bar, meeting room. Popular with visiting yachts. Glass-bottom boat, windsurfing, and many other water sports.

Hotel Royal Bora Bora. *Moderate.* Box 202, Vaitape, Bora Bora; 67.71.54. Old hotel on lagoon in Vaitape village with 8 Polynesian-style bungalows, 6 tiny rooms with common bath, restaurant and bar.

Revatua Club. *Moderate.* Box 159, Vaitape, Bora Bora; 67.71.67, Telex 417FP. Located between Anau and Faanui districts, about 35 minutes by car from Vaitape and 8 minutes by speedboat. Opened Dec. 1985, with 16 double or triple rooms on the mountain side, and an overwater restaurant, bar, and boutique, all built in the 1930s colonial style. The rooms all face the lagoon and are complete with fans, bathrooms, and a small terrace. *Chez Christian* restaurant, the hotel's dining room, offers the best French cuisine in Bora Bora—with seafood specialties—at rather expensive prices. Activities include canoe trips on the lagoon, picnics on a private *motu*, windsurfing, snorkeling, small boating, waterskiing, fishing from the hotel's pontoon or on the reef; daily shuttle service to Vaitape village.

Bungalows Are. *Inexpensive.* C/o Madame Are Siou Moun, Matira, Nunue, Bora Bora; 67.70.73. 5 bungalows with 2 double rooms each, living room, equipped kitchen and bathroom with hot water and electricity, located across road from a beautiful white-sand beach between Hotels Bora Bora and Matira. Excursions and picnics can be arranged as well as transport to Vaitape village. 3 of the bungalows are available only July-August.

Chez Fredo. *Inexpensive.* C/o Alfredo Doom, Vaitape, Bora Bora; 67.70.31. In Viatape village, a 5-minute walk from boat dock, on mountain side. 4 housekeeping bungalows on lagoon, plus a house with 3 rooms where you can rent a single bed with kitchen privileges. Low rate for bed and breakfast. Popular with international budget travelers and French military from Tahiti.

Chez Nono. *Inexpensive.* C/o Noel Leverd, Box 12, Vaitape, Bora Bora; 67.71.38. 2 large and 2 small bungalows, including equipped kitchens and bathrooms at a private home at Pointe Matira Beach. Activities arranged upon request, including trips on the lagoon by motor boat, sailboards and transfers to Vaitape village.

Chez Robert Tinorua. *Inexpensive.* Nunue, Bora Bora; 67.72.92. The last house at Pointe Matira, with Bora Bora's most beautiful white-sand beach and lagoon at the doorstep. A modern house with two bedrooms, kitchen, bathroom, living/sleeping room, and big terrace overlooking beach and lagoon. Can sleep 9 maximum, but water shortage poses problems in dry season of July–October. Outrigger canoe visits around lagoon, to reef, picnics on *motu* or around the island.

HUAHINE

Bali Hai Huahine. *Expensive.* Box 2, Fare, Huahine; 68.82.77. For reservations: P.O. Box 26, PaoPao, Moorea; 56.13.59, Telex 331FP. Near village of Fare (0.6 mile) on long white-sand beach and adjacent turquoise lagoon. 1.8 miles from airport. First-class Tahitian-style bungalows on stilts, very nicely constructed and decorated with indoor gardens in all bathrooms, which are sunken to ground level. Hotel is in midst of several acres of gardens and lakes, crisscrossed with bridges over fish-filled lakes and pools decorated with lily pads and water hyacinths. Excavations on premises have revealed important archeological finds from prehistoric Polynesian society, with artifacts displayed in hotel's mini-museum. Restaurant, boutique, bar, excellent swimming in lagoon, with *Liki Tiki* excursions for snorkelling and shelling, plus sunset cruises. Large swimming pool, tennis courts, games room, Tahitian music nightly. Long pants required for men after 6 P.M.

Huahine Nui. *Moderate.* Baie de Maroe, Huahine; 68.84.69. 6 large bungalows on mountainside overlooking Maroe Bay. American bar, restaurant featuring fresh seafood. Meeting room, tennis, swimming pool and marina.

Relais Mahana. *Moderate.* Box 30, Fare, Huahine; 68.81.54, Telex 300FP. This 12-bungalow hotel is situated on Huahine's most beautiful white-sand beach, which stretches for miles alongside a magnificent coral-flowered lagoon. This is at Avea Bay, one mile from Parea village on Huahine-iti, 1-hour by car from the Huahine airport or Fare village. Efficiently operated by a French family from New Caledonia, the food, ambiance, and language are definitely French. The clean, modern rooms can sleep 3 persons, with one bungalow designed for the handicapped. Restaurant, bar, boutique, tennis court, long pier, excellent snorkelling, windsurfing, pedal boats, outrigger canoes, Hobie cat, water-skiing, ping-pong, and games. Bicycles, rental scooters, and cars available on premises. Disco dancing in lounge each evening.

Chez Lovina. *Inexpensive.* C/o Lovina Bohl, Fare, Huahine; 68.81.90. In the middle of "downtown" Fare, right on the harbor front, Lovina has 7 clean and attractively decorated rooms for rent with electricity, private bathrooms, and double beds. She also has 3 housekeeping bungalows for rent, by the ocean and in a garden. Lovina speaks English, serves meals and gives tours if desired. Great lagoon swimming and white-sand beach across street to right of hotel.

Chez Temeharo. *Inexpensive.* C/o Madame Amelie Temeharo, Parea, Huahine; 68.81.87. In village of Parea, 28 km. (17 miles) from airport and Fare. 5 rooms in big two-story house in center of village. All toilet and shower facilities in common and meals are served family style in large dining room. Long and beautiful white-sand beach 5-minute walk from pension, and trips to nearby *motu,* picnics, and other excursions can be arranged.

Hotel Bellevue. *Inexpensive.* Box 21, Maroe, Huahine; 68.82.76 or 68.81.70. In district of Maroe, 3.6 miles from Fare and 6 miles from Huahine airport, on hillside overlooking Maroe Bay. 1-story building with 8 rooms and 15 bungalows built around a swimming pool. Solar electricity, restaurant featuring local seafood caught by Chinese-Tahitian owner, who will take guests along on his fishing expeditions, or take them by boat to a *motu* where there are white-sand beaches and great swimming and snorkelling. Hotel also has small bar, ping-pong, *petanque,* and tours of the island.

Pension Enite. *Inexpensive.* C/o Martial Lafourcade, Fare, Huahine; 68.82.37. This pension is very popular because of its great cuisine, served next to lagoon and white-sand beach at Fare, right at the entrance to the main village. There are 6 rooms in a big building with beds for 17 people, with bath facilities in common. Besides the restaurant and bar there are excursions around the island and windsurfing. 2-day stay required and meals are AP and MAP.

Pension Huahine. *Inexpensive.* C/o Pierre Colombani, Fare, Huahine; 68.82.69. 2-story building with 10 rooms in the center of Fare, overlooking harbor. Some rooms contain private bathrooms with cold water, which is scarce during dry months of July–October. Beds are very uncomfortable, sagging in middle, and maid service is nonexistent while rooms are occupied. Hotel is very popular with international surfers and budget travelers who find a certain charm about the place.

Pension Tarapapa. *Inexpensive.* C/o Adolphe Bohl, Maeva, Huahine; 68.81.23 (Huahine) or 48.12.52 (Tahiti). 10 housekeeping rooms in Maeva district, at Lake Fauna Nui, 7 km (4.2 mi) from Fare village. 1 building of 4 rooms is located on lake side and another building of 6 rooms is across street, next to a food store. All rooms are equipped with electricity, kitchens, bathrooms, fans, TV, double beds, and terraces. Excursions can be arranged with owners. Beautiful white-sand beach and lagoon swimming found on ocean side of long *motu* opposite the lake.

MANIHI

Kaina Village. *Expensive.* Box 2560, Papeete, Tahiti; 42.75.53 (Tahiti), Telex 339FP. Located on the same *motu* where the airport strip is located, this hotel is across the lagoon from the main village. 14 overwater self-contained *fares* have balconies from which you can watch the colorful fish feeding on coral formations in the aquamarine lagoon. A superb restaurant, separate bar and billiards room, boutique, lagoon excursions, line fishing; visits to village, pearl farm fish park; and picnics on lovely *motu.* All the white-sand beaches and excellent lagoon swimming anyone could wish for.

Chez Rei Estall. *Inexpensive.* Turipaoa, Manihi, Tuamotu Archipelago, French Polynesia; no telephone. 2 rooms in private house in Turipaoa village. Electricity, toilets and shower in common with family, as well as meals.

Chez Marquerite Fareea. *Inexpensive.* Turipaoa, Manihi, Tuamoto Archipelago, French Polynesia; no telephone. 1 double bungalow with bath and 2 bungalows sharing bath on Motu Topiheiri, 20 minutes by speedboat from main village. Meals and lagoon excursions. Reservations required.

MARQUESAS ISLANDS

Fatu Hiva

Chez Francois Peters, Chez Kehu Kamia, and **Chez Joseph Tetuanui.** *Inexpensive.* C/o Omoa Village, Fatu Hiva, Marquesas Islands, French Polynesia. 3 private homes in Omoa Village who rent 2 bedrooms each to visitors. Meals included if desired. Join in family activities, rent horses or go on a wild pig hunt.

Chez Tehau Gilmore. *Inexpensive.* Omoa Village, Fatu Hiva, Marquesas Islands, French Polynesia; no telephone. House with 2 bedrooms he rents very low priced, no meals included. In village with river running behind that is often used for bathing purposes as well as swimming and catching fresh river shrimps. Prepare food yourself or arrange with nearby families. Black volcanic-sand beach often has very rough undertow and heavy breakers.

Chez Veronique Kamia and **Chez Yvonne Tevenino.** *Inexpensive.* C/o Hanavave Bay, Marquesas Islands, French Polynesia. 2 houses in Hanavave Bay with rooms to rent in their homes, meals included. Swim from black-sand beach at beautiful Bay of Virgins beneath shadow of sculptured mountain peaks.

Hiva Oa

Atuona Mairie Bungalows. *Inexpensive.* C/o Guy Rauzy, Atuona Village, Hiva Oa, Marquesas Islands, French Polynesia; telephone AT332. 5 bungalows operated by the town hall of Atuona in center of village, equipped with kitchens, refrigerators, bathrooms, and electricity.

Chez Bernard Heitaa. *Inexpensive.* C/o Puamau Village, Hiva Oa, Marquesas Islands, French Polynesia; no telephone. Private house with 2 bedrooms, kitchen, bathroom in common, and electricity. Located in the valley of Puamau, with the possibility of visiting stone *tiki's* by land rover. Swimming in surf bordered by black volcanic-sand beach just below village homes. Full board pension available.

Chez Saucourt. *Inexpensive.* C/o Atuona Village, Hiva Oa. telephone 333. One bungalow with kitchen and bathroom.

Nuku Hiva

Keikahanui Inn. *Moderate.* C/o Frank and Rose Corser, Box 21, Taiohae, Marquesas Islands, French Polynesia; telephone 382. Almost a mile from the boat pier, situated on a bluff overlooking Taiohae Bay and a long black volcanic-sand beach. 3 Polynesian-style bungalows with private bathrooms, hot water, and refrigerators. No credit cards accepted. Horses for rent and 4-wheel-drive vehicle for excursions. This small hotel is owned by two yachting Americans who know where to buy the best carvings and tapas.

Chez Fetu. *Inexpensive.* C/o Fetu Peterano, Box 22, Taiohae, Nuku Hiva, Marquesas Islands, French Polynesia; telephone TA 366. 300 meters from boat dock in the Vallee Française, three houses, with accommodations for 3 people each, including equipped kitchens and private bathrooms. Swimming from black-sand beach at Taiohae Bay, or nearby white-sand beach close to village.

Hotel Moana Nui. *Inexpensive.* Box 9, Taiohae, Nuku Hiva, Marquesas Islands; telephone 330. Located 1 km. from dock in main village, facing ocean, across road from long black-sand beach with pretty bay for swimming. 7 simple rooms, some with bathrooms, bar and restaurant downstairs. Reservations required for meals, which are usually steak and French fries.

Pension Yvonne. *Inexpensive.* Hatiheu Village, Nuku Hiva, Marquesas Islands, French Polynesia; no telephone. This pretty little village is one hour by boat from Taiohae Bay or a good half-day's ride across the rutted mountain roads. 3 bungalows with bathrooms and petrol lamps in village facing ocean, black-sand beach noted for *nonos* (stinging sand flies). Meals are served in pension's well-known restaurant and include fresh river shrimp and lobsters. Rental horses to visit *tiki's* or excursions into valley.

Tahuata

Chez Naani Barsinas. *Inexpensive.* Vaitahu Village, Tahuata, Marquesas Islands, French Polynesia; no telephone. 3-bedroom house in village with salt-and-pepper sand beach and bay swimming in front of village. Meals served, with emphasis on fresh fruits and fish, lobster, and river shrimp. Boat excursions arranged.

Ua Huka

Chez Joseph Lichtle. *Inexpensive.* Vaipaee Village, Ua Huka, Marquesas Islands, French Polynesia; no telephone. 3-bedroom house, kitchen, electricity, toilet, in village of Vaipaee. Meals and monthly rentals if desired. Horses available for hire.

Chez Joseph Lichtle. *Inexpensive.* At 5 km from Vaipaee, in Haavei, Mr. Lichtle has a lovely setting with a long white-sand beach, gentle swells, and 3 bungalows along beach and 2 houses on the hill overlooking beautiful bay and bird island. Meals are provided from his plentiful garden, fruit trees, and livestock supply, plus an abundant ocean. No other houses around.

Chez Laura Raioha. *Inexpensive.* Vaipaee Village, Ua Huka, Marquesas Islands, French Polynesia; no telephone. A big 4-bedroom house with double accommodations in each room, plus kitchen, electricity, and communal bathroom. Meals served if desired, and horseback riding provided. In village, with swimming from black sand beach in open swells.

Chez Miriama Fournier. *Inexpensive.* Vaipaee Village, Ua Huka, Marquesas Islands, French Polynesia. 3-bedroom house with bathroom, electricity, and kitchen. Meals can be served by family and excursions arranged. Swimming from black-sand beach and often strong current of open bay.

Chez Vii Fournier. *Inexpensive.* Hane Village, Ua Huka, Marquesas Islands, French Polynesia; no telephone. A house with 2 double rooms, toilet, kitchen with refrigerator, plus a "passage hut" with 2 beds and a toilet for those in transit. Monthly rentals available. Meals taken with family. Excursions to *tiki's* in valley. Black-sand beach at foot of village offers swimming in open surf.

Ua Pou

Chez Juliette Bruno. *Inexpensive.* Hakahau, Ua Pou, Marquesas Islands, French Polynesia, telephone HA 391. 2-bedroom house with kitchen and bath. Black-sand beachfronts the village with lovely white-sand beaches nearby.

Chez Rosalie. *Inexpensive.* C/o Mrs. Rosalie Tata, Village of Hakahau, Ua Pou, Marquesas Islands, French Polynesia; telephone HA 311. Lively restaurant in center of Hakahau village. One double room for 4 persons in big family house. Meals taken with family and excursions arranged.

Chez Samuel and Marie Jeanne. *Inexpensive.* Hakahau, Ua Pou, Marquesas Islands, French Polynesia, telephone HA 316. 2-bedroom house with bath, kitchen and electricity. Tours available by car and boat with chauffeur to visit historic and photographic sites.

MAUPITI

Chez Anua Tinorua. *Inexpensive.* Maupiti, French Polynesia; no telephone. 2 double rooms in family home close to the schoolhouse in principal village of Vai'ea. Complete pension with Tahitian family.

Chez Papa Roro. *Inexpensive.* C/o Teroro Raioho, Maupiti, French Polynesia; no telephone. Located in the main village of Vai'ea, 500 meters from schoolhouse, with 1 house with 4 rooms and private baths, 1 house with 6 rooms and communal baths and 1 big house with 3 rooms and a common bathroom. Restaurant and bar on premises and swimming in lagoon across street.

Chez Teha Teupoohuitua. *Inexpensive.* Maupiti, French Polynesia; no telephone. A big house by the lagoon in the village of Farauru, with a capacity for 14 people in 5 rooms and toilet and shower facilities in common. Full pension meals.

Hotel Auira. *Inexpensive.* C/o Mme. Edna Terai, Maupiti, French Polynesia; No telephone. 8 bungalows built in Polynesian style with double bed. 3 of these are located on very white sand beach, with private bathrooms and the 5 garden bungalows share facilities. Hotel has restaurant and is located on Motu Hu'apiti, across the lagoon from main island.

Pension Tavaearii. *Inexpensive.* C/o Mme. Vilna Tavaearii, Motu Tiapaa, Maupiti, French Polynesia; no telephone. Accommodations for 16 people in 2 bungalows with 4 double rooms each, plus 3 showers and 2 toilets in common, a communal dining room, solar lighting and petrol lamps. Located on Motu Tiapaa, an islet across the lagoon from main island, with beautiful white sand beaches and excellent swimming in lagoon. Outrigger canoes and windsurfing.

MOOREA

Sofitel Tiare Moorea. *Deluxe.* Box 1019, Papetoia, Moorea; 56.19.19, Telex 441FP. Opened in 1987, this self-contained complex of overwater suites, beach bungalows, and a colonial-style hotel will have 150 rooms, a leisure area with 2 restaurants, 2 bars, banquet room, swimming pool, and many sports activities. Located on northwest side of Moorea, close to Club Med, 20 minutes by air-conditioned bus from Moorea airport.

Bali Hai Moorea. *Expensive.* Box 26, Moorea, French Polynesia; 56.13.59, Telex 331FP. At entrance to Cook's Bay on small white-sand beach, 6 miles from Moorea's airport. 63 Tahitian-style bungalows in 4 acres of gardens, along beach, and over the fish-filled lagoon. Busy and popular bar, restaurant, boutique, outrigger canoes, bicycles, volley ball, tennis, diving, excursions on raft *Liki Tiki,* frequent picnics, friendly management and personnel. Sunday noon Tahitian feast with folkdance show. Swimming pool with barstools in the pool. Tahitian music nightly.

Climat de France. *Expensive.* Box 1017, Papetoai, Moorea; 56.15.48, Telex 339FP. Next door to Hotel Residence Tipaniers, along white-sand beach in Haapiti district. 40 rooms in motel-style buildings, with air conditioning or fans, plus 43 bungalows with kitchenettes. Rooms are homey and cheerful, with fridges and some bathtubs. Restaurant, bar, swimming pool, tennis, water-skiing, windsurfing, and all other water sports. Nightly movies on large video screen, often in French.

Sofitel Kia Ora Moorea. *Expensive.* Box 28, Temae, Moorea; 56.11.73 or 56.12.90, Telex 390FP. 82 thatched-roofed, attractive and spacious bungalows are spread throughout almost 25 acres of coconut palm trees, lush tropical gardens and a white-sand beach almost a mile long. This deluxe resort hotel includes executive suites, 2 restaurants, gourmet cuisine, bar, well-stocked boutique, all water sports in clear turquoise lagoon, glass-bottom boat, outrigger canoes, picnics, tennis, frequent Tahitian shows and *pareu*-tying demonstrations. Watch the sun rise behind Tahiti each morning from this beautiful site 5 minutes from Temae Airport in Moorea.

Club Bali Hai. *Moderate.* B.P. 26, Moorea, French Polynesia; 56.13.68 or 56.13.59, Telex 331FP. Located on a small white-sand beach near village of Pao Pao at famous Cook's Bay with fabulous panorama of mountains and bay. Formerly Hotel Aimeo, this 19-unit hotel is now managed by the Bali Hai group as a vacation interval ownership program. Swimming pool, tennis court, restaurant, two bars, outrigger canoes and *Liki Tiki* cruises.

Club Méditerranée. *Moderate.* B.P. 575, Papeete, Tahiti; 42.96.99, Telex 256FP. 45 mins. by bus from Moorea airport on large white-sand beach at Haapiti. The completely rebuilt village has 700 beds, a huge restaurant, bars, boutique, disco, theater, and sports complex, plus almost constant organized activities.

Coconut House. *Moderate.* Box 2329, Papeete, Tahiti or Maharepa, Moorea; 56.15.44. 12 bungalows in the district of Maharepa, a 5-minute walk from Hotel Bali Hai. On mountain-side of road, with white-sand beach and lagoon across street. Hotel has very popular restaurant, bar with piano, boutique, swimming pool, hot water, video, outrigger canoes, and snorkeling equipment.

Hibiscus. *Moderate.* Box 1009, Papetoai, Moorea; 56.12.20 or 56.14.09. 29 *fare*-type thatched-roof bungalows scattered spaciously throughout palm-dotted gardens, with huge banyan tree shading part of the immense white sand beach beside a clear lagoon. Next door to Club Méditerranée in Haapiti district, this hotel is noted for its *l'Escargot Restaurant and Sunset Beach Bar.* Swimming pool and all water sports available.

Hotel Residence Les Tipaniers. *Moderate.* Box 1002, Haapiti, Moorea; 56.12.67. In district of Haapiti next door to Climat de France and close to Club Méditerranée, on long white-sand beach with beautiful lagoon. 20 bungalows, 9 equipped with kitchenettes, plus excellent restaurant featuring Italian, French, and Polynesian specialties. Beach snack bar and water skiing center.

Ibis Moorea. *Moderate.* B.P. 30, Moorea; 56.10.50, Telex 361FP. 76 rooms built in "neo-colonial" style with restaurant, bar, color TV in rooms, swimming pool, Hobie cats, sailboards, sunset cruises, "gym-tonic" classes and game room, with picnics to the *motu.* Located in Cook's Bay next door to *Keke III* dock. Part of French hotel chain ACCOR.

Moorea Lagoon. *Moderate.* B.P. 11, Moorea; 56.14.68 or 56.11.55, Telex 327FP. Hotel reopened July 1986 under new ownership and management. All of the 45 thatched-roof bungalows, built along a pretty, white-sand beach and scattered amidst 12 acres of gardens, have been rebuilt, with new furnishings and bathrooms. Located between Cook's Bay and Opunohu Bay, 9.5 miles from village of Pao Pao, with restaurant, bar, boutique, bicycles, outrigger canoes and *Aqua 6* surface submarine for underwater viewing.

Moorea Village. *Moderate.* Box 1008, Papetoai, Moorea; 56.10.02. 19 miles from Moorea airport on large white-sand beach at Haapiti. This hotel is Tahitian owned and operated, with 50 thatched-roof bungalows, including 15 with kitchenettes. Swimming pool, tennis courts, restaurant, bar, boutique, picnics on the *motu* and all water sports. *Maa Tahiti* (Tahitian food) served each Sunday at noon, followed by Tahitian dance show. This hotel is popular with local families from Tahiti and French military personnel.

Residence Linareva. *Moderate.* Box 205, Temae, Moorea; 56.15.35. Telex 537FP. 4 housekeeping bungalows in Polynesian style on long white-sand beach in Haapiti district. Each *fare* is equipped with electricity, color TV, barbeque grill, bathroom, kitchenette, and linens. Accommodations for 3–8 people, with outrigger canoes, sailboards, bicycles, Hobie cats, sunfish boat, motor boat, and scuba diving facilities. Minimum of 2 nights required.

Le Kaveka. *Inexpensive.* Box 13, PaoPao, Moorea; 56.18.30, Telex 361FP. Located next to *Keke III* boat dock in Cook's Bay, this 24-bungalow hotel has an overwater bar and restaurant, plus a marina with aquatic sports activities. Small whitesand beach. Very good salad bar with barbequed steaks.

Chez Billy Ruta. *Inexpensive.* Haapiti, Moorea; 56.12.54 or 56.16.98. These 11 bungalows, beside the lagoon and white-sand beach near Club Med, are complete with 2 single beds each, bathrooms, and linens. Three of the bungalows have kitchenettes.

Hotel Pauline. *Inexpensive.* Afareaitu, Moorea; 56.11.26. About 5 miles from Moorea airport, on mountain side, near the Mairie or city hall of Moorea's capital village, Pauline's is noted for its local-style cuisine. 7 rooms are located in an old South Seas gingerbread-style home complete with verandah. Bathrooms and showers are in common. Beds are rather lumpy and tend to dip into a V in the middle. Pauline's house is also a sort of Polynesian museum, with stone *tiki's* from Moorea's valleys.

Hotel Residence Tiahura. *Inexpensive.* Box 1068, Papetoai, Moorea; 56.15.45, Telex 537FP. Located 300 meters before Club Med, across street from long whitesand beach. 24 Polynesian-style bungalows, 18 with equipped kitchenettes including small refrigerators. Windows are not screened. Swimming pool, boutique, small restaurant-grill, and snorkeling equipment.

Motel Albert. *Inexpensive.* PaoPao, Moorea; 56.12.76. Situated in the village of PaoPao, across street from Club Bali Hai, on mountain side. Family operated motel-type rooms with communal or private bathrooms. Total of 24 rooms including 2 houses, some equipped for cooking. Two night minimum is required and no credit cards accepted.

RAIATEA

Bali Ha'i Raiatea. *Expensive.* Box 43, Uturoa, Raiatea; 66.31.49. For reservations, Box 26, Moorea, French Polynesia, Telephone 56.13.59, Telex 331FP. Built on the lagoon 0.6 miles from village of Uturoa, 2 miles from airport. 36 units, built Tahitian style as rooms in a 1-story building or bungalows over the water and beside the lagoon. No beach. A sitting pool, bar, restaurant, boutique, game room, bicycles, volley-ball, table tennis, outrigger canoe shuttle to nearby white-sand beach *motu,* boat excursions to Fa'aroa River and nearby island of Tahaa, frequent fire walking ceremonies and children's folkloric dance show.

Chez Greenhill. *Inexpensive.* C/o Marie-Isabelle and Jason Greenhill, Box 598, Uturoa, Raiatea, 66.37.64. A bungalow for 4 and a 3-bedroom villa located in a flower garden beside the beautiful Faaroa River. Swimming pool. Meals, transfers and excursions provided by Greenhill family.

Le Motu. *Inexpensive.* Box 549, Uturoa, Raiatea; 66.34.06. 7 basic but clean rooms, plus a very good French restaurant located on second floor of old building in middle of downtown Uturoa. Billiards parlor and disco night club downstairs. Frenchman Roger Bardou came from New Caledonia with his family and took over the abandoned Hotel Hinano building, cleaned it up and refurbished the rooms, which can sleep 3 maximum, and have private showers and lavabos, with common toilets next to the hallway. The restaurant faces the public wharf and public gardens, with flamboyant trees outside. Water-skiing, windsurfing, deep-sea fishing, guided tours, picnic trips to the *motu,* boating excursions available, plus rental scooters and cars. Cuisine is seafood, French and Tahitian specialties.

Pension Ariane Brotherson. *Inexpensive.* Box 236, Uturoa, Raiatea; 66.33.70. 2 rooms for 3 persons each located in a private home, complete with meals, at P.K. 8, Avera, 4.8 miles from Uturoa center. Share the bathing facilities and meals with Tahitian family, and swimming across the street in clear lagoon. Bicycles, island tours, and all nautical activities available.

Pension Marie-France. *Inexpensive.* C/o Marie-France Philip, Box 272, Uturoa, Raiatea; 66.37.10. 2 rooms in a private home on the lagoon 3 minutes from the center of Uturoa. Electricity, with bath facilities in common, all meals if desired, plus picnics and lagoon diving excursions with professional instructor.

Pension Yolande. *Inexpensive.* C/o Madame Yolande Roopinia, Avera, Box 298, Uturoa, Raiatea; 66.35.28. Popular accommodations with Tahitian family 6 miles from airport on pretty lagoon. One large Polynesian-style bungalow with 4 rooms and 3 single beds each, plus a bathroom and equipped kitchen and electricity. No maid service and no lunch served. MAP includes Chinese and Tahitian foods, grilled meats, and picnics on the nearby *motu,* excursions to the *marae* (Tahitian temple), windsurfing and sailing, outrigger paddle canoes, and bicycles available.

Raiatea Village. *Inexpensive.* Box 282; 66.31.62 or 66.33.60. 12 bungalows with kitchenettes located at Fa'aroa River in district of Avera, 11 km. (6.6 miles) from downtown Uturoa. Owned and operated by Tahitian family, who provide transport to the airport, plus excursions around the island, lagoon trips, visits to archeological sites and serve meals if requested. Clean and attractive bungalows are built along a man-made white-sand beach beside the lagoon or just behind in the gardens. Snorkeling equipment, outrigger paddle canoe, bicycles and rental cars available on premises.

RANGIROA

Hotel Sofitel Kia Ora Village. *Expensive.* Box 706, Papeete, Tahiti; 42.86.72 or 42.86.75, Telex 306FP, telephone on premises 384 Rangiroa. 30 first-class attractively designed and decorated bungalows, situated along a very white sand beach and dotted throughout several acres of gardens and coconut palm forests. 15 minutes by boat from Tiputa village and 15 minutes by bus from Avatoru village, 10 minutes by bus from airport. Very good restaurant, overwater bar, boutique, barbeque, all water activities, including glass-bottom boat, diving facilities and lessons, snorkeling through the passes with sharks and fishes swimming below in the very swift current. Tahitian music several nights a week. Friendly management who take good care of their clients.

La Bouteille a La Mer. *Moderate.* Box 17, Avatoru, Rangiroa; 43.99.30 or 334 Rangiroa, Telex 537FP. 11 beach bungalows in typical thatched-roof and bamboo-wall design, on very long white-sand beach beside turquoise lagoon, very close to airport. Family-style meals, French atmosphere, with emphasis on do-it-yourself entertainment, with water sports the main theme.

Hotel Rangiroa Village. *Moderate.* Box 8, Avatoru, Rangiroa; telephone 383 Rangiroa. 9 traditional bungalows on white-sand beach. 0.5 miles from Avatoru village. Restaurant, bar, water sports, and lagoon excursions. Tahitian owned.

Village Sans Souci. *Moderate.* C/o Greg & Louise Laschelle, Avatoru, Rangiroa; 42.48.33 (Tahiti). Life on a *motu* can be experienced in this 15-bungalow complex located one hour by speedboat from Avatoru village, across immense lagoon. These simple *fares* are made of coconut thatch and have petrol lamps, communal toilets with cold water showers, do-it-yourself housekeeping. Linens provided. Complete pension plan with emphasis on fresh seafood from plentiful lagoon surrounding motu islet. Activities include fishing, snorkelling and scuba diving.

Chez Jimmy Estall. *Inexpensive.* Box 597, Papeete, Tahiti; 42.88.44, 42.88.11 or 42.43.73 and 316 Rangiroa. Four traditional individual bungalows, complete with electricity and bathrooms, located between the ocean and the lagoon, 2 km. from the city hall of Tiputa. Family-style meals served at long picnic tables under thatched shelter. Lagoon excursions and fishing expeditions arranged. Very pleasant pension hotel.

Chez Marie Richmond. *Inexpensive.* Avatoru, Rangiroa; telephone 394 or 392 Rangiroa. 7 Polynesian-style bungalows with private baths, located beside lagoon 5 km from airport. Restaurant-bar open every day, with full board, featuring fresh seafood from lagoon. Boat rentals for line fishing and excursions across immense lagoon.

TAHAA

Marina Iti. *Moderate.* Box 888, Uturoa, Raiatea; 65.61.01, Telex 537FP Attn-Marina-Iti. At the entrance of Apu Bay in Vaitoare, this attractive pension on a point facing the sunset is easily accessible when arriving by boat from Raiatea. Open, spacious sitting lounge, with bamboo and rattan South Pacific-style furnishings. 4 rooms for 3 people each, *table d'hôte* French cooking, all sorts of excursions on the lagoon and water sports, including 4 new charter yachts. Operated by three French yachtsmen.

Chez Mata Marae. *Inexpensive.* Patio, Tahaa (no telephone). 2 rooms in a private home in the village of Patio, next to the Protestant temple. Showers and toilets in common. Meals taken with Tahitian family.

Pension Hibiscus. *Inexpensive.* Box 151, Haamene, Tahaa; 65.61.06. Family pension and *Restaurant Hibiscus* operated by Gilbert and Marie-France Marchand, a young French couple who have owned restaurants in many parts of the world. 4 newly built individual bungalows, restaurant, bar, and boutique on the mountain side between the bays of Haamene and Faaaha. A fun atmosphere, with picnic trips to the *motu*, fishing on the reef, windsurfing, bicycling, tours of the island, and rental cars. Full pension possible, with escargots, lobster and fondue Bourguignonne on menu. No beach, and bay here is rather choppy due to wind gusts sweeping through.

Tahaa Iti Village. *Inexpensive,* Tiva, Tahaa; 65.61.00 Located between villages of Tiva and Tapuamu, facing Bora Bora and providing clear view of magnificent sunsets. 7 small thatched-roof bungalows are built on stilts over the beautiful, clear lagoon where tropical fishes can be seen feeding among the colorful coral gardens. These old bungalows, now being reconstructed, are very simple, with tiny balconies and bathrooms and showers in common in the gardens. A new thatched-roof building is the dining room and kitchen, where one of French Polynesia's best chefs serves up sumptuous meals, *table d'hôte.* Tours of the island, excursions on the lagoon, picnics on the *motu,* outrigger canoes, bicycles, and mountain hiking can all be arranged.

TETIAROA

Tetiaroa Village. *Moderate.* Box 2418, Papeete, Tahiti; 42.63.02. This is Marlon Brando's private atoll, 17 minutes by airplane from Tahiti. The hotel consists of a private airstrip, plus 14 thatched-roof bungalows complete with electricity, private bathrooms and hot water, plus 5 A-frame bungalows with none of the above, sharing facilities in common. There is a dining room, reception area, boutique, and kitchen with a beach bar on the blindingly white sand beach, close to a magnificent lagoon. Activities include trips to bird island by boat across turquoise lagoon, sailboards, snorkeling equipment, Hobie cat, and boat rental with driver.

CAMPING. There are now organized campgrounds on Tahiti. At Mahina, 6.5 miles from Papeete, is a 50-tent camp near a black-sand beach with good swimming, and communal showers and toilets; additional camping near the Club Med on

Moorea with fresh water and spartan facilities, but a lovely beach and lagoon, and bus service is available to the boat dock. A dozen or so tents are always set up in Huahine, in a clearing beside the beach and lagoon between the Hotel Bali Hai and the village of Fare. No fresh water or bathrooms available on the premises. On Bora Bora Chez Pauline Youssef, Box 215, Bora Bora, operates a campsite at beautiful Matira Beach. Common facilities include a bungalow for games and reading, a bungalow for cooking and dining and another for bath facilities. Philippe Selio Vaino also has a beach campsite 2 km south of Anau village, with hot and cold water and daily bus service to Vaitape village.

RESTAURANTS. Dining out in Tahiti is one of the most popular pastimes for visitors and residents alike. Since there are so many cultures, it naturally follows that the choices of foods available are varied and interesting ones. The most popular restaurants for visitors are usually those serving French food—Papeete is noted for its French restaurants. Chinese food is a favorite anywhere and Tahiti is no exception, as shown by the many Chinese restaurants scattered over town. Tahitian food is a little harder to find, because it is usually prepared at home by the families. Many of the hotels do feature Tahitian feasts or "tamaaraas" frequently to give the visitor a taste of smoked breadfruit, taro, "fei" or mountain bananas, "fafa," their version of spinach which is very good when cooked with chicken and served with their young suckling pig, and "poisson cru," or marinated fish served with coconut milk, or "poe," a starchy pudding made of papaya, mango or banana.

Good old fashioned steak and French fries can be purchased almost anywhere that serves food and the quick-service hamburger shops have discovered Tahiti, with the opening of Big Burger and several stand-up sidewalk shops. A very popular place to eat, especially at night with the locals, yachties or those on low budgets, is on the "trucks" called "Les Roulottes." These are lunch wagons that are parked on the waterfront where the boats load for Moorea. Some have stools and they all serve basically the same foods—steak and fries, chicken and "poisson cru," brochettes or shish kebabs, which are heart of veal barbequed on the spot. For breakfast or a snack, try the French pastries found in the "salons de thé." Sweeping tax cuts in late 1987 brought Tahiti's once-horrific restaurant and bar prices down to comfortable levels. At the same time, many restaurants revamped their menus to provide excellent, but budget, meals.

Price categories are as follows: *Deluxe*, over $20. *Expensive*, $14–$20. *Moderate*, $6–$14. *Inexpensive*, $4–$6.

Bloody Mary's. *Expensive.* Located on Bora Bora between Vaitape Village and Hotel Bora Bora; 67.72.86. This highly popular seafood restaurant and bar has a huge thatched roof, white-sand floor, rough-hewn tables and coconut log stumps. Fresh fish, lobsters and other seafoods are barbequed on grill while clients watch. Chicken and steaks also available. Many world-famous people have dined here. Free transportation from hotels. Reservations requested. Closed Sundays. Accepts major credit cards.

Chez Christian. *Expensive.* Located on Bora Bora between villages of Anau and Faanui at Hotel Revatua Club; 67.71.67. An overwater 1930s colonial-style restaurant that serves excellent seafood, French cuisine, and extravagant desserts. Open daily. Reservations preferred. Accepts *American Express, Carte Bleue, Visa.*

Coco's. *Expensive.* On the lagoon at P.K. 13, Punaauia, 7.8 miles from Papeete; 58.21.08. A colonial-style restaurant and separate bar/lounge owned by two Frenchmen. French nouvelle cuisine is served, featuring such dishes as *aiguillettes de canard* and *choux farcis aux noisettes d'agneau au miel et citrons verts.* Closed Sunday evening and Monday. Reservations a must. Accepts *American Express* and *Visa.*

La Cremaillère. *Expensive.* On Blvd. Pomare in Quartier Patutoa, 2 blocks from lagoon heading inland, 42.09.15. Excellent nouvelle cuisine Française served in this small, air-conditioned restaurant off the tourist track, in a neighborhood close to Papeete. Serves lunch and dinner. Closed Sundays. Reservations recommended. Accepts *American Express* and *Visa.*

Jade Palace. *Expensive.* Located on ground floor of Vaima Center on Rue Jeanne d'Arc, immediately across street from Tahiti Tours, ½ block inland from Papeete waterfront; 42.02.19. This is the Chinese restaurant most tourists are directed to by hotel travel desks, so reservations are required. Open for lunch and dinner, closed Sundays. Accepts *American Express, Diner's, Visa.*

Lagoonarium. *Expensive.* Seafood restaurant built over lagoon at P.K. 11,5 in Punaauia, 7 miles from Papeete; 43.62.90. Tahitian dance shows Friday nights and Sundays at 2:00. Popular with large groups from ships and incentive programs. Closed Mondays. Reservations recommended. Accepts *American Express, Diner's,* and *Visa.*

La Maribaude. *Expensive.* On the heights of Pamatai, overlooking Papeete, Moorea, and Point Venus. Take Pamatai Road from circle island road and follow up mountain about 15 minutes until you see the entrance to restaurant; 42.82.52. French gastronomic cuisine featuring salmon with butter and leeks, chicken legs stuffed with foie gras, and duck breasts. Swimming pool, cool mountain air, and jazz music with dinner every Friday night. Free roundtrip transportation. Closed Sundays. Reservations required. Accepts all major credit cards.

Moana Iti. *Expensive.* On Blvd. Pomare on Papeete waterfront, between Ave. Bruat and Rue de la Canonniere Zelée; 42.65.24. Excellent French cuisine, with specialties including *paté de la maison,* rabbit simmered in red wine sauce, and steak au poivre. Closed Sundays. Reservations recommended. Accepts *American Express, Carte Bleue, Diner's,* and *Master Card.*

Nuutere. *Expensive.* Located in Papara district at P.K. 32.5, 20 miles west of Papeete on mountain side; 57.41.15. A wonderful gastronomic destination for those with transportation. A pleasant restaurant featuring French cuisine with a Bretonne touch. Many mouth-watering chef's specialties, plus fresh seafood dishes and T-bone steaks. Closed Tuesdays. Reservations requested. Accepts *Visa.*

La Petite Auberge. *Expensive.* At the Pont de l'Est, on Rue des Remparts, just around corner to right from Rue de Marechal Foch, going east from Papeete toward Mamao; 42.86.13. A small, intimate French country-style inn with air conditioning and service not usually found in Tahiti. The most "French" restaurant on the island, featuring cuisine from the provinces of Normandy and Brittany, with a fine selection of wines. Duck conserve a specialty. Serves lunch and dinner. Closed Saturdays. Reservations required. Accepts *American Express, Diner's,* and *Visa.*

Acajou. *Moderate.* Downtown Papeete, on corner of Blvd. Pomare and Rue Georges Lagarde; 42.87.58. This indoor/outdoor restaurant is usually filled with a lively group of American tourists or the European-Chinese-Tahitian-American residents of Tahiti. Owner-chef Acajou, formerly with Pitate, is famous for his French onion soup, seafood cassoulet, steak roquefort, shrimp in champagne sauce, and delicious pepper steaks. Serves breakfast all day, plus lunch and dinner. Closed Sundays. Reservations recommended. Accepts *American Express, Diner's Club,* and *Visa.*

Amandine. *Moderate.* Centre Aline, Blvd. Pomare on Papeete waterfront, in interior courtyard behind Tahiti Art; 43.85.53. A favorite lunch or refreshment stop for shoppers and office workers, this small *salon de thé* is also a patisserie and confiserie, serving deliciously baked French pastries and chocolate candies, ice cream, and sorbets, plus 30 kinds of perfumed teas. Closed Sunday. No reservations. No credit cards.

Le Belvedere. *Moderate.* Located 600 meters (1,800 feet) high in the mountains, up the Fare Rau Ape valley in Pirae district east of Papeete; 42.73.44. This restaurant offers the best bargain for tourists as the price includes transportation to and from hotels, a delicious meal with wine, coffee and dessert, a swimming pool, and happy atmosphere. The beef fondue is a specialty. Second and third helpings of beef, French fries, salad, and wine are cheerfully brought on request. Other selections include French onion soup, mahi mahi, cous-cous, and pepper steak. The ride up the mountain is an unforgettable experience as the bright yellow Le Truck winds around the numerous curves, overlooking all of Papeete and the harbor. Closed Tuesdays. Reservations required for transport. Accepts *American Express, Diner's, Visa,* and travelers checks.

Dahlia. *Moderate.* In Arue district, east of Papeete, at P.K. 4,200, lagoon side, just after Camp d'Arue French military base; 42.59.87. This very popular restaurant is always busy because it serves the best Chinese food in Tahiti. Try roast suckling pig in coconut milk, or crystal shrimps. Open for lunch and dinner, but get there before 1:00 or 8:30 P.M. Closed Sundays. Reservations recommended. *American Express, Carte Bleue, Diner's, Visa.*

Dragon d'Or. *Moderate.* On Rue du Colette, across from Papeete City Hall between Rue Paul Gauguin and Rue des Écoles des Freres de Ploermel, two blocks inland from harbor; 42.96.12. A very popular, well-established Chinese restaurant that serves excellent cuisine for lunch and dinner. French dishes also available. Closed Mondays. Reservations requested. Accepts *American Express, Carte Bleue,* and *Visa.*

Le Gallieni. *Moderate.* Located in Hotel Royal Papeete on Papeete waterfront street, Blvd. Pomare; 42.01.29. Noted for excellent breakfasts. California prime-rib featured for lunch or dinner each Thursday, Friday and Saturday, with other specialties including cous-cous, pineapple duck, and hot apple pie. Reservations needed for specialty days. Open every day. Accepts *American Express, Carte Bleue, Diner's, Master Card, Visa.*

Lou Pescadou. *Moderate.* On Rue Anne-Marie Javouhey, 2 blocks inland from Papeete waterfront; 43.74.26. Mediterranean, Provençal, and Italian cuisine and very noisy, lively, popular pizzeria, where free drinks are served while waiting for a table. Open for lunch and dinner, first come, first served. Closed Sundays. Accepts *American Express, Visa.*

Mandarin. *Moderate.* On Rue des Écoles, 2 blocks inland from Blvd. Pomare and Papeete waterfront; 42.99.03. A nicely decorated, air-conditioned restaurant serving excellent Cantonese specialties. Ask to be seated in the dining room upstairs, which is even more elegant and offers excellent service. Closed Sundays. Reservations recommended. Accepts *American Express, Diner's, MasterCard,* and *Visa.*

Restaurant du Musée Gauguin. *Moderate.* Built over the lagoon at K.M. 50,500 in the district of Papeari, 30 miles from Papeete, overlooking the Tahiti-iti peninsula; 57.13.80. A favorite luncheon stop for people touring the island, this beautifully located restaurant is close to the Paul Gauguin Museum. Roger and Juliette Gowan serve fresh and deliciously prepared hot and cold dishes, shrimp curry, and other seafood specialties, varied buffets, plus fruits and homemade pies. Most tourist groups eat here. Open every day for lunch, closed for dinner. Group reservations required. Accepts *American Express, MasterCard* and *Visa.*

Les Tipaniers. *Moderate.* Located at Hotel Residence Les Tipaniers on Moorea, in Haapiti district near Club Med; 56.12.67. Unpretentious surroundings with excellent Italian cuisine. Fresh pasta, lasagne, pizza and other Italian favorites, plus Continental cuisine. Closed Tuesdays. Reservations preferred. All major credit cards accepted.

Les Roulottes. *Moderate.* Located on Papeete's boat docks, all along the quay and parking area next to Papeete harbor. These lunch-wagon type vehicles usually have stools for sit-down eating. Many of them serve barbequed shish kebabs, steaks, and chicken legs, while others serve Chinese food, pizzas, hamburgers, crêpes, waffles and ice cream, Tahitian food, and veal on a rotisserie. A fun way to watch the people pass by while dining under the stars, before, during or after a night on the town. Most of the roulottes begin serving dinner as soon as the sun goes down and continue to the wee hours of the morning, or all night on weekends. No reservations. No credit cards.

TOURIST INFORMATION SERVICES. There are two dozen travel agencies in French Polynesia that can provide information and assistance for anyone wishing more specific information on Tahiti and Her Islands. Some of the larger ones are: *Tahiti Nui Travel,* B.P. 718, Papeete, Tahiti, 42.68.03; *Tahiti Tours* (the American Express Agency), B.P. 627, Papeete, Tahiti, 42.78.70; *Tahiti Voyages,* B.P. 485, Papeete, Tahiti, 52.57.63; *Voyagence* (also known as *AmiTahiti*), B.P. 274, Papeete, Tahiti, 42.72.13; *Marama Tours,* B.P. 6266, Faaa Airport, Tahiti, 43.96.50; and *Paradise Tours,* B.P. 2430, Papeete, Tahiti, 42.49.36. The best source for general information and brochures about French Polynesia is the *Tahiti Tourist Promotion Bureau,* B.P. 65, Papeete, Tahiti, 42.96.26. Inquiries regarding lodging with local families in the islands, how to immigrate to Tahiti and/or get a job, how to visit the islands as cheaply as possible, or whether you can bring your pet with you should be addressed to either the Tahiti Tourist Promotion Bureau in Papeete or their office at Tele Flora Bldg., 12233 West Olympic Blvd., Suite 110, Los Angeles, CA 90064, (213) 207-1919, or telex 497 1603. (There is no ZIP code used in the addresses in French Polynesia.)

Embassies and Consulates. No embassies exist in French Polynesia and the consulates, which are primarily honorary titles, represent European and Scandinavian countries, with the addition of Chile and the Republic of Korea. There are no consulates for the United States, Great Britain, Canada, New Zealand or Australia. The nearest American Embassy is located at P.O Box 218, Suva, Fiji.

HOW TO GET AROUND. By air. *Air Tahiti,* 42.24.44, the domestic airline, connects Tahiti with neighboring islands (Moorea, Huahine, Raiatea, Bora Bora, Maupiti), distant islands of the Gambiers, and remote archipelagoes (Tuamotu atolls of Rangiroa, Manihi, Takapoto, Anaa, Makemo, Tikehau, Hao, Kaukura, Apataki, Mataiva, Fakarava, Tatakoto, Pukarua, Reao, Nukutavake, Fangatau, Napuka, Arutua, Fakahina, Vahitahi, Tureia, and Pukapuka; Austral Islands of Rurutu and Tubuai; and the Marquesas Islands of Nuku Hiva, with connections to Ua Pou, Ua Huka and Hiva Oa), using ATR42 and F-27 turbo-prop and Twin Otter planes. There is also an air taxi service between Tahiti and Moorea, operated by *Air Moorea,* 42.44.29, with planes leaving frequently throughout the daylight hours.

By sea. (See also "Cruises," below.) Between Tahiti and Moorea—the *Keke III* (tel. 42.80.60), an air conditioned, sleek motor launch with bar and hostesses, makes three round trips daily. Departures from the Papeete boat dock to the nearest Moorea harbor of Vaiare Bay leave Tahiti at 7 A.M. and 5:15 P.M. for a 45-minute crossing, and the "tourist special" departs each morning at 9:15 for the 60-minute trip to marvelous Cook's Bay, leaving for Papeete at 4 P.M. The *Moorea Ferry II* (tel. 43.73.64), which takes passengers and motor vehicles, departs from the Papeete boat dock every day except Tuesdays for Vaiare Bay, leaving Tahiti at 8 A.M. and 2 P.M., with a supplementary departure every Friday and Sunday at 5 P.M. The new *Tamarii Moorea VIII* (tel. 56.13.92) car and passenger ferry leaves from its anchorage near the Keke III on Papeete's boat dock four times daily Monday through Saturday and three times on Sundays. The Tamarii Moorea II and *Tamarii Eimeo* (tel. 42.83.79) also make several daily crossings and only one Sunday voyage.

The Leeward Society Islands of Huahine, Raiatea, Tahaa, and Bora Bora are served from Tahiti by a car ferry and two passenger/cargo ships. The *Raromatai Ferry* (Compagnie Maritime des Iles Sous Le Vent, B. P. 9012, Papeete, Tahiti, 43.90.42), which offers a restaurant plus a choice of airplane-type seats, semi-private or private cabins with beds, leaves Papeete each Tuesday and Friday at 8:30 P.M., arriving in Huahine the following morning at 6 A.M. and continuing the stops in Raiatea and Tahaa, finally completing the 17-hour trip to Bora Bora at 1:30 P.M. One-way fare for a seat is 3.000 CFP and 8.000 CFP for a semi-private cabin. The *Temehani II* (Societe de Navigation Temehani, Motu Uta, Tahiti, 42.98.83) and the *Taporo IV* (Compagnie Francaise Maritime de Tahiti, B.P. 368, Papeete, Tahiti, 42.63.93) offer a less expensive way to visit the Leeward Islands, while providing an insight into the normal lifestyle of Polynesians voyaging from island to island, plus the color and excitement of a cargo freighter. The *Temehani II* leaves Motu Uta in Tahiti each Monday and Thursday at 5 P.M., arriving the following morning in Huahine. Accommodations include berths or a place on the bridge. Bring your own food and drinks. The *Taporo IV* leaves Tahiti each Monday and Wednesday at 5 P.M. and each Friday at 6 P.M. for the Leeward Islands, with stops made in Tahaa on the last two voyages of the week. This ship, which is usually crowded with islanders, has a snack bar, TV, and couchette berths in an open room, or a place on the bridge to put down a bedroll or sleeping mat. Rates vary from 1.100 CFP to 2.100 CFP, according to destination and sleeping arrangement. The *Taporo I* (Societe Taporo Teaotea, B.P. 129, Uturoa, Raiatea, 66.35.52), based in Raiatea, operates between Raiatea and Tahaa, Bora Bora and Maupiti, with one voyage every three months to Schilly, Bellinghausen, and Mopelia, returning to Raiatea in three days.

The far-off Marquesas Islands can be reached from Tahiti by the 264-ft. air-conditioned 17-cabin passenger/cargo/copra ship *Aranui* (Compagnie Polynesienne de Transports Maritimes, B.P. 220, Papeete, Tahiti, 42.62.40), which departs Tahiti every 25 days for a 17-day voyage through the Taumotu atolls of Manihi and Takapoto to the Marquesas Islands of Ua Pou, Ua Huka, Nuku Hiva, Hiva Oa, Tahuata, and Fatu Hiva. Not recommended for those who need all the comforts of a passenger liner, but highly recommended for adventurers of all ages, as this offers the best way to visit islands that still merit the cliche "paradise." Rates begin at 125.700 CFP for a mattress on the bridge deck and range up to 350.000 CFP for the ship's best cabin for two persons, all meals and land excursions included.

The less tourist-oriented and less expensive ship, *Taporo V* (B.P. 368, Papeete, Tahiti, 42.63.93), departs Tahiti every 15 days for a direct voyage to the Marquesas, arriving back in Tahiti 10 days later. A one-way fare on the bridge costs 15.000 CFP and in a cabin 20.500 CFP, both fares including meals. The Austral Islands of Tubuai, Rurutu, Rimatara, and Raivaevae are served by the *Tuhaa Pae II* (Societe Anonyme d'Economie Mixte de Navigation des Australes, B.P. 1890, Motu Uta, Papeete, Tahiti, 42.93.67), with about two voyages a month and a stop in distant Rapa once a month. The average round-trip without Rapa lasts for 6–7 days and costs 13.000 CFP on the bridge and 22.750 CFP for a berth in a cabin. Meals are 2.400 CFP per day.

The Tuamotu Archipelago is served by several small ships called *goelettes* that take merchandise to these atolls and bring back copra and fish to Tahiti. It is sometimes possible to secure deck space and occasionally a berth on these cargo vessels, but do not expect anything fancy or comfortable. The *AuuraNui* (Sane Richmond, B.P. 9196, Papeete (Motu Uta), Tahiti, 43.92.40), plies its trade in the northeast and central Tuamotus, with voyages lasting three weeks. The *Manava II* (Societe des Transports Maritime des Iles, B.P. 1816, Papeete, Tahiti, tel. 43.83.84), also covers some of this area with 15–17 day voyages. And the *Tameni* (C/o Jean Charles Tekuataoa, B.P. 2516, Papeete, Tahiti, 43.86.82) makes 3–4-week passages to the southern Tuamotus and the Gambier archipelago. Fares for these voyages are determined by the super cargo.

By car. On the islands of Tahiti and Moorea it is relatively easy to rent cars and four-wheel drive vehicles of recent vintage. *Avis* (tel. 42.96.49) and *Hertz* (42.04.71) have offices at the Tahiti-Faaa International Airport and at the larger hotels of Tahiti. Other rental agencies in Tahiti are: *Andre* (42.94.04); *Budget* (42.66.45); *Europcar National Car Rental* (42.48.97); *Pacificar* (42.43.64); *Robert* (42.97.20); *Tahiti Rent A Car* (42.74.49); *Toyota* (43.70.22); and *TTT* (42.87.66), with chauffeur if desired. Automobiles, jeeps, vespas, and bicycles can be rented at all the Moorea hotels, as well as at the Temae Airport and at the boat docks in Vaiare and Cook's Bay. Agencies in Moorea include: *Arii Rent A Car* (56.11.01, 56.10.01, or 56.16.02); *Pierre* (56.12.48); and *Billy Ruta* (56.16.98). On Bora Bora, cars, jeeps or minimokes, vespas or mobylettes, and bicycles can be rented through the hotels or at the 3 agencies on the island: *Bora Bora Rent A Car* (67.70.03); *Chez Alfredo Doom* (67.70.31); and *Otemanu Locations* (67.70.94). Bicycles or cars are definitely recommended as opposed to vespas or other motorized two-wheeled vehicles, as many tourists have ruined their vacations by suffering severe accidents or at the least "road rash." On Huahine, *Kake Rent-A-Car* (68.82.59) has mini-mokes, cars, scooters, and small Hondas; *Budget Rent A Car* (68.81.47) rents cars only; and *Dede*, in Fare, rents Honda motorcycles and small scooters. On Raiatea contact Suzanne Guirouard at *Garage Motu Tapu* (66.33.09) for car rentals or *Charles Brotherson* (66.32.15) for motorcycle, scooter, and bicycle rentals. On the island of Tahaa car rentals or excursions can be arranged through the *Tahaa Iti Village* (65.61.00) or the *Tahaa Lagon* (65.61.06). Henri Tupaia in Poutoru rents cars and Petit Tetuanui in Tiva arranges excursions. On other islands ask at your hotel or with the mayor of the village concerning transportation needs. Major credit cards are accepted in Tahiti and Moorea and at the Budget agency in Huahine, but most of the other rental agencies accept only cash and require a deposit.

By taxi. There is taxi service available in Tahiti, Moorea, Huahine, Raiatea, and Bora, the most visited islands. The fares are high and in Tahiti the prices double between the hours of 11:00 P.M. and 5:00 A.M. Taxis can usually be found outside the airport in Tahiti, outside the larger hotels, in front of the Centre Vaima at the corner of Blvd. Pomare and Rue Jeanne d'Arc in downtown Papeete, behind the public market downtown, and in front of the Jasmine Bar on Blvd. Pomare. To call for a taxi telephone 43.19.61. In Moorea, *Frederic Pahi* (56.17.15) offers taxi service, or you can ask the hotels to call a taxi; in Raiatea, *Rene Guilloux* (66.31.40) has taxis; *Ioata* (68.80.94) and *Enite* (68.32.37) provide taxi service in Fare, Huahine, and in the other islands just ask at your hotel desk.

By Le Truck. Local buses, called Le Truck, offer an inexpensive and often entertaining way to get around Papeete, and to and from your hotels in Tahiti. They leave from the central market downtown and go in all directions, making stops all along the way, taking people home. There is no set schedule for these trucks except for those going to the other side of the island, and you don't want to be on these

Le Trucks unless you have a definite way to return when you want to. Service operates from very early in the morning throughout the day and for the hotels on the west coast, up until midnight or sometimes later. You pay the driver when you get off. Public transportation by Le Truck is offered also on Huahine and Raiatea, but not on Moorea or Bora Bora, although Le Trucks are used to transport passengers between the boat docks and the hotels.

INTERISLAND CRUISES. (See also "How to Get Around by Sea," above.) *Association des Professionels du Tourisme Nautique des Iles Sous le Vent* is comprised of several charter yachts and sports fishing boats in the Leeward Society Islands. Members include 56-ft. Columbia ketch *Aita Peapea,* 55-ft. catamaran *Katiana,* 65-ft. cruiser *Danae III,* 72-ft. motor yacht *Maliga,* 37-ft. sloop *Vanessa,* fishing boats *Toerau, Mokalei, Aquaholics,* and *Te Aratai II,* plus the Moorings fleet of yachts. P.O. Box 590, Uturoa, Raiatea; 66.35.93, Telex 422FP.

Aranui, B. P. 220, Papeete, Tahiti, Tel. 42.62.40, offers 17-day cruises to the Marquesas Islands, departing Papeete every 25 days in 264-ft. A/C 17-cabin passenger/cargo/copra ship. See How to Get Around for details.

Exploration Cruise Lines, 1500 Metropolitan Park Bldg., Olive Way at Boren Ave., Seattle, Wa. 98101; 800–426–0600; in Seattle, 624–8551, Telex 32–9636, offers year-round island hopping aboard the *Majestic Tahiti Explorer.* First-class 4-, and 5- and 7-day cruises from Tahiti to Moorea, Huahine, Bora Bora, Tahaa and Raiatea, aboard 152-foot, 44-stateroom, 4-deck ship. Fly and cruise programs available in cooperation with UTA from Los Angeles.

Moana Adventure Tours, Nunue, Bora Bora. Glass-bottom boat trips, water skiing, speedboat rides, visits to coral reef, fishing, scuba diving inside lagoon and outside reef. Write to Erwin Christian, C/o Hotel Bora Bora, Nunue, Bora Bora, 67.70.28.

Sea and Leisure, B. P. 3488, Papeete, Tahiti; 43.97.99. This floating office along the Papeete waterfront, across from the Post Office, has information on every aspect of water sports in Tahiti and her Islands. Boats, fully equipped for deep-sea fishing for marlin, sailfish, tuna, and other game fish can be chartered here. Sailboats, Hobie Cats, surfboards, and windsurfing equipment, glass-bottom boats, waterskiing and diving expeditions can all be arranged.

The Moorings, 1305 U.S. 19 South, Suite 402, Clearwater, FL 33546; 800–535–7289 or 813–535–1446. World's largest yacht charter company operates a bareboat sailing fleet of 20 yachts based in Raiatea. Formerly South Pacific Yacht Charters, the sailing fleet consists of specially designed Moorings yachts, plus a few Endeavor 37-ft. boats, Nautical 39-ft. boats and Peterson CSY 44-ft. yachts. Provisions, captain, cook, and crew available if desired, for chartering in the Leeward Islands of the Society group. Telephone in Raiatea is 66.35.93.

Tahiti Aquatique, BP6008, Faaa, Tahiti; 42.80.42. Double Polynesian canoe used as glass-bottom boat for lagoon cruises, snorkeling, sunset or "funset booze cruise," dinner cruises. Complete line of nautical sports including scuba diving and underwater photography lessons. Located at Maeva Beach Hotel.

Tahiti Cruising Club, B.P. 1604, Papeete, Tahiti; 42.68.89. Skippered- or bareboat sailing in new or recent yachts ranging 32–83 ft. long. Hotel accommodations, airline connections, and all other conveniences arranged for you.

Tahiti Yacht Services. Box 4256, Papeete, Tahiti, 53.33.92; Telex 260FP. A group of 12 first-class yachts offers sailing excursions to Marlon Brando's Tetiaroa atoll and to all the Society Islands, Marquesas, Tuamotus, Australs, Gambiers, Pitcairn, Hawaii, and New Zealand.

Windstar Sail Cruises, Ltd., 7415 N.W. 19th St., Miami, FL 33126 (305-592-8008); Telex 522.289. The Windsong, a 440-ft., 4-masted steel-hull sailing ship for 150 passengers, offers sailing programs from Tahiti to Society Islands. Fares start at $US2,800 per person. Flight and cruise programs will be combined with pre- and post-cruise hotel accommodations.

TOURS. Circle Island Tour. Any travel agency or hotel desk in Tahiti can arrange a tour of the island, with or without meals and/or admissions to the museums, for a half day or full day. The average tour leaves the hotel at 9:30 A.M., stopping at One Tree Hill, historic Point Venus, pointing out the Blowhole of Arahoho, cascading waterfalls deep within the lush green valleys, the marker of Bougainville's landing in Hitiaa and rainbow-colored Tahitian homes surrounded by gardens of dancing color. A visit to the Paul Gauguin Museum in Papeari can be included before or after lunch, followed by a walk through the Harrison Smith Botanical Gardens or a smaller garden with verdant tropical foliage and a roaring waterfall. The latter half of the tour passes by the Atimaono Golf Course with a refreshing stop at the cool fern grotto of Maraa Point, then a roadside view of Tahiti's lovely and wealthy west coast districts of Paea and Punaauia, with old Polynesian style homes of pandanus and woven bamboo beside the lagoon and multimillion dollar modern homes in the mountains. The tour ends at the hotel, usually around 3:30 or 4 P.M.

Interior Mountain Tours. *Tahiti Rainbow Tours* (58.44.09) and *Mafatu Fenua Excursions* (58.44.80) offer half-day mountain, valley, and waterfall tours in A/C four-wheel-drive vehicles. *Sea and Leisure* (43.97.99), located in the floating office across from the Papeete Post Office, can arrange exciting and challenging hiking and mountain climbing tours to explore Tahiti's interior valleys, grottoes, and lava-tubes. *Moorea Activities* (56.10.50) leads various walking, hiking and mountain-climbing tours through Moorea's heights.

Helicopter Tours. *Pacific Helicopter Service* (43.16.80 and 43.84.25) and *Tahiti Helicopters* (43.34.26 or 42.61.22) provide aerial sightseeing of Tahiti's ancient vol-canoes, spectacular mountain peaks, lush valleys, and tropical waterfalls. Pilots are trained for still and motion photography flights.

SEASONAL EVENTS. Two of the major events on Tahiti's annual schedule are listed here. In **July,** *Tahiti's Festival* is in full swing when the month begins and the pace accelerates with competitive sports, singing, and dancing events. All over French Polynesia there are parades, games, contests and colorful shows, with special food, dancing and gambling *baraques* constructed for the occasion. The highlight of the festival is the International Pirogue Race, with competing teams from many countries.

In **December** is *Tiare Tahiti Day.* Tahiti's national flower, the white gardenia, is featured, with a gardenia being presented to everyone on the streets of Papeete, in the hotels and at the airport, culminating in an all-night ball with Tiare Tahiti flowers decorating the ballroom, the tables and even the performers.

SPORTS. Many sports are available in conjunction with your hotel. See Accom-modations. The climate is very favorable all year for outdoor sports, and the lagoons are the centers of sporting activities. In Tahiti there are sailboats for rent by the hour, day or week at *Tahiti Cruising Club,* B. P. 1604, Papeete, Tahiti; Tel. 42.68.89 and Sea and Leisure's floating office on the waterfront across from the Papeete Post Office, 43.97.99. There are water sports facilities located at the Hotel Tahiti Beach-comber (43.86.23) and at Tahiti Aquatique, located at the Hotel Sofitel Maeva Beach, (42.80.42). Both locations have small sailboats, water-skiing, sightseeing la-goon tours, glass-bottom boat rides, line fishing in the pass or on the coral reef, and deep sea-fishing expeditions. Tahiti Aquatique also offers diving instruction and expeditions.

On the waterfront in downtown Papeete there are numerous deep-sea fishing boats for hire, and the Haura Club, Tahiti's official organization for sports fishing, holds annual International Billfish Tournaments, associated with the International Game Fish Association. Contact Dave Cave, P. O. Box 582, Papeete, Tahiti, 42.49.29 or 42.89.10.

American snorkeling and shelling expert Ron Hall, B. P. 98, Pao Pao, Moorea, Tel. 56.11.06, guides Moorea visitors to the best snorkeling and shelling spots, giv-ing extensive lessons for beginners. Snorkeling and diving expeditions can also be arranged at Hotel Linareva in Moorea, 56.15.35; with Erwin Christian of Moana Adventure Tours in Nunue, Bora Bora, 67.70.28; and with the Hotel Kia Ora Vil-lage on the Tuamotu atoll of Rangiroa, RA 384, where guests enjoy diving in the passes along with hundreds of sharks and fishes.

Airplane rentals are possible through the Aeroclub de Tahiti, B.P. 1500, Papeete, Tahiti, Tel. 42.58.02, and with *Tahiti Conquest Airlines,* Tel. 43.84.25.

The Vol-Libre Polynesian Club, B.P. 5374, Pirae, Tahiti, 43.72.01, a **hang-gliders** association, offers another form of flying.

A **bowling alley** is located between Papeete and the Tahara'a Hotel (42.93.26).

For the **golf** enthusiast, the course at Atimaono (57.40.32), 45 minutes by car from the center of Papeete, is open year round and is located between the lagoon and the mountains in a very colorful setting. There are 18 holes (6,950 yards) and par is 72 for men and 73 for women. A club house with bar and snack bar, pro-shop, lockers, driving range, clubs, hand cart rentals and lessons are all provided.

Mountain climbing expeditions can be arranged through Sea and Leisure, B. P. 3488, Papeete, Tahiti, 43.97.99. On Moorea, contact Bruno, Moorea Activities, Box 30, Moorea, 56.10.50; Telex 361FP.

Riding. Horseback riding and lessons are available in Tahiti at the *Club Equestre* (42.70.41) and *L'Eperon de Pirae,* (42.79.87), both located next to the Hippodrome in the district of Pirae. Wendy Pratt, a young American woman, operates Te Anavai Ranch in the district of Papeari, (Tel. 57.20.20), giving riding lessons and leading trail rides through Tahiti's most beautiful tropical forests. La Petite Ferme on Huahine is located between the airport and the Hotel Bali Hai, B. P. 12, Huahine, Tel. 68.82.98). Riding lessons, hourly rides, and 2–4 day camping trail rides can be arranged. Horses are a common mode of transportation in the Marquesas and horses, with or without saddles, can easily be rented on all the Marquesan islands.

Tennis. There are tennis courts and clubs at Hotel Tahara'a (48.11.22); Hotel Tahiti Beachcomber, (43.86.23); Hotel Sofitel Maeva Beach, (42.80.42); Hotel Te Puna Bel Air, (42.09.00); and at the Tennis Club in Fautaua, (42.00.59). On Moorea there are tennis courts at the Hotel Bali Hai, (56.13.59); Club Bali Hai (56.13.68); Hotel Sofitel Kia Ora Village, (56.12.90); Club Méditerranée, (56.15.00); Climat de France, (56.15.48); and Moorea Village, (56.10.02). The Hotel Bora Bora has a tennis club (67.70.28); and the Hotel Bali Hai (68.82.77) and Relais Mahana (68.81.54) in Huahine have tennis courts.

Spectator Sports

Soccer, the favorite sport of Tahitians, can be seen on almost all the islands. In Tahiti, enthusiastic crowds gather at the Fautaua Stadium or the Stade Pater, both located in Pirae, near Papeete, on week nights and during weekends to cheer their team to victory. As there are many athletic clubs in Tahiti, it is best to call the local newspapers (*La Depêche de Tahiti,* 42.43.43) to find out what sporting events are taking place and where. Reservations and advance purchase of tickets are not needed. *Horseracing.* Tahitian-style horseracing is held on special occasions at the Pirae Hippodrome, where jockeys sometimes ride bareback, wearing only a brightly colored Pareo and a crown of flowers. Parimutuel betting exists, but the payoffs are very small. *Cockfighting* is another Sunday afternoon event. Although officially illegal, the fighting rings are out in the open and all the hotels can help you to find out where the action is taking place. Recent spectator sport to thrill the trail bike enthusiasts is the opening of an international motorcross course at Taravao. Other regularly scheduled spectator sports include *archery, bicycling, boxing, outrigger canoe racing, volleyball, sailboat racing* and *track* events.

MUSEUMS AND GALLERIES. *Musée de Tahiti et Des Îles,* 58.34.76, at Pointe des Pêcheurs in Punaruu P.K. 15.7, about 10 miles from town, is located on the site of a former *marae* and has displays of the ocean floor and the Polynesian islands. The bountiful nature that exists in these islands is featured—life on the coral reefs and in the lagoons, in the highlands and on the atolls, as well as the flowers and trees. The history of Polynesia after the arrival of the Europeans is also a main theme here. Open 9:30 A.M.–5:30 P.M. daily except Mondays. Admission charge. The *Paul Gauguin Museum,* B.P. 7029, Taravao, Tahiti, 57.10.42 or 57.10.58, is located 30 miles southeast of Papeete at P.K. 51.2 in the district of Papeari. This is Tahiti's most famous museum. The story of this famous artist's life and artistic activities is told with the help of photographs, reproductions of his most famous works, documents and furniture. Open every day 9 A.M.–5 P.M. Admission charge. *Tahiti Perles Center,* 43.85.58, on Blvd. Pomare, next to Protestant Temple of Paofai, is a jewelry store and a new museum for the black pearl. Open Mon.–Fri. 7:30 A.M.–noon and 1:30–5 P.M., Sat. 9 A.M.–noon. Closed Sun.

Art galleries in Tahiti are: *Galerie Winkler,* 42.81.77, located on Rue Jeanne d'Arc between the waterfront street of Blvd. Pomare and the Catholic Cathedrale; *Galerie Vaim'antic,* 43.68.96, located on the lower plaza of the Vaima Center in

Papeete; *Galerie Noa Noa,* 42.73.47, on Blvd. Pomare in front of the Tahiti Tourist Office; *Galerie Etienne Siquin* (Chouchou), 42.09.81, located across from Mandarin Restaurant on Rue des Écoles; and *Galerie Oviri,* 42.63.82, located at P.K. 12,700 in Punaauia, on the mountain side, fourth house on the left. Art exhibits are often held at Fare Manihini in the Tahiti Tourist Bureau and in the large hotels.

In Moorea the *Galerie Aad Van Der Heyde* is located at P.K. 7 in PaoPao (56.14.22); *Galerie Api* in the district of Haapiti (56.13.57) combines artwork with hand-painted clothing. On Bora Bora, at the entrance to Point Matira, is the *Jean Masson Museum,* featuring the works of this famous French artist, whose widow, Rosine Temauri, also exhibits her own paintings and hand-painted clothing.

GARDENS. The *Harrison W. Smith Botanical Gardens* are located adjacent to the Gauguin Museum in Papeari, 30 miles from Papeete. In these 340 acres you will find hundreds of varieties of trees, shrubs, plants and flowers from tropical regions throughout the world.

SHOPPING. With the introduction of shopping centers in Papeete, the merchandise displayed in the stores is very much what you find in Parisian boutiques, including the price tag. There are no real bargains to be found here. French perfumes are less expensive than in the United States. There are some local products such as the exquisite Marquesan wood carvings, the dancing costumes, shell jewelry and Tahitian perfumes that will make nice gifts or souvenirs of your visit to Polynesia. An especially nice inexpensive purchase is the Monoi Tiare Tahiti, which is the coconut oil scented with Tahiti's national flower. This can be used as a moisturizing lotion, a perfume, suntan lotion, mosquito repellant, hair dressing, massage lotion— some people have even considered drinking it! The brightly patterned *pareu* fabrics that make the traditional Tahitian *pareo* are available in dozens of shops.

Tahiti's biggest export is the South Seas black pearl, which is also the most sought-after souvenir item. Exquisite jewelry fashioned of black pearls, 18-karat gold and frequently with diamonds, or unset pearls of all sizes, shapes, quality and prices can be purchased in French Polynesia. Shops selling these pearls are found on practically every block in downtown Papeete, in addition to all the hotel boutiques on all the tourist islands.

The *Centre Vaima,* located in the middle of downtown Papeete, occupies a city block between the Blvd. Pomare on the waterfront, Rue Jeanne d'Arc, Rue du General De Gaulle and Rue Georges Lagarde. This 3-level shopping complex is the largest in Papeete. Here you will find *Popsy,* a *tres chic* boutique for ladies; *Armandissimo,* with Italian and French ready-to-wear for men and women; *Anita* for high fashion ladies clothes and shoes; *Polynesian Curios* for local wood carvings and mother-of-pearl jewelry; *Islands Treasures* for authentic Polynesian artifacts and dance costumes; *Optique Surdite* for instant repair of eyeglasses or purchases of French-style sunglasses; *Vaima Junior* for children's clothes; *Anemone and Vaima Shirts* for hand-painted Tahitian style clothing; *Cordo Express* for repair of luggage, handbags, and shoes; *Elegancia* for French shoes; *Polynesie Perles* for black pearls; *Vaima QSS Photo* for one-hour photo development; *La Cave à Cigars* for cigars from Havana, Brazil, and Sumatra; *Tahiti Duty Free Shop* for French perfumes; *Le Kiosque* for international newspapers and magazines; and *Aux Ducs de Gascogne* for foie gras, patés, French Armagnac, and other gourmet items.

Aline's, Tahiti's only department store, has a small shopping mall. It is located one block from the Vaima center, on Blvd. Pomare. Also on this waterfront street, between the Vaima center and Aline's, is *Tahiti Art,* with exclusive and lovely fabrics, dresses, and shirts. *Marie Ah You,* on Blvd. Pomare one block toward the public market from the Vaima center, sells elegant original gowns, using their own designs of fabric and fashion. For beautiful Tahitian fabrics to sew yourself, try *Tapa Tissus,* on Rue du General de Gaulle, across from the Vaima center.

The boutiques on Moorea carry a good selection of the hand-painted muumuu type dresses, as well as bikinis, T-shirts, beach cover-ups, and other elegantly casual wear, created by the artisans who live on this neighboring island. Try *Shark's Tooth Boutique,* the boutique at the Sofitel Kia Ora Village, and *Dina's Boutique,* all on Moorea. On Bora Bora, Alain and Linda sell their own clothing designs and wall hangings, hand painted by brush; and *Martine's Boutique* has a good selection of hand-painted T-shirt dresses. *Moana Art* near the Hotel Bora Bora also carries a line of elegant island fashions. Shops, boutiques, jewelry stores, and art galleries all maintain the normal working hours of the South Seas. This means they are open early in the morning, around 7–7:30; they close for a couple of hours at noon or just before; then are open in the afternoon until 5:30–6:00. Usually they are open on Saturday mornings and closed on Sundays.

NIGHTLIFE. Papeete is a swinging town after dark and the crowds in the restaurants and nightclubs seem to really enjoy themselves. Most of the hotels feature Tahitian dance shows several times a week and a band that plays dance music nightly. For discotheque dancing, go to the *Club 106* above the Moana Iti Restaurant on Blvd. Pomare, between Ave. Bruat and Rue de la Canonniere Zelée; the popular *Too Much Club* in the Centre Vaima, entrance on Rue du General de Gaulle; the select *Le Retro Disco* behind Le Retro Restaurant on the corner of Blvd. Pomare and Rue Georges Lagarde; or the young "jet-set" *Mayana Club* upstairs at the Centre Bruat on the corner of Ave. Bruat and Blvd. Pomare.

La Cave, located at the other end of Blvd. Pomare, on the ground floor of the Hotel Royal Papeete, has both a disco and a large dance hall with a live Tahitian band that plays on weekends and special events. Tourists of all ages will feel comfortable here and will enjoy the ambiance while dancing to a Tahitian beat of fox trots, waltzes and the hip-shaking *tamure.*

The *Bar Lea* on the ground floor of the Hotel Pacific on Blvd. Pomare has live Tahitian music with popular singers performing on weekends. *Le Paradise Club,* a couple of doors away, has live entertainment and feature nights. *Chaplin's,* just next door, has live jazz music. *Star Circus* is a popular weekend nightclub, with Tahitian and disco music inviting the dancers in during the wee hours. Located at Le Bougainville Restaurant behind the Catholic cathedral, *Le Pub,* on Avenue Bruat, attracts office and government workers for happy-hour cocktails and dancing to Tahitian orchestra or disco music. Next door is *Le Pitate,* at the corner of Ave. Bruat and Blvd. Pomare. This noisy dance hall, with a very lively band, gets going late, as do most of the nightclubs, but is always filled with a mostly Tahitian crowd.

For another view of Papeete-by-night, try the other end of town, where young French military men often dance with Tahiti's transvestites and watch Papeete's entertaining *mahu's* or third sex, reign in all their flamboyance. *The Piano Bar,* on Rue des Ecoles, welcomes tourists to their transvestite strip show. Also on this street are several other bars and discos, including the *Bounty Club* and *Le Lido,* mostly military hangouts. Several other waterfront type discos and dives are located along Blvd. Pomare, between Ave. Prince Hinoi and Ave. du Chef Vairaatoa. The *Princesse Heiata* is a hotel in Pirae, about 3 miles from downtown, where an after-hours disco operates each weekend until 5 A.M. Very crowded and noisy. The *Hotel Tahiti* often has very nice dinners and dances on Saturday nights, in conjunction with a contest to elect a beauty queen or to celebrate a sports event.

THE COOK ISLANDS

Tourist Town

by
GRAEME KENNEDY

Tiny Rarotonga, in the Cook Islands midway between Hawaii and Auckland, Fiji, and Tahiti, was 15 or 20 years ago the Pacific's most enviable destination. If you'd been there, you could really impress travellers hooked into the Fiji-Tahiti-Hawaii sun circuit, for the Cooks were then an undiscovered place of tropical beauty and peace right off the track and thus able to impart the prestige exclusivity brings.

How things have changed. These days, if you want to meet your neighbor or workmate, go to Raro. Chances are he or she will be there or just got back or is packing to go.

The change started in 1973, when New Zealand built the Cooks an international airport just outside the main town of Avarua on Rarotonga. A trickle of regular visitors began to stay in the handful of motel-guesthouses scattered around the 32-kilometers-circumference, reef-ringed island where you could have whole white sandy beaches to yourself. The trickle became a torrent when the Rarotongan Resort Hotel opened in 1977, funded by the New Zealand government as a means of generating revenue to aid an ailing economy. Within five years, tourist numbers had rocketed to almost 18,000—ironically the Cooks' 1986 population.

Visitor numbers climbed 29 percent to 25,600 in 1984, then more modestly as new motels sprung up behind almost every palm tree. Following the devastation of Cyclone Sally in early 1987, visitor arrivals increased by only 3 percent, to 32,100. Recovery was, however, rapid and storm-damaged hotels were expanded as they were rebuilt—the Edgewater Resort at Arorangi Beach now claims to be the biggest motel complex in the Pacific.

In 1986, innovative former Premier Sir Tom Davis—an island-born doctor who worked in the United States on early NASA space programs—signed a management agreement with New Zealand's *Ansett Airlines* to establish flag-carrier *Cook Islands International;* it now operates a weekly Boeing 727 to Sydney and Auckland, bringing to four the number of airlines serving Rarotonga.

Tourist authorities on Rarotonga insist there is room for more visitors, that Cook Islanders are aware of tourism's negative impact, and that cultural and environmental values will be maintained. But Rarotonga, with an area of only 41.6 square miles, is very tiny and more than 600 tourists were on the island every day of 1987, an average of seven days each.

The Cooks desperately need tourism to ease a long dependence on foreign aid—but some island leaders wonder if it will be worth the cost in social terms.

Now, though—while there's still room on the beach—the Cooks are an attractive proposition. The exchange rate is favorable, especially for Americans and Australians, the lagoons are clean and warm, the sand is white and clean, and the living is pretty easy.

The Cooks' 15 islands occupy just 93 square miles in 750,000 square miles of ocean from Pukapuka, Rakahanga, and Penrhyn in the north to Rarotonga, Mauke, and Mangaia in the south. In the north, the islands are storybook coral atolls; in the south, all are of volcanic origin, with jungled basalt spires and fine lagoons.

Folklore puts the Cook Islanders' origins back to the early 1300s, when two chiefs, from Tahiti and Samoa, arrived almost at the same time to claim the new land. Without a battle, they divided Rarotonga equally and lived harmoniously, while the territorial boundaries were eventually broken down and the new race emerged. Legend has it that seven canoes of Cook Islanders left Muri Lagoon about 1350 and navigated to New Zealand to begin the Maori race after a growing population on the small island created food shortages and tribal wars.

Captain Cook visited the islands that were to bear his name in the 1770s and was followed by the missionaries and traders in the 1800s. The Cooks became a British colony and remained so until 1901, when they were turned over to New Zealand, whose administration was notable only for its neglect. The small Pacific nation became independent under Premier Albert Henry in 1965. An individualistic and volatile character often accused of nepotism, he was known as Papa at home until his death in 1978, when Sir Tom Davis succeeded him. Rarotongans are proud of their Albert Henry Museum in Avarua, where mementos of the old man's iron reign are displayed.

Avarua is a busy waterfront town with public buildings and shops, old homes in spacious tropic gardens, the inevitable guesthouses, and the almost-anything-goes Banana Court bar, tavern, cabaret, and meeting place still run by former Pacific heavyweight boxing champion Apiro Brown. Outwardly a friendly chap, Apiro has little trouble in his well-run establishment.

Under the towering basalt peak known as the Needle, and its jungle-draped lesser brothers, Rarotonga lies warm and happy, encircled by its reef, lagoon, and villages like Titihaveka, Ngatangiia, Matavera, Arorangi, and Muri.

The Cooks' other islands, spread over almost 20 degrees of latitude, are accessible only by irregular cargo ship—services can take weeks. These atolls, with enchanting names like Manihiki, Rakahanga, and Suwarrow, lie far to the north, and, unlike their southern neighbors, will probably never see a guest bungalow.

But good hotels and motels have been developed closer to Rarotonga, especially on Aitutaki, said to have the finest lagoon in the Pacific. Regular air service brings visitors to nearby Atiu and Mauke, tiny islands rapidly becoming more popular. Peaceful and unhurried they can still be; Pacific-enchanting they will hopefully remain—if they are not overtaken by the wave of tourism looming over Rarotonga.

PRACTICAL INFORMATION FOR
THE COOK ISLANDS

WHEN TO GO. Apart from December through March, when rainfall regularly exceeds 10 inches a month, the Cook Islands have a pleasantly warm and sunny climate, temperatures and humidity peaking with February's average 84°F maximum and easing to a 77°F minimum in August. Stormy weather hits the Cooks infrequently, but the rain can be spectacular. Take a light raincoat even in the dry season.

Average Temperature (°Fahrenheit) and Humidity

Rarotonga	Jan	Feb	Mar	Apr	May	June	July	Aug	Sept	Oct	Nov	Dec
Average max. day temperature	84°	84°	83°	81°	79°	77°	77°	77°	77°	79°	80°	82
Days of rain	15	15	16	14	13	11	10	11	11	12	13	14
Humidity, percent	79	81	80	79	77	77	75	74	73	74	75	76

General hints: The best tourist season is May through October. Temperature is warm and humid, tempered by trade winds.

WHAT TO WEAR. Other Polynesian islands are a good guideline. Light, breezy, and casual day and night, but please, no swimwear or bare chests in public places. Minimum winter temperatures in the 60s in August may require a light wrap or cardigan at night.

HOW TO GET THERE. The Cooks' new flag-carrier, *Cook Islands International*, flies weekly from Sydney and Auckland; *Air New Zealand* flies from Auckland, Nadi, and Papeete; *Polynesian Airlines* flies from Papeete and Western Samoa. *Hawaiian Airlines* from Honolulu and Pago Pago.

ENTRY REQUIREMENTS. All visitors except New Zealanders need passports for stays up to 31 days. Entry permits are not needed provided visitors have onward tickets showing they do not intend to stay longer. Application can be made in Rarotonga for longer visits. Vaccination certificates are not needed.

Duty-free allowance in the Cook Islands is 200 cigarettes, ½ lb. of tobacco or 50 cigars, and two liters of spirits or wine or 4½ liters of beer. The Cooks are free of serious plant and animal diseases and pests, and all plants, fruit and animals brought into the country will be inspected.

CURRENCY. The Cook Islands use the New Zealand dollar, worth about US67¢. Coins are minted for local use, including the dollar coin bearing the image of the god Tangaroa, which has become popular with coin collectors. All credit cards are accepted.

ELECTRICITY. Available voltage is 230 volts, 50 cycles, the same as in New Zealand and Australia. However, a two-pin plug may be required at some accommodations. Provision for 110-volt AC electric shavers is made at several hotels and motels.

TIPPING. This will offend in the Cook Islands.

LANGUAGES. Cook Islands Maori is the local language, but almost everyone is fluent in English.

TIME ZONE. Greenwich Mean Time, plus 10½, or 2 hours behind U.S. Pacific Standard.

ACCOMMODATIONS. *Deluxe* means NZ$100 and up for a single room; *expensive,* NZ$60–NZ$100; *moderate,* NZ$30–NZ$60; *inexpensive,* below NZ$30.

Rarotonga

Rarotongan Resort Hotel. *Deluxe.* Box 103 Rarotonga. Phone 25.800. The island's top hotel, with 150 rooms and four beachfront suites 12km from Avarua town. Rooms have one double and one single bed and are fully self-contained with refrigerator and tea-coffee-making facilities. Hotel has restaurants, bars, games room, swimming pool, shop, tennis, wind surfers, and outrigger canoes. Conference facilities are also available. Tour and travel desk and hourly bus service to Avarua.

Ariana Bungalows. *Expensive.* Box 434. Phone 20.521. In Upper Tupapa, eight minutes' drive from town, six self-contained pole-construction cottages and two family units in spacious tropical gardens. Swimming pool, barbecue, store with basic groceries.

Edgewater Resort Motel. *Expensive.* Box 121. Phone 25.437. 84 self-contained units with fully equipped kitchens minutes from Avarua on four-acre private site with sandy safe swimming beach. Squash court, swimming pool, games room adjacent to bar, nightclub, and restaurant.

Lagoon Lodges. *Expensive.* Box 45. Phone 22.020. Just 400m from Rarotongan Resort Hotel, set in two acres of garden with 10 self-contained bungalows, four with two separate bedrooms. Pool, barbecue, opposite lagoon.

Little Polynesian. *Expensive.* Box 366. Phone 24.280. On the white-sand beach at Titikaveka 12km from town, nine self-contained units beside pool; liquor license.

Manuia Beach Hotel. *Expensive.* Box 700. Phone 27.652. Redecorated and modernized, on sandy beach at Arorangi Village 8km from Avarua. Restaurant, airport transfers, bar with 20 self-contained villas.

Muri Beachcomber. *Expensive.* Box 379. Phone 21.022. On sparkling Muri lagoon, 10km from Avarua, with six double and four twin self-contained and serviced units. Pool, barbecue on 1.25 acres of garden.

Palm Grove Lodge. *Expensive.* Box 23. Phone 20.002. In garden setting with swimming pool opposite private beach, two self-contained bungalows, and two island-style units 15.3km from Avarua. Handy to restaurant and shop, regular bus service.

Puaikura Reef Lodge. *Expensive.* Box 397. Phone 23.537. Twelve self-contained units sleeping four each opposite white-sand beach 10.8km from town. With freshwater pool and barbecue.

Raina Village Motel. *Expensive.* Box 1047. Phone 20.197. Opposite safe white beach, spa pools, wind surfers, barbecue. 14km from town, four luxury units with own balcony and sun deck.

Rarotongan Sunset. *Expensive.* Box 377. Phone 28028. 20 rooms with cooking facilities, pool. On lagoon at Arorangi village.

Tamure Resort Hotel. *Expensive.* Box 17. Phone 22.415. Has 35 newly decorated twin and double rooms on the beach 2.5km from town. All are at ground level and contain tea-coffee-making facilities, refrigerator, fans, and all amenities. The Tamure offers bicycle, motorbike, and car rentals, secretarial service, tour desk, and entertainment four nights a week, usually local dancing.

Turangi Reef Lodge. *Expensive.* Depot 8, Ngatangiia, Rarotonga. Phone 26.560. Eight self-contained units 7.3km from Avarua with shore frontage but no beach.

Arorangi Lodge. *Moderate.* Box 51. Phone 27.379. Eight self-contained units in Arorangi Village, just past airport.

Kii Kii Motel. *Moderate.* Box 68. Phone 21.937. On the beach only 2.6km from Avarua, nine roomy self-contained units that sleep up to four. Swimming pool and barbecue area in gardens.

Mana Motel. *Moderate.* Box 72. Two self-contained units, 3km from Avarua.

Matareka Heights. *Moderate.* Box 587. Phone 23.670. Away from beach, in foothills 3km from town. One communal unit and two self-contained with bathroom facilities.

Onemaru Motel. *Moderate.* Box 523. Across road from swimming beach in quiet gardens 11.7km from Avarua. Two self-contained units with twin beds.

Paradise Inn. *Moderate.* Box 674. Phone 20.544. Only accommodation in Avarua with 16 self-contained split-level units on beach.

Tiare Village Motel. *Moderate.* Box 489. Phone 23.466. Opposite airport on inland road 3km from town, 2km from beach; three fully equipped chalets.

Whitesands Motel. *Moderate.* Box 115. Phone 25.789. Six self-contained units with cooking facilities 10km from Avarua and 7km from Rarotongan Resort Hotel on sandy beach.

Are-Renga and Airport Lodge. *Inexpensive.* Box 223. Phone 20.050. At the airport 8.5km from Avarua with six self-contained units.

Dive Rarotonga Hostel. *Inexpensive.* Box 38. Phone 21.873. Barry and Shirley Hill run this budget facility with special washing, drying, and storage for dive equipment. Six twin rooms, one double, and two singles. Communal kitchen; lounge, washing and toilet facilities.

Aitutaki Island

Aitutaki Resort Hotel. *Deluxe.* Box 342, Rarotonga. Phone 22.713. 25 fully self-contained cottages in tropic garden on own private island, linked to Aitutaki by causeway. Full bar and restaurant with games room, native-craft center, gift shop, marina, swimming pool, and glass-bottomed boat. All water-sport and diving facilities and adjacent to a nine-hole golf course.

Rapae Cottage Hotel. *Moderate.* Box 65 Rarotonga. Phone 22.888. Close to main Aitutaki village in tropic garden. 12 units with one double and one single bed, two catering for families of up to six. All self-contained and include insect screens, ceiling fans, and sundecks. Hotel has restaurant and bar and features weekly island feast and dancing. Cruises, fishing, and diving available.

Tiare Maori Guesthouse. *Moderate.* Box 65, Rarotonga. Phone 26.300. Six rooms at Ureia, three-minute walk from post office and shop.

Atiu Island

Atiu Motel. *Moderate.* Box 79, Rarotonga. Two self-contained units with tennis courts; motorcycles for hire.

Mauke Island

Tiare Holiday Cottage. *Moderate.* Write Tiare Cottage, Mauke, Cook Islands. Four cottages with share cooking and bathroom block.

Mauke Lodge. *Inexpensive.* Two self-contained units with cooking facilities.

HOW TO GET AROUND. There is no transport problem for the tourist on Rarotonga, with public and private vehicles readily available.

A local **bus** company operates an hourly service around the island (21 mi. clockwise, 20 mi. on the inside lane in the opposite direction) from 7 A.M. to 4 P.M. weekdays and 7 A.M. to noon on Saturdays. Most hotels have their own bus services to Avarua.

Cook Islandair's Britten-Norman Islander **aircraft** fly scheduled services from Rarotonga to Aitutaki, Atiu, Mitiaro, and Mauke, and *Air Rarotonga* flies a Beechcraft twin to Aitutaki, Atiu, Mauke, and Mangaia. Charter aircraft are available for island hopping and scenic flights.

A local **shipping** company operates overnight voyages to the outer Cook Islands; however, because of varying cargo demands and weather, services are not definite until a few days before departure.

Rarotonga has several reliable **taxi** services available 24 hours a day. Fares are government controlled and are displayed in each cab.

Most stores and hotels rent **bicycles,** which are convenient, since the round-Rarotonga road follows the lagoon and is quite flat.

Several **rental-car** companies are well established in Rarotonga and are always in high demand. Car bookings should be made before arrival. The major companies: *Budget,* Box 607, phone 20.888; *Cook Islands Rental Cars,* Box 326, phone 24.442; *Avis,* Box 74; Phone 22.833; *Tipani Rentals,* Box 49, phone 22.327; *Vaima Rentals,* Box 1043, phone 22.2222; *Ace Rent-a-Car,* Box 257, phone 21.901.

Driving is on the left, and tourists must have a current Cook Islands' driving license, available from the police station in Avarua on presentation of their own license.

TOURIST INFORMATION. *Cook Islands Tourist Authority,* Box 14, Rarotonga; Phone 29.435.

TOURS. Rarotonga, small though it is, offers a variety of organized and special-interest tours including a cross-island walk through the mountainous interior, a round-island sightseer, reef walks, beach barbecues, and a day trip to Aitutaki. Book through *Stars Travel,* Box 75, phone 23.669; *South Seas Travel,* Box 49, phone 22.327; *Tipani Tours,* Box 4, phone 22.792; *Union CITCO,* Box 54, phone 21.780; *Trans Pacific Travel,* Box 511, phone 20.660.

Cruises. Deep-sea fishing is immensely popular out of Rarotonga, and a number of companies offer specialized service.

Blue Water Adventures. The 32-ft. *Don Quixote* takes an unspecified number of fishing enthusiasts for a three-hour voyage under the command of Trevor Nicholson. Lunch and drinks provided at $NZ50 a person. Box 94; phone 21.225.

Aquaholics IV. Chris Mussell hires his boat out at $NZ250 and prefers groups of four. Food and drink are provided—and fish are guaranteed. Phone 22.161.

Don Beer Charters. Don charges $NZ40 a person for a five-hour fishing trip on his 24-ft. *Tangaroa II,* preferring groups of four. Lunch provided but bring your own drinks. Box 384; phone 21.525.

Seafari Charters. Elgin Tetachuk hires the 34-ft. *Seafari* to a maximum of six anglers for $NZ55 each and trips up to five hours. Snack lunch but bring your own drinks. The *Seafari* is also available, at $NZ350, for photographic cruises catering to up to 15 people. Box 148; phone 20.328.

All deep-sea-fishing cruises share catches with tourist-fishers.

Diving. Rarotonga waters are warm and clear and teem with fish and coral. *Dive Rarotonga* (Box 38; ph 21.873) operates a 29-ft., flat-top catamaran on daily scuba/snorkeling trips. Equipment rental, tank filling, and instruction. Dive Rarotonga also runs its own hostel.

SPORTS. A beachside nine-hole golf course and grass tennis courts are available in Avarua, but most sporting activities in the Cooks are ocean oriented—swimming, diving, sailing, fishing, wind surfing, with equipment available for hire at most hotels and from tour operators.

The intervillage athletic competition, "kumete," is on June 2; the annual international lawn bowls tournament on June 26; the Rarotongan Open Golf Championship in July; the Nike 15km road race on Easter Monday; and the round-Rarotonga road race on November 8. All events attract international competitors.

NIGHTLIFE AND RESTAURANTS. Cook Islanders excel at dancing, singing, and drumming and all major hotels feature regular island nights with feasts of native food. Don't miss an evening or two at the quaint old *Banana Court* tavern-lounge in central Avarua, right alongside the betting shop. Open 11 A.M. to 11 P.M. Mondays and Tuesdays and until midnight other days; closed Sundays. Dancing Wednesday through Saturday nights with live local bands. Discos have sprung up in Rarotonga during the past two years, catering to younger visitors. Notable are the *First Club,* with a polished stainless steel dance floor and mirrored walls, and *TJ's,* featuring a spectacular light, sound, and video show. Both are in Avarua.

Quality restaurants have proliferated on Rarotonga to cater to visitors staying at the high proportion of motels on the island where it is estimated they eat out four or five nights a week. Almost 20 restaurants have grown up on the round-island road, so that none is more than 20 minutes' drive from anywhere. *Brandis,* one of the Rarotongan Hotel's three restaurants, is regarded as the island's best and is popular with tourists and locals alike, offering traditional and European meals. For a change, try the Mexican fare at the *Hacienda,* Chinese at the *Tangaroa* and *Hibiscus House,* Italian at the *Portofino,* and grills and seafood at the *Vaima.*

The *Sundowner Bar,* on the beach at Arorangi, is the place for an evening drink before a steak and seafood dinner at the *Outrigger,* opposite. Around the lagoon is the *Tumunu* —one of the island's best European dining spots—and *Polyanna's,* attached to the Edgewater Resort.

DEPARTURE TAX. NZ$20.

AMERICAN SAMOA

Polynesia Imperfect

by
GRAEME KENNEDY

Step out of a cab in Fagatogo after the 30-minute drive along the stunning seascape from Tafuna Airport and you know you're still in Samoa—but a very different Samoa from the one to the west you might have just left. For unlike Apia, with its leisurely, Old World charm and pace, **Pago Pago** bears the unmistakable stamp of the Stars and Stripes and all that goes with them. This doesn't make American Samoa better or worse—just different.

This U.S. territory (a domestic flight from Honolulu), has a total land area of just 76 square miles spread over six islands ranging from the tiny atoll Swains Island (population 34 at last count) in the north, through the 54-square-mile Tutuila, to the eastern Manua group of Tau, Olosega, and Ofu.

Pago Pago Bay, on Tutuila, recognized as the Pacific's most spectacular deepwater port—and therefore maintaining a major U.S. Navy presence—is dominated by 2,142-foot Mount Matafao to the west and 1,609-feet Mount Alava atop the eastern coast of the bay, reached from Pago's downtown area, Fagatogo, by a cable car on the world's longest unsupported aerial tramway. The town, a mixture of modern and old, clings to the harbor shores under steep jungle curtains, their tops often hidden by the clouds that bring the 120 inches of annual rainfall which prompted Somerset Maugham's classic short story "Rain." The tale was dramatized and

73

filmed as *Sadie Thompson,* after a Pago Pago prostitute and town character whose name now adorns the lounge-bar at the Rainmaker Hotel, built
at the port entrance under 1,178-foot Mount Pioa—Rainmaker Mountain.

Pago is a happy town across the bay from three fish canneries where
Korean, Japanese, and American deep-sea-fishing fleets come and go with
their catches of tuna. With the U.S. sailors, the Asian fishers lend the Polynesian territory an exotic and colorful atmosphere.

The U.S. government pumps millions of dollars into its Samoan territory annually, and it shows. American television is beamed live by satellite
into the most remote villages; the first major building you'll pass on the
drive in from the airport is the Lyndon B. Johnson Tropical Medicine Center; Fagatogo supermarkets are crammed with American goods; and the
U.S. flag flies high over the town.

Less influenced is the Manua group to the east, relatively undeveloped
and with only one tourist motel on each of its three islands—Ta'u, Olosega, and Ofu. The territory's highest peak, 3,050-foot Lata Mountain, towers over the main island, Tau, where the twin villages of Si'ufaga and
Luma were the object of anthropologist Margaret Mead's studies that led
to her book *Coming of Age in Samoa.* Published in 1928, it depicted the
Samoan people as sexually guilt-free, relaxed, highly intelligent and adher-
ing to their thousand-year-old lifestyle. Mead died at 77 in 1978, five years
before New Zealander Derek Freeman published his *Margaret Mead: The
Making and Unmaking of an Anthropological Myth.* He argued that Samoans were, in fact, jealously violent and often turned to rape, murder, as-
sault, and suicide.

It is still debated whether Manua or Savaii was the true ancient Samoa,
the cradle of Polynesia from which these handsome people grew. Many

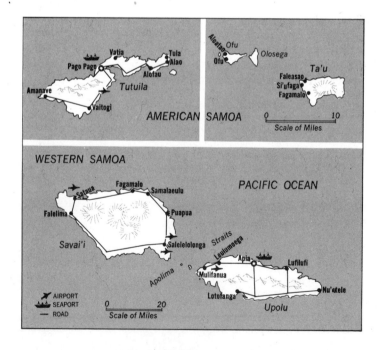

legends and stories that are the basis of Samoan tradition and ceremony can be traced to incidents that occurred on Tau island.

Archaeologists believe that Polynesians had established themselves on the eastern shores of Tutuila about 600 B.C. and lived peacefully isolated from the western world until Dutch navigator Jacob Roggeveen became the first European to see the islands, in 1722.

Roggeveen sailed on without landing after inaccurately fixing their position, and Samoa remained undisturbed for another 40 years before whites "rediscovered" the islands. They avoided them for decades after learning of the massacre of eleven members of a French scientific expedition led by Captain Jean François La Pérouse at Aasu, near Fagasa, across Tutuila from Pago Pago, in 1787. The site is now known as Massacre Bay, and a monument and cross erected by the French government in 1883 still stands.

The first real outside influence arrived with missionary John Williams and his ship *Messenger of Peace* in 1831. The islanders grasped Christianity with enthusiasm and were prepared when they were caught up in the wave of colonial expansion in the late 1830s. The United States, seeking suitable coaling ports in the Pacific, took over Tutuila in 1900 and the Manua group four years later while Germany gained possession of Upolu and Savaii to the west. With no official colonial administration, President McKinley declared the islands the responsibility of the U.S. Navy, with Commander B. F. Tilley formally accepting the deed of cession from all but one of the major chiefs, Tuimanua, from Tau. He did not sign for five years; then his people were granted the privileges of their new association with the United States.

With World War looming, Tutuila took on a new importance, and Pago became a vital training and staging area for the Marine Corps. Roads, air strips, docks, and hospitals were built, shattering the Samoans' quiet lives for all time. Many Samoans joined the Marines and began the flood of islanders who would migrate to the United States and build new lives there.

The military left in 1945 as suddenly as it had come, and Tutuila reverted to its prewar peace and quiet.

Administration was moved from the navy to the Department of the Interior under President Truman, and for more than 10 years the distant territory stagnated until, in 1961, President Kennedy sent a new governor, H. Rex Lee, to Pago Pago with instructions to get the islands moving. That he did, bringing the islands into the twentieth century and building the foundations for the Polynesian-American society that thrives today.

Tutuila is a surprising piece of the United States. Set in the South Pacific with soaring green-jungled mountains, crashing waterfalls, and superb beaches backed up by an efficient tourism infrastructure—it's not pure Polynesia, but it is fun.

PRACTICAL INFORMATION FOR
AMERICAN SAMOA

WHEN TO GO. American Samoa's rainfall is notorious, with more than 14 inches falling in an average December and more than 12 inches a month until April, when trade winds strengthen, humidity drops, and the dry season begins. Wet-season temperatures average around 80.5°F, falling to the high 70s midyear. Even in the rainy season, long periods of sunshine can be expected.

Average Temperature (°Fahrenheit) and Humidity

Pago Pago	Jan	Feb	Mar	Apr	May	June	July	Aug	Sept	Oct	Nov	Dec
Average max. day temperature	87°	86°	86°	87°	85°	84°	83°	83°	84°	85°	86°	86°
Days of rain	25	22	22	24	20	18	19	18	18	22	21	23
Humidity, percent	76	76	76	76	76	77	75	74	73	76	76	75

General hints: The tourist season starts April-May; June to October are considered the most pleasant. Remember, Samoa is close to the equator, and the weather is tropical, warm and humid. It rains most of the year, but the bursts last only an hour or so.

WHAT TO WEAR. Anything comfortable and informal is the standard, with cotton or light washable clothes ideal all year. A light plastic raincoat is essential. Samoans have their own clothing standards, and bikinis or short shorts should not be worn outside your hotel.

HOW TO GET THERE. *Hawaiian Air* from Honolulu and Auckland; *Polynesian Airlines* and *South Pacific Island Airways* from Western Samoa; *Air Pacific* from Fiji. **Ferry** sails several times a week from Western Samoa. Pago Pago's Tafuna International Airport is 6 miles from town.

ENTRY REQUIREMENTS. U.S. nationals need no travel documents; others need passports and visas. You can bring in one gallon of liquor and 200 cigarettes, 50 cigars, or one pound of tobacco.

CURRENCY. The U.S. dollar is used in American Samoa.

LANGUAGE. Both English and Samoan are spoken fluently.

TIPPING. This is not encouraged.

TIME ZONE. GMT less 11 hours; 3 hours behind U.S. Pacific Standard.

ACCOMMODATIONS. Rainmaker Hotel. Box 996, Pago Pago. Phone 633.5413. 164 air-conditioned rooms and 36 beach *fales* up to U.S.$100 a double, set on Goat Island Point at the entrance to Pago Harbor and under Rainmaker Mountain, a short walk to downtown Fagatogo. Bars, restaurants, pool, private beach.

Apiolefaga Inn. Box 336, Pago Pago. Phone 699.9124. 12 self-contained, air-conditioned rooms, on coast 20 minutes from downtown, 10 minutes from airport. Restaurant, pool, live entertainment. About $50 for a double.

Herb and Sia's Family Hotel. Box 430, Pago Pago. Phone 633.5413. 15 air-conditioned rooms in downtown Fagatogo. Island-style hospitality for about $30.

Each of the three islands of the Manua group has reasonably priced (from $25 to $30 a double) comfortable accommodations. On Olosega, **Don and Ilaisa's Motel** has five rooms. Box 923, Olosega. Phone 655.1120. On Ofu, **Vaoto Lodge** has 10 rooms, c/o Vili Malae, Ofu. Phone 655.1120. The eight-room **Niumata's Guesthouse** is on the island of Ta'u.

HOW TO GET AROUND. *Samoa Air* and *Manua Air Transport* operate twin-engined **aircraft** from Tafuna International Airport on the 45-min. flight to the islands in the Manu'a group.

On Tutuila, public **"aiga" buses** run frequent but unscheduled services from Fagatogo to outlying villages. The service stops at 5 P.M.

Cars can be rented by the day, week, or month from *Avis* (Box 3457; phone 633.1630), *Budget* (Box 3204; phone 633.2482), *Royal Samoan* (Box 727; phone 633.4545), *Hertz* (Box 968; phone 633.4323), *Morris Scanlan Rentals* (Box 367; phone 633.5520), and *Pavitt-U-Drive* (Box 3255; phone 699.1456).

Cabs are plentiful and fares are government-regulated.

When in Pago, don't miss the spectacular cable car ride across Pago Harbor to the summit of 1609-ft. Mt. Alava. It leaves from Solo Hill, above Government House in Fagatogo, daily except Sunday between 8 A.M. and 4 P.M. and Cost: $2.50.

TOURIST INFORMATION. Contact the *Office of Tourism,* Box 1147, Pago Pago, American Samoa.

TOURS. Visitors can easily arrange sightseeing and cultural tours throughout Tutuila and the Manua group, taking a half-day or several to take in the islands' seascapes, mountains, rain forests, and beaches. Massacre Bay at Aasu, the scenic mountain pass at Afono, Vaitogo village, and the ancient chiefs' burial ground at Fagiatua are some of the popular stops.

Tour companies can also arrange for visitors to spend a night with a Samoan family in an outer village to experience their culture firsthand.

Contact *Samoa Holiday and Travel Centre* (Box 968; phone 633.4692), *Paradise Travel* (Box 298; phone 633.9228), *Samoa Tours* (Box 727; phone 633.5884), *Nomura's* (Box 1238; phone 633.2235), *CDI Travel* (Box 1390; phone 633.2421), *Pacific Island Tours* (Box 3994; phone 633.4660), *Pritchard's Travel* (Box 290; phone 633.4222), or *South Seas Travel* (Box 1875; phone 633.2878).

SPORTS. The conditions are excellent in American Samoa to engage in any water sport. Swimming, diving, sailing, and fishing are the most popular pursuits.

Underwater visibility can exceed 100 feet, giving superb views of coral reefs and the colorful fish that abound in the warm tropical waters.

Chuck Bergmen (phone 633.2010) operates fishing and diving trips, or a combination of both, in his 28-ft. launch. Day-long fishing trips cost $50 with a minimum of three people. He can provide all scuba and tank equipment for wreck, night, and reef dives. Mike Crook (Box 3700; phone 633.1701) sails his launch *Leilani* out of Pago for fishing excursions. Minimum of six people; $200 for a five-hour trip, $350 for 12 hours.

For big game fishing, contact the president of the American Samoa Game Fishing Association, Box 1180, phone 96799.

Ashore, the 18-hole, par-70 championship golf course at Lava Lava, near the airport, welcomes visitors to the greens as well as to its restaurant and bar. There are public tennis courts at Tafuna and at the nearby Ava Club. Hiking trails through the jungled mountains are popular, though the climb to the peak of Rainmaker Mountain is suitable only for serious climbers.

Spectator sports include rugby, boxing, American-style football, basketball, and the unofficial national sport of *kirikiti*—a Polynesian game of cricket played with a three-sided bat and hard rubber ball by teams which have in the past numbered more than 100.

SHOPPING. The Samoan Village at Pago Pago Park is a collection of fales built by American Samoa's old people and is devoted to traditional handicrafts such as shellwork, weaving, and carving. Aged citizens work at the center and sell their wares there. Good buys include puke and paper-shell necklaces, tapa prints, and woven pandanus ware such as place mats, bags, and baskets. Carved wooden kava bowls and tortoise shell are also of high standard.

American Samoa is a duty-free port, and several stores in Fagatogo and neighboring Utulei, as well as at Tafuna Airport, specialize in perfumes, cameras, and stereo and radio equipment.

NIGHTLIFE AND RESTAURANTS. Like their neighbors to the west, American Samoans know how to enjoy the nightlife from the cultural to the cut-loose.

Traditional *fia-fias,* with dancing and vast native feasts of roast pig, breadfruit, taro, and palusami, are held regularly at the *Rainmaker, Herb and Sia's Motel,* and the *Apiolefaga.* Visitors with less exotic tastes can try the Terrace restaurant at the *Rainmaker, Soli,* and *Mark's* (with its great harbor view). Other options include the very good Korean barbecue at *Malaloa* or a drive around the harbor to Atu'u to partake of the Chinese menu at the *Ramona Lee.*

Pago and its harbor suburbs abound with food outlets—take-out bars, lunch wagons, and bar-restaurants. In Fagatogo, the *Ala Moana* and *Big Jake's* have food to go, while *Hot Dog City* and the *Icewich Fale* speak for themselves. You'll find *Matai's Pizza Fale* and *Milovale's Drive-in* in the Nu'uu shopping center, *Lydia's Snack Bar* near the hospital at Fagaalu, and *Te'o Fuavia's Place* past the fish-packing sheds at Atu'u.

The action starts in Pago after dark at the *Purple Onion* at Tafuna, the *Sadie Thompson Bar* at the Rainmaker, and the Mexican disco with its stunning light show at *Evalani's* in Pago. Check out the *Seaside Garden Lounge* in Fagatogo, not far from a new fun-palace of good food, music, and drinks above the legendary Miss Thompson's old rooming house. It's called, naturally, *Sadie's*.

WESTERN SAMOA

Where It's Really At

by
GRAEME KENNEDY

"You lie on a mat in a cool Samoan hut and look out on the white sand under the high palms and a gentle sea, and the black line of the reef a mile out and moonlight over everything. . . .

"And then among it all are the loveliest people in the world, moving and dancing like gods and goddesses.

"It is sheer beauty, so pure it is difficult to breathe in it."

Rupert Brooke, one of the many men of literature to become besotted by Samoa, wrote those lines almost 100 years ago; yet they remain just as relevant today.

For Western Samoa, the magic islands of Savaii and Upolu is Polynesia at its most pure. Savaii, they say, is the legendary Hawaiki from which the original Polynesian people set out to conquer the Pacific and settle north in Hawaii, south in the Cook Islands and New Zealand, and east in Easter Island.

Now the old migration is reversed, with tourists coming from America and Europe, Australia and Japan, New Zealand and Asia, all lured by the glistening beaches and lagoons that might be models for all others in the South Pacific, the clear freshwater inland lakes, high waterfalls, tumbling rivers, and lush-green highlands—and for Samoa itself. It is often said that the best thing about Samoa is simply being there, feeling the warmth of the people and the land, surrounded by the beauty Brooke and others wrote of and caressed by the heady scents of frangipani, poinciana, ginger flowers, bougainvilleas, and countless other tropical flowers filling the air.

They come to the new Faleolo international airport, opened late 1985 to 747 standards, a 40-minute drive from the island nation's capital, Apia. Since then, motels and cheaper accommodations have sprouted like mushrooms. A new 200-room hotel, the Royal Samoan, is on the drawing board, and the government is dedicated to developing a tourist industry compatible with the Samoan's age-old customs and tradition.

Apia, a busy waterfront town of more than 30,000 people on the north coast of Upolu, is flanked to the east by its deepwater port and the impressive Fono (parliament buildings) on Mulinuu Point to the west. Once a center of intrigue where foreign consuls plotted the annexation of the South Pacific by colonial powers, and a gathering place for trading schooners, sealers, and whalers, Apia is still a romantic South Seas port town. Modern office buildings now stand alongside colonial wooden structures, with their wide verandas and palm trees. The old post office and the Burns Philp store are wonderfully preserved examples of early-1900s architecture.

Apia stretches itself, warm and lazy, around the bay to embrace the colorful, noisy New Market, where villagers bring their produce, fish, live turtles, and handicrafts for sale from predawn until late, late night. There are restaurants, bars, memorials, parks, shops, and government offices within Apia's arms, shared with tourist hotels such as the Tusitala and Aggie Grey's, both bearing the names of Samoan legends.

Aggie, who died in 1988 at the age of 90, was the Pacific's last living legend, whose name became synonymous with Bloody Mary from Michener's *Tales of the South Pacific*.

Michener and Aggie were good friends, and although his Mary of book, stage, and screen was actually an old tobacco-chewing harridan from the New Hebrides (now Vanuatu), she could easily have been modeled on the incredible Aggie. Aggie first met Michener when he was serving with the U.S. Navy during World War II and, like thousands of others, found a home away from home at Aggie's then-modest guesthouse on the waterfront. A luxury guest fale at her now-magnificent hotel is named for the author, as are others for actress Roberta Hayes and actor Gary Cooper, who shared her hospitality when they starred in the sixties movie adaptation of Michener's *Return to Paradise,* filmed across Upolu at the dramatically beautiful Lefaga Beach. Twice widowed and left with six children at the height of German colonization, Aggie pestered the authorities until she was granted a license to run a club where Samoans could meet, talk, and drink together.

The Americans and their military machine marched up the Pacific toward Japan in the early 1940s, and they all ended up at Aggie's, transforming it into a U.S.-style hamburger bar and beer hall. That was the beginning, and now the soldiers, sailors, and airmen of the war years return as elderly tourists to toast her memory.

The Scottish novelist Robert Louis Stevenson is also a legend in Samoa. They called him Tusitala—the teller of tales—and his tomb atop Mount Vaea, overlooking Apia and the bay, is almost a national shrine. It bears his immortal requiem: "Under the wide and starry sky/dig the grave and let me lie. . . . Home is the sailor, home from the sea, / and the hunter home from the hill."

Stevenson, suffering from tuberculosis, came to Samoa from Honolulu in 1888 in search of a place to recover his health and continue writing.

He wrote to a friend, "I go there only to grow old and die; but when you come, you will see it is a fair place for the purpose." Already famous, with *Treasure Island* published, Stevenson built a fine house at Vailima, at the foot of Mt. Vaea, and wrote prolifically in his last five years, producing novels such as the controversial *The Beach at Falesa, The Ebb Tide,* and *The Wrecker.* He died on December 3, 1894, while preparing a salad for dinner. A steep track has been cut up the mountain to his tomb; tourists are advised to make the journey in the early morning, before the heat of the day. Vailima, beautifully restored, is the official residence of the head of state, the Malietoa Tanumafili. Permission to visit Vailima and its flowered, parklike grounds can be obtained from the Prime Minister's Department in Apia.

But Western Samoa is much more than Apia and Vailima—Michener wrote that even the journey from Faleolo, past the 72 village churches, into town was "the most beautiful drive in the South Pacific." The road hugs the coast past neat villages, rugged seascapes, lagoons, and quiet pools until it bursts into the bustling Apia suburbs. Continuing east, the road weaves through some of the island's most colorful villages and scenery, climbs to Mafa Pass and its stunning views and on to the magnificent 160-foot Falefa Falls before plunging to the white sands and clear lagoon at Aleipata on the eastern tip of the island.

There, soak in the warm Pacific and gaze at the tiny off-shore islands Nuulua, Nuutele, Fanuatapu, and Namua. Return to Apia through dreamlike Mulivai Beach and savor its wide lagoon. The once-lovely Samoan Hideaway resort on the beach is deserted and in disrepair since its sale almost two years ago.

Don't miss the sliding rocks at Papaseea, just five miles from Apia, where natural-rock water chutes give thrilling rides into a cool, shaded freshwater pool similar to that at Piula Cave, where cold, crystal waters flow from beneath the village Methodist church just a 30-minute drive inland from Apia. The same distance is Lake Lanoto'o, where you can swim in clear, fresh water teeming with goldfish. Difficult to reach, but it is worth the effort—engage a guide through your hotel.

The "big island" of Savaii is 1½ hours, or 13½ miles, to the west by ferry from Mulifanua, near Faleolo Airport. It's just seven minutes, by Polynesian Airlines, from Apia's air strip by the golf course at Fagalii, to the main town of Salelologa. Polynesian also flies several times daily to a new airstrip built over the lagoon at Vaisala on the northwest of Savaii to service the hotel there which has become Western Samoa's best beach resort since the Hideaway's closure. Here are beaches and lagoons you've dreamed about—white sand that rarely bears a footprint, bird-filled forests unchanged since time began, lagoons so clear they can't be real. But to shake yourself back into the twentieth century (well, almost), be on the Salelologa wharf when the ferry docks from Upolu. Guitar-playing Samoans, with pigs, chickens, crates of beer, and much singing and laughter make every arrival a festival.

Wonderful islands, these, first sighted by Dutch navigator Jacob Roggeveen in 1722 and named the Navigator Islands by the Frenchman Bougainville 64 years later. Samoa's modern history began, as did many island's, with the pioneer missionary John Williams' arrival in 1830, and a stone cairn in Savaii's Sapapalii village marks the spot where he first set foot on the Samoas. Ten years later, the German trading firm Godeffroy and Sons established itself in the islands to trade in copra and encourage the Samoan people to grow produce for export as well as their own use.

Meanwhile, warring tribal factions under rival kings sought aid from the British, German, and U.S. powers in Apia in the late 1800s, prompting a show of naval force, wiped out by the great 1889 hurricane, which sank all but one ship (British) and ended what could have become a major confrontation. As a result, Germany administered Western Samoa, the United States the east, and Britain quietly withdrew. Good colonists, the Germans established vast coconut plantations now operated by a Western Samoan quasi-government organization. World War I broke out in 1914, with New Zealand taking charge as the Germans retreated homeward. An unlikely colonial power, New Zealand's administration caused much friction, creating the Samoan chiefs' Mau movement, which culminated in a waterside confrontation in which more than a dozen Samoans were shot dead by New Zealand militia. A change of government in Wellington and the overpowering U.S. influence during World War II were the catalysts to Western Samoa's becoming the first independent Polynesian nation in January 1962. Thus began a gradual, graceful emergence into the twentieth century.

The population of 160,000 now includes the world's largest number of full-blooded Polynesians. Samoan is the purest surviving Polynesian type. A dignified people who love to sing and dance in the traditional way, they have adapted their lifestyle, based on Fa'a Samoa—the way of the ancestors—to western influences. The very basis of Samoan life is the aiga (*eye-ing-a*), or family, which extends far beyond parents and children to embrace a vast group of blood, marriage, and adopted members. At the head of each aiga is the matai, the acknowledged head of the family selected by consensus and responsible for directing the family's future, lands, and other assets.

Within the aiga is an unwritten law binding its members to house, feed, clothe, lend money to, or fight for others in the group if necessary, creating a philosophy toward property incompatible with western ideas. But it works well in Samoa, where most live on the land in the traditional style, growing their own food outside their thatched fales, catching fish in the lagoons, and selling a little produce at the markets for cash. Drive through any Samoan village and you will see women weaving and men carving and tilling their soil in the old way—and you realize that they are not doing this for the tourist.

It is the way of things.

It has been said that if a Samoan man has healthy children, a neat and comely wife, a house of his own, a canoe, a coconut palm, banana trees, and a few pigs, he has the intelligence to know he's well off.

And that isn't bad.

PRACTICAL INFORMATION FOR

WESTERN SAMOA

WHEN TO GO. Since it is close to the equator, Western Samoa's climate is hot and humid, although the fresh trade winds in the May-to-October dry season make life pleasantly comfortable despite an 84°F average. Temperatures average 86° and humidity soars in the November-to-April wet season, when rain will fall more than 75% of the time. Sea temperatures are ideal all year—mostly in the low 80s and rarely falling below 75°F.

Average Temperature (Farenheit) and Humidity

Apia	Jan	Feb	Mar	Apr	May	June	July	Aug	Sept	Oct	Nov	Dec
Average max. day temperature	86°	86°	86°	86°	86°	85°	84°	84°	85°	85°	86°	86°
Days of rain	24	24	19	24	13	13	11	11	21	18	15	22
Humidity, percent	84	85	84	84	83	82	80	80	80	82	83	84

General hints: There is little climate variation between the two Samoas, although American Samoa has a heavier rainfall. Best time for visit in Western Samoa is June through November.

WHAT TO WEAR. Lightweight summer clothes with a light cardigan or sweater for cooler midyear nights are ideal. Apia is generally informal, and men seldom wear ties. Shirts and shorts are acceptable almost everywhere. In keeping with Samoan custom, women should wear dresses outside their hotel and should not be seen in the main streets wearing bikinis or other bathing suits.

HOW TO GET THERE. National flag carrier *Polynesian Airlines* links Western Samoa with Boeing services to Tahiti, Rarotonga, Pago Pago, Auckland, Fiji, Tonga, and Sydney. Other international airlines operating into Faleolo include *Air New Zealand, Air Pacific,* and *Hawaiian Air. South Pacific Island Airways* flies daily between Pago Pago and Faleolo.

ENTRY REQUIREMENTS. A passport and onward travel bookings are required for stays of up to 30 days. Longer visits will require an entry permit obtainable from the immigration officer in Apia, Western Samoa, the high commissioner in Wellington, New Zealand, the consulate in Auckland, or from the Samoa mission to the United Nations in New York.

Visitors must make written declarations and are allowed one bottle of spirits and 200 cigarettes. Firearms, drugs, and indecent publications of any kind are prohibited.

Yellow fever vaccinations are necessary only if arriving within six days of traveling through an infected area.

LANGUAGE. Samoans generally use their own soft, musical Polynesian language, although English is the accepted language for government and commerce. English is widely spoken and understood in the most remote villages.

ELECTRICITY. About 50 square kilometers around Apia is served by hydroelectric and diesel-generated power. Supply is scarce in outlying districts, although some villages and hotels have their own generators. Current is 240 volts AC, 50 Hz. Electric shaver adaptors are available in most hotels.

CURRENCY. Western Samoa's decimal currency is the *Tala,* broken into 100 sene. At press time, one American dollar buys 2.2 Tala. Foreign currency is accepted at major hotels and larger stores or can be exchanged at the Apia banks during business hours, 9:30 A.M. to 3 P.M. All credit cards are accepted at larger establishments, but check first with smaller restaurants.

TIPPING. This is not done in Western Samoa.

ACCOMMODATIONS. For double rooms, *Expensive* means US$35–US$50; *Moderate,* US$20–US$30; *Inexpensive,* below US$20.

Aggie Grey's Hotel. *Expensive.* Box 67, Apia. Phone 22.880. The best hotel in the Samoas—and probably in Polynesia. 130 air-conditioned rooms, suites, and fales on the Beach Rd. waterfront in flower-garden setting with large swimming pool, two bars, and airy, elevated dining room. Now managed by Aggie's son Alan, the hotel retains its Polynesian charm alongside modern facilities. A WS$2 million building program is due to be completed by the end of 1988.

Tusitala Hotel. *Expensive.* Box 101, Apia. Phone 21.122. Has 96 air-conditioned double rooms on the waterfront, a short walk to the west of downtown. Swimming pool, conference room, bars, dining room.

The Apian Way. *Moderate.* Box 617. Phone 21.482. Five minutes' walk from Apia, with one double and five single air-conditioned rooms.

Seaside Inn. *Moderate.* Phone 22.578. Self-contained units, bar, one minute from Palolo Deep.

Vaiala Beach Cottages. *Moderate.* Box 1157. Phone 22.202. This popular swimming beach is a mile from downtown Apia, just past the wharf with seven cottages in garden grounds. All are self-contained and have cooking facilities. Good diving at Palolo Deep, 300 yards away.

Harbour Light Hotel. *Inexpensive–Moderate.* Box 8. Phone 21.103 or 21.933. 30 air-conditioned rooms, licensed restaurant and bar at wharf end of Apia waterfront.

Betty Moor's Guesthouse. *Inexpensive.* Box 18. Phone 21.085. Inland near wharf and 100 meters from Vaiala Beach with five single rooms, four twins, and two doubles. Share cooking facilities and showers.

Olivia Yandall's Casual Accommodation. *Inexpensive.* Box 4089. Phone 22.110. Two self-contained units, each with one single and two double bedrooms.

Savaii Island

Safua Hotel. *Expensive* (but rates include meals). Box 5002, Salelologa. Phone 24.262. Just north of Salelologa, on the beach in parklike grounds with restaurant, bar, and nine self-contained fales. Visitors are welcome in the nearby picturesque villages of Safua and Lalomalava.

Salimu Hotel. *Expensive.* On beach with canoeing and snorkeling gear for hire. Bookings through travel agents in Apia.

Savaiian Guest Fale. *Expensive* (but rates include breakfast and dinner). At Salelologa, comfortable island-style accommodation. Book through travel agents in Apia.

Salafai Inn. *Moderate.* At Salelologa with guest-house-style accommodation, double rooms on spectacular beach. Meals available. Book through travel agents in Apia.

Vaisala Hotel. *Moderate.* Box 570, Apia. Phone 22.027. Built on one of Savaii's prettiest beaches on the northwest corner of the island, featuring 18 self-contained units, restaurant, two bars, facilities for all water sports.

HOW TO GET AROUND. Internal **air services** to Savaii are operated by *Polynesian Airlines* using twin-engined light aircraft.

The *Western Samoa Shipping Corporation* has daily **ferry services** between Upolu and Savaii and a twice-weekly schedule to American Samoa. The service and departure times are irregular, and passengers should contact the corporation by phoning in Apia 20.935.

Public-transport buses are colorful wooden-seated and open-sided old vehicles ideal for tourists looking for a bit of adventure. They leave irregularly from the bus stand at the new market in central Apia. A 30-sene fare will take you through the town area or up into the hills through neighboring villages and plantations. Fares to the most distant villages are a maximum of about WST1.60. Buses also serve the coastal villages on Savaii Island.

Rental cars are plentiful. The license of your own country is acceptable, driving is on the right, and all signs are in English. Car-rental companies include *Pavitt's U-Drive* (phone 21.766), *Gold Star* (phone 21.711), *Avis Rentway* (phone 22.468).

A host of richly decorated stereo-blasting **cabs** are available in Apia and include two radio-controlled services. Cabs can be telephoned or picked up at ranks outside the major hotels, downtown, and at the airport.

TOURIST INFORMATION. Contact the *Western Samoa Visitors Bureau*, Box 862, Apia. Phone 20.471.

TOURS. Guided bus and car tours are available to all places of major interest on Upolu. A limited tour service operates on Savaii, and travel agents in Apia should be contacted for information.

Tour companies on Upolu include: *Retzlaff's Tours.* English- and German-speaking guides in this long-established Western Samoan company. All entrance fees included in costs. Box 145; phone 21.724 or 21.725.

Gold Star Travel and Tours. Half-day tours available through Apia, to Stevenson's tomb, sliding rocks, Felafe Falls, and Piula Cave, full day to Mulivai, Aleipata Sands, Paradise Beach, and the Togitogiga Falls. Meals not included. Box 185; phone 20.466.

Samoa Scenic Tours. Specializing in two to four-hour tours, one taking in Apia township, royal tombs, Stevenson's home, Vailima, coffee plantations, the sliding rocks, and other attractions along the north coast to the east to Falefa Falls, plantations, the Mafa Pass, and return via Piula Cave Pool. Private car available. Box 669; phone 22.880.

Janes Tours. Jane Leungwai operates tours throughout Upolu from 2½ to 6 hours, taking in all places of interest and popular spots. Minimum numbers are eight in a coach and four by car. Box 70; phone 20.954 or 20.218.

Union Travel and Tours. Operating station wagons and specializing in groups, Union offers half- and full-day tours of Upolu. Box 50; phone 21.787.

SPORTS. Western Samoa has surprisingly excellent sporting facilities, dominated by the huge Apia Park stadium and tennis-court complex built to accommodate the South Pacific Games in 1983. Almost every village has a sports club, and rugby, soccer, basketball, netball, volleyball, hockey, and American football are played vigorously. Squash is becoming popular, and courts in Apia are a short stroll from Aggie Grey's toward the wharf. Phone 23.780 for reservations.

The *Apia Park tennis courts* are open every day, including Sundays, and cost 50 sene per player per half-hour. Reservations can be made on 22.571.

The *Royal Samoan Golf Club* at Fagalii in suburban Apia is the site of the Royal Samoan Open Golf Championship every August. Visitors are welcome, and arrangements to pay greens fees can be made at your hotel.

Lawn bowls are popular in Samoa and hotels or tour companies can direct you to the *Apia Bowling Club,* which has greens next to the Tusitala Hotel and at Apia Park.

Lasers, Hobie Cats, and Windsurfers can be hired from *Samship Charters,* near the Tusitala Hotel. Phone 21.700.

SHOPPING. Samoan families have always made a wide range of articles for their personal use, and these are becoming increasingly popular to tourists for their quality and beauty of woods and fibers. The Samoan siapo (tapa) cloth, made from mulberry bark and painted with natural dyes, is a particular example. Woven mats and baskets, hand-carved bowls, shell jewelry, and bright native prints are all attractively priced in the handcraft store on Beach Rd. and at the family stalls in the New Market in downtown Apia.

The Philatelic Bureau above the main post office sells examples of Samoa's prize-winning postage stamps, and commemorative issues of Samoan coins are available in mint sets from the Treasury Department.

All duty-free items are available from two stores at Faleolo Airport.

NIGHTLIFE AND RESTAURANTS. Apia is a swinging nighttime town, with more liquor licenses, rock bands, bars, and clubs per square mile than any other Polynesian island outside Hawaii. Add to those the thundering fia-fias held almost nightly at one hotel or another, and you've got a lot of nightlife.

Fia-Fias

Fia-fia literally means "fun" and an opportunity to take in a huge slice of Western Samoan culture and excitement in one gulp. Friday night at *Aggie Grey's Hotel* is the scene for the islands' most spectacular fia-fia, with centuries-old drumming underlining warlike dancing led by heavily-tattooed Dominic, who doubles as a head-waiter in the hotel dining room. He is followed by the women's performance, often led by Marina Grey, who demonstrates the traditional siva—a dreamy and sensuous dance not unlike Hawaii's hula. The climax of the show is a drumming, whirling fire dance, an electrifying performance. Next comes the feasting—mountains of whole spit-roasted pig, chicken, fish, hams, salads, and that Polynesian delight palu-sami, young taro-leaf tops steamed with coconut cream to be savored with any dish. The Tusitala hotel has a similarly rousing fia-fia.

Cocktails

Predinner drinks are almost compulsory in Samoa, and Apia abounds in pleasant bars, most on the waterfront and facing the sunset. Try *Otto's Reef* (phone 22.691), but don't expect the Ritz, just good drinks and plenty of fun, especially if Otto is there. The *Tusitala's* bar is cavernous and, open both sides, attracts the cooling evening breezes. Almost next door is the *Beachcomber,* relatively new and happily run American-style by Tessa and Horst. The bar at *Aggie's* is comfortably airy.

Restaurants

Eateries are many and varied, from the seemingly endless range of western and Samoan dishes offered at *Aggie's* to the fine steaks at *Amigo's,* on Vaea St. at Saleufi (23.140). The *Apia Inn,* on Beach Rd. overlooking the harbor, is air-conditioned, with cool decor and splendid service specializing in European dishes (21.010), while at *Le Godinet,* the lobster mornay would do credit to a Parisian chef. Reef crab, swimming in rich black bean sauce and served whole is the sensational speciality at Apia's *New Canton* restaurant.

Late Night

Late-nighters in Apia have no excuse to simply sit in their hotel rooms—you can rock way past midnight here.

Start at the popular *Surfside* nightclub, just a short stroll toward the wharf from Aggie's, where there's good music and a laid-back atmosphere.

A five-minute walk in the cool night breezes toward town brings you back to *Otto's,* where, on Friday and Saturday nights and for a WST1 door charge, you can hear top Apia rock bands playing their own compositions. Very loud but much fun. Just two doors down is the *Love Boat* (24.065), with music, cold beer, inexpensive yet interesting meals and friendly atmosphere.

Get a WST1 cab from the Love Boat into Apia and *Donovan's Reef* (23.187), a wonderfully wild and wacky bar with live band and dancing. But be wary of the exterior flight of wooden steps when you're leaving.

There are several other so-called nightclubs in Apia, featuring deafening disco and live music in dark, gloomy interiors. Don't go.

For something totally different in late-night entertainment, head for the *New Market* and follow your nose. Food stalls abound, it seems, open 24 hours a day and offering such Samoan fare as barbecued mutton flaps and chicken backs with fried vegetables and island chop suey—vermicelli with meat, soya sauce, and spices—all starting at around WST3. Don't expect china and silver cutlery, but it's fun.

DEPARTURE TAX. WST20.

TONGA

Ancient Polynesia Still

by
GRAEME KENNEDY

The Pacific's only surviving monarchy and the only island group never colonized, Tonga sprawls poor but proud just east of the International Date Line between 15 degrees and 23.5 degrees south, a scattering of 169 islands in 140,000 square miles of ocean.

With a total land area of just 258 square miles and only 36 islands inhabited, the 92,000 native Tongans subsist as Polynesia's poorest people. The biggest problem is a lack of land. Under Tongan law, every male over 16 is entitled to an 8¼-acre allotment on which to plant crops and eventually raise a family. There is simply not enough land to go around, but large-scale emigration is prevented by strict entry laws and quota systems in favored countries, notably New Zealand.

So Tongans are trapped at home—with a 3.6 percent annual population growth and a fragile agricultural economy based on erratic export prices for copra, bananas, and coconut products. Tonga is actively encouraging tourism as a reliable source of foreign exchange, although the economy is still propped up by cash aid grants and development projects from wealthier nations, especially New Zealand, Australia, and West Germany. Tonga, though, offers the tourist no more—and in many areas a lot less— than other Polynesian destinations, and this is probably why the kingdom welcomed fewer than 4,000 guests last year.

Tonga's outer island groups, especially Vava'u and Ha'apai, have wonderful beaches and superb lagoons—but so do other Pacific islands that have much more rewarding exchange rates with the U.S., Australian, or New Zealand dollars.

But Tonga is quaint and historic. Its ruler, King Taufa'ahau Tupou IV, is able to trace his origins back to the Tu'i Tonga chiefs who reigned more than 1,000 years ago, and archaeologists believe the islands were inhabited as early as the fifth century. The first Europeans there were the Dutch navigators Schouten and Lemaire in 1616. They were followed by Tasman, Wallis, and Cook, who named the group The Friendly Islands. Captain Bligh had cause to remember Tonga—the *Bounty* mutiny occurred in Tongan waters.

The missionaries arrived in the 1820s, and their influence helped in 1845 to end the savage tribal wars that had raged for 50 years. King George Tupou I was proclaimed ruler, beginning the dynasty that survives today under Tupou IV—a big 22-stone (308-pound) man who needs two aircraft seats whenever he flies overseas, which is often. Tongans accept and revere their royal family, despite the vast and obvious differences in living standards and wealth: Three-quarters of the working population are employed on plantations, and others seek a livelihood from the sea. Able navigators and fishers, Tongans until recently still hunted whales with hand harpoons.

The women are skilled at mat weaving, basket work, and producing tapa cloth, although the younger population, eyes opened to the twentieth century by tourism and stories from their contemporaries who have experienced the great mecca that is Auckland, New Zealand, often show little interest in continuing with traditional pursuits.

Men and women in Tonga wear the skirtlike *tupanu,* or *vala*—men to the knee and women to the ankle. Women wear a decorative waistband, the *kiekie,* and men a woven mat, the *ta'ovala,* tied with belts of coconut fiber. Both are signs of respect for elders and the royal family.

Since the first missionaries came to Tonga around 180 years ago, Christianity has dominated local life and stamped it with attitudes approaching priggishness. Until recently, swimming and dancing were banned on Sundays and even now any loud activity is discouraged on Sundays, when no public transport operates, international airline flights are banned, inter-island shipping is canceled—and you won't find a drink anywhere outside the bigger hotels. Almost every Tongan will attend church on Sunday, and harmonized hymn singing is almost the only sound heard throughout the islands. The official church is Wesleyan, with Tupou IV its head, but almost all denominations are represented here. The Mormons, especially, have a huge following.

Tongatapu, the most populous island (with 61,000 people), is quite flat and covered by coconut plantations. It has cliffs to the south but a wide lagoon embracing 12 small islands along its northern coast. Here is Tonga's capital, Nukualofa, a ramshackle town with a handful of modern buildings housing the Bank of Tonga and some administrative departments. The king's 120-year-old Victorian-style royal palace and chapel, surrounded by tall Norfolk pines, dominates the waterfront just along from Queen Salote Wharf, where cruise ships occasionally tie up. Almost in the center of town are the much-photographed royal tombs, where Tongan royalty has been buried since 1893.

Other monuments left by ancient kings remain on Tongatapu. At the ancient capital of Mu'a is the Langi—the vast terraced tombs where the Tu'i Tonga were laid to rest in huge slabs of hewn rock to create the closest thing to a pyramid in Polynesia.

Farther around the coast, at Tongatapu's northeast corner, is the 1,000-year-old Ha'amonga trilithon—a 5-meter-high gateway of carved coral rock topped by a 6-meter rock lintel. The stones are estimated to weigh about 40 tons each, and legend says they were brought by canoe to Tonga from Wallis Island. Deep-etched lines in the crosspiece point directly to the rising sun on the longest and shortest days, indicating that the ancient kings might have used the trilithon as an early seasonal calendar.

Across the island and nine miles from Nukualofa are the blowholes, known as *Mapu-'a-Vaea,* or Chief's Whistle, for the whistling noise made by the surf as 18-meter geysers blast into the air as far as you can see along the coastal cliffs. Near Mu'a, on the inland lagoon and 12 miles from town, is the old 'ovava tree under which Captain Cook rested when he visited Tonga in the *Endeavour* more than 200 years ago. A monument was placed at the spot in 1970.

Along the north coast on roads made reasonable by overseas aid programs, one of the strangest tourist "attractions" on any island is a collection of tall trees at the beachside village of Kolovai, where thousands of bats, or flying foxes, spend the day hanging upside-down, chattering and smelling. They are sacred and can be hunted only by members of the royal family. Visitors will miss little by avoiding the bats' pungent, stringy, tough flesh.

Eua Island, 40 kilometers southeast of Tongatapu, is a complete contrast to the main island, with rolling hills, high cliffs, and streams tumbling through a natural forest that is the home for a variety of tropical birds, particularly the Eua parrot, kingfishers, and blue-crowned lorikeets. Population is around 4,000.

The Haapai group, 160 kilometers north of Tongatapu, is a flat, thin archipelago featuring the live volcano Tofua and the extinct Kao. It has many fine beaches, lagoons, and reefs and is home to about 10,000 Tongans.

Another 112 kilometers north is the Vavau group, the finest among the Tongan islands and with a population around 13,000. The seas around the main island are sprinkled with 17 others, smaller and separated by deep, narrow channels leading into the fiord-like approach to the main town, Neiafu. This natural harbor has been known for centuries as Port of Refuge and is one of the Pacific's most beautiful. The Paradise International Hotel lies at its head, and jungle-clad Mount Talau rears above, giving spectacular views across freshwater Lake Tuanuku and the group's larger islands, Pangai Motu, Kapa, Nuapapa, and Hunga.

A Tongan friend once explained that "Nukualofa is the worst of our country—but Vavau is the best."

He was not wrong.

PRACTICAL INFORMATION FOR TONGA

WHEN TO GO. Tonga's climate is slightly cooler than that of most other tropical islands, but it shares their seasonal division into "summer" wet and "winter" dry seasons. The dry months are May, June, and July, when the average temperature falls to 21, 22, and 23°C—about four degrees below the wet-season averages. Rainfall drops from around 2,450mm in Feb. to only .860mm in June. In the capital, Nukualofa, the mean annual temperature is 24.7°C, humidity 76.9%, and rainfall 1,775.5mm. Temperature, rainfall, and humidity increase in the northern island groups.

Average Temperature (°Fahrenheit) and Humidity

Nukualofa	Jan	Feb	Mar	Apr	May	June	July	Aug	Sept	Oct	Nov	Dec
Average max. day temperature	83°	84°	83°	82°	79°	78°	76°	76°	76°	78°	80°	82°
Days of rain	17	17	20	15	14	12	12	12	12	12	12	14
Humidity, percent	76	78	79	77	74	74	72	72	71	70	71	73

General hints: Best tourist months are May through November. Heavy rains begin in December and last through March; humidity is high in this period. It's a good idea to have a sweater along for the cool July and August evenings.

WHAT TO WEAR. Tongans, like other Polynesians, adhere to the teachings of the early missionaries in their attitudes to modesty. The law here forbids any person from appearing in a public place without a shirt or blouse, and this is strictly enforced. Brief shorts, bikinis, and other swimwear are fine at the beach or poolside but are frowned upon in public. Although Tonga is cooler than other tropical islands, casual dress is recommended; however, a light pullover or stole should be packed for evenings in the June-to-September dry season. Bring an umbrella or a light raincoat at any time of the year.

HOW TO GET THERE. *Polynesian Airlines* and *Air New Zealand* fly into Tonga's Fuaamotu Airport from Apia, and Auckland, New Zealand. *Air Pacific* flies in from Auckland, Nadi, and Suva. *Hawaiian Air* serves Tonga from Honolulu and Pago Pago.

ENTRY FORMALITIES. Visitors must have passports, ongoing tickets, and adequate funds to qualify for a 30-day permit, extensions to which can be granted up to a maximum of six months. Visas are required by all but citizens of Commonwealth or European Economic Community countries. Health certificates are no longer required in Tonga.

CURRENCY. Tonga's unit of currency is the *pa'anga*, which is tied to no fixed rate of exchange with any other country. It is totally worthless outside Tonga. The *pa'anga* is divided into 100 units called *seniti*, so that the terms dollars and cents ($T) are frequently used. Foreign currency and traveler's checks can be changed at the Bank of Tonga in Nukualofa or Vavau. $US1 gets you about T$1.45.

ELECTRICITY. Electricity is diesel generated and available in Nukualofa and at larger hotels. Current is 230 volts AC, 50 Hz.

TIPPING. This is not encouraged in Tonga.

LANGUAGE. Most Tongans understand and speak some English, but that does not necessarily end the language problem. A Tongan "yes" can mean a "no," since Tongans will often say what they think will please you rather than what they mean. This can be frustrating.

TIME ZONE. GMT plus 13 hours; 21 hours ahead of U.S. Pacific Standard.

ACCOMMODATIONS. The Tongan Visitors Bureau regularly inspects accommodations offered to ensure they maintain standards justified by the prices charged. Most have flush toilets, but don't expect hot water in the smaller, cheaper guesthouses. Boil water before drinking in areas outside Nukualofa. Tonga offers a variety of hotels, motels, and guesthouses, but Tonga veterans will advise you to pay a little extra rather than try to subsist in "budget" accommodations. Based on prices for single accommodation, categories are: *expensive,* $45 and up; *moderate,* $25–$45; *inexpensive,* $15–$25; and *budget,* below $15.

Eua Island

Fungafonua Motel. *Inexpensive.* Box 1, Ohonua, Eua. Ten rooms with private facilities.

Haukinima Guest House. *Budget.* Futu, Eua. Ten rooms, near the Ohonua wharf.

Ha'apai Island

Fonongava'inga Guest House. *Budget.* Pangai, Ha'apai. Five rooms, a 10-minute walk from Taufa'ahau wharf.

Seletute Guest House. *Budget.* Four rooms, a half-mile from the wharf.

Evaloni Guest House. *Budget.* Pangai, Ha'apai. Three rooms near the wharf.

Tongatapu Island

Kahana Lagoon Resort. *Expensive.* Box 137, Nuku'alofa; 21–144. Eleven rooms at new coastal development 5km from downtown. Full kitchen facilities and a good beach.

Royal Sunset Resort. *Expensive.* Private Bag, Nuku'alofa; 21–254. Fourteen beachfront units, a restaurant, bars, entertainment. On 8-acre Atata Island, 10km from Nuku'alofa wharf.

Captain Cook Vacation Apartments. *Moderate.* Box 838, Nuku'alofa. Six self-contained two-bedroom units, 1.5km from town center.

Fafa Island Resort. *Moderate.* Box 42, Nuku'alofa; 22–800. Eight fales on island reached by a 30-minute launch trip, 6.4km from Nuku'alofa. Restaurant featuring French cuisine, bar; good beaches.

Friendly Islander. *Moderate.* Box 142, Nuku'alofa; 21–900. Twelve modern suites, fully equipped kitchens, private balconies, fans, radio, and phone. One of the better motels.

International Dateline Hotel. *Moderate.* Box 39, Nuku'alofa; 21–411. Famous old hotel on the waterfront with 76 air-conditioned rooms, bars, and a restaurant. Pool in attractive garden setting.

Ramanlal Hotel. *Moderate.* Box 74, Nuku'alofa; 21–344. Twenty-nine self-contained, air-conditioned rooms in central district, with bar, restaurant, and nightclub.

Sunrise Guest House. *Moderate.* Box 132, Nuku'alofa; 21–141. On the waterfront at Kolomotua, 2km from downtown, with six modern rooms.

Joe's Tropicana Hotel. *Inexpensive.* Box 1169, Nuku'alofa; 21–544. Fourteen self-contained rooms, with two bars and restaurant, around the corner from the Dateline Hotel.

Keleti Beach Resort. *Inexpensive.* Box 192, Nuku'alofa; 21–179. Eight fales on a good beach 10km from Nuku'alofa. Bars and licensed restaurant.

Nukuma'anu Motel. *Inexpensive.* Box 390, Nuku'alofa; 21–491. Four rooms 2km from downtown.

Pangiamotu Island Resort. *Inexpensive.* Private Bag, Nuku'alofa; 21–155. Comfortable fales on 32-acre island 15 minutes by boat from Nuku'alofa.

Way In Motel. *Inexpensive.* Private Bag, Nuku'alofa; 21–834. Ten rooms in center of the commercial district, with Chinese restaurant.

Budget guest-houses in the Nuku'alofa area include the **Baby Blue,** Box 249, 22–349; **Beach House,** Box 18, 21–060; **Fasi-Moe-Afi,** Box 316, 22–829; **Good Samaritan,** Box 36, 41–022; and **Sela's,** Box 24, 21–430.

Vava'u Island

Paradise International Hotel. *Expensive.* Box 11, Neiafu, Vava'u. Tonga's superb hideaway on the kingdom's most beautiful island, the Paradise—once known as the Port of Refuge Hotel—has 32 units with magnificent views, freshwater swimming, and a small, safe beach.

Tongan Beach Resort. *Moderate.* Box 104, Utungake, Vava'u; 70–380. Fales on the beach at the island of Utungake, 9 miles from Neiafu.

Stowaway Village, *Inexpensive.* Box 102, Neiafu; 70–137. Overlooking harbor near center of town, with six units in tropical garden.

Vava'u Guest House, *Inexpensive.* Box 148, Neiafu; 70–300. Opposite the Paradise.

Tufumolou Guest House. *Budget.* Neiafu.

Niuatoputapu Island Guest House. *Budget.* Hihifo, Niuatoputapu. Five rooms on a superb out-island of the Vava'u group.

TOURIST INFORMATION. Tonga Visitors Bureau, Box 37, Nukualofa, tel. 21–733.

HOW TO GET AROUND. Depending on the island you are visiting, transportation can range from comfortable sedan to bicycles and horses. On the main island of Tongatapu, buses, taxis, rentals, and the colorful—if uncomfortable—open-air three-wheel taxis known as *ve'etolu* are available. Public transport is very limited on the other islands and, along with shipping and air services, does not operate on Sundays. The other six days of the week, buses are cheap and run regularly through Nukualofa and Tongatapu. Inter-island ferries operated by the Shipping Corporation of Polynesia, Warner Pacific Lines, and several private companies link Nukualofa with the other island groups, but advance bookings cannot be made because schedules often change due to weather or other commitments.

Rental cars, mostly Japanese, are available from *Gateway Rental Cars* (Box 956, tel. 22333), *Friendly Island Rental Car* (Box 142, tel. 21–900). *Avis* (tel. 21720) and Teta Tours (tel. 21688).

Cabs are readily available, but be warned—fix a price for the trip before departure.

Domestic air services are provided by *Friendly Island Airways* to Vavau, Eua and the Haapai group with a 22-seat-turbo-prop Spanish CASA–22 and a British Islander aircraft.

Because Tongatapu is quite flat, bicycles are an ideal form of transport and can be hired cheaply in Nukualofa. Horses can be hired from Queen Salote Wharf when cruise ships are in. On other occasions, the Tonga Visitors Bureau can assist.

TOURS. *Tongatapu Island.* Tour operators provide a wide range of sightseeing and excursion tours and will be happy to bend regular itineraries to suit personal preferences. The Tonga Visitors Bureau, however, warns that some "operators" are not always reliable and visitors should arrange movements well in advance and have them confirmed in writing, especially outside Tongatapu.

All ground-tour operators on Tongatapu take groups on the most popular excursions. These include:

The Nukualofa Capital tour to the royal palace, the royal tombs, the Langa Fonua handicraft center, the Talamahu fruit and vegetable market, and the Havelu desiccated-coconut factory. Time is 2 hours and distance 16km.

The historical tour through the ancient capital of Mua and the burial grounds of the old kings to the trilithon and Captain Cook's landing place. Time is 3 to 4 hours and covers about 50km;

A cultural tour that enables visitors to meet Tongans in their villages and watch them preparing meals, making tapa cloth, and weaving baskets or mats. Time is 2½ hours, and distance depends on which villages are chosen;

The Hufangalupe tour to one of Tonga's most attractive sea vistas with a huge natural-coral bridge, towering cliffs, sandy beach and profuse bird life, which takes about 90 minutes and covers 30km;

Local identity Oscar Kami's Oholei Beach Feast, which is the one Tonga attraction not to be missed (visitors dine on traditionally cooked suckling pig, crayfish, and fruit in Hina's Cave, a natural theater formed from an ancient ocean blowhole) 5 hours for the 40km tour and feast;

The spectacular blowholes, the hideously impressive trees with flying foxes hanging like bunches of grapes at Kolovai, and lunch, a swim, and snorkeling at either Haatafu Beach or the Good Samaritan Inn; can be either a half- or full-day tour.

Tongatapu's ground tour operators include *Oholei Beach Tours* (Box 330, Nukualofa, tel. 21–707), *Moana Travel* (Box 115, tel. 22188), *Vital Travel and Tours,* (Box 838, Nukualofa, tel. 21–616), *Maamafo'ou Tours* (Box 229, Nukualofa, tel 21–425), *Teta Tours* (Box 215, Nuku'alofa, tel. 21688).

Pangaimotu Cruises operates the 2½-hour cruise and visit to Pangaimotu Island, which features swimming on fine white beaches, snorkeling, water skiing, and picnic lunches under the coconut palms. Check with Earl Emberson, Box 740, Nukualofa.

Nuku or Leo's Island is about an hour's launch trip from Nukualofa for a day trip of fishing, swimming, snorkeling, and picnicking on the perfect island to do just about anything. Contact *South Seas Travel and Cruises,* Box 581, Nukualofa.

Vava'u Island. Most Nukualofa-based tour operators will organize special trips on Vava'u. Give yourself either 3 hours or all day for the visits to Keitahi and Eneio beaches—both superb white sandy tracts and crystal-clear coral water. Visitors are driven across the island from Neiafu through native villages and plantations for picnics.

Give yourself 3 hours for the scenic coastal drive through the villages of Feletoa, Tefisi, and Longomapu and enjoy the stunning views of Port of Refuge Harbour and its many islands.

Just 14.5km from Neiafu, visitors can savor *lapila,* or kingfish, caught by hand and pan fried on the shores of the freshwater lake Teanuku. Set about 3 hours aside for this excursion.

Vava'u's highest peak is Mount Talau, towering behind Neiafau. A steep path leads climbers to the table-top summit for a wonderful view of the town and many of the group's other islands. Three hours should suffice for this side trip.

Thousands of swallows find the multicolored cave on the island of Kapa their sanctuary during autumn. Take 2 hours by boat, down the spectacular Port of Refuge Harbor, to drift inside their amazing grotto.

Experienced divers are enthusiastic about the drowned caves on the island of Nuapapu, where guides take them down through a heart-shaped entrance into an ethereal, blue-lit cavern. Veterans of this dive say the allotted 3 or 4 hours is not long enough.

Haapai Islands. There are very few organized tours here, but worth visits are Felemea village, on Uiha Island, where visitors can take part in octopus hunts, *kava* ceremonies, feasting, dancing, and other post-partying pursuits.

Pangai town, once the seat of the Tongan royal family, is a delightful old village, skirted by white, sandy beaches, and will always merit an hour's stroll.

SPORTS. Tongans have been represented at international competition level by boxers, rugby players, and handballers, but visitors should confine their sporting activities to the water—there are few facilities available for other pursuits. A low-standard nine-hole golf course is on the inland lagoon a few miles south of Nukualofa, and tennis courts are found mostly in the residences of foreign high commissioners.

NIGHTLIFE AND RESTAURANTS. Don't look for a lot of nightlife in Tonga, where until recently even swimming was banned on Sundays and you could have been thrown in jail for dancing and singing on Sunday. With tourism, times have changed, however, and visitors now have ample opportunity to kick up their heels—even if it is all a bit basic.

Loud, pop-style bands are featured at the *Dateline* and *Joe's Tropicana* on Fridays and Saturdays. Dine-dance nights are also held occasionally at the *Yacht Club* in Nukualofa, and the *Good Samaritan Inn.*

Restaurants and snack bars have increased in Nukualofa with the growing numbers of tourists. They include the *Basilica Restaurant,* for snacks or full meals under the basilica in the cultural center at St. Anthony of Padua, Taufaahau Rd.; The *Beach House,* for home cooking in the old Vuna Rd. boardinghouse; *Cafe Fakalato,* which offers snacks and meals on Wellington Rd.; *Dateline Hotel,* with a full restaurant, poolside snack bar, and Thursday-night barbecue; *Fasi-Moe-Afi Cafe,* offering a sea-front garden setting for substantial snacks on Vuna Rd.; *Good Samaritan Inn,* serving seafood and French dishes at Kolovai Beach; *Joe's Tropicana,* with its seafood specialties in the Latai Room; *John's Place,* serving snacks and take-away food in Taufahau Rd.; *Ha'atafu Beach Motel,* with its restaurant offering superior meals and service; *Onetale Snack Bar,* serving simple fare opposite Talamahu Market on Salote Rd.; and *Sela's Guest House,* with traditional Tongan food. Relatively new are the *Seaview,* offering seafood in garden setting, and Nukualofa's French restaurant, *Chez Alisi and André.*

Off Tongatapu, some hotels offer meals, including the *Kaukinima Motel* and *Lei-pue Lodge* on Eua, the *Seletute Guest House* on Haapai, and, on Vavau, the *Paradise International Hotel* and the *Stowaway Village.*

DEPARTURE TAX. $T5.

NIUE ISLAND

Hidden Coral Wonderland

by
GRAEME KENNEDY

Fly into Niue, and your first sighting will be of a badly made concrete sponge cake sitting quite alone in an awesome vastness. It appears dry and harsh (which it is) and inhospitable and totally uninteresting (which it certainly is not.) Initial impressions of Niue are misleading—you must look within this fascinating island to find its magic.

Niue is the world's largest single block of coral—259 square kilometers (about 100 square miles) of it sitting atop a giant of an undersea volcano in the middle of a triangle formed by Samoa, Rarotonga, and Tonga. With a population of around 2,500, Niue is bigger than either Rarotonga or Tongatapu. Most of the inhabitants live on the western side of the island near its busy little main center, Alofi.

Unlike its neighbors, Niue has no jungle-draped mountains sweeping down to glistening white lagoons, no rivers, lakes, or waterfalls. But treasures are hidden here.

Over the centuries, rainwater has leaked through the coral, leaving stunningly beautiful sea caves in the high cliffs with their feet on a coral shelf, creating magnificent subterranean grottoes, caverns, and freshwater lakes 100 feet below the arid surface.

Niue was once a coral atoll embracing the tip of its volcano pedestal. In some prehistoric movement of the earth's crust, Niue was thrust upward, and the lagoon is now a central plateau, the old reefs and islets forming a rugged escarpment rising more than 200 feet above the sea.

The cliffs, pierced by cathedral-like sea caves open to the coral shelf and the Pacific, are the treasures. The underground lakes in their vaulted caverns, accessible from the old interior lagoon, are wonders of the South Pacific.

Niue was first sighted by Captain Cook in 1774. He named it Savage Island when his attempted landing was fiercely opposed by the natives, who, having enough trouble eking out an existence from their sparse land, did not want to deal with strangers.

The name was changed when the world got to know the natives better—but even that took some time since missionaries, traders, and administrators passed the island by until the early nineteenth century. The Niueans remained aloof from the rest of the world until Samoan missionaries brought Christianity to the island in 1846, followed 17 years later by the London Missionary Society, who defended their tiny land from invaders.

In 1900, Niue was granted protection by the British crown, and the following year it was annexed to New Zealand, to be administered as part of that country's overseas territories. The island has run its own affairs since 1974 through a legislative assembly that meets regularly in Alofi under the leadership of longtime premier Sir Robert Rex. Visitors are sometimes surprised to find that Rex is an affable, stately man who enjoys a whiskey with friends and visitors alike in the modern Niue Hotel.

Since the early sixties, Niue has been moving into the twentieth century, with computer technology, satellite communications, and modern health and education services. The opening of Hanan International Airport was a big event for Niue, but tourism was then unknown.

Tourism Minister and Premier Sir Robert Rex realizes that the island's fragile social fabric could be torn apart by a torrent of relatively wealthy foreign visitors, and he has always opted for controlled development. The small number of beds available on the island is a built-in control in Lui's efforts.

Meanwhile, a New Zealand company has taken a long lease of the 20-room Niue Hotel and is encouraging scuba divers to experience some of the clearest and most colorful water in the Pacific. With virtually no beaches, underwater visibility is uncluttered by sand, and the lack of rivers means no soils or other pollution in seas teeming with tropical fish and Technicolor-bright corals.

Niue is no place for the elderly and infirm, although the Tourist Department is undertaking to build negotiable paths and steps down the cliffs to the more spectacular caves and seascapes.

I think of Avaiki as a Walt Disney sea cave; the colors and natural architecture suggestive of scenes from *Fantasia*. Here, vast limestone caverns open like a theater stage onto the Pacific breakers exploding on the reef edge 50 meters away. The theater balcony opens onto a crystal pool, alive with tiny fish darting like liquid sapphire. You can swim here under stalactites that hang like rock icicles, droplets of water continuously falling and sounding like tiny bells. It has relatively easy access from the round-island road, 4.5 kilometers from Alofi.

Just 150 meters north is Palaha, the soaring sea cave, for all the world like a gigantic opera house, with a huge arch supported by giant pillars of long-dead coral.

On to Hio, a pocket-sized coral-sand beach, a craggy clamber from the road near the village of Vaipapahi, and one of the very few beaches on Niue. It is quite beautiful and worth the effort of getting there.

The road swings up into the escarpment, through air heady with the perfume of lime and passionfruit plantations to Hikutavake, village of old people and children who do not smile until you do—then you can't stop them. Here is the majestic Matapa Chasm, a towering cleft in the cliff and the legendary bathing place for the ancient kings. Here you can float in gentle swells, which are calmed by bus-sized boulders blocking the chasm entrance from the big Pacific seas that explode against the cliffs outside.

The arches at Talava are another of the dozen or so wonders of Niue on the northeast of the island, where huge coral bridges leap over acres of deep clear pools on the coral shelf; again, a place for the sprightly. Access is through a narrow, slippery cavern, which emerges high up the towering cliff-face with the Pacific thundering at its base and exposing a coral amphitheater. At the landward side of the coral arena, a rock hole scarcely large enough to admit a person plummets straight down for almost 15 feet, then angles away in a limestone tunnel barely high enough to crawl through. This is not for claustrophobics, but those who undergo the ordeal are rewarded with a sight few Europeans have seen—a subterranean cave lit from above with an ethereal beauty, a pool so clear that tiny pebbles on the bottom 12 feet down are magnified among brilliant white sand, those electric-blue mini-fish, and greenery creeping in with the sunlight.

Catch your breath and go on to Togo, about 2½ miles north of the east-coast village of Hakupu, where you cross a cliff-top moonscape of jagged gray dead coral until there, in its midst, you find a white coral sand oasis 50 feet below sheer rock cliffs. Coconut palms rise beside a freshwater pool and stream rising from somewhere under the coral.

Pass through the Huvalu Forest and through neat villages like Avatele, Liku, Lakepa, and Mutalau, and wonder at the magnificent old churches that dominate the clifftop landscape. But the jewel of Niue is a magic cave named Vaikona. The rough track into Vaikona starts 2½ miles south of Liku. Walking it, with the stink of old coral in your nose and thorns and spikes barring your way, you wonder why you have bothered to come. But Vaikona is the one natural challenge you must conquer if you go to Niue. Drop through a rock hole on the high jungle floor barely wide enough to squeeze through and carefully make your way across an underground cliff face, wet and slippery from the incessant water dripping from the limestone just above your head. How far down if you slip? It's mercifully too dark to see. Edge forward until, at last, you turn a corner and stand atop yet another cliff at least 15 meters below the surface, and you are faced with one of the most breathtaking sights you will ever see—above or below the earth.

A vast cavern opens before you, and a jagged crack in the "ceiling" high above sends shafts of sunlight lancing to the bottom of a deep, clear lake at the bottom of this massive vault. The jungle has found its way in, and vines and deep green leaves cling halfway down the limestone walls. You swim in the cold, clear water and wonder at what forces centuries ago created this beautiful place. Then the climb back out doesn't seem so hard.

It is sad that today almost 9,000 Niueans have deserted their homeland and settled among the bustle and bright lights of New Zealand's biggest city, Auckland. But there are jobs there, and New Zealand aid money can provide only so much employment out of Alofi. Yet those who remain are a pleasant people, busying themselves with their government jobs, their sports, and their bush gardens, blocks of land up in the interior where they grow taro, bananas, coconuts, limes, and passionfruit for their own needs and a little for export to Auckland's Karangahape Rd. shops. Everyone—even cabinet ministers and Sir Robert Rex himself—adheres to the old custom of spending time each week weeding, digging, planting, or harvesting in their high, hot bush gardens.

Niueans also go to sea in outrigger canoes—stored in high cliff caves, away from the pounding seas—and catch tuna and Spanish mackerel, big game fish that fight and test every inch of the Niueans' courage and skill. And they have one of the world's rare delicacies simply walking around, ready to be picked up (carefully), cooked, and eaten. It's the coconut crab, or *uga*—pronounced *"oonga"*—a creature as delectable as it is ugly. It eats only coconut meat, tearing the nut apart with its huge claws, and its white flesh is delicately flavored by the tropical fruit.

Bees thrive on Niue and, feeding mainly on passionfruit and lime flowers, produce a unique, thin, dark honey of tantalizing taste.

Increasing numbers of tourists, mainly divers from New Zealand, are discovering this unique destination. It's not easy to reach but it all seems worthwhile when, after a day of underwater excess, you can sit at the bar of the Niue Hotel, gaze across the wide Pacific, and share a cool drink with the Premier.

PRACTICAL INFORMATION FOR NIUE

WHEN TO GO. Like all tropic islands, Niue has two seasons—the wet season from December to March and the dry season in the remaining eight months, when temperatures average 24°C. after wet-season highs of 27°C. Niue has the southeast trades, which create warm temperatures by day and a comfortable coolness by night. Average rainfall is 2,780mm a year. Humidity is highest during the wet season.

WHAT TO WEAR. The early missionaries left their mark on Niue, and swimwear is still unacceptable in public, such as in the shops. The coral and rugged terrain make thongs unsuitable, and sneakers or tennis shoes are recommended. Casual, comfortable clothing is standard for day and night—walking shorts, socks, and short-sleeved shirts for men and light cotton frocks for women. A light pullover will be useful in the cooler evenings.

HOW TO GET THERE. Weekly flights by *Air Nauru* operate only from Auckland, New Zealand.

ENTRY REQUIREMENTS. Passports are required for 30-day visitors' permits. Onward travel booking is essential; permit extensions can be obtained from the police department in Alofi. Visas and health inoculation certificates are not required. Baggage searches are mandatory to protect Niue's fragile agriculture-based economy from imported pests.

CURRENCY. The New Zealand dollar is Niue's official currency. The Westpac Banking Corporation opened a branch in Alofi in mid-1987. A bank authorization is required for the export of foreign currencies, and they must be declared on departure. The Niue Hotel accepts Amex and Bankcard.

LANGUAGE. Niueans speak their own Polynesian dialect and are fluent in English.

ACCOMMODATIONS. Built in 1978 for the South Pacific Forum meeting, the Niue Hotel is 3km south of Alofi and has 20 modern and self-contained rooms on the cliff top overlooking the Pacific. It has a full-sized swimming pool and a dining and entertainment center offering excellent meals including local dishes and a weekly smorgasbord, usually on Tuesdays. Lunch boxes are provided for day tours. Island nights, with traditional dancing, are features at weekends. Rates are $NZ55 single, $NZ58 double or twin, $NZ96 executive suite (sleeps 5). Box 80, Alofi; tel. 91 or 92. The **Hinemata Motel** consists of three rooms serviced daily, with shared kitchen and bathroom. On the coast near Alofi. Budget rates. Box 81, Alofi; tel. 167. A three-room house with shared facilities between Alofi and the Niue Hotel, the **Pelenis Guest House** serves European and island-style meals with complimentary fresh fruit in season. Guests are encouraged to accompany the owner, Mr. Talagi, in his daily routine—to church and his plantation—to experience authentic island life. Box 11, Alofi; tel. 135. **Esther's Village Motel,** at Avatele, 7 km from Alofi, has two self-contained units with cooking facilities. Rates—$NZ30 single, $NZ38 double, $NZ25 extra adult.

TOURIST INFORMATION. The *Niue Tourist Board,* Box 67, Alofi, and the *Niue Consular Office,* Box 68–541, Newton, Auckland, New Zealand, are both good sources of information.

GETTING AROUND. There is no regular transport service on Niue, but cabs and rental cars and motorcycles are readily available. A local guide may be necessary to take you to some of the more out-of-the-way places of interest. Cabs charge around $NZ1 a kilometer and can be called on either Alofi 58 or 70W. Rental cars cost between $NZ35 and $NZ45 a day and motorcycles between $NZ15 and $NZ25 a day. Bicycles are about $NZ7 a day.

Rental-car companies are *Niue Rentals,* tel. 58; *Maile Rentals,* tel. 271 or 85, and *Russell and Ama,* tel. 167 or 608.

TOURS. *Niue Adventure Tours* offers almost every Niuean sport, leisure, and cultural activity in its range of tours. Uga-hunting and bat- and pigeon-shooting expeditions cost $NZ25 a person. Tropical-fish collecting is $NZ30, and fishing at night for flying fish is $NZ50. Scenic tours by van are $NZ20 a person, and scuba diving is $NZ60. Niue Adventures offers a wide range of fishing and diving tours with all equipment, including air tanks, masks, fins, underwater cameras, and fishing tackle available for hire. An air tank fill is $NZ5. Contact *Niue Adventures;* Box 141; tel. 102.

SPORTS. Niueans are versatile and enthusiastic sportspeople, engaging in organized competition in softball, soccer, rugby, netball, and a local version of cricket played with a club-shaped bat and a hard rubber ball by teams of 30. Watch a game at any village in the evenings. All visitors are welcome at the *Niue Sports Club,* opposite the airport-entrance road, where they can try their skill on the nine-hole golf course or grass tennis courts. Clubs, tees, balls, and bag can be hired from $NZ5 to $NZ10 a day. Two tennis racquets, and two balls cost $NZ8 a day. The sports club has a friendly, well-stocked bar where visitors are honored guests.

SHOPPING. Niue is known throughout Polynesia for the high quality of its woven wares. Basic materials are young coconut palm fronds and the leaves of the pandanus palm. Woven with great style and finish, mats, baskets, and hats are colored with natural dyes and can be bought at moderate prices. In the Alofi stores, visitors can buy a wide range of products, generally more cheaply than in Australia or New Zealand. Duty-free shopping has not been introduced to Niue, but the low duties levied do allow bargain buying.

NIGHTLIFE AND RESTAURANTS. You won't find anything resembling Las Vegas here. Apart from island nights at the Niue Hotel, several island social clubs hold entertaining evenings where visitors are welcome. In Alofi, the *Crab Inn* has long been a popular restaurant-meeting place. In 1987 expatriate New Zealand journalist Stafford Guest opened *Sails* eatery.

DEPARTURE TAX. $NZ10.

WALLIS AND FUTUNA

French Fantastic

by
GRAEME KENNEDY

The road to Aka-Aka from the coastal flatlands and the long coral runway of Hihifo Airport sweeps upward past green leafy hillsides. Old horses and young pigs scamper in and out of the banana and taro and onto the manicured lawns that seem to float around villages, and fine old white colonial buildings hang in a blue-green haze at the coastal main town of Mata-Utu, on the mideast shore of this handsome island.

Your jeep climbs, juddering on the potholed white coral road and groaning upward through jungle so lush it is impossible to see more than a few yards ahead; yet above you're told there are deep, cold freshwater lakes held in extinct volcano craters and drenched in tropical flowers inhabited by parrots, lorikeets, and other vivid native birds.

With every turn of this road, the lagoon expands in both view and beauty far below until there is an explosion of color that strikes the senses like a physical blow. Blues, greens, reds, yellows, and startling whites of the coral shimmer under a transparent sea in which tiny islets with palm trees float inside the reef, where the Pacific thunders in white detonations almost a mile out.

You stop, breathless, at Lomipeau—a modest yet unique restaurant, open sided so that the jungle, lagoon, and ocean present a living mural. Warm scented zephyrs flirt with the red-and-white-checked tablecloths while you wait with a cold drink at the matey little bar.

It is the home of Christian Ruotolo, the darkly handsome fiftyish French-Algerian who made this his home after years of pouring wine for other tourists from Italy to Noumea. He knew what he was doing when he moved 21,000 kilometers from Paris, 2,200 kilometers from New Caledonia to this beautiful, tiny tropic island to the north of Fiji and the Samoas. Christian and his Wallisian wife, Paola, have been here since the mid-seventies and have gradually expanded their little restaurant; it now has 15 air-conditioned double rooms and is a large part of the entire Wallis tourist plant. In a typical menu, the Ruotolos offer baby lagoon scallops pampered in oil, garlic, and parsley; New Zealand lamb with taro and island herbs; and French vanilla ice cream drenched in Kahlua or Cointreau, all washed down with good Bordeaux for around 2,200 French Pacific francs (about $US15).

Wallis is a treasure island of fewer than 10,000 people, a far outpost of France which pours millions of francs every year into this little-known territory for one purpose—to keep control of the strategically important runway at Hihifo. The islanders don't seem to mind the French motives, for they are secure and happy. With the territory comes Futuna, just over an hour's flight to the southwest, more mountainous and jungled than Wallis but with the same perfect white beaches and lagoons. The bones of the Pacific's first saint, St. Peter Chanel, now rest at the Futuna village of Poi, where he was hacked to death in 1841.

Discovered by English navigator Captain Samuel Wallis during his 1766 to 1770 voyage of exploration to find the mythical great southern continent in the Pacific (he also discovered Tahiti), the archipelago that bears his name was made a French protectorate in 1886 as the major powers scrambled for new colonies. The United States built the air strip at Hihifo during World War II and more than 5,000 American servicement were once based there. Wallis and Futuna became a French overseas territory in 1961.

A popular port of call for wandering South Seas yachtspeople, Wallis has never been on the convenient tourist trails. One jet flight comes to Wallis each week, in an aging Caravelle from Noumea through Fiji's Nadi. But a trickle of visitors do come, enough to maintain Lomipeau and two smaller properties (the Tanoa Hotel is closed). In the late seventies, there were plans to build a Club Med–style resort at the Tanoa, but they seem to have been forgotten. I'm pleased about that.

PRACTICAL INFORMATION FOR
WALLIS AND FUTUNA

WHEN TO GO. Expect hot, humid, rainy weather in the traditional Pacific wet season from November through March, with temperatures up to 31° C; it will be more comfortable from June/July through September, with an average high of 24°C. Farther north past both Fiji and the Samoas, the oppressive wet-season heat is countered by refreshing midyear trade winds.

WHAT TO WEAR. Light, comfortable, informal clothes are adequate all yearround. Bring a sweater for cooler evenings and a plastic coat or umbrella for unexpected showers. Shorts and swimwear are not acceptable as evening wear at restaurants.

HOW TO GET THERE. Noumea-based *Air Caledonie International* operates a weekly (Tuesday or Friday) service to Wallis's Hihifo Airport via Nadi in Fiji; return service is on (Tuesday or Friday) via Nadi, Fiji. Air Caledonie has an office in Nadi, Fiji (tel. 72899 or 72145). A shipping service leaves Noumea about every 35 days.

ENTRY FORMALITIES. No visa is required, but passport and onward or return tickets are necessary, for stays of up to 30 days. Yachtspeople should contact the high commissioner, 1, ave. Marechal Foch, Noumea, New Caledonia, before their voyage.

ELECTRICITY. As in all French Polynesia, electric current is 220 volts AC, 50 Hz. A two-prong plug is necessary.

TIPPING is not encouraged.

LANGUAGE. Most Wallisians speak French and their own Tongan-based Polynesian dialect. Fluent English speakers are difficult to find.

CURRENCY. Wallis and Futuna's monetary unit is the French Pacific franc (CFP). Notes are CFP5,000, CFP1,000 and CFP500. Coins are CFP100, 50, 20, 5, 2, and 1. One U.S. dollar is about CFP103.

TIME ZONE. GMT plus 11 hours; 20 hours ahead of U.S. Pacific Standard.

ACCOMMODATIONS. About 6km from Hihifo Airport and 800m from the center of the main town, Mata-Utu, at Aka-Aka, the **Hotel Lomipeau** has 15 air-conditioned rooms with private facilities, television, and radio. Marvelous restaurant, with bar and tour desk. Rates: Single CFP 7,000, double CFP 8,000. Box 84, Aka-Aka, Wallis Island; tel. 72–20–21; telex ALPAC 076 WF. **Hotel Mohanahou,** at Liker has 4 air-conditioned rooms. **Hotel L'Albatross,** at Hihifo, 7 km from Mata-Utu, has 5 air-conditioned rooms.

GETTING AROUND. Unscheduled village buses run around Wallis from Mata-Utu, where limited rental cars are available at moderate cost. Check at hotel desk. *Air Caledonie International* operates a 1-hour, 18-seat Twin Otter to Futuna on Mondays, Wednesdays, and Fridays. Internal transport on Futuna is haphazard.

TOURIST INFORMATION. New Caledonia Tourist Office, 25, ave. Marechal Foch, Noumea, New Caledonia (tel. Noumea 27–2632).

TOURS. Individual tours around the lagoon, to the crater lakes, to villages, and for general sightseeing can be arranged through your hotel desk to suit personal preferences and timetables.

SPORTS. You've come to the wrong island if you're looking for championship-standard golf courses and Wimbledon-style tennis courts. You have it right, though, if you're after superb snorkeling and diving, sailing, or any other water sport you can think of. All equipment can be hired through your hotel.

NIGHTLIFE AND RESTAURANTS. Nightlife is extremely limited on Wallis and unknown on Futuna. Hotels have live bands and dancing once or twice a week, and a native disco with no known name on the hill outside Mata-Utu is a happy, noisy place. Elaborate Wallisian dancing and *kava* ceremonies are not to be missed.

Hotel Lomipeau specializes in an imaginative French-style menu with tantalizing Polynesian overtones. Several smaller eateries of unknown origin flourish in Mata-Utu.

FIJI ISLANDS

By
GRAEME KENNEDY

It is difficult to detect exactly when beautiful, balmy, tropical Fiji began to self-destruct.

Some farsighted thinker might have seen it coming 110 years ago when the British, who annexed the islands in 1874, decided to import Indian labor to work the sugar and cotton plantations for their English and Australian owners. But the seer's warnings were ignored.

With the plantation economy booming and manpower desperately short—the native Fijians had no wish for such work—almost 63,000 Indian "coolies" were brought to Fiji beginning in 1916. They thrived in their new environment, and less than 20,000 accepted the offer of repatriation to their native land.

Others migrated, no doubt attracted by tales of a paradise in the South Seas, and throughout the 1920s and 1930s maintained a remarkably high birthrate in their adopted country.

The impending racial collision should have been foreseen by 1950, when Indians began to outnumber the native Fijians. But they were tolerated by the carefree indigenous population and became the islands' farmers, storekeepers, lawyers, doctors, executives, and, very quietly, its politicians.

The Fijians were left to get on with simply being Fijians as they always had done.

Indians and Fijians rioted in the streets of Suva when stately Ratu Sir Kamisese Mara became the new nation's first prime minister after Britain granted Fiji independence in 1970. This followed sporadic outbreaks of

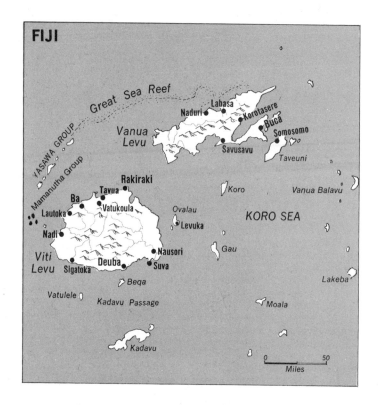

violence between the two races during the previous ten years. But despite the persistent and often explosive demonstrations of discontent, no one moved to seek a positive solution to the conflict.

Then, in 1977, the inevitable happened.

The Indian-dominated National Federation Party beat Mara's Fijian Alliance 26–24 in the general election and won the right to form a government. The governor-general of the day, however, swept the election result aside, reappointed Mara as prime minister, and held new elections in which the shocked Fijians reinstated their Alliance Party.

Mara won again in 1982, but five years later Dr. Timoci Bavadra, a gentle Fijian doctor from Viti Levu's west coast, led his Indian-dominated Federation-Labor coalition to power and became prime minister.

But the real destruction of Fiji came on May 14, a month after Bavadra's 1987 victory, when an army lieutenant colonel, Sitiveni Rabuka, led a troop of armed and masked soldiers into Suva's Parliament House and marched the prime minister and his aides away at gunpoint.

The armed coup was staged not for political reasons but for blatantly racial ones. The majority of voters had democratically elected Bavadra and his party, but Rabuka, like so many others before him, chose to overturn that basic freedom with a gun.

Despite the colonel's bullying and threats, the Indian sugar-cane growers refused to harvest. Others burned their cane and the $20 million sugar export industry collapsed.

Tourism quickly followed, with few hotels boasting better than 5 percent occupancy in the usually packed months after the coup. Airlines stopped flying through Nadi International Airport, where a young Indian with dynamite strapped to his body attempted to hijack an Air New Zealand Boeing 747 in late May 1987. The attempt ended when a crew member slugged him with a full bottle of duty-free Scotch whiskey.

Despite Rabuka's promises of a speedy return to democracy, the military regime rounded up hundreds of his opponents and threw them into army and civil jails without trial.

A part-time solution was to have been a joint governing body comprising both Alliance and Coalition members, but the militant, thuggish Taukei (Fiji for Fijians) movement saw this as weakness and forced Rabuka to stage a second armed coup on September 25.

Abolishing the constitution, Rabuka declared Fiji a republic and himself head of state. His armed soldiers kept Governor-General Ratu Sir Penaia Ganilau and other administrators under house arrest and again threw opponents in jail.

Soldiers set up roadblocks, patroled tourist hotels, guarded major buildings, and enforced a night curfew. Rabuka forbade any activity on Sundays—including sports, picnics, and gardening—other than worship, preferably in a Methodist church.

The British Commonwealth, which, after its Rhodesia and South Africa experiences abhors racism and racist governments, expelled Fiji from its membership.

Amazingly, Rabuka declared former Governor-General Ganilau the new republic's first president and installed the durable Mara as its founding premier. Their job was to write a new constitution, one that would give indigenous Fijians political power in perpetuity, disenfranchising the Fiji-Indian majority.

Rabuka continued to maintain that Fiji would return to a civilian democracy—but there are very few who believe that, or that Rabuka will not always be in the shadows, pulling the strings Ganilau and Mara dance to, always with the threat of yet another coup if things do not go his way.

Rabuka, who promoted himself to brigadier after Coup Two, remains a racist dictator with the army's guns at his ready. Recent tourism figures reflect a decided preference for other destinations: Visitor arrivals for 1987 were down 26.4 percent and were expected to slump 20 percent in 1988.

Travelers to Fiji are advised to holiday at an out-island resort such as Musket Cove or Plantation Village in the western Mamanuca group or at Treasure or Beachcomber Islands in the Yasawas, where happenings on Viti Levu seem light-years away.

Tourists will miss little by avoiding the grubby little port of Suva, the scene of much of the post-coup bloodshed and violence.

Unemployment is high among the city's 160,000 residents, many of them young people drifting into town from the depressed agricultural economies of their villages. Suva abounds with bars and noisy, gloomy nightclubs; watch your wallet anywhere in the city.

Almost all of Fiji's tourist sites are located to the west and southwest of Viti Levu, which—with smaller Vanua Levu to the north—is the heart of the 300-island cluster 3,000 miles from Honolulu, 2,000 miles from Sydney, and 1,100 miles south of the equator. Nadi International Airport, in the hot, dry sugar belt of the west coast, is the gateway for almost all visitors, and many high-standard hotels have sprung up here.

Fiji's second-largest city, Lautoka (pop. 40,000), is 20 miles north and is dominated by foul-smelling sugar processing mills. This is Indian territory, where pitifully small plantations earn workers an average of $1,500 a year.

It is also the departure point for the delightful Yasawa cluster of islands and resorts, and of the famous Blue Lagoon cruise ships. To the south, only a few minutes by air from Nadi, are the Mamanucas—picture-book tropical atolls with fine resorts, reefs, and lagoons.

Queen's Road, the 130-mile sealed highway to Suva, runs south and east from Nadi through sugar-cane fields to the Coral Coast, with white-sand beaches and more tourist hotels.

This is where Fijian tourism began in the boom times of the 1950s and 1960s. The little riverside town of Sigatoka has grown to service the area and the industry.

Most hotels here have regular *meke* nights, with native Fijian dancing displays, feasts of traditional food—reef fish and whole pig cooked over hot stones in an earth oven called a *lovo*—and much *yaqona* drinking. Also known as *kava,* and pronounced *yang-gona,* it is mildly narcotic rather than alcoholic and is made from the root of the pepper plant. *Yaqona* tastes like watery mud.

Offshore is the island of Beqa, home of the Fijian fire-walkers who, protected by the god Veli, walk barefooted and apparently unharmed across red-hot stones. They can sometimes be seen at Coral Coast resort hotels on special *meke* nights. Hindu Indians of the Madrasis sect also practice fire-walking, but as a religious rite. These followers of Maha Devi induce a trancelike state and pierce themselves with needles before treading the hot rocks in a purification ritual.

Fiji's other islands have recently developed tourist facilities, notably on Vanua Levu, which for many years was regarded as being fit for growing copra and sugar and little else. But the country's second-biggest island has become popular, with secluded resorts on quiet lagoons and beaches where scuba divers can enjoy some of the Pacific's best underwater sport.

Taveuni, just east of Vanua Levu, now claims seven recommended hotel-guest houses while Ovalau, with Fiji's old capital, Levuka, and even Kadavu, south of Suva, are actively seeking tourist dollars.

But the hunt for those dollars has become difficult since the Rabuka coups and the armed oppression of the nation's Indians. Until that day in May 1987, Fiji tourism was looking forward to another record year, with receipts almost matching that of sugar exports. The industry's future looked assured, as tourism to the whole Pacific region increased dramatically with the specter of hijacking and terrorism in the Northern Hemisphere and the huge numbers of visitors attracted by Australia's bicentennial in 1988.

But the coups and ensuing racism-by-decree ended those high hopes. Fiji's international image is now one of gunpoint power, not the long-held perception of a warm, friendly South Seas destination with lagoons, palm trees, white beaches, and happy people.

PRACTICAL INFORMATION FOR FIJI

HOW TO GET THERE. The international airport at Nadi in western Viti Levu is the gateway to Fiji. A shuttle service links it with the capital, Suva, where Nausori Airport can handle narrow-bodied twin-engined jets and light aircraft.

Fiji's national carrier, *Air Pacific,* runs scheduled flights to New Zealand, Australia, Vanuatu, the Solomons, and Tonga. It has regular services between Nadi and Suva.

Other international carriers flying into Nadi are *Qantas, Air New Zealand, Canadian International,* and *Air Caledonie.*

CLIMATE. Warm and pleasant without great extremes of heat or cold. The temperature averages 27.5°C (87°F) November to April and 24.4°C (75.7°F) May to October.

Rainfall varies markedly. It is usually abundant in the wet season (November to April), especially over Viti Levu and Vanua Levu, but deficient the rest of the year, especially in the dry zone on the western and northern sides of Viti Levu and Vanua Levu. Tropical cyclones, which have caused considerable damage in recent years, are most likely to hit Fiji between January and March.

Average Temperature (°Fahrenheit) and Humidity

Nadi

	Jan	Feb	Mar	Apr	May	June	July	Aug	Sept	Oct	Nov	Dec
Average max. day temperature	88°	88°	87°	87°	85°	84°	83°	83°	84°	85°	86°	88°
Days of rain	21	19	24	20	17	14	10	12	14	14	16	17
Humidity, percent	75	78	80	80	77	79	76	71	69	66	67	69

Laucala Bay (Suva)

Average max. day temperature	86°	86°	86°	84°	82°	81°	79°	80°	80°	81°	83°	85°
Days of rain	12	13	15	14	9	7	6	5	8	8	10	10
Humidity, percent	81	81	83	82	80	81	79	78	79	78	78	79

CURRENCY. Fiji's unit of currency is the Fiji dollar. Denominations of Fiji notes are $20, $10, $5, $2, $1. The Fiji dollar fluctuated wildly after the 1987 coups, but at press time $US1 bought F$1.45.

ENTRY FORMALITIES. All visitors to Fiji must have a passport valid for at least six months from date of entry. They must produce an onward ticket out of the country, and proof may be required of sufficient funds for maintenance while in Fiji.

Visas are required from nationals of only a few countries. A temporary visa may be obtained to stay for one month, and it may be extended up to six months. Business travelers are required to obtain a work permit after seven days from date of arrival.

Inoculations are not required unless visitors are entering from a designated infected area. Children under a year are exempt.

LANGUAGE. English is commonly spoken although Fijian and Hindi are also official languages.

ELECTRICITY. The current is 240 volts AC. Plugs are three pronged, set at an angle. Most electrical supply shops sell adaptors. Hotels generally have 110-volt converters for appliances.

COMMUNICATIONS. Fiji is particularly well served with a modern communications network handling telephone, telegraph, facsimile and telex services worldwide.

TIPPING. Tipping is optional.

DRINKING LAWS. A wide range of beers, wines, and spirits are available at licensed outlets—hotels, restaurants, and clubs. Local liquor laws should not inconvenience adult (over 18) visitors.

TIME ZONE. GMT plus 11 hours; 20 hours ahead of U.S. Pacific Standard Time.

USEFUL ADDRESSES. *Fiji Visitors Bureau,* head office: Thomson Street, Suva. GPO Box 92. Telephone 22–867 Suva and 72–433 Nadi Airport. Other bureau offices are in Auckland, Box 1179, telephone 732–134; Sydney, 38 Martin Place, telephone 231–4251; Los Angeles, 6151 West Century Boulevard, suite 524, telephone (213) 417–2234, telex 759972; London, 34 Hyde Park Gate SW7 5BN, telephone 584–3661; Tokyo, NOA Building (10th floor) 3–5.2 Chome, Azabudai, Minato-ku, telephone (03) 587–2038.

Fiji Hotel Association, Box 2001, Government Buildings, Suva. Telephone 38–1093.

American Embassy, 31 Loftus St., Suva. Telephone 31–4466.

FESTIVALS. *Bula Festival:* an annual event in Nadi Town each July (Bula means welcome). *Hibiscus Festival:* Held in Suva each August to coincide with the first week of the school holidays; this is a carnival week of traditional entertainment, sports, and shows. The week ends with the Hibiscus Ball and the crowning of Miss Hibiscus. *Sugar Festival:* Lautoka, the sugar city, celebrates the harvest in September. *Diwali:* the Hindu festival of lights (October–November) is preceded by an annual spring cleaning of houses. Oil lamps and colored lights decorate the houses. Hindus celebrate the holy festival with devotion—fasting is observed, and prayers and offerings of sweets and fruits are given to Lakshmi, the goddess of wealth.

ACCOMMODATIONS. Fiji offers a wide range of accommodations from luxury resorts to dormitories at cheap rates. The traveler with a limited budget has plenty of choice. Based on prices for double accommodations, hotels are graded: *Deluxe* $100 plus; *Expensive,* F$60–F$100; *Moderate,* F$30–F$59; *Inexpensive,* up to F$30. (All room rates subject to 8% government tax.)

VITI LEVU ISLAND

Coral Coast

The Fijian Resort Hotel. *Deluxe.* Private Bag, Nadi Airport; 5–0155. 364 rooms. Luxury resort on 100-acre island 35 miles from Nadi. A one-stop holiday spa. Outstanding hotel staff. Good food. Dining rooms, bars, shops, tennis courts, 2 swimming pools, 9-hole golf course, lawn bowling, water sports, horse riding, dancing nightly, fire walking.

Hyatt Regency. *Deluxe.* Box 100, Korolevu; 5–0555. 249 rooms. Delightful beach setting with human-made off-shore island. Dining rooms, bars, shops, tennis courts, 9-hole pitch and putt, water sports, entertainment, fire walking.

Hide-a-Way Resort. *Expensive.* Box 233, Sigatoka; 5–0177. 15 bures. Beachside hotel on more modest scale. Informality stressed. Dining room, bar, shop, swimming pool. Dormitory accommodation available: $F8. Complete renovation underway.

Man Friday Resort. *Expensive.* Box 20, Korolevu; 5–0185. Traditional-style thatched bures by beach. Restaurant, bar, mini-golf, water sports, entertainment.

Naviti Beach Resort. *Expensive.* Box 29, Korolevu; 5–0444. 144 rooms. Attractive hotel at water's edge. Dining room, bar, tennis courts, water sports, swimming pool, 9-hole golf course, shops, fire walking.

Reef Hotel Resort. *Expensive.* Box 173, Sigatoka; 5–0044. 72 rooms. Close to coral reef. Restaurant, bar, stables, swimming pool, golf course, coral viewing.

Casablanca Beach Hotel. *Moderate.* Box 164, Sigatoka; 50766. Eight air-conditioned rooms with pool, restaurant, bar. Close to tennis, golf, scuba, and horse-riding.

The Crow's Nest. *Moderate.* Box 270, Sigatoka; 5–0230. 18 apartments beachside. Dining room, bar, swimming pool, snorkeling, children's playground.

Tambua Sands Beach Resort. *Moderate.* Box 177, Sigatoka; 5–0399. 19 bures beachside. Dining room, bar, swimming pool. Dormitory available: $F8.

Tubakula Beach Resort. *Inexpensive.* Box 2, Sigatoka; 50097. 24 rooms with cooking facilities, pool with most sports able to be arranged.

Budget accommodation ($F5–$F22): **Sigatoka Hotel,** Box 35, Sigatoka; 5–0011. 3 rooms. **Waratah Lodge.** Box 86, Korotoga; 5–0278. 5 bures. Swimming pool, restaurant. **Vakaviti Units and Cabins.** Box 5, Sigatoka; 5–0526. 5 units and dormitory. Swimming pool, cooking facilities.

Deuba

Pacific Harbour Villas. *Deluxe.* Postal Agency, Pacific Harbour; 4–5022. Luxury accommodation at one of Fiji's most exclsuive resorts. See Pacific Harbour International Resort.

Pacific Harbour International Resort. *Expensive.* Postal Agency, Pacific Harbour; 4–5022. 84 rooms and 20 villas. Magnificent resort on coast with championship golf course; air strip, shopping complex, five restaurants, cultural center, and resident doctor. Villas fully self-contained. Swimming pool, tennis courts, water sports, entertainment, fire walking.

Fiji Palms Beach Club Resort. *Expensive.* Postal Agency, Pacific Harbour; 4–5050. 14 self-contained apartments. Swimming pool. Access to Pacific Harbour. Time shares available.

Coral Coast Christian Camps. *Inexpensive.* Postal Agency, Pacific Harbour; 4–5178. 6 rooms and 8 budget cabins close to beach. No alcohol permitted.

Lautoka

Anchorage Beach Resort. *Moderate.* Box 9472, Nadi Airport; 6–2099. Beachside near "Sugar City." Dining room, bar, swimming pool, water sports. Dormitory accommodations available at $F12 (cooking facilities).

Cathay Hotel. *Moderate.* Box 239, Lautoka; 6–0566. 42 rooms. Dining room, bar, swimming pool. Golf and tennis can be arranged. In Lautoka town.

Saweni Beach Hotel. *Moderate.* Box 239, Lautoka; 6–1777. 12 self-contained units on beach, 12 minutes from Nadi. Dormitory $F6. Dining room, bar.

Waterfront Hotel. *Moderate.* Box 9211, Nadi Airport; 64–777. Modern hotel in central Lautoka, ideal for overnights or excutives. 20 rooms with pool, good restaurant and bar.

Nadi–Lautoka Offshore

Matamanoa Island Resort. *Deluxe.* Box 9729, Nadi Airport; 6–0511. 20 bures on lovely beach. Dining room, bar, swimming pool, water sports, coral viewing.

Castaway Island Resort. *Expensive.* Box 9246, Nadi Airport; 6–1233. 15 miles offshore. 66 bures. Dining room, bar, swimming pool, tennis, water sports, gymnasium, sauna, spa, day trips to neighboring islands, deep-sea fishing.

Club Naitasi. *Expensive.* Box 9147, Nadi Airport; 7–2266. Relatively new resort on Malolo Island. 28 bures and 9 luxury villas. Dining room, bar, swimming pool, cooking facilities, water sports, half tennis court. Beach beautification program underway.

Mana Island Resort. *Expensive.* Box 610, Lautoka; 6–1455. 22 miles offshore. 132 bures beachside on delightful bay. Dining room, bar, swimming pool, water sports, water scooters, tennis.

Musket Cove Resort. *Expensive.* Private Bag, Nadi Airport; 6–2215. 24 attractive self-contained bures and four luxury villas. Dining room, water sports, weekly three-island cruise, swimming pool.

Navini Island. *Expensive.* Box 685, Lautoka; 62–188. Offshore resort with 10 bures with all facilities, bar, restaurant, all sports. A 48-ft. cruiser is available for charter.

Plantation Island. *Expensive.* Box 9176, Nadi Airport; 7–2333. 20 miles offshore on Malolo Lailai Island. 90 rooms. Dining room, bar, swimming pool, horse riding, water sports, water scooters. Dormitory $F12.

Treasure Island. *Expensive.* Box 364, Lautoka; 6–1599. Idyllic little island. 69 bure units and bungalows. Dining room, bar, mini-golf, water sports, deep-sea fishing.

Beachcomber Island Resort. *Moderate* (meals included in rates). Box 364 Lautoka; 6–2600. 11 miles offshore, five sandy acres. Popular with young people. 14 bures, 8 lodge rooms, and dormitory ($F35 including meals). Dining room, bar, water sports.

Nadi

The Regent of Fiji. *Deluxe.* Box 441, Nadi; 7–0700. 294 rooms. Luxury beach resort (Denarau Island) for those who like to holiday in style. Dining rooms, bars, shops, swimming pool, water sports, archery range, golf course, tennis courts, resident nurse, entertainment, fire walking.

Sheraton Fiji. *Deluxe.* Box 9761, Nadi Airport. Opened late 1987 adjacent to Regent with 300 air-conditioned rooms, conference facilities, three bars, restaurants, and 15 shops.

Castaway Gateway Hotel. *Expensive.* Box 9246, Nadi Airport; 7–2444. 93 rooms. Recently renovated comfortable hotel ideal for in-transit stopover. Dining room, bar, TV rental, swimming pool, tennis, spa pool.

Fiji Mocambo. *Expensive.* Box 9195, Nadi Airport; 7–2000. 124 rooms. Imposing hotel handy to airport. Dining rooms with varied and interesting menu, bars, tennis, golf range, swimming pool, entertainment, fire walking.

Nadi Airport TraveLodge. *Expensive.* Box 9203, Nadi Airport; 7–2277. 114 rooms. Dining room, bar, swimming pool, tennis. Handy to airport. Ideal transit hotel.

Tanoa Hotel. *Expensive.* Box 9211, Nadi Airport; 7–2300. 102 rooms. Good standard accommodation close to airport. Dining room, bar, tennis, swimming pool, spa, sauna, entertainment. Cooking facilities in villas.

Dominion International Hotel. *Moderate.* Box 9178, Nadi Airport; 7–2255. 85 rooms. Attractive hotel set around big swimming pool. Dining room, bar, pitch-and-putt golf, horseback riding available. Tennis court, archery range, and jogging track.

Seashell Cove Resort. *Moderate.* Box 9530, Nadi Airport; 5–0309. 14 rooms 17km from Nadi on white-sand beach. Simple facilities. Swimming pool, tennis, water sports. Dormitory $F8. Camping available.

Skylodge Hotel. *Moderate.* Box 9222, Nadi Airport; 7–2200. 48 rooms. Garden setting. No frills. Dining room. Swimming pool, spa, minitennis, golf pitch. Good budget accommodation.

Fong Hing Private Hotel. *Inexpensive.* Box 143, Nadi; 7–1011. 22 rooms. In Nadi town. Tidy budget accommodation. Restaurant with Chinese and European food.

Nadi Sunseekers. *Inexpensive.* Box 100, Nadi, 7–0400. 21 rooms and dormitory. Budget accommodation with swimming pool, restaurant, tour desk and game room.

Sandalwood Inn. *Inexpensive.* Box 445, Nadi; 7–2553. 25 rooms. Also for the low-budget traveler. Swimming pool. Some rooms share facilities.

Suva

Suva Courtesy Inn. *Expensive.* Box 112, Suva; 31–2300. 56 rooms. Good-quality hotel in downtown Suva. Dining room, swimming pool, video.

Suva TraveLodge. *Expensive.* Box 1357, Suva; 31–4600. 134 rooms. Best hotel in Suva. On water's edge near town center. Full facilities.

Capricorn Apartment Hotel. *Moderate.* Box 1261, Suva; 31–4799. 25 rooms. Two small apartment-like blocks in downtown Suva, overlooking swimming pool. Facilities include a dial-a-meal service. 10 additional rooms planned for 1988.

Grand Pacific Hotel. *Moderate.* Box 2086, Government Buildings, Suva; 2–3011. 72 rooms. Somerset Maugham atmosphere, but past its best. Thrift accommodation also available.

Outrigger Apartment Hotel. *Moderate.* Box 750; 31–3563. 20 air-conditioned rooms with cooking facilities. Bar, restaurant, shops, and spa pool.

The President Hotel. *Moderate.* Box 1351, Suva; 36–1033. 44 rooms. Ocean views from attractive hillside setting. Dining room, bar, swimming pool.

Southern Cross Hotel. *Moderate.* Box 1076, Suva; 31–4233. 31 rooms. Overlooking downtown Suva. Dining room, swimming pool.

Suva Peninsula Hotel. *Moderate.* Box 888, Suva; 31–3711. 39 rooms. Good-quality accommodation with swimming pool, dining room, room service, and baby-sitters.

Pacific Grand Apartments. *Inexpensive.* Box 875; 25583. 13 basic rooms with cooking facilities and dormitory.

South Seas Private Hotel. *Inexpensive.* Box 157, Suva; 2–2195. 30 rooms. Spartan facilities at budget prices—$F11 twin. Dormitory-style.

Sunset Apartment Motel. *Inexpensive.* Box 485; 23021. 12 air-conditioned apartments with cooking facilities. Tour desk, laundry, baby-sitter.

Suva Apartments. *Inexpensive.* Box 12488, Suva; 2–4281. 12 rooms. Simple self-contained apartments aimed at the budget conscious.

Townhouse Apartment Hotel. *Inexpensive.* Box 485; 22661. 28 air-conditioned apartments with cooking facilities. Hotel as bar, restaurant and tour desk.

Tropic Towers Apartment Hotel. *Inexpensive.* Box 1347; 25819. 29 air-conditioned apartments with cooking facilities. Restaurant, bar, pool, tour desk.

NORTH COAST

Ba Hotel. *Inexpensive.* Box 29, Ba; 74000. Modest 13-room accommodation with air-conditioning, restaurant, bar and pool.

Rakiraki

Rakiraki Hotel. *Moderate.* Box 31, Rakiraki; 94101. Quality budget accommodation with 36 rooms, pool, restaurant, bar, bowling green, tennis and nine-hole golf course nearby.

Nananu Beach Cottages. *Inexpensive.* MacDonald's Private Mail Bag, Rakiraki; 22672. Five self-contained cottages on the beach at nearby Nananu-i-ra Island.

Tavua

Tavua Hotel. *Inexpensive.* Box 4, Tavua; 91122. 11 air-conditioned rooms, restaurant, bar and pool. Golf and tennis can be arranged.

VANUA LEVU ISLAND

Labasa

Coral Island Resort *Moderate.* Box 7, Nasea, Labasa; 82955. 11 units on Nukubati Island. Restaurant, bars, paddle boats, fishing, horse riding, wind surfing.

Hotel Takia. *Moderate.* Box 7, Labasa; 81655. 36 air-conditioned and self-contained rooms. Restaurant, swimming pool and bar.

Crand Eastern Hotel. *Inexpensive.* Box 641, Labasa; 81022. 25 rooms, restaurant, bar.

Savusavu

Na Koro Resort. *Expensive.* Box 12, Savusavu; 86188. 25 bures with all facilities. Bar restaurant, gift shop. All sports, with big-game fishing and yacht charters.

Namale Plantation Resort. *Expensive.* Box 244, Savusavu; 86117. Just 10 private bures set in jungle gardens around swimming pool, bar, restaurant and tennis court.

Hot Springs Hotel. *Moderate.* Box 208, Savusavu; 86111. 48 air-conditioned rooms and bar with windsurfing, deep-sea fishing, scuba and snorkel diving.

Kontiki Lodge. *Inexpensive.* Box 244, Savusavu; 86262. Eight bures on attractive beach. Pool and all watersports.

Lesiaceva Point Beach Apartments. *Inexpensive.* C/o GPO, Savusavu; 86250. Just two self-contained apartments close to lagoon for reef walking and coral viewing.

OUTER ISLANDS

Taveuni

Matagi Island Resort. *Expensive.* Box 83 Taveuni, Suva; booking office 27384. Up to 13 bures to be completed by late 1988. Restaurant and facilities for all water sports and game fishing.

Castaway Gardens. *Moderate.* Box 1, Taveuni; 87286. 30 air-conditioned rooms with pool, restaurant, bowling green and tennis courts. Fishing, water-skiing, wind-surfing and horse riding all handy.

Dive Taveuni. *Moderate.* C/o Matei Post Office, Taveuni; 406M. Especially for diving enthusiasts, with accommodation for 10. Tanks and back-packs supplied but bring wetsuits, flippers, and masks.

Maravu Plantation Resort. *Moderate.* Postal Agency, Matei, Taveuni; 401J. Three self-contained bures with pool, restaurant and bar.

Matei Plantation Lagoon Resort. *Moderate.* Matei Post Office; 401G. Game fishing specialists with one luxury guest house with all facilities and one bure on headland offering great views.

Kaba Guest House. *Inexpensive.* Box 4, Taveuni; 8758. Budget accommodation with cooking facilities close to supermarket, 10 miles from airport.

Ovalau Island

Levuka Holiday Resort. *Moderate.* Lawakitoki, Ovalau; 44329. Dormitory accommodation and three bures with cooking facilities and bar.

Old Capital Inn. *Inexpensive.* Box 50, Levuka; 44057. Island tours and fishing can be arranged from humble five-room hotel with bar and restaurant serving European and Chinese meals.

Rukuruku Holiday Resort. *Inexpensive.* Box 112, Levuka; 311491. Four bures and four cottages with budget accommodation. Restaurant, bar, barbecue, fishing and snorkeling.

Qamea Island

Qamea Beach Club. *Deluxe.* C/o Matei Post Office, Taveuni; 87220. Eight private bures all facing the beach and containing one or two king-size beds and overhead fans. Activities include windsurfing, diving, sailing and crab hunts.

Namena Island

Moody's Namena. *Inexpensive.* Private Bag, Suva; 388RP6M. Four bures on beach, handy to diving, beachcombing, fishing and birdwatching.

Kadavu Island

Plantation Hideaway. *Inexpensive.* Lagalevu Estate, Kadavu. Three bures and camping facilities. Shared facilities. Fishing, diving trips to Great Astrolabe Reef.

TOBERUA ISLAND

Toberua Island Resort. *Deluxe.* Box 567, Suva; 4–9177 or 2–6356. 14 bures. Idyllic beach-side accommodation. Dining room specializes in local seafood and native foods. Fishing and excursion boats.

NAIGANI ISLAND

Mystery Island Resort. *Expensive.* Box 12539, Suva; 4–4364. 22 rooms. Good-quality accommodation off northeast coast of Viti Levu an hour by air from Suva. Excursions to Ovalau Island. Dormitory $F10.

YASAWAS

Turtle Island Lodge. *Deluxe.* Box 9317, Nadi Airport; 7–2921. 12 bures. Exquisite island setting ideal for a sun-and-sand holiday. For adults only. Transfer by seaplane. Rates include meals and all drinks.

RESTAURANTS. Fiji offers a wide variety of food—American-English, Indian, Chinese, Japanese, and Indonesian. Generally the quality is good and prices are very reasonable. Tourists tend to dine at the better-quality hotels, particularly outside Suva and Nadi, where most restaurants can be found. But in the two main cities it's possible to dine out in style or within a tight budget or to buy good quality take-out food.

Hotels and resorts usually hold specialty nights featuring ethnic dishes. Some offer the *lovo*—a traditional feast in which the food is wrapped in banana leaves and cooked slowly in an earth oven with hot stones. A whole pig may be the pièce de résistance. One of the most popular local dishes with tourists is *kakoda*—raw Spanish mackerel marinated in lemon juice, coconut oil, peppers, tomatoes, and spices.

You can spend as much or as little as you like. At the top end, dinner for two with wine can cost $F120. The average would be $F20–$F30.

Following is a selection of restaurants not attached to hotels or resorts. As a general rule American-English restaurants will cost upwards of $F30 a couple and Chinese or Indian restaurants will be cheaper.

Nadi

American/English: *Club Room,* Nadi Airport, 73027.
Chinese: *Fong Hing,* Vunavou St., 71011; *Poon's* Main St., 70896.
Indian: *Curry Corner,* Clay St., 70690; *India Curry House,* Main St., 71717; *Maharaja,* Namaka, 72962.
Japanese: *Suekiro,* Andrews St., 71956.
Italian/Spanish: *La Hacienda,* Namaka: 72902.

Sigatoka

American/English: *Crow's Nest,* Queens Rd., 50230.
Italian/Spanish: *La Hacienda,* Queens Rd., 50766.
Seafood: *The Sea Lounge,* Main Rd., 50592.

Suva

American/English: *Scott's,* 26 Bau St., 312708; *Red Lion,* 215 Victoria Parade, 319268. *Tiko's Floating Restaurant,* Stinson Parade, 31362.
Chinese: *Wan-Q,* 25 Cumming St., 23155; *Sichuan,* 6 Thompson St., 26316; *Samraat,* 9 Ellery St., 314070. *Ming Palace,* Old Town Hall, 315111. *Great Wok of China,* Flagstaff, 312285.
French: *Le Normandie,* 36 Cumming St., 313172.
Japanese: *Sakura House,* Pacific Harbour, 45300.
Indian: *Curry Place,* 16 Pratt St., 313885; *Star of India,* Waimanu Rd., 25411.
Indonesian: *Java Room,* 46 Gordon St., 24932.
Italian: *The Pizza Place,* 207 Victoria Parade, 22418.
Mexican-American: *Traps,* 305 Victoria Parade, 312922.

HOW TO GET AROUND. Nadi International Airport is the gateway to Fiji, and almost all visitors arrive there. *Air Pacific* (tel. Nadi 72–499, Suva 24624) maintains a 30-minute shuttle service between Nadi and Suva's airport at Nausori. Typical fare is $F40.

Fiji has more than 15 airports and the main outer islands can be reached by air. Air Pacific has daily services to and from Nadi, Suva, and Labasa. *Fiji Air* (tel. 22–666) is the main island service. *Sunflower Airlines* (tel. 73–016) serves several islands from Nadi. *Turtle Airways* (tel. 72–988) operates island resort transfers and seaplane sightseeing. *Pacific Crown Aviation* (tel. 36–1422) has a helicopter-charter service based in Suva.

The offshore resort islands can also be reached by ship or launch, and transfers are usually part of the accommodation package. Yachts and cabin cruisers are available for charter (see Tours). Government and private shipping companies operate freight and passenger services linking the outer islands, but don't expect luxury. For information on government vessels call the Marine Department (tel. 22–818).

Taxi services are geared to take visitors from Nadi and Suva airports to hotels and resorts on Viti Levu. Taxis are metered in towns and are required to carry a fare table for long distances. It's best to agree on a price before taking a long taxi trip. You can expect to pay about $F11 from Nausori to Suva, $F30–$F50 from Nadi to the Coral Coast resorts, and F$65 to Deuba.

Buses operate right around Viti Levu and on the other main islands as well as town and suburban routes. Bus between Nadi and Suva is $F20. Air-conditioned coaches on this route are operated by *United Touring Fiji* (tel. 72–811), *Tradewinds Tours* (tel. 72–056), *Pacific Transport* (tel. Nadi 7–0044, Suva 2–5425). Rental cars are readily available to explore Fiji's 1,950 miles of roads. Visitors with a current domestic license are eligible to drive. There are 11 rental-car agencies, most of which have offices at Nadi Airport, Suva, and Lautoka. You can expect to pay a minimum deposit of the estimated rental charge. Rates vary from about $F30 a day, with unlimited mileage. Agencies include *Hertz* (tel. Nadi 7–2771 or Suva 2–3026), *Thrifty* (tel. 7–2935), *UTC* (tel. Nadi 7–2811 or Suva 2–5637), *Budget* (tel. Nadi 7–2735 or Suva 31–5899), and *Avis* (tel. Nadi 7–2688, Suva 31–3833).

TOURS. Cruises. *Blue Lagoon Cruises* (Box 54, Lautoka; 6–1268/6–1622) offers four- and seven-day cruises to the beautiful Yasawa Islands from Lautoka. Opportunities for swimming, snorkeling, and fishing, plus visits to Fijian village and limestone caves. Four-day cruise from around $F300 plus tax; seven-day from around $F600 plus tax. Rates include meals.

Islands in the Sun (Fiji) Ltd. (Box 364, Lautoka; 6–1500) offers a variety of ways to explore the Fiji islands. A cruise and resort package (around $F350 plus tax) offers three nights at Beachcomber Island. You can take a day cruise to Beachcomber Island (around $F135), and there's a day trip from the Naviti Beach Resort on the Coral Coast to Vatulele Island, renowned for its red prawns.

South Sea Cruises (Box 718, Nadi; 7–2988) has day cruises to Mana. Bar, boutique, and island-style entertainment. Barbecue or smorgasbord lunch included. The *Jungle Princess* will take you upriver to a wilderness area (around $F1). Game fishing can also be arranged.

Daydream Cruises Ltd. (Box 9777, Nadi Airport; 7–3441) offers shopping tours to Nadi from the Coral Coast and a visit to Malamala Island. Swimming, snorkeling, lunch, and entertainment, around $F31.

Coral Sea Cruise (tel. 36–1250). The glass-bottomed vessels *Coral Sea* and *Tropic Sea* offer coral garden viewing, swimming, and snorkeling, with luncheon. Depart daily from Tradewinds Hotel, Suva, 9 A.M. Costs: around $F26 for a full day; under $F20 for a half day.

Sightseeing Tours. *Orchid Island Fijian Cultural Centre* (Box 1018, Suva; tel. 36–1128). Offers half-day coach tour to picturesque Orchid Island. Opportunity to see Fijian history and culture and enjoy *yaqona* (kava drinking) ceremony.

Rainbow Tours (tel. Suva 31–1233) offers half-day tour of the Rewa Delta including Nasilai village, where Fijian pottery making is demonstrated. Tour includes visit to Hindu temple on return to Suva.

Wilderness Adventures (Fiji) Ltd. (Box 1389, Suva; 31–3500). Offers whitewater rafting on the Ba River daily except Sunday and full-day canoe trip on Navua River. Also four-day treks into interior Uih Levu. Age limit 15 years to 50.

Coral Coast Railway Co. (tel 5–0757). The restored train Fijian Princess provides a 12-mile scenic trip from Yanuca (near the Fijian resort hotel) to Natadola Beach along an old sugar-cane route. $F38 fare includes barbecue lunch. Full-day return excursion.

United Touring Fiji Ltd. (tel. 7–2811) offers a variety of coach tours including a five-day trip around Viti Levu with shopping and sightseeing excursions. A full-day guided tour from Nadi to Suva and return takes in the main scenic attractions of the capital. Pick up at all major Coral Coast resorts. A half-day tour from Nadi explores the Cannon Route—the historic Momi gun battery with its tremendous view of the Mamanuca Islands.

Road Tours of (Fiji) Ltd. (Box 9268, Nadi Airport; 7–2935). Full-day trips to Suva, Pacific Harbour, the Emperor gold mine; and the Sigatoka Valley, the heartland of Fiji's agriculture. Half-day trips include the Lautoka sugar mill, the Sigatoka highlands, and the Vuda lookout north of Nadi. Also offers three-day tours around Viti Levu.

Turtle Airways (tel. 7–2988) operates a daily seaplane sightseeing service from Newtown Beach or Regent of Fiji Hotel to the Nadi offshore resorts. Also charter flights.

Sun Tours Ltd. (Box 9403, Nadi Airport; 7–1266, Suva 31–2300) offers seven-day adventure holidays off the beaten track to Vanua Levu, Taveuni, Ovalau, and Naigani islands. For tourists who don't like to laze around.

SPORTS. Every sport to be enjoyed in sun, sea, and sand is readily available in Fiji. Many resort hotels have their own tennis courts, some championship golf courses, and horseback riding. All, of course, have warm tropical water for diving, boating, windsurfing, sailing, canoeing—or just splashing around.

More adventurous visitors, however, have plenty of opportunity for a sporting holiday on the water, or below it. Dive, game fishing, and yacht charter companies abound.

Diving. *Pacific Island Divers,* C/o PO, Savusavu, 86188. Beginners' courses and daily dive charters. *Scubahire Ltd.,* Box 777 Suva; 361088. Based at Suva and Pacific Harbor, operates two launches for dive excursions from half-day to two weeks. *Aqua Trek Adventures,* Box 9176, Nadi; 72333. Full instruction courses servicing Plantation Village, Musket Cove, and Club Naitasi. *Dive Center,* Box 3066, Lami; 314599. Day and night dives, instruction from Beachcomber and Treasure Islands. *Sea Sports,* Box 65, Korolevu; 50598. Daily charters from Hyatt Regency, Fijian Resort, and Naviti with 10 qualified instructors. *Dive Expeditions,* Box 502, Lautoka; 60496. Six-day trips to the Yasawas with divers' accommodation on Waya Island. *Dive Taveuni,* c/o Box Taveuni; 406M. Dives on famous Rainbow Reef from a 30-ft. catamaran. *Mana Divers,* Box 610, Lautoka; 61246. Specializes in reef dives off Mana Island. *Qamea Dive,* Box Matei, Taveuni; 220. Daily dive trips to nearby reefs. *Matagi Island Dive,* Box 83, Waiyevo, Taveuni; 87260. Two live-aboard launches for hire with excursions with certificated guides.

Game Fishing. *Dau Wai* and the *Dau Siwa.* Fast sport-fishing vessels based at the Regent Hotel; tel. 7–1445. *Fleet Lady.* 43-footer based at the Fijian; tel. 5–0155. *Commander One.* 42-ft. Suva-based vessel; tel. 36–1128. *Serenawai.* Based at the Hyatt Regency, a 27-footer available Mon.–Sat.; tel. 5–0555. *Sereki Mai.* 48-ft. De Fever cruiser at Navini Island; tel. 6–2188. *MV Marau* and *Marau* 11-ft. and 32-ft. vessels, each with twin fighting chairs, based at Pacific Harbour; tel. 4–5357.

Yacht Charters. *La Violante,* 103-ft. schooner. Stardust Cruises, Private Bag, Nadi Airport; tel. 6–2215. *Whale's Tale,* 100-ft. schooner, Oceanic Schooner Co., Box 9625, Nadi Airport; tel. 7–2455. *Tau,* 94-ft. schooner, Tradewinds Marine, Box 3084, Lami; tel. 36–1796. *Mollie Dean,* 75-ft. power launch, Mollie Dean Cruises, Box 3256, Lami; tel. 36–1562. *Rainbow,* 36-ft. ketch, *Kita,* 35-ft. ketch, Emerald Yacht Charters, Box 15, Savusavu; tel. 8610. *Seax of Legra,* 45-ft. ketch, Warwick and Dianne Bain, Box 89, Taveuni; no phone.

Spectator Sports

Rugby, played in the cooler months from May to September, is the national sport. Fijian teams have toured New Zealand, Australia, Britain, France, and Wales. Soccer, played between March and October and culminating in the interdistrict tournament during Independence weekend in October, is a close second. Cricket is a summer sport attracting major competition from Suva, Nadi, and Lautoka.

GARDENS, MUSEUMS, HISTORIC SITES. Suva. *Fiji Museum,* through the Thurston Gardens near the Grand Pacific Hotel, has many relics of Fiji's history from pre-European days. Open daily 8:30 A.M. to 4:30 P.M. Small entrance fee. *Thurston Gardens* has an outstanding collection of flora.

Colo-I-Suva, a forest park 7 miles from Suva, has nature walks, picnic areas, and swimming holes in Waisila Creek. Special permission is required to stay at this licensed campsite; contact the Forestry Department, tel. 2–2777.

Orchid Island, in a river 7 miles from Suva, has an extensive collection of tropical plants, timber, coral, and seashells. Fauna includes mongoose, iguanas, monkeys, and local snakes. The island also features a traditional Fijian village.

Deuba. *Cultural Centre and Marketplace of Fiji* (Postal Agency, Pacific Harbour; tel. 4–5083) re-creates traditional Fiji with dance theater, fire walking, and a village. Market specialty shops include quality handicrafts.

Nadi. *Waqadra Gardens* is a 70-year-old tropical botanical garden around an old family homestead. Tours at 10 A.M. and 11 A.M. Monday to Saturday.

Viseisei Village, where Fijians are thought to have first landed is near the Vuda lookout. Sights include a native house, a church, and a chief's home.

Momi Battery is the site of World War II guns used to guard Nadi. Great view.

Nadarivatural in the mountainous heart of Viti Levu, is a must for nature lovers. Camping is allowed with permission of Forestry Department.

SHOPPING. Duty-free bargains can still be found in Fiji, particularly in electronic goods, jewelry, and perfumes. Visitors are advised to shop with caution, especially in the main commercial areas—Cumming Street in Suva, along Lautoka's Vitoga Parade, and in the main street of Nadi village.

The National Duty Free Merchants Association warns shoppers to refuse approaches on the street by "touts" who offer to take them to shops with "special" prices. Visitors should deal only with stores displaying the association's official membership sticker on front windows. Buyers should also obtain a guarantee with the seller's name and address and a receipt showing the name of the shop, a full description of the goods bought, and the full price paid.

Native handcrafts are relatively cheap, popular with tourists, and of good quality if purchased from reputable stores such as Jacks Handicrafts in Nadi and Sigatoka. Tapa cloth, mats, and baskets woven from pandanus leaves, shell ornaments, and native wood carvings are favorites. But beware of street hawkers, especially the notorious sword-sellers of Suva, who will, on a pretext of friendship, block your path, engage you in conversation, and insist that you buy an unwanted 18-inch wooden sword he has already carved your name on. Their selling techniques are overzealous and no one is obliged to buy a sword simply because it has his or her name on it. Swords and masks should be bought only from sellers with a numbered badge of the Souvenir Sellers of Fiji Association. They must also have a current license and identification.

ENTERTAINMENT AND NIGHTLIFE. There's plenty of entertainment at all resort hotels, which regularly feature the traditional Fijian *meke*—a spectacular show of song, dance, and drums usually accompanied by a native-style feast. Many hotels put on special nights, such as the Nadi Mocambo's Mongolian Barbecue, the lobster and curry nights at the Travelodge, and Chinese and Thai buffets at the Hyatt Regency.

But for real nightlife, venture out after dark to one of the many nightclubs and experience Fiji in the raw. They're thunderously loud, and very dim, but generally free-wheeling and much fun. There's an old saying here that prostitution is practically unknown because there are too many enthusiastic amateurs—you'll see why.

The Golden Dragon on Suva's Victoria Parade has been packing them in for at least 20 years with its unique lighting, spacious dance floor and ample bar. Don't miss it. It's had competition since the mid-Seventies from *Lucky Eddie's,* just along the Parade, and its slightly more sophisticated "twin", *Rockefeller's,* which has table service. You have until 1 A.M. nightly to sample *Screwz* and *The Engine Room,* both with disco and live bands.

Several Nadi hotels feature discos, but the "in" place at the airport is the *Bamboo Terrace,* air-conditioned and with a glass dancefloor. In Lautoka, it's *Hunter's Inn* with its cave-like decor and glass floor. At Ba, the *Club Tropicana* features disco and live band to 1 A.M. Thursday to Saturday, while on the Coral Coast the Regency's *Hibiscus Lounge* and the Black Marlin bar at the *Fijian* are relatively sophisticated night spots with merriment and dancing, ideal after a day out in the sun.

DEPARTURE TAX. F$10.

KIRIBATI AND TUVALU

Recently Independent Nations

by
LOIS K. BRETT

Lois Brett is a California-based writer specializing in the South Pacific.

Until 1976, the Gilbert and Ellice Islands were a British colony, and transportation companies treated them as one territory. But they are now independent and separate, and they have new names: The Gilberts are Kiribati (pronounced "kiribas"), and the Ellice Islands are Tuvalu. Most Kiribati people call their republic Tungaru.

Kiribati and Tuvalu, which includes Ocean Island and the Phoenix and Northern Line islands, are situated in the southwest Pacific around the point where the date line cuts the equator. Although the total land area of these two countries is only about 283 square miles, they are scattered over more than two million square miles of ocean, and distances between them are enormous. Christmas Island (part of Kiribati), due south of Hawaii, is 2,000 miles from Ocean Island. The islands are remote from large centers of civilization and are off the major air routes. Tarawa (the capital of Kiribati) is about 2,500 miles from Sydney, Australia, and 1,400 miles from Suva, Fiji.

All these islands except Ocean Island rise no more than 12 feet above sea level; all are coral atoll lagoons, arcs of coral sand, devoid of hills or streams. Were it not for the masses of towering coconut palms, they would appear as little more than sand banks. If you steamed three miles out to sea, the islands would disappear from your horizon. In most of the atolls the reef encloses a lagoon; on the eastern side are long, narrow stretches of land varying in length from a few hundred yards to some ten miles and in width from one or two hundred yards to nearly a mile. The sea around the islands and in the lagoon swarms with fish, which form an important part of the islanders' diet. Not much grows here; the vegetation is poor. However, the coconut palm thrives on these islands and supplies a good deal of food and drink. The main diet consists of taro, bananas, uncultivated coconut, breadfruit, and seafood—everything else is shipped in. There is no native fauna, apart from birds.

There are 56,000 inhabitants of Kiribati; most of them are Micronesians. The 8,000 Tuvaluans are Polynesians who occupy nine islands with a land area of only 10 square miles.

The islands were first sighted by Europeans in 1765, but it was not until 1856, with the coming of the missionaries, was there any real European contact. The waters of the Gilbert Islands were a favorite with the whalers. Some of the crews deserted and settled, but there was no great interest in colonizing the islands at the time. In the 1860s "blackbirders" carried off about 400 islanders from the Ellice group for work in Peru. Other islanders were recruited to go to work on plantations in Fiji, Tahiti, Hawaii, and Australia. These incidents almost depleted the islands of their male population. This era also brought European diseases, particularly measles, against which the islanders had little resistance. With the people's consent, the islands became a British protectorate in 1892, in hope of eliminating blackbirding and the islanders' incessant tribal battles. A simple code of laws was drawn up based on earlier mission legislation, and a council of old men became the native courts to administer them.

When phosphate was discovered on Line Island in 1900, Ocean was annexed by Great Britain and placed within the jurisdiction of the protectorate. With this rapidly growing phosphate industry, headquarters were transferred from Tarawa to Ocean Island. Over the years, other islands were annexed, including Christmas Island in 1919. In 1925 the colony was placed under the jurisdiction of the governor-general of New Zealand. The British drained the riches of the phosphate island of Ocean; today the island is the producer of 99 percent of Kiribati's income, but the phosphate will soon be depleted and leave the islands with no cash income. It is hoped that low-scale tourism will help.

The islands remained a British protectorate until 1941, when the Japanese invaded and took control of the Gilbert Islands. The Ellice Islands escaped because they were off the beaten track the Japanese had established for themselves.

The islands became very familiar to Americans when, two years after the Japanese armed forces landed on Tarawa in 1941, the Americans set up an advanced base on Funafuti in the Ellice Islands. On November 21, 1943, Americans launched their first penetration of Japan's ring of island defenses. At dawn, the United States Second Marine Division landed on the Tarawa islet of Betio. After four days of fierce fighting, the Marines overwhelmed a strongly entrenched Japanese garrison. The Japanese lost 5,000 men killed in action or dead by suicide, and the Americans suffered 990 fatalities and 2,296 wounded. This was one of the bloodiest battles in the Pacific, and it was a major turning point in the war for the Americans.

There are three major islands of interest to tourists: Christmas Island, the largest coral atoll in the world, is three hours' air time or 1,300 miles due south of Honolulu. Tarawa and Abemama are near the point where the date line and the equator meet—about a five-hour flight from Christmas Island.

Tarawa

Tarawa is the capital island of Kiribati. You reach the islet of Betio by a half-hour drive from the Otintai Hotel (one of the two hotels on the island). A memorial on Betio honors the American war heroes on a point overlooking the harbor—a short walk from the ferry dock. A small park leads the way to the memorial. Along the shore line at Betio, huge bunkers, overgrown with shrubs and plants, are grim reminders of 40 years ago.

A returning veteran would hardly recognize the island. In World War II, the island was totally destroyed. Not a house or a palm tree was left standing. All the Europeans and most of the local people had either left before the Japanese invaded or were killed. Only a few people were left to do service at Japanese insistence. Today, most of the people of the republic live on Betio. The rest of the people on the island of Tarawa are spread along both the lagoon and the ocean side of the island. There is a fairly good road from Bairiki to Bonriki. Beyond Bonriki, you travel by foot or by boat to the few settlements along the way to the tip of the island at Naa.

Returning veterans will find that Tarawa is a lovely island, studded with thousands of palm trees along the white-sand beaches. They will also find to their pleasant surprise very friendly, shy people who, through some amazing gardening technique, are able to grow taro and bananas and who live mainly on uncultivated coconut, breadfruit, and seafood. Most islanders are outrigger sailors and fishers and spend much of the time on their boats. Fish are caught with traps, nets, and lines or speared in the lagoons, along the reef, and in the open sea. With the lack of large crops and the occasional drought, the people live a difficult but proud life.

American veterans wishing to view World War II battlefields will find that a mass of American and Japanese hardware is still conspicuous along the beaches. Hardware abounds at Nukufetau, Nanumea, Abemama, Tarawa, and Butaritari (which the American military labeled Makin). But a concentration of war relics may be found in Betio, at Tarawa, where 6,000 people occupy one square mile. You can circumnavigate Betio on foot along its beaches in about an hour. The best time to find portable war memorabilia is at low tide—but be sure to wear old tennis shoes to minimize the risk of gashing your feet on anything from shards of barnacle-encrusted Coke bottles of the mid-1940s to torn metal and empty cartridges.

Because the entire nation has only some 70 hotel rooms, there is a limit to the number of visitors Kiribati can handle. Kiribati is not for everyone. There is no place here for the demanding tourist or for those in a hurry. Kiribati is a fragile destination, intent on retaining its culture, and it's best suited to travelers who care about wonderful, underdeveloped places off the beaten track.

What tourists will find, wherever they travel in this country, are people who genuinely enjoy tourists, mostly because they see hardly any. They are unjaded, and their smiles and laughter are irrepressible.

Abemama

Robert Louis Stevenson and his wife loved the island of Abemama and lived here for a while in 1889. It probably hasn't changed much since those days, though now you arrive by plane rather than by boat.

Abemama is a coral atoll with a lagoon of clear, warm water, lots of palm trees, and plenty of white-sand beaches. It's only 100 air miles from Tarawa, and the Trislander flies there every day but Sunday.

The Robert Louis Stevenson Hotel is 9 miles from the airport, near the site where the Stevensons lived. Guests are met and transported from the airport in whatever transportation is available that day. If it is a truck, you toss your luggage in the back and plop yourself on top of it for the trip to the hotel. Along the way, you'll most probably pick up anyone who flags down the truck. Since there are no buses, this is the way people get around. Otherwise, most people stroll barefoot along the roads.

As you turn in to the hotel grounds, you are greeted by a huge overhanging sign that welcomes you to the Robert Louis Stevenson Hotel. It's just the type of hotel where Stevenson might have stayed. The cottages are built in a unique style with walls about four feet high, made of the spines of the coconut tree. Above is a latticed criss-cross open-air window pattern; the roof is thatched. The open-air cottages are on the lagoon surrounded by white sand overlooking the brilliant aqua water.

Abemama is a relaxing spot for couples or families. The atmosphere of the island is catchy. With no modern technology to get in the way, people seem to enjoy the simple things in life. There's time to snorkel, to swim, or to study the stars at night. Food is simple, most probably the fish caught that day or some combination of what comes from the hotel's simple larder, but you will not go hungry. With reminders of Stevenson's pictures in the hotel's lounge–dining room–bar and the whole atmosphere of the place, somehow food doesn't seem to matter.

Each cottage is simple but attractively furnished. There are a lanai, a bedroom where you sleep under mosquito nets, and a bath with only tepid but very refreshing water. (Be sure to bring plenty of bug repellent and soap.) If you imagine living a very simple Robinson Crusoe life but in a comfortable and very relaxing setting, you're at the RLS Hotel. The shy staff tries to entertain you at night but they prefer that you join them in song or contribute what talents you have. There's a piano-organ, and it's a perfect place to have singalongs as you relax under the stars, or in the common room.

The staff can arrange for fishing or snorkeling, but you must bring your own equipment. Pack plenty of books and expect to amuse yourself. Except for exploring and getting to know the local people, there is nothing to do but relax. If you are adventurous, this is one of the most idyllic getaway-from-it-all islands on earth.

Christmas Island

Captain Cook spotted Christmas Island on Christmas Day and so named it in 1777. Around 1837, whalers began to settle, setting up shops. By the 1860s there was a flourishing trade in coconut oil and copra.

Only three hours south of Hawaii, Christmas is a "sleeper" in American terms. Protective legislation makes it and the surrounding areas "tropical oceanic sanctuaries." The seas and the lagoons abound with fish. The island and small islets are also sea-bird sanctuaries, with hundreds of thousands of birds, unmatched by any other island in the Pacific.

Visitors stay at the Captain Cook Hotel, a rather plain, small place. The fishing and the bird watching make up for anything the hotel lacks. The rooms are clean, have small refrigerators and bottled water.

A hotel barbecue is held once a week under the trees near the ocean—charcoal-broiled lobsters, other seafood, chicken, and steak. All seafood is fresh, and the hotel will cook your own catch every night—you can even have your fish for breakfast and lunch if you wish. On barbecue night, the hotel puts on an outstanding Kiribati cultural show. The music and choreography are usually taught by a senior villager, whose pride in retaining the culture is strong. Bring lots of film for this colorful show.

Fishing and bird watching are the big things on Christmas, and Hawaiian Islanders sneak down here for a week at a time for a change of pace. The Captain Cook Hotel has facilities to fast-freeze your catches, including the huge lobsters, all of which can be taken back with you on the plane. (*Air Tungaru* offers a special seven-day fishing package.)

Bird watchers will find Christmas Island a haven. You can walk right up to the nesting birds, who have no fear of humans. A few beautiful white fairy terns will follow you around, then go back for companions, and all will investigate your every move.

There is only one weekly flight, so you must come prepared, but your week's stay will be one of the most rewarding experiences of your life. Bring lots of film; you can't buy it there. Also, this is where a tape recorder comes in handy—to capture the bird-life sounds.

Tuvalu

Nine islands make up Tuvalu, which has been an independent nation since 1978. The group is about 1,200 kilometers north of Suva in Fiji. Funafuti is the capital and main island. All but Niulakita are inhabited—about 1,000 people on each of the islands—for a total population of around 10,000.

The islands were originally named after a nineteenth-century politician, Edward Ellice, member of Parliament and owner of the ship *Rebecca,* in which Captain Arent De Peyster discovered Funafuti Atoll in 1819. A few of the other islands were spotted as early as 1528, but not until the nineteenth century did whalers, beachcombers, and missionaries begin to settle in.

Christianity arrived in the 1860s, and the islanders became British subjects in 1877. For most of the colonial period, the Ellice Islands consisted of a single administrative district with its headquarters on Funafuti. The islands were not captured by the Japanese because they were not included in Japanese plans. However, Americans used the islands as a base in 1942, and it was from there the colony was administered until the Japanese were driven from the Gilbert Islands by the American marines in November 1943. The Americans built the first air strip on Funafuti, and it has since been restored. After the war, many of the Ellice Islanders migrated to the Gilbert group because they needed work, but many stayed behind and started proceedings toward independence. They succeeded in separating themselves legally from the Gilbert and Ellice Islands group and became known as Tuvalu in 1975.

The people are Polynesians, most with a Samoan a heritage. Many Samoan customs and traditions still prevail.

Funafuti, the capital, is a pear-shaped atoll enclosing a lagoon. It is only 13½ miles by 10 miles, with 30 islets. Everyone lives near Fongafale, the main center of the island. It was here that Professor Sir Edgeworth David put down a 1,100-foot bore in 1897–1898 to prove Darwin's theory of the origin of coral islands. The island still has some of the remnants of the British colonial days—administration offices, the jail, and a hospital (the old hospital was destroyed by a hurricane in 1972, but a new one was opened in 1975). Prince Charles, following attendance at Fiji's independence celebration, made a four-day visit to Funafuti in 1970.

There's only one hotel on Funafuti—the Vaiaku Lagi Hotel; it's small and inexpensive. Facilities include dining room, bar, tennis courts, and a few small shops. Swimming is in the lagoon. The hotel is near the beach and only a five-minute walk from the airport. Bring your own entertainment to this very pleasant but isolated island.

PRACTICAL INFORMATION FOR
KIRIBATI AND TUVALU

WHEN TO COME. The weather stays much the same year round—mid 80sF. Best time to visit is between March and October, the season of the northeasterly trade winds. Westerly gales bring rain and sticky discomfort from November through February.

TRAVEL DOCUMENTS. Kiribati: Passport and Visa required. Visas are U.S.$28.80 and are valid for three months. You must have ticket to leave with confirmed onward reservations and necessary document to depart to a third country. *Health requirements:* Cholera and yellow-fever inoculation required. No airport tax.
    Tuvalu: Passport required. Visa: $US33. You must have ticket to leave and enough funds to stay. Airport tax: $A2.50.

HOW TO GET THERE. Christmas Island: via *Air Tungaru* from Honolulu. **Tarawa:** Air Tungaru from Majuro, Marshall Islands, and Tuvalu to Tarawa; *Air Nauru* from Nauru to Tarawa. **Tuvalu:** *Air Pacific* from Suva and from Tarawa via Air Tungaru. For up-to-date information on air fares and schedules contact: Air Tungaru, Box 274, Bikenibeu, Tarawa, Kiribati; or 4767 Farmers Rd., Honolulu, HI 96816; (808) 735–3994; (800) 345–1564.

DRINKING WATER AND ELECTRICITY. Drink only bottled or boiled water or the palatable and wholly sterile juice from a freshly opened coconut. Electricity is geared for Australian and British-type outlets—three prong, 240 volts, 50 Hz. On Abemama, electricity is by generator. Don't count on it for electric razor or hair dryer.

WHAT TO PACK. Modesty in dress is essential. Lightweight casual clothing, preferably cotton. Bikinis are not recommended except for swimming. Women's shorts are never seen in town. Men usually wear walking shorts and open-necked cotton shirts; long trousers are worn in the evening or for formal occasions. Bring sunglasses, lots of film and tapes (you can't buy them here), Lomotil, insect repellent, batteries, flashlight, and candles. Shoes for beach and coral walking. Perhaps some balloons to share with children or small tablets and pencils to give away.

TIPPING. No tipping unless for extraordinary service.

CURRENCY. At present, the Australian dollar is used. $A1 = $US.76.

LANGUAGES. Local languages and English. Because of a local courtesy, English is not spoken in the company of anyone who does not speak it; thus the tourist should be prepared for one-to-one conversations.

TIME ZONE. Tarawa is GMT plus 11 hours; 20 hours ahead of U.S. Pacific Standard Time. Christmas Island is GMT minus 10, 2 hours behind PST.

ACCOMMODATIONS. Kiribati: The *Otintai Hotel* on Tarawa has 28 a/c rooms. Be sure to book well in advance. Box 270, Bairiki, Tarawa, Republic of Kiribati, Central Pacific. For reservations cable: OTINTAAI; tel 28084; tlx 77032. There are a good restaurant, and a bar; airport shuttle. Car and motorbike rentals and excursions can be arranged. Rooms in the new wing all have balconies overlooking the lagoon. *Hotel Kiribati* at Betio, 10 rooms. For reservations cable: JKKBS

BETIO. Box 504, Bairiki, Tarawa, Republic of Kiribati, Central Pacific. $23 up. Bar; dining room serves Chinese and English-style meals. Rent cars or motorbikes; airport transportation can be arranged. *Captain Cook Hotel* on Christmas Island has 36 rooms. For reservations cable: COOKHOTEL. $40–$47. Clean, plain rooms with refrigerators. *Robert Louis Stevenson Hotel* on Abemama; for reservations write: Box 462, Abemama, Rep. of Kiribati, Central Pacific; tel. 26305; tlx 77029; cable: COMPROSE. From $14. Bar, dining room, fishing, boating, snorkeling. Charming open-air thatched cottages.

Tuvalu: *Vaiaku Langi Hotel,* Funafuti, Republic of Tuvalu, Central Pacific. Be sure to book in advance. Rates start at $A20.

TOURIST INFORMATION. Kiribati: Government of the Republic of Kiribati, Ministry of Natural Resources Development, Box 64, Tarawa, Kiribati. Bairiki, Tarawa, Kiribati, Central Pacific. Tlx K177039 RESOURCES; cable RE-SOURCES. **Christmas Island:** Write *Air Tungaru,* 4767 Farmers Rd., Honolulu, HI 96816. Tel. (800) 345–1564. Tlx 296808 AIRTG HR; cable TUNGAIR HNL. **Tuvalu:** Tuvalu High Commission, Box 1495, Suva, Fiji. Tel. 2–2697/8.

TOURS. Christmas Island: *C.H.R. Ltd.,* 4767 Farmers Rd., Honolulu, HI 96816. Contact: Carol Farrow, above address, or tel. (800) 345–1564. Tlx: 296808 AIRTG. According to Bob and Carol Farrow, operators of the tours to Christmas Island, fishing at Christmas is "ranked the number-one spot in the world with fly and spin fishermen." Popular catches include bonefish, trevalle (ulua), and wahoo. Fish can be flash-frozen and taken home. Their 7-day tours cost $1,675, including meals, transportation (air and ground), boats, etc. Flights leave Honolulu every Wednesday at 5 A.M. and return the following Wednesday at noon. Optional day trip to bird island sanctuary available for $45. This is a fantastic opportunity to visit the largest bird sanctuary in the Pacific. Includes guide.

HOW TO GET AROUND. Kiribati: *Air Tungaru* operates a special service for arriving and departing passengers to and from airport. Fare: $A2.50. Regular buses run between Bonriki and Bairiki. Fare is $A0.65. Bus on Betio circles the atoll frequently. Fare: $A0.30. There is very limited taxi service. Car rentals can be arranged at your hotel. Best to order before you arrive. **Christmas Island:** There is no public transport. Rental trucks or minibus available for hire through Air Tungaru. **Tuvalu:** Write *Tuvalu High Commission,* Box 1495, Suva, Fiji. Tel. 2–2697/8 for information regarding transport and other services, or write to the *Vaiaku Langi Hotel* (see above). Note: It is possible to hire local people for their transport—land or sea. Settle *fairly* on price beforehand. On **Tarawa,** it's possible to take a voyage from Tarawa to a distant island in a *baurua*— a large, twin-sailed ocean-going outrigger canoe, centuries old in design.

SHOPPING. There are few handicrafts: baskets, table mats, fans, or items made from coconut shells. There are also a few weapons and artifacts worth looking for. Among tools of war, the Kiribati shark-tooth sword is claimed to be unique in concept and craft. The swords, in great demand by collectors of both artifacts and militaria, are of polished coconut wood, with drilled shark teeth, filed to razor sharpness, lashed to the two edges. The hilt and sometimes the entire length of the sword is covered with finely woven dye-patterned pandanus into which, for good luck, a plaited strand of a woman's hair is sometimes woven. Sword length varies from 12 to 36 inches.

A prized Tuvalu artifact is the carved wooden *tuluma,* also spelled *turama,* an oval miniature sea chest, 18 to 24 inches in diameter, with hermetically fitting lid, in which treasured possessions were carried on transoceanic canoe journeys. Miniature models (4 to 10 inches in diameter) have been used for decades in the South Pacific as humidors and, in recent times, as containers for cameras. A comparable sea chest in the Gilberts is named *bookai.*

Business Hours: Mon.–Fri. 8 A.M.–noon and 1–5 P.M.; Saturday 7 A.M.–noon.

VANUATU

The Timeless Islands

by
KATHLEEN HANCOCK

New Zealander Kathleen Hancock is a freelance journalist and photographer covering travel, trade, and current affairs in the territories of the South Pacific.

In 1606 Pedro Fernandez de Quiros, the finest navigator of his time, came upon Espiritu Santo, northernmost island of the New Hebrides group. He believed he had discovered the great southern continent hinted at by Ptolemy and Marco Polo, outlined on ancient maps as stretching right across the South Pacific. The Portuguese Quiros was looking for land and gold for his sponsor, King Philip III of Spain, and souls for the Church of Rome.

Not a man to be intimidated by immensities of ocean, he had christened the Pacific the Gulf of Our Lady of Loreto on leaving the coast of Peru. And four months later he made landfall in the northern New Hebrides at Gaua in the Banks Group. Gifts were exchanged with the friendly local people, but in the Spanish manner Quiros took hostages against the chance of sudden attack, putting them in the stocks for the night and, worst indignity of all for a Melanesian, shaving their heads and beards.

Sailing south, Quiros found more land and a great bay with a good port. The terrain was mountainous, and he was sure this was the continent he sought. He named it Terra Australis del Espiritu Santo. A great gathering of Melanesians lined the beach to see the strange creatures in their huge ships of 150 tons. The local people refused to let the Spaniards approach them on the beach but laid down their bows and arrows and indicated that the visitors could get water, giving them presents of fruit and vegetables.

But soon there was trouble. Muskets were fired in the air to frighten the increasing numbers of excited people who gathered in the surrounding bush. A Spaniard fired too low and killed a Melanesian. There was some parleying. A line was drawn in the sand, and a chief indicated that his people would lay down their arms if the Spaniards would do the same. But Quiros' admiral, one Torres, mishandled the situation, arquebuses were fired, and a chief dropped dead. He was hung from a tree "that he might be seen by all."

From this point there was never a chance of reconciliation between Quiros' men and the people he called "courageous and sociable." He broke the most sacred taboos of the people, beginning with the shaving of heads on Gaua. At Espiritu Santo his men stole carefully husbanded supplies of food from hill villages where they might have bartered for them successfully. Small boys were kidnapped to take home to Spain. And "he even broke the rules of war so far as to kill a chief." (Tom Harrisson: *Savage Civilisation*).

Quiros took possession of the "continent," named the great anchorage the Bay of St. Philip and St. James, set up an altar, and christened the city-to-be Nuova Jerusalema. But there were more killings, kidnappings, and ambushes. Local resistance persisted. Many of Quiros' men fell ill with fish poisoning. Discontent, unrest, and nostalgia for home unsettled the crews. Fifty days after their arrival in Espiritu Santo the *Almiranta* sailed out of what is now called Big Bay, bound for South America and ultimately Madrid. After seven years spent petitioning the King of Spain for recognition of his great discovery and compensation for its cost, Quiros died penniless and without honor.

For some reason Quiros' findings were suppressed, and it was 162 years before these islands were visited again by European explorers. Bougainville sighted Maewo, Pentecost, Espiritu Santo, and Malekula in 1768 and established clearly that this was no continent. Four years later Captain James Cook discovered the southern islands of the group and charted the whole archipelago, giving the islands their inappropriately dour Scottish name.

A mixed bag of missionaries, whalers, and sandalwooders followed Cook; then the "blackbirders" moved in with their ugly trade. By 1885 missionaries and planters, mostly British and French, were settling in increasing numbers on most islands in the group and problems arose over their personal safety. Murders were commonplace, with missionaries and traders the usual victims.

In 1877 John Higginson, an Irish-born trader but a naturalized French citizen, was urging the French Government in New Caledonia to take over the New Hebrides, but this idea met with cries of outrage from the well-established British missions and especially from neighboring Australia. Finally the British and French governments got together in 1888 and set up a joint naval commission to keep law and order in the group. Then German interests appeared on the scene with a vigorous campaign to extend their influence in this part of the Pacific. To counter this threat the French and British governments set up the Franco-British Condominium in 1906.

Joint "Pandemonium"

This jointly controlled administration known in the Pacific as the "Pandemonium" with its two sets of laws, two education systems, and two official languages and pidgin as well, was clumsy and expensive to run and functioned at a pace that any self-respecting snail could have bettered. But it did keep the peace and introduce limited education and a system of hospitals and clinics to a wild and remote part of the Pacific.

News of World War I took three months to reach the remote New Hebrides and had little effect on these islands. But the outbreak of World War II was a different matter. The French administration of the New Hebrides was among the first of France's overseas territories to rally to de Gaulle. And when Japan entered the war in 1941, these islands became a forward base for U.S. troops, with attention concentrated on Espiritu Santo.

The Segond Channel, a strait between Espiritu Santo and Aore, was found capable of harboring hundreds of ships. Roads, airfields, and docks were built. Workshops, floating cranes, hospitals, and sawmills were set up. The rain forest was cleared to establish hundreds of acres of market gardens to feed the troops in the New Hebrides and the Solomons. On Espiritu Santo the village of Luganville (or Santo, as it's commonly known) was the staging point for U.S. army, navy, and Marine forces advancing on the Solomons. In 1943 there were around 40,000 U.S. troops in Santo, later joined by about 1,400 New Zealanders, mostly airmen. Men, ships, and supplies poured into the once sleepy backwater. French planters sent their nubile daughters to a safer island.

Independence was granted by Britain and France to the duly elected government of the New Hebrides on July 30, 1980, and the new state was christened Vanuatu, meaning "our land." In the first flush of independence there was some political unrest on Espiritu Santo and Tanna, but both are now back to normal. Efate was never affected.

The ni-Vanuatu (the new name for the Melanesian inhabitants) are now emerging from a confused and confusing period of sporadic contact with a motley array of European explorers, traders, sandalwooders, missionaries, colonists, civil servants, soldiers, sailors, and airmen. Within the passing of less than a century they have left the stone age behind to confront European living, languages, and legal systems. Whatever the rate of emergence into the hard light of social, economic and political reality, one thing is for sure. The great Melanesian gifts of common sense, goodwill, honesty, and humor will prevail.

These are a sturdy, proud, and independent people, with a strongly developed sense of fair play. Even a fleeting encounter with them is a rewarding experience for the traveler looking for a different scene. In these islands it's worth considering the answer given to an early missionary by a man of Tanna. "Why do you put that paint on your faces?" asked the missionary. "Why do you put those clothes on?" asked the Tannese. "This is our way of clothing; that is yours."

The Economy

Vanuatu is a potentially rich area. These islands are incredibly fertile, and the climate, though tropical, is a pleasant one with a predictable rainfall. Copra heads the list of exports, with fish not far behind and cocoa coming on strong. A good way behind come beef and coffee, but production here is increasing and capable of much greater development. The recent growth of tourism has brought another source of income to the group, and the popularity of the area as a tax haven has also had a considerable effect on the economy.

Most of the meat eaten in Vanuatu is produced locally, and there are great strides being made to improve local herds. Cattle were first introduced as a cheap form of weed control in the coconut plantations, but both European planters and Melanesian villagers have discovered that a little care in sowing good grasses and the purchase of good quality breeding stock makes for an extra source of income at not much additional expense. With the introduction of pedigree Charolais and Hereford bulls, as well as Brahmin cross-bred cattle, herds have improved greatly.

Plantation labor is pretty scarce in these islands. It's one of the few Pacific territories that is underpopulated, and to aggravate this, local workers have long been accustomed to spending fairly long periods in New Caledonia, where nickel is king.

Life in Vanuatu and especially in remote Espiritu Santo still ambles on in the same lazy way that it has for nearly a century. In Vila you can buy luscious brandied cherries at the trade stores and ivory and jade and gold jewelry at the Chinese shops. But in the bush villages elsewhere in the group, pigs are both capital and power. While a jazz combo belts out its rhythms on a hotel dance floor, not far away in the hill villages the thump of a hundred feet shakes the ground in a "custom dance."

Tourism in Vanuatu is undergoing something of a rebirth. Since independence in 1980, local leaders have had their hands full sorting out development priorities after the years of "pandemonium." Tourism has now reached the top of the list and a concerted drive is being made to attract visitors, mainly from Australia and New Zealand. Tourism planners have tagged Vanuatu "The Timeless Islands" and are pushing it as a place to put your feet up or pursue a wide variety of fascinating activities.

Exploring Vanuatu (formerly the New Hebrides)

Captain Cook was never much of an original thinker when it came to christening all those islands he discovered in the Pacific 200 years ago. But he seems to have struck rock bottom when he gave such an unimaginative name to the 80 islands of that enchanting archipelago known as the New Hebrides. Now, of course, his error has been corrected by the new independent government.

This offbeat, slightly raffish, totally fascinating collection of islands lies east of the Coral Sea, scattered north to south in the southwest Pacific like confetti. This is a territory where tourists are not yet processed, where you can still wander along a white beach on the edge of an impossibly blue lagoon with only the lap of the tide to break the silence. Two of the resort hotels in Vila modestly face the lagoon. The third spills down the gentle slopes of Iririki Island in Vila Harbour. A little investigation will disclose a few gourmet restaurants and the ambience is as near to the traditional picture of a South Pacific island as you're likely to find.

On the short flight to Vanuatu from Australia, New Caledonia, Fiji, or New Zealand, it's hard to imagine that in about two or three hours you will be descending over Efate Island's endless acres of coconut palms. Your first hint of the important part these islands played in the Pacific war comes as you disembark at Bauer Field, named in honor of a gallant American airman. Melanesian officials, brown and sturdy, in their new green uniforms, whisk you through the few formalities with a minimum of fuss.

Old Vila hands stay at Le Lagon. Newly christened Le Lagon Pacific Resort, this lovely cluster of thatched roofs on Erakor Lagoon has been totally rebuilt and refurbished. This is a notable hotel in anyone's language. At the height of the winter season, or ticking over quietly between times, Le Lagon never gives any sign of hustle or crowding. But for lovers of peace and solitude, the rooms and bungalows dotted among huge trees and slender palms provide a blissful escape from the worries of day-to-day life.

The new Iririki Island Resort on the island of that name looks over the harbor to Vila Town. Bungalows nestle among big trees and flowering shrubs, climbing the hill to restaurant and bar. There are a big pool and a small beach, the ambience is upscale and elegant, and the cuisine gourmet, with dancing nightly to the hotel duo.

The Intercontinental Island Inn at Tassiriki is set at the far end of the lagoon. The need for more rooms for visitors to Vila has been obvious for some time, since the word about the fascinations of Vanuatu began to filter through the Pacific, and this new hostelry will certainly help to meet the growing demand. There is an excellent hairdresser here and a lively disco operates nightly in the Ravenga Room. Yachtsmen and diving groups tend to stay in town at *Rossi's* on the waterfront. A snack menu is available on the terrace. Another modestly charming hostelry near Vila township is Solaise—also a favorite gathering place for locals. If economy is uppermost in your mind, one of the small rooms in this single-story complex set around a shady swimming pool could well suit you. Overlooking beautiful Vila harbor, the Vate Marina, a few minutes from the post office, is a good place for budget-conscious travelers. And the old Vate Hotel (renamed The Olympic) right in town has been almost gutted and totally refurbished with excellent cooking facilities. The restaurant on the ground floor is popular with discriminating diners.

If you want a change from your hotel, take off aboard trimaran or ketch for a three-day cruise around Efate and the small offshore islands, visiting tribes, buying mats, diving, fishing, and picnicking. Ask at your hotel's tour desk about this. If one day on the ocean is enough, try a relaxing sail on a cruiser with a picnic lunch and all the sun you can soak up to loosen those knots you came here with.

Excursions by road outside Vila are not as smooth as excursions by sea. But if you are looking for a day out, drive around the island either by rental car or with one of the many tours, stopping at Eton Beach for a swim and lunch.

Closer to Vila, Susan Barnes' Whitesands Country Club at Rentabao offers riding through the rain forest, swimming 200 yards from the Clubhouse. Succulent lunches are available on order. An idyllic scene, the mounts are first rate, and both experts and beginners are welcome. Or you can eat at Nagar Hall right on the beach at Paunangisu where fresh seafoods, grills, and chicken are featured on a moderately priced menu.

Among resorts near Vila is Hideaway, a minuscule island retreat on a five-acre atoll about half an hour by water taxi from the township, or less if you drive the 15 minutes by road to the jetty that looks over toward the island. But don't settle for a day trip—stay a few nights. Lush vegetation and your own private piece of lagoon make this an informal resort to dream about. Snorkel; go coral viewing on Mele Bay. The surrounding waters are densely populated with marine life—they're also a marine reserve. Diving is becoming a feature of this small resort island. The emphasis is on local foods, admirably cooked.

Erakor Island, set on an atoll opposite Le Lagon, is a delightful little bungalow resort run by Australian Val Ireland in conjunction with Erakor village. Great food, comfortable accommodations, and an extra bonus in the form of a ruined chapel and missionary graves.

Manuro Paradise is different—30 miles from Vila, with the most unusual beach scene in the area. The Pacific has carved a rectangular lagoon through the coral rock, sloping up to a sugar-white beach. Bungalows dot the grassy sward, and the food is great. Check to be sure it's open, though.

Back at Vila, shopping in the little township is an adventure. Travelers browse in the Chinese and Vietnamese shops, dark aromatic treasure-houses. Serious collectors of artifacts and shells investigate Island Crafts and Handikraf Blong Vanuatu. A colorful market opposite the Government Building sells shells, artifacts, clothing, and produce on Wednesday, Friday, and Saturday. The Cultural Center has an interesting display of artifacts and shells.

French influence ensures you'll eat well in this far-flung series of dots on the wide Pacific. There's a handful of excellent restaurants in Vila. Good French cooking is the norm, varied by Italian, Vietnamese, and European. You can also buy delicious cheeses and fresh bread in town from the two big trade stores—Burns and Philp and Ballande—both on Kumul Highway, the main street, or collect takeaways at the *Solaise Motel.*

It's a relaxed scene in Port Vila. The atmosphere is informal, there's no tipping, and tariffs are very moderate by today's standards. This is a duty-free area too, and bargains abound.

Leave yourself plenty of time in these islands. This is a destination where things tend to crop up, adventures materialize, opportunities arise. You'll meet a new kind of people—warm-hearted, eccentric, generous, and hospitable. It's Jack London country, large as life and twice as crazy.

The Outer Islands—Tanna

The next stop on your exploration program could be Tanna, where Captain James Cook saw the glow from the sacred volcano Yasur miles out to sea. The copper-skinned Tannese call their lush island "the navel of the world." You can fly down to Tanna from Vila with Air Melanésie in about an hour, with a possible way stop at Erromanga, "the martyr isle," dubiously distinguished for wholesale murders of missionaries last century.

The plane approaches Tanna over a coastline jumble of red and black boulders washed by the aqua and emerald colors of the reef. You skim over the treetops of the rain forest. From the air the grassy airstrip looks like a cricket pitch, but it's twice the size of the one I landed on the first time I visited Tanna a few years ago.

At the reed and thatch bungalows at Epul Bay, *Tanna Beach Resort* offers good accommodations, a Vila-class restaurant, and cold beer from the bar. It's a lovely spot—rustic, but civilized. The bungalows are scattered among the coconut palms on grassy slopes rolling to a spectacular black sand beach.

At Whitegrass, Chief Tom Numake's bungalows overlook a rocky cove. A small restaurant serves wine and food, and your host will arrange excursions.

In the hill villages behind Epul Bay a cautious approach will pay dividends. These are proud and dignified people, not to be intruded upon with impunity. But as everywhere, good manners are a key to friendly acceptance. A pocketful of candy helps, too.

Villages are the ultimate in primitive living. Bamboo and nipa huts stand a mere five feet at the ridgepole. A rough barrier of logs keeps the pig population out of the dark and smoky interiors. Once Tannese reserve is breached you may be given oranges, and you can occasionally buy a mat or a Tannese grass skirt. If your village neighbors approve of you, there's a chance you might be invited to a "custom" dance—a nightlong feast of primeval music, color, and excitement.

The island is incredibly fertile. Tanna's ten-foot topsoil grows yams six feet long. In the rain forest the margin of a deep pool makes a perfect picnic spot. The indigo ocean crashes in white foam on glistening beaches, black and white. Herds of magnificent wild horses roam at White Grass, and the mighty stallions snort defiance at you, as you are driven by the tourist bus over the high plateau.

There's even a pocket volcano thrown in, with performance almost to order. The area around the volcano is also the headquarters of the Jon Frum movement, a cargo cult that originated on Tanna during the war. A belief arose that Jon Frum would ultimately appear, probably by plane, in the form of refrigerators, trucks, canned food, cigarettes, and all the enormous variety of material goods that had suddenly begun to pour into these islands as part of the American war effort. Jon Frum symbols, which include crosses painted red, may be photographed but should not be touched. Permission to climb the volcano must be obtained from the neighboring village. Tour Vanuatu and Air Tropicana run day tours.

The Outer Islands—Espiritu Santo

You can find a lot of adventure in a couple of weeks in Vanuatu; Espiritu Santo, largest island in the group, presents a picture totally different from either Efate or Tanna.

You fly into Santo from Vila with Air Melanésie or from Honiara with Solair, over a canopy of rain forest, interrupted here and there along the coast by the orderly ranks of coconut plantations. Relics of the Pacific war are everywhere on this island. The remains of fighter planes rust in the dense bush. And the jungle has overtaken the miles of market gardens that once supplied New Zealand and U.S. troops. Now, however, the dogs of war are silent in the Coral Sea, and today Santo sleeps in the sun.

Bokissa Island is a real hideaway, separated from the Santo mainland by the big island of Aore. Fifteen minutes by runabout and you find a Crusoe situation, but with all the amenities. Great swimming and diving, easy walks, a pool, and excursions. Good cooking, a varied library, and all the board games you've ever heard of.

The Hotel Santo will be your base on the mainland. It's small, modern, but full of atmosphere. The locals gather at the bar before lunch and dinner. You'll hear tall tales of the Pacific from Scottish supercargoes, Fijian first mates, Melanesian administration officers, Chinese storekeepers. Look around at the paintings, the montages, the ancient artifacts on the walls. Decoration is by Marcel Moutouh, who completed his paintings for the 22 bedrooms in an incredible two-month burst of effort.

Your choice of restaurants in this little township is limited, but the food is as intriguing as Santo itself. Down at the end of the empty main street, is Pinocchio, a typical French bistro. Little Saigon is new, too, with a Vietnamese menu. The formidable Mme. Harbulot dispenses fresh local food in the French manner at a new venue at Chez Lulu.

This island is a storehouse of local custom and wartime history. It's for travelers who like to find their own adventure. Shorter trips include Fanafo village, and the heavily forested South Santo coast where you may still see a "man bush" in traditional dress walking along the coral road. Santo isn't the thriving copra and cattle center it was before independence—only 200 Europeans remain there now—but for the adventurous traveler it still offers much of interest.

Divers will find plenty to do in Santo. There are myriads of fishy wonders, an infinite variety of shells to be gathered, and also the immense wreck of the 32,000-ton troopship *President Coolidge* to be explored. She lies on her side in the Segond Canal, the bow in 80 feet, the stern in about 240 feet of water. This area is an underwater paradise for both reef and wreck divers. Their contact will be Allan Power, who can be reached at the hotel. Resident in Santo for many years and keeper of the local underwater monuments, Power is a world-famous diver who knows the wrecks and the fish who inhabit them. His underwater photography has been featured in *International Photography*.

In Santo there's lots of lovely gossip, as in all Pacific outposts. The coconut wireless may give a garbled version of the truth, but what it lacks in accuracy, it makes up for in color. Given access to local rumor, you'll never need to open those paperbacks you brought with you. Regional half-truths are much stranger than fiction.

PRACTICAL INFORMATION FOR VANUATU

HOW TO GET THERE. *Air Caledonie International* flies to Vila from Sydney (Mondays and Saturdays), from Melbourne (Sundays), from Brisbane (Fridays), from Auckland (Sundays), and from Noumea (daily except Wednesdays). *Air Pacific* flies from Nadi (Tuesdays and Saturdays). *Air Nauru* flies from Auckland (Sundays). *Solair* flies from Honiara twice a week. *Ansett* flies from Sydney (Sundays). *Air Vanuatu* flies from Sydney (Saturdays).

CLIMATE. Semi-tropical with average of 70° May-October, 80° November-May. Humid and often rainy January-February.

Average Temperature (°Fahrenheit) and Humidity

Vila	Jan	Feb	Mar	Apr	May	June	July	Aug	Sept	Oct	Nov	Dec
Average max. day temperature	85°	87°	85°	83°	81°	80°	78°	79°	79°	82°	83°	85°
Days of rain	22	20	23	20	19	18	17	14	16	15	17	19
Humidity, percent	75	76	78	76	74	73	72	70	70	68	69	69

General hints: Note that the seasons are reversed from the northern hemisphere. May to October are good months for tourists. Humidity is high year-round.

CLOTHING. Informal the year round. Daytime, cotton dresses or slacks for women, slacks or shorts for men. No ties. Evening, light long or short dresses for women; for men, slacks.

CURRENCY. Monetary unit the vatu; current rate: 100 vatu = $US1.04.

ENTRY FORMALITIES. A passport is required of all visitors. No visas required for stays of 30 days or less. Onward tickets required.

HEALTH. Medical services available in most areas likely to be visited. It is advisable to take anti-malarial tablets once weekly, starting one week before arrival and continuing for four weeks after leaving the area. As in all tropical regions, it is advisable to equip yourself with remedies against upset stomachs. There are no dangerous animals or insects in Vanuatu.

WATER. The Government Water Board assures visitors it is safe to drink from the tap, but if you are prone to digestive disorders, it may be best for you to boil tap water or stick to the bottled variety.

LANGUAGES. English and French are spoken. Pidgin English and many other dialects are also used in Vanuatu.

ELECTRICITY. 220–240 volts, 50 cycles, 2 prong plugs.

TIPPING. Not in Vanuatu, please. It is contrary to Melanesian customs.

POSTAGE. The post office is located on Kumul Highway, the main street. Hours: 7:30 A.M.–11:15 A.M.; 1:15 P.M.–4:30 P.M. Saturday 7:30 A.M.–11 A.M. Postage rates: Australia and New Zealand, letters 35 vatu, postcards 30 vatu; U.S., letters 45 vatu, postcards 40 vatu; Europe, letters 55 vatu, postcards 50 vatu.

TIME ZONE. GMT plus 11 hours, or 19 hours ahead of U.S. Pacific Standard Time.

ACCOMMODATIONS. With the reawakening of tourism in Vanuatu has come an upgrading of accommodations. Vila now boasts three hotels that can fairly claim to be expensive by world standards. *Le Lagon* alone has spent $US24 million on refurbishing and the *Intercontinental Inn* and smaller *Rossi's* and *Solaise* have had extensive renovation. The motel-apartment scene is also attractive, especially for families, ranging from apartments right in town to tiny islands where you can swim, snorkel, or just lie in the sun. The price categories are as follows: *Expensive,* $US96–$US123; *moderate,* $US32–$US50; *Inexpensive,* $US16–$US30. Most hotels accept American Express, Diners Club, Visa, or MasterCard, but it's wise to take cash to outer-island resorts.

Vila

Intercontinental Island Inn. *Expensive.* Erakor Lagoon. Box 215; 2040. 166 rooms, air conditioning, all facilities, room service, 2 restaurants, 2 bars, pool. Shops, hairdresser, tour desk. Golf (9 holes), tennis. Conference facilities. Bank, boutique, disco. All cards.

Iririki Island Resort. *Expensive.* Box 230, 3388. Telex 1080. Situated in lovely Vila Harbour, 5 minutes by hotel's own 24-hour ferry from Vila waterfront. Deluxe bungalows, air conditioning and fans, in-house video, restaurant, poolside bar, dancing at night.

Le Lagon. *Expensive.* Erakor Lagoon. Box 86; 2313. Telex 2313. 115 rooms, 25 bungalows on Erakor Lagoon. Air conditioning, all facilities, refrigerator. Some suites, to accommodate 5. The Michoutouchkine restaurant for fine cuisine and a verandah cafe. 2 bars, pool. All water sports, golf course (9 holes), cruises, films, dancing daily in the *Pilioko* piano bar. Conference facilities. Shops, tour desk. Both restaurants offer excellent cuisine. AE, DC.

Erakor Island. *Moderate.* Box 24; 2983. In the lagoon of the same name. Simple bungalows, great food. 24 hr. boat service to mainland. American Express.

Olympic Hotel, *Moderate.* Box 709; 2464. Telex 1090 OLYMPIC. Right in town, popular with business people. Well-equipped apartments overlooking town and harbor. Secretarial services, telex, AE, DC.

Rossi's. *Moderate.* Rue Higginson. Box 11; 2528. Oldest established hotel in Vanuatu. 32 rooms, air conditioning, and all facilities. Restaurant, bar. Undergoing extensive modernization. All cards.

Solaise. *Moderate* Rue Picardie. Box 810; 2150. Telex 1065 SOLAISE. 16 units 5 min. from town, each with shower-room, refrigerator. Light breakfast included. Fans. Restaurant, bar, pool, garden. Weekly rates after two weeks. Varied menu, excellent cooking. AE, DC.

Coral Apartments. *Inexpensive.* Box 810; 3569. Telex 1065 SOLAISE. Self-contained studio apartments. 5 minutes from P.O. American Express, Diners Club.

Marina Motel. *Inexpensive.* In town on Erakor Road, Box 56; 2566. Telex 1111 VANTEX MARINAVILA. 12 air conditioned apartments, pool, harbor view.

Out of Town

Hideaway. *Moderate.* Mele Island. Box 875; 2963. Telex 1052 VLITRS. 6 miles from Vila, 3-minute ferry service to island. 10 bungalows, restaurants, bar, tariff incl. Swimming, snorkeling, diving, good food. AE.

Teouma Village Holiday Resort. *Inexpensive.* Box 651; 3241. Telex 1072 TEOU-MA. Charming garden complex of 2 bedroom apartments on Erakor Lagoon. Safe swimming, baby-sitters. AE, DC.

Vila Chaumieres. *Inexpensive.* Box 400; 2866. Bungalows, good facilities, popular bar.

Santo

Bokissa Island Resort. *Moderate.* Box 261, Boulissa. Telex 1099. 4 miles offshore from Santo, 8 attractive bungalows, pool, good food, snorkeling, fishing. A Crusoe Scene. AE, DC.

Hotel Santo. *Moderate.* Box 178, Luganville; 250. Ten minutes from airport. 22 rooms. French restaurant, bar, swimming pool, curio shop, game room. Air conditioned. Tours arranged. AE.

Tanna

Tanna. *Moderate.* Tanna Beach Resort; bookings Tour Vanuatu, tel. 2745; or Air Melanésie, tel. 2643, both Kumul Highway (main street). 9 bungalows at Epul Bay. New management. Licensed bar and restaurant, fresh local food—lobster, fish, steak. Volcano excursions, wild horses. AE.

Chief Tom Numake's Bungalows. *Economical.* Box 5, Lenakel. Bookings Air Melanésie, tel. 2643, or Tour Vanuatu, tel. 2745, both Kumul Highway (main street). Small restaurant and bar. Tours to volcano, wild horses; Tom's a good host.

RESTAURANTS. Vila. Even though Vila is a small town of around 15,000 inhabitants, these include about 10,000 Melanesians, 2,000 Europeans, and a smattering of Vietnamese, Chinese, Gilbertese, Fijians, Tahitians, and Tongans, and eating out is therefore an adventure. It must be stressed that in these remote islands changes are frequent. But you are pretty certain to find good and often superb cuisine in the unpretentious eating houses of your choice. Service will not be swift in this languorous ambience, but it will be pleasant, and after all this is not a place to come if you must rush madly around. We note the best of a surprisingly wide choice of restaurants and snack bars. Most restaurants in the *Expensive* or *Moderate* categories accept major credit cards, but check before you book. Price categories for dinner (wine not included): *Expensive,* $US20–$US27; *Moderate,* $US16–$US18; *Inexpensive,* $US10–$US15.

Expensive

Kwang Tung. Rue Carnot (Chinese Alley); 2284. Good Chinese cooking. Evenings daily.

L'Houstalet. Erakor Road; 2303. French cuisine.

Michoutouchkine. Le Lagon Hotel; 2313. Extensive menu, wonderful outlook over Erakor Lagoon. Evenings only.

Pandanus. Teouma Road; 2552. Beautiful setting at the head of the lagoon.

Reflections. In Olympic Hotel; 3639. Good cooking.

Rendezvous. Central Vila; 3045. First-class French cuisine and seafood.

Reriki Restaurant. At Iririki Island resort; 3388. Elegant, great food, music with dinner. 24-hr. ferry operates here.

Tassiriki Room; Intercontinental Hotel; 2040. Charming restaurant *intime.* Reservations.

Moderate

La Cabane. Wharf Road; 2763. Rustic restaurant, good food, Tahitian ambience, a warm welcome from Felix Tehei. Spontaneous music after dinner most nights.

Ma Barkers. Right in town opposite taxi rank; 2399. Familiar menu, excellent fish and grills, well presented. Reasonable.

Rossi's. Next to ANZ Bank on main road; 2528. Blackboard menu at reasonable prices. On The Terrace overlooking Vila harbour.

Teppanyaki. Airport Road; 3373. Piano bar.

Trader Vic's. Beautiful setting on harbor. Fine food.

Waterfront Restaurant. Next door to Yachting World; 3490. A roundhouse set on the shore of Vila Harbour, a step from town centre. Select your own steak, fish, or chicken to be barbecued; big salad bar.

Inexpensive

Binh Dan. Freshwater Road en route to Intercontinental Inn; 2287. Vietnamese specialties; new and popular. Dinner only.

Bloody Mary's. Main Road (Kumul Highway). At the market. Excellent quick food, reasonable.

Chalet. Main Road (Kumul Highway). Excellent snacks. Also main dishes like goulash and wiener schnitzel cooked under the eye of M. Brenner, late of Czechoslovakia via Papua-New Guinea.

Ichise. Wharf Road; 2470/2699. Delicious traditional Japanese food and service. Parties can book small dining room.

Solaise. Rue Picardie; 2150. A blackboard menu in a relaxed ambience, a short walk from the center of town. Pizza, crêpes, fresh-caught fish. Also take-aways.

La Tentation. Salon du Thé in Raffea Building. Sinfully delicious patisseries.

La Terrasse. Main road (Kumul Highway). Snacks, French-café ambience, excellent menu, reasonable.

Santo

In a township that is little more than a hamlet,—you can still eat well. Check for new restaurants when you arrive—like Vila, but on a much smaller scale, the eating out situation in Santo changes frequently. If the cook hasn't just left, the food will be excellent, and prices will be moderate.

Chez Lulu. Close to Hotel Santo on back road; 4215. Features local foods. Access by boat. Good eating here.

Hotel Santo Restaurant. Main street; 250. Not the gourmet restaurant it once was, but reasonably good plain food.

Little Saigon. Main street. A shoebox of a restaurant serving tasty Vietnamese food.

Pinocchio. Main street. A new addition to the Santo scene. Small French café-bar-restaurant, attractive menu changes daily. Seafood is a specialty.

Oceania. Main street. Good Chinese food, next to Hotel Santo.

HOW TO GET AROUND. By air: *Air Melanésie* (tel. 2643) flies regular schedules to many parts of the group; charter services available. *Air Tropicana* (tel. 2836) also covers groups on regular basis or charter.

By car: Taxis, depot in town, available from all hotels. Rental: Avis, tel. 2533; Hertz, tel. 2244, Box 128. National Car Rental at Socametra, tel. 2977; Budget Rent-a-Car, minimokes, tel. 3170. **By bike:** *I.S. Rentals,* for mopeds or motorbikes, is on the corner of Wharf Road, next to Ichise Restaurant.

In Santo, **by bus and car:** Regular bus service from wharf to town on cruiseship days and mini-buses operated by hotels, transfers to Pekoa airstrip. **Taxis:** large number of taxis fitted with meters, reasonable charges. Check fare for longer trips before hire. *Melanesia Rent-a-Car* —contact Mary Miu, tel. 325. And remember to drive on the right.

SEASONAL EVENTS *February 14th.* Jon Frum, Tanna Island. Jon Frum cargo-cult rituals on Tanna Island, mainly at Sulphur village, include dances, parades, feast for the expected return of Jon Frum.

May (generally). Land-Divers of Pentecost Island, several times yearly. Diving from 70-ft. tower built around a tree. Vines are attached to ankles to break the fall. Usually performed by the pagan village of Bunlap (South Pentecost). Arranged by Tour Vanuatu, Vila, at a high cost. The 23-meter *Concoola* conducts 6-day Pentecost Jump cruises, generally in April and May. For information, contact Box 611; tel. 3271.

July 30th. Independence Day, Military parade, speeches, ball at night.

End of August. Toka Dance, Tanna Island. Impressive native feast according to custom. Includes dances, killing of pigs by clubs, etc. Circumcision ceremonies are usually held during this period at Tanna.

September. Tanna Agricultural Show.

October. Vila Agricultural Show.

December 23–25. Christmas festivities. Arrival of Père Noel at Vila. Church services, choir singing and ball in main centers.

Holidays. All government offices, banks, and most private offices are closed on the following days—sometimes on the day before and after, too.

January 1—New Year's Day. Easter. May 4th—Ascension Day. July 30th—Independence Day. December 23rd–25th—Christmas holidays.

TOURS. *Vanuatu Visitors Bureau,* Box 209, Port Vila.

Pentecost Land Divers: This event, usually held in May, can be scheduled for special occasions at different times of the year. A trip worthwhile to see these fabulous Pentecost divers. Men dive from 70-foot tower (head first) with vines attached to their ankles to break the fall.

Vila Township: (1½ hours) Drive covers downtown Vila, residential area, courthouse, college, police barracks and a native village. Before returning to hotel, tour continues to top of Klems Hill for a harbor view of Vila with a short stop at another small village. *Mele Village* (full day): Travel to Mele Village. Meet local people. Trip also includes ride on outrigger canoe. Time for swiming, shelling, snorkeling, or loafing. Picnic lunch (included in price) before returning to Vila. *Efate Safari* (Full day): Travel 76-mile route through some of the most rugged terrain of Vanuatu. Tour east coast past beaches to Forari for a view of the islands of Mao, Pele, and Kukula. Visit Church of All Denominations, drive through several villages and plantations. Picnic lunch before returning to Vila. *Volcano Skyrama* (2½ hours): An extensive view of Vanuatu's volcanoes. *Air Melanesia* aircraft leaves at 5:30 A.M. and flying between the peaks of Mataso Island, heads toward the island of Tongoa to view underwater volcano. Tour continues toward Lopevi, one of the most active volcanoes in the islands, to see red-hot lava flowing down sides into steaming sea. View the island of Ambrym to see smoking volcano Benboy and other nearby volcanoes, back to Vila, passing coast of Malekula, home of primitive Big Nambas tribe. *Glass-Bottom Boats* (2 hours): Tour sea world of Erakor Lagoon aboard *Coral Sea* glass-bottom boat. Underwater life specialist describes tropical coral and sea life. *Primitive Tanna Island* (Full day): Fly *Air Melanesia* or *Air Tropicana* to Tanna Island. Transfer to four-wheel Land Rover for plantation tour, then continue through dense jungle bush through the mountains to Kings Cross (the island center). Cross the ash plain of Siwi Lake to Yasur volcano. Drive almost to crater edge for view of lava. Also visit subterranean volcanic tubes, until recently considered taboo. *Hideaway Island Cruise* (full day): Cruise aboard 41-foot catamaran to Mele Bay to Hideaway Island. Snorkel, swim before lunch at resort before return to Vila harbor via Pango Coast and Fila Island. Departs Sunday, Tuesday, Thursday. *South Pacific Cruises:* 3-day cruise round Efate, outlying islands; or 6–12 days to Ambrym, Pentecost, Santo in sailing ship *Coongoola. Vaterama:* (45 min.) *Air Melanesia* flight with panoramic views of Efate, the capital island of Vanuatu. Follow coast road by air with views of the outlying islands of Mele, Nguna, Mataso, Moso, and Hat Island. Also views of wartime airstrip of Coin Hill and Havannah, with pass over the international hotel Le Lagon. *Air Tropicana* for variety of Air Adventure Tours—Tanna, Santo, Ambrym and local sightseeing round Efate. All these tours may be booked by Tour Vanuatu at their office on Kumul Highway (main street), tel. 2745, 3096, or 3035, or at their offices at the Hotel le Lagon and the Intercontinental Island Inn.

Valor Tours, 10 Liberty Ship Way, Sausalito, CA 94965. Specializes in veterans' tours with organized programs throughout the South Pacific (and the world). Future plans include sending a number of units who served in the Pacific Theater to that area. They work with national and civic leaders of the host country. Write for complete details on individual or group tours to World War II sites.

Other tour operators include *Tour Vanuatu,* tel. 2745; *Frank King Tours,* tel. 2808; *Pan Tours,* tel. 3160.

TOURS AROUND VILA. Reef, fishing, and sailing expeditions: *Frank King Tours,* opposite the market, next to the government buildings. This tour agency has a great variety of interesting tours including glass-bottom-boat tours, sunset cruise, wine and cheese, coral viewing by underwater floodlight. Also enjoy Frank's *L'Espadon II* luxury cruise, which includes snorkeling, swimming, and lunch on Hideaway Island. *Escapade:* a 43-ft. game fishing cabin-cruiser, twin Diesel fitted for diving, top class fishing equipment, day-trips, and charter. *Nautilus Dive Shop,* N.Z. U.A. instructors, scuba diving, snorkeling for both experts and beginners; tel. 2398. Other tours: *Vila Roundabout Bus Tour; Nature Walks; Frank King's Visitors Club,* free services and restrooms for tourists; opposite the market.

SPORTS. *Vila Tennis Club,* on Freshwater Road; *Le Lagon Golf Club* (free to guests); *Port Vila Golf Club,* Mele Beach (green fees 500 vatu; *Squash Courts* (BESA Club), behind the post office; Horse riding, *Whitesands Country Club,* on the Rentabao Road, past the second lagoon; skin-diving, *Dive Action,* on the waterfront, Box 816, tel. 2837; *Nautilus,* on the Kumul Highway (main road), Box 78, tel. 2398; *Yachting World,* harborside next to Waterfront Restaurant; cruising and big-game fishing on Charlie Laub's *Rendezvous II,* Box 828, tel. 2124, or Gordon Neal's *Pacific Dream,* tel. 2745; *Scuba Holidays,* Hideaway Island, Box 875, tel. 2963.

SHOPPING. Vila may be small, but the real traveler with an inquiring mind, a degree of patience, and a nose for a bargain can have loads of fun in the shops, boutiques, and trade stores in-between swimming in that fabulous lagoon and indulging the flesh in the town's restaurants and nightclubs. Vila is a tax-free area for most luxuries. When budgeting be prepared for local 10% tax on tourist services and a 1,000 vatu (approx. $US10) departure tax.

If artifacts are your thing, and you yearn for a puppet from Malekula, an ancestor figure from Ambrym, or an intricately carved comb from Tongoa, then your first stop in Vila town will be at *Island Carvings,* Judith Wood's crowded shop, now in former U.T.A. premises on the Olympic Hotel Corner. You know you'll get the real thing here—this lively Australian does her own buying on trips that range from Tonga to the Trobriands, with emphasis, of course, on local Melanesian crafts. Prices are realistic and a chat with Judith Wood is an added bonus—she is one of the most knowledgeable dealers in the Pacific.

There are dozens of Chinese merchants up the narrow nameless streets of Vila. Jade, gold, ivory, transistors, tape recorders, portable hair dryers, cameras—all at duty-free prices. At the two big trade stores, British and French, look at kitchen gear, fabrics, and perfume; buy French cheese and pâtés to eat for lunch with a loaf of French bread; investigate the range of French and Spanish wines and bottles of tiny mandarines or plums in cognac. For stereo and electronic gear, *Sound Centre* is helpful.

In the Pilioko building *Sun Fashions* sells informal wear for women. At smaller establishments, the range won't be wide and you'll probably have to hunt for your size. Big news on the fashion scene is Australian Trudy Pohl for top-class leisure and swimwear from Europe and Israel.

Prouds, duty-free shop on the main street, sells jewelry, silver, and trinkets of every kind.

ART GALLERIES. Big news on the thriving Vanuatu art scene is the opening of *L'Atelier* by Suzanne Bastien, longtime resident of Vanuatu, friend of Crocq, Frank Fay, and Tatin, whose last show she organized and set up in Tahiti just before his death in 1982. This charming woman is greatly respected for her knowledge of art in all its forms and her understanding of what is best in an area well-known for its painters. She has the absolute eye of the real art lover. Look in at her gallery opposite the entrance of the Olympic Hotel for as exciting a collection of paintings as you will find anywhere in the South Seas.

A mile or so from Le Lagon Hotel along the road skirting the lagoon lies a trap for art lovers. The thatched "atelier-musée" of Nicolai Michoutouchkine sits among a collection of immense slit-gongs in the midst of a tangle of tropical trees and herbiage. French born, of Russian parentage, Michoutouchkine is a painter of originality and power. You can almost feel the miasmic vapors of the rain forest in his wildly colorful oils. His companion, Pilioko, comes from the island of Wallis, and was once the painter's protegé. These days this muralist, weaver of tapestries, and designer of fabrics stands on his own feet. In their shop in the Pilioko Building you can buy shirts, dresses, and pareos designed by Eliza Keil and hand printed by Vanuatu's most famous couple.

NIGHTLIFE. *L'Houstalet Disco,* Erakor Road; *Le Lagon* (Saturday-night disco and dancing in the Pilioko Piano Bar nightly); *Intercontinental* (disco nightly in the Ravenga Room); dinner dancing at *Iririki Island,* ferry takes five minutes from Vila.

NEW CALEDONIA

The Island of Light

by
KATHLEEN HANCOCK

When Captain James Cook discovered New Caledonia in the course of his second voyage to the Pacific in 1774, he found a stone-age Melanesian culture. The population of this 250-mile-long, cigar-shaped island was estimated to be about 50,000 and consisted of a number of warring tribes speaking 32 mutually unintelligible dialects. Papuan/Australoid in racial type, the New Caledonian was a rugged warrior, and in times of war a headhunter and a cannibal.

However, the tribe that met Cook when he landed at Balade on the east coast were unarmed and shy. Cook needed supplies of food, wood, and water, but all he could get was water because there was no food or firewood to spare. Apart from the fertile strip around the coast, this was a sterile land where mineral deposits overlaid by a cover of bush made the soil impossible to cultivate. Cook was delighted by the island, however. "So variegated the scene," he wrote, "that the whole might afford a picture for romance." The friendliness and honesty of the inhabitants also impressed the crew.

D'Entrecasteaux followed in Cook's wake some years later. He heard the night cries of seabirds on reefs north of the Loyalty Group off the big island's east coast and hastily made off in the other direction to anchor at Balade in 1793. However, unlike Cook, he found the people surly, dishonest, and warlike and could hardly believe Cook's report of them. But it seems that this extraordinary alteration in the tribes of Balade was caused not by any basic change in the nature of the New Caledonians, but by the famine, drought, and intertribal wars that had intervened.

No one worried much about New Caledonia for the next 50 years. Then French Catholic missionaries established themselves at Balade in 1843, but pillage, arson, and murder were the order of the day, and cannibalism was commonplace. Many a sandalwooder was killed, baked, and eaten with a side dish of yams. However, a little research into early accounts of the goings on of sandalwood crews and traders reveals that their behavior wasn't calculated to create a friendly climate in these islands, and it was generally their own fault that they ended up in the earth oven.

Hot on the heels of the missionaries, John Paddon, English ex-seaman, set up as a trader in New Caledonia, and in 1845 he bought Ile Nou and established his trading station there. Dealing in sandalwood, whale oil, and tortoise shell, he brought groups of settlers from Australia to the as yet unclaimed island in his own ships. It looked as though the scene was set for a new British colony.

But the British delayed; neither the Colonial Office nor Queen Victoria was interested in acquisition. And the French had their own ideas about this remote island. The massacre of 17 naval personnel in the northwest in 1850 had enraged public opinion in France. Further, the establishment of a naval base in the southwest Pacific seemed a good thing. Finally, most pressing of all, the setting up of a prison colony with a climate less hostile than the pestilential vapors of infamous Guiana was felt in Paris to be an urgent matter.

So in 1853 the tricolor was raised at Balade by Admiral Febvrier Despointes. Ten years later the first shipload of convicts were building their own prison on Ile Nou, sold by Paddon to the French for a tidy sum. About this time the French realized that three British missionaries were firmly established in the Loyalty Islands only 50 miles off the New Caledonian mainland. A small "force de frappe" set off for Lifou, where they were confronted by 500 islanders led by the Rev. Macfarlane, a fiery Scots parson. After a bit of skirmishing, the better-armed French subdued the islanders and their leader, declaring the group French territory.

Until penal transportation was abolished in 1898 there were, in any year, between 7,000 and 10,000 able-bodied criminals in the colony, engaged for the most part in mining the nickel that had been discovered by Jules Garnier in 1865. They were also employed on public works—many of New Caledonia's older public buildings date back to this time.

The deportees' lot was regarded in those days as not too uncomfortable. It wasn't unusual to see 50 prisoners controlled only by a man in uniform carrying a white umbrella. And 20 years later, George Griffiths, an English traveler, found Nouméa's nonchalant acceptance of the concerts provided by the prison band in the Place des Cocotiers "quite bizarre." He remarked that the "chef d'orchestre" had cut the heart out of a man he considered his rival in his wife's affections, got her to cook it, and dined off it with her before revealing its origin.

Legend has it that a Comte des Baue, at Les Beaux, in Provence established this gastronomic precedent, serving the head of his wife's lover to his adulterous spouse.

But not all the deportees were common criminals. The Communards, who were sent out in the thousands after the collapse of the Paris Commune, were birds of a very different feather, honest workers and intellectuals for the most part. The Arabs who were exiled after the Kabyle revolt in Algeria were also political prisoners. But few of these were imprisoned at Ile Nou. Some were confined on the Ducos peninsula, but most finished up on the Isle of Pines, where they enjoyed comparative freedom on one of the loveliest and healthiest islands in the Pacific. The great majority of Communards were pardoned and returned to France after the amnesty of 1879.

For a good while after annexation, the Melanesians resisted the French, but there was only one uprising of any importance—the great "canaque revolt" of 1878, which cost the French 200 lives during a guerrilla campaign lasting more than a year. There is no record of Melanesian losses, but many villages were burned and crops destroyed during a long-drawn-out campaign that finally drew to a close when the Canala chiefs threw in their lot with the French.

From this time on the great mineral wealth of New Caledonia was developed in earnest. To fill the gap in the labor pool, Indonesian, Japanese, and Indo-Chinese indentured laborers were brought into the country on contract. Many of the Japanese remained when their time was up, intermarrying with European and Asian women. Most of the Vietnamese, however, chose to return after the end of World War II, when the French held a referendum enabling them to make a choice between returning to southeast Asia or remaining in the Pacific.

The Modern Scene

The outbreak of war in the Pacific led to great changes in this French colony. The island was stunned by the fall of France and shocked by the presence of the Vichy government in Nouméa. Feeling ran high, and finally Henri Sautot, French Resident Commissioner in the nearby New Hebrides, now Vanuatu, took steps. Supported by most of the populace of Nouméa and a great force of "broussards," or bush farmers, from the interior, he deposed the pro-Vichy regime and firmly placed New Caledonia on the side of Free France. In March 1942 he cordially received General Patch, who arrived in the sleepy harbor with 40,000 men in 15 large battleships, 10 cruisers, and several escort vessels.

Nouméa became an important American base, rated second for tonnage in the Pacific after San Francisco. Admiral Nimitz called the country the bastion from which the American offensives in the Solomons and the Philippines were launched. In New Caledonia they described it differently. "You couldn't pee behind a tree without peeing on an American," they complained. And no wonder, with something upward of 250,000 American troops in and around Nouméa at one time. But let it be said that there is still a great reservoir of good feeling and gratitude toward the thousands of Americans and New Zealanders who passed through New Caledonia during the war years.

Education is free and compulsory for all up to the age of 16. The little blue minibuses that scurry round Nouméa day and night are used by citizens of every color and income level. Round the tables at the city's restaurants and nightclubs you'll see blue-black Somalis and pale Europeans; sloe-eyed Vietnamese and sturdy Melanesians; dusky Martiniquai and Chinese-Tahitians. It's an atmosphere you can breathe in.

The Economy

Upcountry New Caledonia is pretty well a solid lump of minerals for the whole of its 200-mile length. It's a case of scratch a mountain and you find a mine in this big cigar-shaped island. Nickel, iron, cobalt, chrome, coal, manganese, antimony, copper, lead, and gold—you name it, they have it. Heading the list however, in vast quantity, is nickel, closely followed by chrome. The drop in world demand for chrome in the sixties caused the bottom to fall out of chrome mining, in spite of large deposits that are 50% pure ore. Today nickel has hit another low, and tourism is playing the major part in the country's economy. However, the big chrome mine at Tiébaghi has now reopened, mainly supplying the Chinese market.

Following their occupation of New Caledonia in 1853, the French wasted little time in investigating the mineral resources of the island. Jules Garnier, a government mining engineer, was sent out in 1863 and covered on foot and on horseback practically the whole of the wild and mountainous terrain of the new colony. He reported huge deposits of iron ore, copper, and chrome, but he is famous principally for his discovery of the nickel ore that now bears his name—Garnierite. His report on his findings, published in 1867, is a historical document, and he also developed methods of smelting nickel ore that were used by the first smelters built near Nouméa.

Garnier's discoveries were followed by the establishment of the Société le Nickel by John Higginson, an Irish-born entrepreneur who later became a French citizen. "Le Nickel" was well-established by the late 1870s, and until a few years ago the company enjoyed a virtual monopoly in New Caledonia. There are a good many independent mine operators, known locally as "petit mineurs," in spite of fortunes running into millions. The "petit mineurs" sell a lower grade ore direct to Japan, where it is processed in Japanese smelters, but this market is threatened today by recent nickel finds in the Philippines and Malaysia that are worked by cheap labor.

Most of the big mines are on the island's east coast, where the nature of the terrain makes the delivery of ore to ship a comparatively simple matter. Mining is open cast, usually high in the mountains or on plateaus well above the narrow shoreline. The ore is recovered by excavators, bulldozers, and power shovels and carried by immense 45-ton trucks to conveyors that send it directly down to the nickel ships on the coast. This economical and efficient method of working the rich deposits was born of necessity. New Caledonia could not produce a labor force large enough to cope with the demand, and almost total mechanization was the only answer.

The "Société le Nickel" draws on many countries for the raw materials required to operate this huge concern. Tankers bring fuel from the Persian Gulf; coal for the coking plant comes from Australia; gypsum is bought from Mexico; New Zealand provides timber for the company's housing schemes.

New Caledonia can view with satisfaction her reserves of ore which have been estimated to be the world's greatest. And "le Nickel" proposes to reopen one of the shut-down furnaces shortly. This promise, together with the reopening of the chrome mine at Tiébaghi, has given New Caledonia's faltering economy a welcome boost.

There are said to be many millionaires among Nouméa's 60,000 citizens. But in spite of all the money lying around, most New Caledonian housewives do their own work. They have to, because the labor shortage that has existed here for nearly a century, together with the highest wage scale of any other Pacific island territory, combine to reduce the domestic labor pool to less than a puddle.

Basic foods are pegged against inflation, and of course, in this French community, wine heads the list of basics. Bread is about the same price as in the U.S. The big difference here is that it comes warm, crusty, and fresh from the ovens twice daily, including Christmas Day, saints' days (of which there seem to be one a week), and all other holidays.

Compared to their Australian and New Zealand neighbors, New Caledonians pay a modest income tax. There's a solid payroll tax for all em-
ployers, worked out at from 25 percent to 30 percent of the pay packet.
This tax, from which all wage earners are exempt except for a 5.5 percent
contribution toward old-age pensions, covers the child benefit, pensions,
maternity allowances, a workers' housing scheme, and sundry other so-
cial-security measures. If you're self-employed—a doctor or lawyer, for
instance—you don't incur this tax, but you don't benefit from social securi-
ty either.

Two notable developments in New Caledonia have been the increase
in the population, which rose from 87,000 in 1963 to around 140,000 in
1979, and the development of tourism during the last ten years. The Melanesian population has risen during this period from about 41,000 to
around 60,500, while an influx of immigrants, mostly from France and
also from former north-African colonies, has boosted the European sector
from 33,000 to around 50,000. Today Polynesians from Wallis and Tahiti
number 17,000, and Vietnamese, Indonesians, ni-Vanuatu, and others
amount to nearly 12,000.

In the last 15 years or so tourism has seen its position in this territory
change from that of a Cinderella neglected in favor of its rich, ugly sister,
mining, to a position where it's regarded as a welcome partner in the economy. Nearby Australia and New Zealand provide most of the holiday visitors to New Caledonia, but the slightly scruffy charm of the city of Nouméa, combined with the beauty of the beaches, the reef, and the outer
islands, is rapidly making this a destination for travelers from further
afield, mainly Japan. Considering the world economic scene, the cost of
a holiday in these parts hasn't escalated nearly as much as might have
been expected.

Government

Today New Caledonia is a French Overseas Territory and an integral
part of France. This status was gained in 1958 following the crisis in
French politics that brought General de Gaulle to power. In response to
de Gaulle's call for a yes/no vote, 96 percent of the registered voters
turned out, and 74 percent of these opted for the new status.

All New Caledonian citizens of whatever race have French nationality,
electing a president of France and sending to Paris two deputies, a senator,
and a representative to the Economic and Social Council. The Mitte-
rand/Chirac government has made a start in buying back large tracts of
land to hand over to the Melanesian people, the cost being shared by the
territory and metropolitan France. France has had its hands full with various separatist organizations which refuse to recognize rule by Paris. Almost 40 people have been killed in clashes between the militant Kanaks
(indigenous people) and French forces. An independence referendum in
late 1987 to remain part of France passed by an overwhelming majority.
Separatists, claiming the support of 40 per cent of the population, boycott-
ed the referendum.

South Pacific Commission

Nouméa is also headquarters of the South Pacific Commission, housed
in the old U.S. Army buildings at Anse Vata Beach. The commission is
a kind of small United Nations of the South Pacific, and it is a heartening
example of cooperation between the nations who administer territories in
the South Pacific, the island territories themselves, and the increasing

number of independent Pacific nations. Its staff of experts advise and assist the territories in their area with problems of health, social, and economic development. It is a nonpolitical body and gives its services only on demand. A visit to its operational headquarters at Anse Vata is well worthwhile for those interested.

Food and Drink

Eating is a passion in New Caledonia, and you'll probably be given plenty of advice on where to find the best *crabe farcie,* the best *quenelles,* the best *couscous.* But since there are around 126 bistros, restaurants, and shrines to haute cuisine on the island, there's not the slightest possibility of your being able to sample the lot. Moreover, the scene changes frequently—they do say in these parts that a new restaurant opens every week and an old one closes. Space forbids a full catalog of eating in Nouméa in our Practical Information section, later. But one thing's for sure—you'll eat well. Costs can vary from moderate to as high as you care to go, but whichever way you play it, you'll revel in the cuisine. And when your liver or your wallet protests, Nouméa's excellent delicatessens and groceries will provide you with a delicious picnic lunch for a very small outlay. With a *baguette* of crunchy bread, a *tranche* of Brie and a bottle of *vin ordinaire,* it's no hardship to economize at lunchtime.

See the *Dining Out* section for editor's choice. Check closing days—they vary.

Exploring New Caledonia

There are lots of good reasons for a holiday in New Caledonia. Obvious ones like sun and sea and fishing, gourmet cooking, the beat of the *tamoure* in dark Tahitian nightclubs, and the scruffy charm of the city of Nouméa all spring instantly to mind. But what you don't expect to find is courtesy, kindness, and that easygoing amiability that's a peculiarly Pacific thing. In this intriguing French Pacific territory, believe it or not, even the taxi drivers are polite!

Early explorers had a name for this island that lies above the Tropic of Capricorn on the fringe of the Coral Sea. They called it the Island of Light. And whether you fly in from Australia, New Zealand, or Fiji, your first sight of land is breathtaking. The strange colors of mineral deposits streak fairytale peaks. A hundred promontories curve their way out to sea. Ten miles offshore the second biggest reef in the world glows jade and turquoise in the translucent ocean. As the aircraft loses height, you glimpse occasional sugar-white beaches between the green belt of coconut palms and the aquamarine waters of the great lagoon.

You're in a different world the moment you step out of the plane at Tontouta. Gendarmes in *képis* and very short shorts give the place a foreign-legion air. But there's nothing military about their duties here—they simply hurry you through entry formalities.

Even at the airport you get a taste of the fascinating complex of peoples that makes up the population of this Pacific outpost. Chic Frenchwomen mingle with brown Melanesians. There's a sprinkling of Indonesian sarongs, and a few tiny women wear the floppy black pants and white jacket of Tonkin. A group of Tahitians straight out of Gauguin stand next to a blue-black Somali off to Paris in a neat business suit.

A new shorter road to Nouméa cuts through rolling country covered with niaouli, cousin of the Australian eucalyptus. The bony, mineral-rich mountains make a dramatic backdrop to the scene. Breadfruit and banana grow by the wayside, and the gardens around the occasional bungalows vibrate with op-art colors—hot-pink hibiscus, magenta bougainvillea, scarlet poinsettia, and citron-yellow allamanda riot everywhere.

Nouméa

For most tourists their first sight of Nouméa is a big surprise. You expect to find a drowsy, humid, tropical town meandering round the shores of the harbor. But the reality is quite startling. Nouméa is a busy little city where the thermometer hovers pleasantly in the mid-seventies. The town clusters round a central square shaded by flame trees. A few tall palms give the Place des Cocotiers (Coconut Square) its name. Colonial buildings of faded pink stone nudge sparkling new structures of glass and concrete. There are chic boutiques with ready-to-wear from the great fashion houses of France. Dark little Indonesian or Tahitian shops are hung with shell necklaces, pandanus hats, and batik or pareu cloth. Chinese stores sell everything from incense burners to men's socks. In the back streets bougainvillea and Burmese honeysuckle spill over garden walls. Here and there among the shuttered houses you catch a glimpse of a cool courtyard.

The citizens of this tropical island are a multiracial mixture—French, Melanesian, Indonesian, Tahitian, Arab, Martiniquais, Somali. In this atmosphere integration is no problem. The population is divided up almost half and half European and Melanesian, with a sizable section of Polynesians from Tahiti and the Wallis Group. Vietnamese, Indonesians, and "others" make up the rest.

One of the foremost attractions of Nouméa is the transport system. From the bus depot on the Baie de la Moselle little blue minibuses scuttle round town and out to the beaches and suburbs. The bus leaves every 15 minutes and the standard fare will take you anywhere in town or the suburbs. The drivers—of every race and racial mixture—are an obliging lot, and a round-trip on a bus is an entertainment in itself.

Within the precincts of the town you realize that there's nothing sleepy about this little Paris of the Pacific. It moves! At 6 A.M. all Nouméa starts thinking of work, for shops and offices open at 7:30 A.M. and for a good half hour before that cars, scooters, and mopeds whizz along the narrow streets in a continuous stream. Most of the population seems to be on wheels, but the standard of living is high in these parts and no one rides the lowly bicycle. At this hour of the morning the balmy air is filled with a truly Gallic blaring of horns and screeching of brakes.

Mind you, all this bustle is largely on the surface—indulged in, one suspects, because of the lovely noise it makes. There's always plenty of time in this part of the Pacific, and the Caledonians have their own ideas about the important things in life—there'd be a riot if those long loaves of bread didn't issue from the bakers' ovens all day long.

The hubbub comes to an abrupt end at 11 A.M. Nouméa goes home, with a loaf of the mid-day baking under arm, and settles down for a lengthy French lunch and siesta. This is where the visitor has to look sharp. Eleven-thirty is the hour for lunch—and alas for the hapless tourist who wanders into a restaurant around 1:30 P.M. hoping to be fed.

New Caledonians live on and in the water. The yacht harbor is a forest of masts. Swimming in the limpid waters that surround this big island, skin diving off the reef, toasting on the white beaches—this is the New Caledonian way of life.

From the bays just out of town you can board a cruiser or catamaran for a day trip to Amedée atoll—a good way of enjoying all the charms of this informal sport-loving island. This isn't a trip for worshipers of muscular activity, it's for lotus eaters—though you can swim around the tiny atoll if you feel inclined. No, it's a place to lie on the sugar-white sand under a hau tree, dunking yourself in the translucent sea at intervals. Either the *Samara* or *Mary D* makes a good trip. *Samara,* captained by Jack Owen, provides the best lunch, cooked by his delightful Tahitian-Chinese wife, Christine, and accompanied by songs from the Tahitian crew.

Patrick and Minerva Helmy are charming bilingual hosts aboard the *Mary D,* for day trips to Amedeé lighthouse. And there's atoll living for naturists on M'Ba Island not far offshore in the great lagoon, offering swimming, snorkeling, volleyball, and other games (through *Hoki Mai* Cruises). You can eat superbly in Nouméa and dance on any night of the week. You'll try Tahitian fish, Indonesian curries, Italian pasta, Spanish paella, and Chinese specialties. You can sample every style of French cooking. The traditional French preoccupation with food and wine leads, of course, to a traditional French health problem. To hear one of the locals bemoaning the state of his liver while consuming an epicurean meal washed down by copious draughts of good red wine—this is an experience. "Too much exercise," mutters the sufferer, spearing another delectable morsel.

The Museum is also a must, with a comprehensive display of Melanesian artifacts, including a *grande case* (a chief's house) in an open court, and a more general display of artifacts from the South Pacific.

Between Anse Vata beach and the Baie des Citrons, Dr. Catala's world-famous aquarium attracts scientists from all over. A new wing dramatically displays the vivid colors of the unique collection of living deep-sea corals, creating the effect of actually being submerged on the night-dark floor of the ocean home of these extraordinary creatures. You will probably have to be dragged away from the fishy and coral wonders that are displayed here with such taste.

On weekends sturdy Melanesian women provide a free show with their cricket matches at the square near the gendarmerie. French citizens of every race and color play *pétanque,* a kind of bowls, under the spreading palms in the Place des Cocotiers. Eating can be expensive at night, but it often costs no more than cuisine of an equivalent standard at home. And a picnic lunch will more than even things up. In addition, you can dance all night in the city's *boîtes* for the price of a drink or two. Tipping is absolutely forbidden in this civilized island.

Down at the docks you can still find the traditional bead-curtained bistros, where a beer or an aperitif can lead to an amiable encounter with the locals. And there's entertainment at the wharves where inter-island ferrys are crowded with outer islanders in a dazzle of gay *muumuus.*

Outside Nouméa

But however intriguing Nouméa may be, it's not the whole story. If you're one for open spaces, Melanesian villages, trade stores, and deserted beaches fringed with rustling palms, then you've got to make another choice. You can fly to Touho on the east coast with Air Calédonie and from there potter up north, either by country bus, if you're rugged, or by rental car.

Up country, inns are small and informal, and mostly operated by the local tribe; the plumbing works, in spite of a tendency for the towel rail to fall to the floor. The food is generally first rate, with the accent on local fish, crab, and oysters. It will be good French bourgeois cooking, and what more could you want? In these parts you come across old churches that look like illustrations to a book of fairytales, and the Melanesian villages have a picture-book quality too.

Finally a geological surprise awaits the visitor to Hienghène, farther up the coast. The road winds through light forest hung with exotic parasites, along shores bordered with casuarina and coconut palms. Bronze hedges of beefsteak plant mark the sites of villages gay with hibiscus, cassia, poinsettia, and tiare. Blue begonia and magenta bougainvillea clamber over the tiny huts roofed with layers of white bark.

Suddenly Hienghène's stark seascape explodes in the lagoon. Oddly unrelated to the mainland, sheer black rocks rise abruptly from the sea to a height of more than 400 feet. From one side you can see them as the towers of Notre Dame. From another you get a picture of a gigantic sitting hen.

A new road has recently been built from Hienghène to loop around the top of the island, connecting up with the west coast road at Koumac. The northern scenery above Poum is spectacular—white beaches, offshore atolls, a denser rain forest—the road up the west coast is paved as far as Koumac, and work is proceeding on the mountain pass between Bourail and Poindimié. Unpaved roads are reasonable, and the surface is good. Rental car rates are reasonable.

Tribal life in upcountry New Caledonia goes on much as it always has—gardens are tended, a new house built from time to time. Coffee plantations shelter under the bigger trees of the forest all the way up the island, and at the right time of the year, villagers busy themselves drying the beans for market. The *gîte,* or country lodging, usually a Melanesian project, is a new development upcountry with basic accommodation at a very modest tariff, in well-built thatched *farés. Alfresco* meals are available, and the cooking will be simple but good, with an emphasis on fresh fish and game. The northernmost gîte is at Poum; the southernmost at Goro. This kind of simple but attractive accommodation can also be sampled in any one of the three islands of the Loyalty Group, half an hour by air from Nouméa. The Gîtes at Ceingeite and Wabao on Mare are delightful. All in all, an experience for the adventurous. The east coast is a favorite area for campers, especially for French families from Nouméa. Apart from mosquitos, there are no stinging or biting things in this favored island.

From Hienghène you can fly straight back to Nouméa if you wish, over the great mountain chain that marches down the center of the island's two hundred and forty-odd miles. Huge deposits of the island's great mineral wealth lie just beneath the surface of the gaunt mountain tops. From the small Air Calédonie plane you can see the winding russet trails traced by prospecting bulldozers. At Thio the towers and turrets of the immense opencast nickel mine look from the air like the red ruins of some ancient city, but as you fly southeast you soon see the familiar ribbon of white coral sand edging the blue-green bays and inlets.

Beyond Nouméa

You can't really leave this area without staying a night or two at an outer island. Ilot Maître, 30 minutes from Nouméa, within the great reef, is easiest to get to. White-roofed bungalows are dotted among the light bush of this little atoll, whose waters are a marine reserve. On the lee side a sandy beach, on the windward side rock pools for fossicking. The cuisine is first rate, served in a beamed, high-ceilinged restaurant overlooking the lagoon. Birds are returning to this island—it's a charming place to unwind.

Isle of Pines

The day trip to the Isle of Pines with Air Calédonie shows you some of the loveliest beaches in the Pacific. Its sugar-white sand skirts blue-green lagoons, and its beauty is world famous. Lunch is included on this excursion, and divers will also find plenty of scope at the Nauticlub, where Swiss-born Albert Thomas and Hilary Root from New Zealand offer picnics (local fish barbecue, diving, swimming and shelling, on off-shore islets). Diving instruction is available, and the rustic ambiance is warm and friendly.

Since the closure of the *Relais de Kanumera,* a number of gîtes, or rural lodgings, have been built on this lovely island. They are small complexes of 3 to 5 bungalows, which are well constructed by members of the local tribes. Meals can be provided—by arrangement—or you can do for yourself. At the Bay of Ouameo, M. Lepers, a former plumber from Paris, dispenses simple but hearty hospitality at the Gîte de Kodjeue—nine sturdy bungalows, excellent meals at a long table under a thatched shelter, a safe beach, plus fishing, pirogues and a grocer's shop, cooking facilities, and a refrigerator cater to cook-your-own types. M. Lepers has extended his domain to a charming rustic restaurant just a step from the fabulous white beaches of Kuto and Kanumera. He will drive guests over for the day—great food and a changing room for swimmers. Also available are trips to Grottoes (Captain Cook's vessel is said to have been spied at sea by islanders peeping through a gap in the wall of one of these caverns) or a visit to the century-old mission at Vao. Nataiwatch is in a leafy grove a few yards from a white beach, and each bungalow is allotted its own private shower and toilet in a nearby block. Here your host is Guillaume Kouathe, teacher of carpentry at the local school, whose craft is well displayed in this delightful cluster of five bungalows.

No visitor to the Isle of Pines should leave without exploring the prison ruins, cemeteries, waterworks, and other relics of the "deportation." Most of the ruins are to be found in the light bush near the isthmus of Kuto.

PRACTICAL INFORMATION FOR
NEW CALEDONIA

HOW TO GET THERE. *UTA* flies to New Caledonia from Paris (Wednesdays and Sundays), San Francisco (Wednesdays), Tokyo (Wednesdays), Tahiti (Mondays and Thursdays), Sydney (Tuesdays and Fridays), and Auckland (Tuesdays). *Qantas* flies from Sydney (Wednesdays and Sundays) and Melbourne (Sundays). *Air New Zealand* flies from Auckland (Saturdays). *Air Calédonie International* flies from Auckland (Sundays), Sydney (Mondays and Saturdays), Brisbane (Fridays), Melbourne (Sundays), Nadi (Tuesdays), and Vanuatu (daily except Wednesdays).

WHEN TO GO. New Caledonian weather is pleasant all year round. December to March are the warmest months, fairly humid but only moderately rainy. Temperatures around 28°C. April to November is generally dryer, with an average temperature of 22°C. June, July, August can be quite cool at times and you may need to pack a sweater or a wrap of some kind for going out at night. Visitors swim all year round. The locals prefer the summer months of November to March.

CLIMATE. Dry season from April to December. Rainy season early February to late March.

AVERAGE TEMPERATURE

	Jan	Feb	Mar	Apr	May	Jun	Jul	Aug	Sep	Oct	Nov	Dec
°F	83.5	84.2	82.9	79.7	77.0	74.5	72.3	72.9	74.1	77.9	80.6	82.6
°C	28.6	29.0	28.3	26.5	25.0	23.6	22.4	22.7	23.6	25.4	27.0	28.1

AVERAGE RAINFALL: (inches)

4¼	4	4¼	5	4¼	3¾	3¼	3	2	1½	1½	2¼

WHAT TO WEAR. Light, informal clothes—women will find sophisticated dressing along these lines in the better restaurants. Long trousers for men at night in restaurants and clubs. Only the casino requires jacket and tie.

CURRENCY. The French Pacific Franc (CFP) is used. At press time, the exchange rate is as follows: $US1 = 125 CFP; A$1.00 = 89 CFP; $NZ1 = 66 CFP; £1 = 188 CFP; Fr. fr. 5.59 = 100 CFP. *American Express, Visa, Diners Club,* and *MasterCard* are generally accepted, except upcountry and on outer islands, where cash is required. You can contact the American Express agent—Max Shekelton—at Center Voyages, 27 Avenue du Maréchal Foch (tel. 28.40.40).

WHAT WILL IT COST? Room costs in this territory are moderate in Nouméa and reasonable in the outer islands and upcountry. Food can be an expensive item, according to your tastes but at the smaller bistros the set menu is pretty reasonable at about 1,200 CFP. The top-class gourmet places will charge you about what you'd pay in similar restaurants at home for three courses and coffee. A bottle of beaujolais or riesling will range between 1600 CFP and 2000 CFP a bottle. You will eat fine food, and the wine list will be extensive.

Drinks aren't cheap either, but it's necessary to remember that by most standards they are doubles—then the price doesn't seem too high. Soft drinks and beer are comparatively expensive and cost nearly as much as a carafe of wine. The remedy is obvious. If you're looking for your money's worth alcoholically speaking, a liqueur is the best buy. They are more like triples and you won't forget in a hurry your first sight of a New Caledonia-size cognac or Benedictine. Nightclub drinks are around $US6, but there is no cover charge as a rule and you can sit or dance over a drink or two all night without being hassled to buy more.

Local transport is fairly reasonable. The bus ride from Tontouta airport to your city hotel costs 1,500 CFP. The remarkable bus service charges a flat rate of 80 CFP from town to Anse Vata beach and runs from 6 A.M. to 6:30 P.M. Taxis charge 420 CFP daytime, after 6 P.M. 450 CFP, for the 2-mile trip from Anse Vata to the city. Air Calédonie's rates are reasonable. Rental cars are a bit more expensive than Fiji, but cheaper than Tahiti.

The all-day trip to Amedeé Lighthouse will cost around 3,850, CFP which includes lunch, wine, entertainment, great swimming, and snorkeling. A three-hour fishing tour will run to 3,000 CFP, while a whole day's scuba diving will set you back about 9,900 CFP It costs 350 CFP to enter the aquarium and the same for entry to the big Olympic swimming pool.

ENTRY FORMALITIES. Valid passport required. Visa required for stay of up to three months, good for multiple entries and extendable upon arrival. Visas may be obtained from your local French consulate or embassy.

LANGUAGE. French is the official language, but English is widely understood.

ELECTRICITY. A.C. 220 v., 50 Hz. (2 prongs).

TIPPING. No tipping, please.

WATER. Modern pipeline supply. Safe in all areas.

TOURIST INFORMATION. *Office du Tourisme,* 25 avenue du Maréchal Foch, phone 27.26.32. Telex: N.C. Turism 063 N M. FAX 2746. Tourist information and literature: *Nouméa Visitors Bureau,* Place des Cocotiers, phone 27.27.03. Also: 39 rue Jean Jaurés, Nouméa.

SERVICE NUMBERS. Police: 17. Radio Taxis: 28.35.12 and 28.53.70. Surcharge 120 CFP. for telephone taxi.

POSTAGE. For letters, stamps, parcels, cables, and telephone: Baie de la Moselle. Airmail rates: U.K. letters, 89 cents, postcards, 56 cents; U.S. letters, 79 cents, postcards, 51 cents.

TIME ZONE. GMT plus 11 hours; 19 hours ahead of U.S. PST.

HOTELS. Most are smallish and intimate, with tariffs ranging from moderate to very reasonable. The newer hotels at Anse Vata and the Baie des Citrons are right up-to-date, and so are a few of the newer bungalow hotels upcountry and in the outer islands. Outside Nouméa at certain times of the year it's wise to carry your own mosquito repellent and a packet of mosquito coils, though the management can usually supply the latter. Hotel categories: *Expensive,* $US60–$US70; *Moderate,* $US45–$US55. *Inexpensive,* under $US40. Room tax (approximately $US1.20) is not included in the categories.

Nouméa

Escapade. *Expensive.* Box 819; 28.53.20. Atoll resort within the lagoon, 30 min. from town by launch. 44 bungalows, swimming, snorkeling, windsurfing, Hobie Cats, pool, floor shows twice weekly. Excellent restaurant.

Isle de France—Apartments. *Expensive.* Anse Vata. Box 1604; 26.24.22. Telex 143NM FRANLAG. 48 apartments, air-conditioning, fans, color TV, IDS tel., private balconies, fully equipped kitchen including iron, full-size refrigerator, and oven. Three pools, 2 tennis courts, brasseries/restaurant. Gym, sauna, fitness center. Down a quiet cul-de-sac, 3 minutes from Anse Vata beach.

Le Surf. *Expensive.* Anse Vata Beach. Rocher à la Voile. Box 4230; 28.66.88. Delightful ambiance, excellent restaurant and piano bar, Pool, casino.

Ibis Hotel. *Moderate.* Baie des Citrons. Box 819; 26.20.55. Charming hotel, excellent restaurant and snack bar, sidewalk café overlooking sheltered beach. Also Japanese restaurant. Rates include American breakfast, water sports, cycles.

Le Lagon. *Moderate.* Route de l'Anse Vata. Box 440; 26.12.55. Air conditioning. Private facilities. Tea- and coffee-making facilities. Telex, convention facilities for 150. Recently refurbished.

Lantana Beach. *Moderate.* Box 4075; 26.22.12. The old Lantana completely rebuilt with two more floors, color TV, video, bar. No restaurant but many nearby. On Anse Vata Beach.

Mocambo. *Moderate.* Baie des Citrons. Box 678; 26.27.01. Close to excellent swimming beach. Completely refurbished. Air conditioning, color TV, tea- and coffee-making facilities. Free transfer to La Rotonde, one of Nouméa's top restaurants. Telex. Conference rooms. No restaurant but many nearby.

Noumea Village Hotel. *Moderate.* 1 rue de Sebastopol; 28.30.06 and 27.32.99. Apartments, parking, restaurant, right in town. Daily poolside buffet lunch good value, free bus to Kuendu Beach.

Nouvata. *Moderate.* Anse Vata Beach. Box 137; 26.22.00. Recently modernized beachfront hotel, 85 rooms, air conditioned, refrigerators. 2 restaurants, one French, one Chinese. Pool, with snack service. Pleasant garden setting. Charlie's American Bar and the excellent French restaurant, both popular rendezvous.

Paradise Park Motel. *Moderate.* Box 234; 27.25.44. A charming complex in the Valeé des Colons; set in 3 acres of garden. Big pool, bar, restaurant, coffee shop. Air-conditioning, kitchenette. Shuttle bus to town and beaches 4 times a day.

Le Paris. *Moderate.* Rue Sebastopol in town. Box 2226; 28.17.00. Convenient hotel. Caters to business clientele. Two nightclubs in complex, restaurant, hairdresser.

Club Mediterrannée. *Inexpensive.* Anse Vata Beach. Box 515; 26.12.00. 550 beds. The Club Med recipe as before, great for investigating Club Med but investigation of Nouméa and the hinterland frowned on. Plenty of well-organized spontaneity, lots of *yé yé,* as the French have it, good food at set hours. A bargain package.

Hotel La Pérouse. *Inexpensive.* In town, top end of Place des Cocotiers. Box 189; 27.22.51. Small, basic, 30 rooms, 18 with shower, air-conditioning extra. Snack restaurant and bar.

Motel Anse Vata. *Inexpensive.* Val Plaisance. 19 Rue Laroque, Box 4453; 26.26.12. 22 fully equipped one-room motel flats with bath and kitchen. Air-conditioning, balcony. Residential area, few minutes' walk from Anse Vata Beach. Good food shops and restaurants adjacent.

Motel Le Bambou. *Inexpensive.* Val Plaisance; 26.12.90. Anse Vata Beach, fully equipped units, fans, in quiet suburb.

Youth Hostel. Situated on a hill behind the cathedral. Box 767; 27.58.79. 60 bunk beds in dormitories. Communal facilities. Lounge, dining room, and recreational center. Members 700 C.F.P. per night, nonmembers 800 C.F.P.

West Coast Hotels

Les Paillottes de Ouenghi. *Moderate.* Boulouparis; 35.17.35. Quiet country retreat on Ouenghi River. 15 bungalows; pool, tennis, riding, canoeing, excellent food. Only 60 kms. from Bourail—a fascinating area for students of history and World War II.

Tontoutel. Airport motel. 35.11.11. Modern, pool, good food.

Upcountry Tribal Lodgings (Gîtes)

Not to be missed for a night or two or even longer are the gîtes, or rural lodgings scattered in the countryside beyond Nouméa and along the palm-fringed beaches of the outer islands, including the Loyalty Islands and the lovely Isle of Pines. These rustic bungalows, usually in a group of four or five, are mostly of traditional construction roofed with thatch, soundly made. Most are owned by Melanesians and built on family land. Some have all facilities, including some means of cooking. Others will provide a communal bathroom. One of the most charming, *Nataiwatch* on the Isle of Pines, offers a solution in the shape of six spanking clean showers, washbasins, and toilets. Nataiwatch is set in a leafy glade bordering the fabulous white sand beaches of the Baie de Kuto. Each bungalow is alloted its own three facilities—in effect a relatively private bathroom. Meals are available every day except Sunday if you don't want to cook. M. Georges Lepers has built nine bungalows along the shore of the *Baie de Ouameo* on the same island. He offers riding and a tennis court, and a pool is under construction. The beach is safe, and you'll eat some memorable meals *chez Lepers*—freshly caught lobster and fish are always on the menu. You'll get first-class French bourgeois cooking, and what more could you ask?

There is much to explore in the offshore islands and upcountry. Melanesians are friendly and helpful to tourists. A little French is useful, but some English will be understood; otherwise sign language does very well. The *Office of Tourism* in Nouméa publishes an excellent brochure on the many gîtes in the territory, both upcountry and offshore. Contact the Nouméa Visitors' Bureau in the rue Jean Jaurés for detailed information on any of the fifteen gîtes in the territory or contact Air Caledonie Gîtes, 19 Avenue Marechal Foch, tel. 28.65.64. If you want to get close to the land and the people, this is your chance.

DINING OUT. Limitations of space prevent a comprehensive listing. So we will present our own choices ranged in rough order of price—which leads to another problem.

It's not easy to categorize New Caledonian restaurants in terms of cost. First-class and even the second rank of eating houses are not cheap, for the raw material of any meal you eat will cost your host a pretty penny. Most meat and vegetables are imported by air from nearby New Zealand and Australia and sometimes even from the West Coast of the United States.

The "elegant decor" required for deluxe rating will often be lacking. But instead, your surroundings will be individual and attractive, and the cooking itself in the better restaurants rates a super-deluxe listing. Fine food is a passion in this country and even the humblest shack on a dusty country road may conceal a cordon bleu cook.

We have therefore not attempted to rate restaurants according to the decor but according to food and service—though in this offbeat French territory you will find that service will mostly be slow. Haste is a bad word here, as it is in most Pacific islands. But one thing is certain—you'll be able to indulge in an orgy of gourmet eating and sample Italian, French, Spanish, Indonesian, African, Chinese cooking. And when your liver or your wallet protests, the excellent delicatessens and groceries in town and at Anse Vata beach will provide you with mouthwatering goodies for a picnic lunch for very little cost.

Price categories: Expensive: $US30 and up; *Moderate:* $US18–$US25; *Inexpensive:* $US10–$US16.

(Check closing days—they differ.)

Expensive

Le Berthelot. 13 rue du Port Despointes; 28.32.70. In charming house in the Vallee des Colons. Fine cooking, interesting menu.

Centre Club. 26 avenue de Maréchal Foch; 27.21.13. Good French cooking just off the Place des Cocotiers. Another shrine for gourmets—best cordon blue cuisine in town.

El Cordobes. 1 rue Bichat; 27.47.68. Spanish dishes a specialty. Try their fish clothed in flaky pastry.

Dodin Bouffant. 29 rue Dusquesne; 28.32.26. Named for the Paris restaurant of gourmet fame. Popular with lovers of fine food.

L'Eau Vive. Route du Port Despointes; 28.61.23. Something different—an unpretentious restaurant run by a missionary order of nuns. Superb food. Moderate prices on the ground floor, fairly expensive upstairs. The sisters import their own wine, Faubourg Blanchot.

Le Grill. Le Surf Hotel, Anse Vata Beach; 28.66.88. Fine cooking, Tahitian dinner-show Thursdays.

Les Helices. Magenta, near local airport; 27.57.41. Specializes in seafood, popular with locals.

Le Petit Train. Baie des Citrons; 26.28.11. Baie des Citrons-gourmet cooking, superb outlook.

La Truffière. Rue Gabriel Laroque, Val Plaisance, near Anse Vata Beach; 26.19.82. First-class cuisine, specializing in the dishes of Périgord.

Moderate

Aux Trois Bonheurs. Avenue de la Victoire; 27.25.32. First-class Chinese cuisine.

Brasserie St. Hubert. Place de Cocotiers; 27.21.42. Toulouse-Lautrec setting for this bar-restaurant in an old colonial building at the top of the Square. A reasonable set menu.

Chez Bianca. Anse Vata, tucked between the bank and the Lantana Hotel; 26.42.44. Good cooking, moderate prices, expensive wine list. Try wine by the carafe.

Esquinade. Rue de Sebastopol, Baie de l'Orpelinat; 27.25.05. This fish restaurant is a favourite eating place for old Nouméa hands. Attractive decor, good cooking.

La Grande Muraille. 71 route de l'Anse Vata; tel. 26.12.28. Good Chinese food in small colorful restaurant.

La Grande Muraille. Ouen Toro; 26.13.28. Cantonese cooking, delightful outlook on point above Club Med.

Maeva Beach. Baie des Citrons; 26.28.11. Excellent cooking and a reasonable set menu.

Mayflower, Nouvata Hotel. Anse Vata Beach; 26.18.70. High-quality Chinese food, friendly.

Nouvata Hotel Restaurant. Anse Vata Beach; 26.22.20. First-class cuisine. Popular with tourists and locals too. Lively bar, the Monins great hosts.

O'Churasco. Route du Port Despointes; 27.35.64. First-class cuisine at a moderate price in the suburbs. Paella a specialty.

Santa Monica. Route de l'Anse Vata; 26.10.35. Near Anse Vata Beach. Abuts the nightclub of the same name.

Eating Out of Town. Almost every wayside café in New Caledonia can offer an attractive meal, but there are a few good restaurants you may like to investigate if you drive to the east coast or even just out of town for the day.

La Siesta. Plum; 43.35.77. A pleasant rustic retreat about ten miles along the Mont Dore road, good food, and a pool.

Vallon Dore. A traditional meeting place for Nouméa's teenagers, chaperoned by watchful parents. Excellent lunches and dinners, and the Sunday tea dance is lots of fun. 14 miles from Nouméa on the Mont Dore road.

Inexpensive Snacks

Béarno. In town, quick service, reasonable. You can get the usual minute steak, but also such dishes as sausages and lentils.

Jamico. Toue de l'Anse Vata, Unassuming little snack bar, friendly service, superb omelettes, as well as hamburgers, steak Tartare, etc. Super Vata Shopping Complex.

La Pergola. 12 rue du Général Mangin. Just off the square, attractive decor, steaks, omelettes, and so on. Reasonable prices, cheerful service.

Anse Vata Beach has blossomed lately with snack bars, pizzerias, boutiques, and a couple of excellent cafés. The problem of a light lunch no longer exists in this area.

HOW TO GET AROUND. *By air:* Air Calédonie maintains regular service from Nouméa to various points on New Caledonia and the surrounding small islands. Points served: Isle of Pines; Mare Lifou, Ouvea, and Tiga in the Loyalty Group, the East and West Coasts. Rates from 6,000–11,000 C.F.P.

By sea: Mary D, 60-passenger tourist boat operated all day; scheduled light-house cruises every Sunday or on request; also lagoon cruises, diving and fishing trips. 35-passenger boat *Samara* for charter, with Jack and Christine Owen, 33 rue de Paris, Val Plaisance. Day trip on well-run boat, with great food. ·

Bus system: From the bus depot buses leave every 15 minutes for the following destinations: Baie des Citrons, Anse Vata, Port Despointes. Trianon, Motor Pool, Magenta Airport. Fare: 80 CFP for any distance, any direction. Pay the driver on boarding the bus. There is a handy bus stop on the square outside new Town Hall.

Car rental: Avis, Europcar, Mencar, Hertz, and *Vata Location* offer reasonable self-drive rates throughout the island. Inquire at your hotel. A current valid driver's license is required. Drive on the right.

Radio-taxis: Phone 28.35.12 and 28.53.70. Fare Anse Vata to town around 420 C.F.P., 450 C.F.P. after 6 P.M. Drive on the right, give way to the right.

FESTIVALS AND SPECIAL EVENTS. *January 1*—New Year's Day is a public holiday and celebrated throughout the country. *Easter* usually starts the sport season with events throughout the New Caledonian winter season. *May 1*—Labor Day; public holiday. *May 12*—Ascension Day: public holiday. *August 28–30,* Agricultural Fair at Bourail. *November 1*—All Saints Day. Families place flowers at grave sites. Public holiday. *November 11*—Armistice Day. *Mid-November*—Round New Caledonia Auto Safari. Teams from Australia, New Zealand, and Japan compete in this highly contested car rally. *December 25*—Father Christmas parades through Nouméa streets in the evening.

TOURS. Tours of Nouméa can be booked by telephone from local agents. Most Nouméa companies have their own cars for touring; some operate buses. The most popular tours are listed here. Tours around the city and environs range from around $US25 to $US55 or so, the latter price including lunch. The *Isle of Pines* day trip, including air fare, will be around $US92. Reliable tour agencies in Noumea are as follows: *Amac Tours,* 2 rue de l'Alma, Nouméa; tel. 27.41.53, telex 021 NM Box A3, Nouméa Cedex. *Center Voyages,* 27 bis avenue du Maréchal Foch, Nouméa; tel. 28.40.40, Telex TRAVEL 146NM; Box 50, Nouméa. *South Pacific Tours,* Shopping Center Vata, Nouméa; 26.23.20; Telex 150NM, Box 4208, Noumea. *Hibiscus Tours,* Nouméa; tel. 28.27.74, Telex NOUVOY 148 NM; Box 4853, Nouméa. *Pacific Holidays,* 27 bis avenue du Maréchal Foch, Nouméa; tel. 27.32.68; Telex PACIF-HOL 160 NM; Box 1524, Nouméa. *Discovery Tours,* 16 Rue du Maréchal Juin, tel. 26.31.31; Telex NOUVATA 145 NM; Box 233, Nouméa. *Shipping & Shore Excursions Agency,* Tel. 28.11.22; Box C2, Telex 163 NM; FAX. 27.85.32.

City-Day Tours of Nouméa and environs: The following tours are available by limousine from local agents. *Nouméa city tour with Aquarium* (3 hours): Includes the world-famous saltwater Aquarium de Nouméa, with tanks duplicating biological conditions of the reef; St. Joseph's Cathedral, built by convict labor; Place des

Concotiers, the central square with its flaming poinciana trees; first settlement of Vallée des Colons; Magenta Bay; Mt. Coffyn Heights for spectacular city-harbor view. *Tuesdays and Thursdays. Mt. Koghi Tour* (4 hours): Travel through tropical jungle to Mt. Koghi for view of Nouméa peninsula, lagoon, and barrier reef. Short jungle walk through rainforest to area waterfalls. Visits via Mont Dore to orchid houses and tropical gardens, lunch at *La Siesta,* continuing to the Parc Forestier and a varied display of tropical bird life. *Thursdays Daily 11 A.M. Mt. Dore Tour* (3 hours): Travel through country, viewing coastal scenery around the Mountain of Gold. Stops at Mission of St. Louis with its native village of thatch-roofed bungalows and dairy farm and La Conception, the oldest church in Nouméa. Daily. *Bougna Feast:* This tour takes you through Nouville peninsula, site of the infamous penal-colony prisons, to Kuendu Beach for a feast of succulent chicken, yams, sweet potatoes, bananas, and papaw baked over hot stones in an earth oven. The meal is prepared by the local Melanesians and served with wine. Kuendu is one of Nouméa's best swimming beaches, and a Polynesian show is included. *Sundays. East Coast Tour* (Full day). Visits cattle-raising area on the west coast, turning at Boulouparis, crossing high central mountain chain to the east, with a stop at a nickel-producing area. (*Note:* New Caledonia is the third largest nickel-producing country, after Canada and Russia.) Visit old mission villages and ghost towns, then on to coffee- and fruit-growing country and tribal villages. The return journey passes through coffee plantations and cattle stations. Seafood lunch at the justly famed restaurant *Paillottes de Ouenghi,* one of Nouméa's favorite weekend spots. *Wednesdays. Amedée Lighthouse Tour.* Full-day tour. Travel by launch to Amedée Lighthouse, built during reign of Napoleon and shipped in pieces to New Caledonia. View coral formations and fluorescent fish. Tour lighthouse before lunch is served under banyan trees. Time for swim, snorkeling, siesta. Daily at 7:45 A.M., weather permitting. Approx. $US42 with lunch and wine. *Hoki Mai Cruises* offer naturist cruises to M'Ba island in the lagoon, day trips or longer. Day trip approx. $US35.

Air Calédonie, Magenta Airport, Nouméa, B.P.212, New Caledonia. Offers regular service to various points within the country: Isle of Pines, the Loyalty Group, the East and West Coasts. The Isle of Pines daytrip is well worthwhile $US112, airfare, lunch, and wine. *Nouméa Yacht Charters* offer a full-day sailing cruise in the huge lagoon, visiting atolls. Lunch with wine, fishing, snorkeling. Departures from Baie des Pecheurs every day, weather permitting.

For general help and information, the Nouméa Visitors Bureau is now in the old "Mairie," or Town Hall, rue Jean Jaurés, on the Place des Cocotiers.

SPORTS. Access to the *Tennis Club du Mont, Coffyn,* the *Cercle Nautique,* and the *Cercle d'Etrier* (riding) must be provided by a member. Inquire at your hotel. The new *Squash Club* at the Baie des Pêcheurs welcomes visitors—bring your own whites—all other gear is available on the premises, 21 rue Jules Garnier, Baie des Pêcheurs, tel. 26.22.18. Water-skiing and wind-surfing can be arranged from your hotel. *Nouméa Yacht Charters* provide bareboat and skippered charters, day sail picnics and diving expeditions in superb Beneteau First 30 and First 38 yachts. Provisioning optional, but reasonable. An enchanting sailing area. Box 848, Noumea, telex 055 NM, tel. 26.17.03. The *Olympic Pool,* just behind Club Med, Anse Vata, is open daily 1–5 P.M., Sun. 10:15 A.M.–4 P.M. Admission charge 120 CFP adults, 60 CFP children under, 14, tel. 26.18.43. Bowling can be found at *Le Commodore,* Anse Vata Beach, tel. 26.26.02. 200 CFP per game. Open every day except Mon., 5–11 P.M. *Municipal tennis courts* are open daily 6 A.M.–9 P.M. Tel. 27.52.32. Admission 300 CFP daytime, 500 CFP nighttime. *Noumea Fishing Center* offers 40-ft. cruising yacht with crew. 8 fishing rods, 2 fighting chairs. For reservations contact Box 1524, tel. (bus.) 28.25.61, or (priv.) 27.16.00, telex 045 NM. *Nauticlub,* Box 18, Vao, Isle des Pins, tel. 46.11.22, telex C/–112 NM Air Cal. Organizes trips for groups of 4 to 8 persons and 10 to 16 persons. Prices include all gear, board including meals and wine. 2 to 4 persons per bungalow. Reservations essential.

AQUARIUMS. Unique in the world for its magnificent fluorescent corals, colorful fishes, and tropical fauna from the nearby lagoon (Anse Vata), from 1:30 to 4.30 P.M. Adults 350 CFP, students 150 CFP, children 50 CFP.

MUSEUMS. The *Museum of Nouméa* is well worth a visit. Featured is a well-displayed collection of Melanesian artifacts. Open every day, except Monday, 10

A.M.–5 P.M. Admission charge 250 CFP adults, 50 CFP children under 12. The museum is at Baie de la Moselle, two blocks from the bus terminal.

ART GALLERIES. There is a great deal of good painting going on in New Caledonia and Mr. Cazalo's *Galerie Galeria* (cr. rues Gallieni and Republique). L'Encardrerie (2 bis rue de Verdun) has the best range by local artists in oil, watercolor, pastel, charcoal, pen, and wash. Look for Nielly, Crocq, Vernande, Michon, Khim, and Bertillon. This gallery is also a treasure house of rugs, tables, carvings, and bibelots from Tibet, Vietnam, Pakistan, and other eastern sources.

The rue Salonique mounts the hill at the top of the place des Cocotiers, as does the rue Anatole France, where you will find *Crea* and many attractive small souvenirs created from local stone, as well as carvings from the area. At *l'Atelier des Artistes* (51 rue Jean Jaurés) a selection of paintings and artifacts. Excellent eating at this gallery/bistro, leisurely service but super food.

SHOPPING. Shopping in Nouméa is fun, and for many, first thoughts in this French territory are of clothes. And clothes, whether dresses or tops or skirts or underwear are a eye-popping temptation as you explore town. On this sport-loving island the emphasis in on casual gear—cotton knits, slacks, swimwear.

Look for the sign "Soldes"—a sale. In Nouméa a sale is a sale. You may pick up a $120 dress for $60 at one of the boutiques displaying the sign.

Océanie, the big supermarket on the rue Clemenceau, is fun to rummage in for everything from Dijon mustard to Italian cotton knits. *Barrau* on the place des Cocotiers, and *Ballande* on rue de l'Alma, both one-time trade stores, are now transformed into department stores—the former is now Prisunic-Barrau. Ballande's kitchenware department will probably fill some gaps in your "batterie de cuisine." This whole store has been refurbished. It carries good sports clothes for men and genuine Lacoste for both sexes.

Perfume is sold almost everywhere in town, but *Rozanne* in the rue Georges Clemenceau just off the square has a tremendous range and is duty free as well. Delightful accessories here too. *Marlene* on the rue de l'Alma and *Bricoles* at the top end of the square are both well-established duty-free shops, and this is one area of shopping where a 30% discount really matters. For wearable ethnic clothing, beautifully made, see *Anna Couture* at 33 bis avenue du Maréchal Foch, just off the place des Cocotiers; this is the New Caledonian answer to Marie Ah You of Tahiti, but at half the price. Expect to pay 4,000 to 6,000 C.F.P. for delectable muumuus, New Caledonian style.

There are plenty of elegant specialty shops for the well-heeled locals where you can pay the earth—the jewelry at *Veyret* on the rue de l'Alma will make your mouth water. But further up the street *Cendrillon* is a treasure house filled with all kinds of precious trinkets within the reach of most travelers. Opposite, *Anémone* displays a most intriguing selection of costume and semiprecious jewelry. *Hippocampe* in avenue Maréchal Foch for unusual bibelots modestly priced. *Hélianthe,* in rue de Sébastopol, almost opposite U.T.A., has an enticing display of gifts and semiprecious baubles.

French and Italian leather handbags are a great buy in Nouméa and many of the duty-free shops carry them. Real leather is the rule, not the exception, and *Le Bagage Calédonien* in the Place de la Victoire, opposite their main store, has a large range at good prices. Ballande's duty-free shop has a wide range of bags, clothing, perfume, and cosmetics.

French children's clothes from birth to adolescence are just as enticing. From doll-size dresses for doll-size French babies to chic toddlers' clothing and fashionable gear for teenagers, French designers have something the others haven't got. But watch out for differences in sizing by years. Multiply by two if you're buying for hefty Anglo-Saxon children. Then shoes! Perhaps, with perfume and handbags, these are the best buy in Nouméa. They run from amusing casual footwear to silver and gold slippers that would grace *Maxim's.* You can buy most of the top French shoe designers—Pierre Cardin, J. B. Martin, and Jourdan—starting at US$60. The *Boty* shops and the Bettina Arcade have the biggest range. On the rue de l'Alma, try *First* for Italian and French shoes, and *Les Champs Elysées* for ready-to-wear and sportswear from the Paris couturiéres. Also try *Les Nanas* at 14 rue de Sébastopol for a small but exclusive selection of footwear. *Courrèges,* in the avenue du Maréchal Foch, often has interesting bargain boxes—Céline shoes, too.

In this town the male shopper isn't catered to as extensively as the female, but casual gear is a good buy, if a trifle expensive. St. Trop on the Rue Vauban isn't cheap, but quality menswear here is good value.

The duty-free shopping is geared to make the traveler's life easier. There is an excellent duty-free store at the airport, but you can also obtain a 20% to 30% discount in a number of licensed shops in Nouméa on purchases totalling 2,000 CFP or over. The Duty-Free Shopping Guide, published by the Tourist Office, supplies a list of these shops, a map of Nouméa with them clearly marked, and a set of rules applying to the purchase of duty-free goods before departure. The range includes jewelery, perfume, clothing, handbags, shoes, cosmetics, cameras, and electronic gear. Tourists must not forget to hand in their duty-free receipts to customs at Toutouta on departure.

NIGHTLIFE. *Commodore Star Truck.* This disco is popular with the young. Tea dancing Sundays 3 to 7 P.M. Entry week nights about $US3, Friday and Saturday $US4.00, which includes your first drink. Promenade Anse Vata; 26.17.54.

Casino Royal. The only casino in the South Seas. Everything from poker machines to blackjack or roulette. Tie and jacket required for the gaming room. In Le Surf Hotel grounds, Anse Vata Beach; 28.66.88. Open 9 P.M. to 2 A.M.

Charlie's American Bar. On grounds of the Nouvata Beach Hotel. Nostalgic decor harking back to World War II in the Pacific.

Etoile. In Le Paris building right in town, drinks cheaper here than in the Papa Club, favored by tourists looking for chacha, tango, and so on. Ask at your hotel for a card to enter these clubs. 45 rue de Sebastopol; 28.28.29.

Le Black Jack. Private club in the Commodore complex. (But your hotel can get you a card to most of the private clubs in Nouméa, if you can afford the prices.) Popular with Nouméa's gilded youth. Promenade Anse Vata; 28.42.86.

Le Métro Club. Attractive decor, really swings from about 11 P.M. Handy to all beach hotels. Drinks around $US5. Anse Vata; 26.22.20.

Papa Club. In the Hotel Le Paris Building. All black glass and subdued glitter. Drinks around $US5. Offbeat shows Thurs., Fri., Sat. around 10 P.M., dancing after 10:30. 45 rue de Sebastopol; 28.20.00.

Santa Monica. An institution in Nouméa and with visitors too. A really Tahitian atmosphere, small, dark, fabulous music from a group, most of whom sit in each night. No entry charge, drinks around $3.50 or so. Pay when you get your drink—there is sometimes confusion if you leave it till later. Anse Vata; 26.19.06.

Le Creole. Perhaps the most sophisticated discotheque in Nouméa; worth a visit. Drinks around $US6.00. The most danceable music in town. 6 rue de Verdun.

Le Joker. Swinging disco, popular with young Nouméa. Le Surcouf building off rue Sebastopol. In rue Frédéric Surleau.

Nightlife in Nouméa is fun and everyone on this island loves to dance. The standard of the bands is high and in the discotheques the records are French and fascinating. You can dance for an hour or two over a couple of drinks and no one will breathe down your neck or hassle you to order more. As with restaurants, closing days vary, so check with your hotel.

SOLOMON ISLANDS

Beauty in the Battlefields

by
SANDY MACDONALD, JEFF GREENWALD
and RONALD CANNARELLA

Jack London, sailing his yacht through the Solomon Islands, was moored off the brooding beaches of the cannibal island Malaita. "If I were king of the world," he mused, "I couldn't think of a finer place to send my enemies."

London might have been one of America's finest writers but, sick with malaria, weary and disillusioned after a traumatic crossing of the Pacific, he was perhaps not the best judge of one of the most fascinating corners of Melanesia.

The Solomons, sadly, are synonymous with war—Guadalcanal is one of the great battlefield victories celebrated by United States forces—and have a dark history dotted with murder, bloodshed, disaster, and abandoned dreams.

But as the 1980s come to a close, the Solomons have buried the past, cast off their stifling colonial ties with Britain, and confidently look forward to taking their place in the Pacific as a stable, energetic, and productive nation.

The double-strand necklace of islands which trickles across the Western Pacific from Bougainville to Vanuatu will never be in the mainstream of tourism—a blessing in itself—and most of the 10,000 visitors a year are dedicated types seeking out the superlative diving and tramping or paying their respects to the war dead of two nations.

The Solomons are perfect for travelers with a sense of adventure. First-class accommodations are available in the capital, Honiara, but in outlying districts visitors will rough it in government guest houses or seedy waterfront hotels. It is still possible to hike for days through the jungle to villages where time means nothing, to island-hop on copra schooners, to dive on wartime wrecks that stand as monuments to the futility of war, or to fly in a small plane over the stunning beauty of the Roviana and Marovo lagoons—mile upon mile of coral strands bordered by places with such exotic names as Munda, Gizo, and Kolombangara.

Moving through the Solomons it is impossible to ignore World War II. After the original capital, Tulagi, was obliterated in battle, the new capital was built on the site of the major U.S. base on Guadalcanal; it, too, was the scene of heavy fighting.

War relics pop up everywhere. Henderson airport still bears its wartime name; heavy rains wash away the thin topsoil and reveal ammunition clips, grenade cases, bullet-ridden helmets, cutlery stamped "U.S. Marines" . . . even the thick-glassed Coca Cola bottles of the era. In the middle of Tambea Village Resort a monument stands where exhausted Japanese troops were taken off Guadalcanal after marching 50 kilometers through the jungle from Honiara. In the mid-1970s a "dead" 500-pound bomb was uncovered in the middle of the capital's hospital grounds; another bomb was found across the road from a midtown gas station. Ghoulish construction workers sell U.S. dogtags unearthed at building sites. It is a legacy that will take a long time to die.

The Solomon Islands are made up of 922 islands, some barely breaking the surface of the sea. The main islands—Guadacanal, Choiseul, Malaita, Makira, New Georgia, and Santa Ysabel—span 800 square kilometers, bracketing the waterway infamously known during the war as The Slot.

The Solomons were first visited by Europeans in 1568 but it took a bloody battle almost 400 years later to introduce the islands to the Western world.

Alvaro de Mendana, on a voyage from Peru, gave the islands their name, hoping to stimulate interest in his discovery by inferring that the legendary King Solomon had gained his wealth in these faraway outposts. Mendana returned in 1595–27 years later—to find a settlement at Graciosa Bay in the Santa Cruz Islands. The village, however, beleaguered by internal strife, was soon abandoned following a fever epidemic. Mendana, himself, was a victim.

Other Europeans, including Abel Tasman, visited the Solomons but it was not until the end of the 19th century that traders and missionaries began to arrive. At the same time, large numbers of the islanders were recruited to work on sugar plantations in Fiji and Australia. Here they were treated like slaves and appalling stories of cruelty drifted back to the Solomon Islands. In retaliation, many Europeans were murdered.

To stop the bloodshed, the British Government established a protectorate in 1893 embracing the islands of Guadalcanal, Savo, Malaita, San Cristobal (or Makira), and New Georgia. The islands of the Santa Cruz group were added later while the Shortland Group, Santa Isabel (or Ysabel), Choiseul, and Ontong Java were transferred by treaty from Germany to Britain in the early 1900's.

The first British resident commissioner, appointed in 1896, set up office on the island of Tulagi, north of Guadalcanal. The headquarters of the British Solomon Islands Protectorate (BSIP) remained at Tulagi until

World War Two when, like many other settlements in the Pacific, it was blasted off the face of the earth by American and Japanese shelling.

World War II

The Japanese advance across the Pacific reached the far western islands of the Solomons in early April, 1942. For the first time, places like Guadalcanal, Henderson Field, "Bloody Ridge," and the Coral Sea became household words around the world.

The Japanese began building an airstrip on Guadalcanal in July, 1942. In August, 1942, American marines landed on Red Beach, took the airstrip within 24 hours and, within a fortnight, the strip was operational. It was named after Major Lofton Henderson, an American hero of the Battle of Midway.

Late in August, the Japanese counterattack led to the famous battle of Edson's Ridge (or "Bloody Ridge" as it was known to the troops). The war on Guadalcanal ended early in February, 1943, when the Japanese evacuated the island and gradually, were forced out of the Solomons island by island. Thereafter, Guadalcanal became a huge American supply base and training centre for the remainder of hostilities. Stark reminders of the war are still to be seen—ships, tanks, vehicles, guns, and aeroplanes—rusting away on the beaches and in the jungle. Iron Bottom Sound, between Guadalcanal, Savo and Florida islands, is probably the world's largest graveyard of men, ships, and planes. Memorials have been built at various battle sites and American and Japanese war veterans often return to the Solomons to pay homage to their fallen comrades.

The war brought great change to Solomon Islands. Honiara (on Guadalcanal) replaced Tulagi as the capital; new roads, bridges, and airstrips were built; the land was opened up to tourists and other visitors; and the beginnings of a national unity began to be felt.

People of the Solomons

The country's population is 220,000. About 200,000 are Melanesian. There are also Polynesians, Gilbertese, Europeans and Chinese. Most Melanesians live on the main islands with the Polynesians living in the outlying islands to the south and east.

Honiara

The first stopping point for any visitor to the Solomon Islands will be Honiara, the capital. It offers a museum, two botanical gardens (one next to the museum, the other behind the prison) and an interesting Chinatown that has the flavor of the old American Wild West. The local market would be a fun event for the early riser; it's best on Saturday mornings. There are no street addresses per se in Honiara; simply tell your taxi driver where you wish to go.

The city is in close proximity to a number of WWII battle sites such as Mount Austin and Bloody Ridge, and the nearby coastline is strewn with sunken transports and abandoned amphibious vehicles. A starkly modern Peace Memorial sits on a hill about ten kilometers from the city center, affording a fine view of the surrounding hills and unique Guadalcanal grasslands.

Tours around the old battle-sites may be arranged through travel agencies at your hotel or in town, and rental cars are also available, although the roads are often quite rough.

For the vacationer seeking a South Seas idyll, the Tambea Village Resort (45 km. from Honiara) is an unspoiled cove run as a cooperative by locals. There are no telephones, and the 24 Melanesian-style bungalows (lovely and comfortable) are lit by kerosene lamps. Horse riding, bush walking, diving, snorkeling, fishing, and canoing are a few of the available activities. The more exclusive Anuha Island resort, a half-hour ride over Ironbottom Sound by twin-engine plane, is a tropical paradise with all the trimmings, including superb cuisine. See details in the Accommodations section.

For the intrepid traveler, the hills, rivers and jungles around Guadalcanal—quite close to Honiara, really—offer some excellent hiking. Kakambona Gorge and the spectacular waterfall up the Mataniko River are wonderful day trips, although it may be necessary to find a local person who can act as a guide. Both hikes require wading through lively rivers; don't carry anything you don't want to get wet.

A Diver's Dream

For scuba divers and snorkelers, the warm ocean lapping against the northern coast of Guadalcanal contains a superb variety of reefs, walls, marine life, and wrecks. But good diving isn't confined to the area around Honiara; far from it. Many other spots, around Tulagi, Nggela, Anuha, Gizo, and the New Georgia islands, offer terrific underwater adventures. The submerged wreck of the *Toa Maru*—a torpedoed Japanese transport not far from Gizo that still contains overturned tanks, piles of *sake* bottles and stacks of unused ammo—should be made into a National Park.

To Experience the Culture

One of the most fascinating aspects of the Solomons is also one of the most difficult things to get a handle on. This is the cultural heritage (or "custom," as it is locally called) of the islands. The large hotels in Honiara have very good shows of customary and Gilbertese dance once or twice a week, and these are well worth attending.

Most Solomon Island dances and songs depict the early traditions and customs, or are based on history and mythology. For example, there are Melanesian dances about head-hunting raids and sharks. On some islands, the people once worshipped sharks. Bonito fishing in the Eastern Solomons is linked with the traditional rituals of the people, as are the dolphin drives off Malaita.

There is a carving center at Betikama, where various traditional items are hewn from ebony and "kerosene" wood; and a two-day excursion to Malaita may include a visit to Langa Langa Lagoon, where traditional shell-money is made.

To really experience the Solomons, though, it is necessary to get off the beaten path and visit the small villages that punctuate the shorelines and hide in the bush. In addition to their local languages—and there are scores of them—most Solomon Islanders speak *pijin,* which can be picked up by an English-speaking person without too much difficulty. Talk to the old men chewing *betel-nut* on their verandas; greet the village women tending to their children or carrying laundry back from the local water tap. The Melanese are friendly and inquisitive, and they love to "story" with visitors. Ask to see their gardens and "custom-houses," the focal points for village activities. Be sure to ask permission before taking photos; some locals resent the fact that westerners have made small fortunes selling pictures to magazines and books, and consider this a form of exploitation.

If by some lucky chance you are invited to spend the night in a village, don't pass up the opportunity. Chances are you will be put with the village's most well-to-do family, and given a comfortable mattress to sleep on. Food is simple, usually confined to rice, taro, sweet potato, Chinese cabbage, and sometimes fish or chicken. Do not offer your hosts money; a 10-kg. bag of rice (about SBD $8, or $US5) from a local shop is a welcome and appropriate gift.

PRACTICAL INFORMATION FOR
THE SOLOMON ISLANDS

HOW TO GET THERE. *Solair* flies to Honiara from Brisbane (Mondays and Thursdays). *Air Niugini* flies from Cairns (Tuesdays and Fridays) and Port Moresby (Tuesdays and Fridays). *Air Pacific* flies from Nadi (Thursdays). *Air Nauru* flies from Auckland (Sundays).

ENTRY REQUIREMENTS. No animal or vegetable products are permitted into the country. Jets are sprayed with a W.H.O.-approved insecticide before passengers may deplane.

A valid passport is required for entry into the Solomon Islands. Entry visas are generally not required for members of the British Commonwealth. Persons entering the Solomon Islands may obtain a visitor's permit upon arrival for a period of seven days and not exceeding two months in any period of 12 months. Visitors should be in possession of adequate funds and onward tickets.

Vaccinations are not normally required for entry unless you are coming from an infected area. Visitors are advised that there is a real danger from malaria. An anti-malarial treatment, such as chloroquine or Maloprim, must be commenced two weeks prior to arrival and continued for several weeks after departure, as per your doctor's instructions. These drugs are available over-the-counter in Honiara. In addition, an injection of gammaglobulin is protection against hepatitis.

CURRENCY. The exchange rate generally is 2 Solomon Islands Dollars (SBD) for $US1. There are many banks in Honiara, and in all of the provincial centers as well. All prices quoted in this chapter, unless otherwise specified, are in Solomon Island Dollars.

WATER. Safe to drink in most parts of the Solomon Islands.

COMMUNICATIONS. The Post Office provides telecommunications within the Solomons while international telecommunications are provided through SOLTEL, a joint venture between the S.I. government and the United Kingdom. Service and clarity via the satellite link are excellent, inexpensive, and available Mon.–Fri. 7:45 A.M.–10 P.M., Sat. until noon. Closed Sun.

ELECTRICITY. Set for 220 volts.

TIPPING. Tipping in the Solomon Islands is not customary. In fact, most local people find the practice patronizing and insulting. Visitors are strictly advised to refrain from it.

WHEN TO GO. The Solomon Islands lie between 6 and 12 degrees south of the equator, and thus experience a tropical climate all year round. This is moderated by the expanse of ocean around them. Southeast trade winds blow from April to November. During the rest of the year the winds are from the northwest and occasionally develop into cyclones. There are exceptions to these patterns; devastating cyclone Namu struck parts of the Solomons in mid-May of 1986.

On Guadalcanal and the larger islands, evening breezes sometimes lower the temperatures to 66°F (19°C). Day temperatures are usually in the 80s. Rainfall in Honiara averages 85 inches a year, the heaviest rains occurring Jan. to March. Some of the other islands average up to 140 inches per year.

Average Temperature (°Fahrenheit) and Humidity

Honiara	Jan	Feb	Mar	Apr	May	June	July	Aug	Sept	Oct	Nov	Dec
Average max. day temperature	87°	86°	86°	87°	87°	86°	86°	86°	87°	87°	87°	86°
Humidity, percent	73	73	80	N/A	N/A	N/A	73	73	73	73	73	73

LANGUAGE. The official language is English, taught in schools throughout the country; but the "official" official language is *pijin,* a unique dialect combining elements of western vocabulary with Melanesian grammar. This is the true language uniting the Solomons, where over 80 separate tribal languages testify to centuries of enmity and polarization. There is a very good primer called *Pijin Blong Umi* (Pijin Belongs to You and Me), for sale at the bookstores.

ACCOMMODATIONS. There are three main hotels in Honiara, several more around Guadalcanal, and at least one in each of the provincial centers. Most hotels have their own restaurants and bars. Rates given here are several months old, and may be a bit lower than what you experience. (All rates are quoted in Solomon Island dollars. To convert to US dollars, multiply by .50).

Honiara

Honiara Hotel. Box 113, Honiara; telephone 21737. The Honiara is a very friendly hotel with a warm and helpful staff. It is 1.5 km from the center of town on the road leading to the airport. There are a variety of accommodations, from fan-cooled rooms with shared bath to fully air-conditioned rooms with telephone, refrigerator, shower, and toilet. There is a swimming pool, restaurant, bar, and nightly video movie. One-day laundry service is available at reasonable rates. Customary and Gilbertese dancing two nights a week. The hotel is within walking distance to Chinatown, and a 15-minute walk from town. Doubles run $48–$56.

Hibiscus Hotel. Box 268, Honiara; telephone 21205. The Hibiscus is in the center of town, close to the post office. During the summer of 1986 major renovations were undertaken to add a pool, lounge and improve other facilities as well. Rates range from $42–$52 for a double. Family units are also available.

Mendana Hotel. Box 384, Honiara; telephone 20071, Telex: HQ66315. The Mendana is Honiara's first-class hotel, situated near the center of town on the beach. There is a swimming pool, and all rooms are fully air conditioned with showers, toilets, and telephones. Refrigerators in deluxe rooms. The Mendana has a good restaurant with a special barbeque on Friday nights, and customary dancing. Car rental and travel agencies, as well as a gift shop, beauty parlor and Island Dive Services, are located in the hotel foyer. A very pleasant place. Doubles from $106, suites from $200.

Central Province

Anuha Island Resort. c/o Pacific Resorts Limited. Box 133, Honiara; A tropic island "paradise" with all amenities and creature comforts. Anuha is a small island just north of Nggela, and the bungalows occupy one corner of it. The entire island is part of the resort, and features some truly breathtaking scenery. All manner of water sports are available and, with the exception of scuba diving and all-day boat cruises, all are included in the price.

There are four classes of bungalows at Anuha. All are comfortable; some, like the honeymooners' suite, are downright lavish. Actually, Anuha would be a great place for a honeymoon; the staff will bring couples to a private island, maroon them there for a day, then pick them up with champagne that evening.

Rates vary widely, depending on the type of bungalow and number of people. A couple in the least expensive accommodation would pay about $110. On the other end of the scale, the honeymoon suite would cost a couple about $250 per night. Write for a rates list.

Meals, prepared by an international chef, are $35 a day, and the menu is absolutely superb. Drinks are extra.

Transportation to Anuha via Solair costs about $30 round trip.

Gizo

Gizo Hotel. Box 30, Gizo, Western Province, S.I., telephone 60199 or 60119. A western-style hotel with amenities, although water is sometimes a problem. Bar and restaurant, with a special crawfish dinner on Friday nights. Adventure Sports, Gizo's multi-facility dive service, is very close by. Rooms begin at $63. A 5% tax is added to these prices.

Phoebe's Guesthouse. Gizo. A clean, small lodge run by a charming local woman. Three bedrooms available; shared toilet, rainwater shower, and kitchen. No meals served, but supplies may be bought in town. The view from the verandah is spectacular. Ask a local person to walk you to Phoebe's; it's about ten minutes from the wharf, up a slight hill. Rates, $15 double.

Q-Island Holiday Resort. c/o Kelton Marketing, Box 320, Honiara; telephone 22902. A tropical island resort situated at the entrance of Wona Wona Lagoon some 22 km. from Gizo. Fly to Gizo or Munda and take a powered canoe. There is fine swimming, diving, and impressive views of Mt. Kolombangara, a huge volcanic crater-cum-island. The resort features three traditionally styled and self-contained bungalow units located a few yards from the sea. Rates $10–$16 pp. double Meals range from $2 (breakfast) to $5 (dinner).

Guadalcanal Province

Tambea Village Resort. Box 506, Honiara; telephone 22231, Telex: HQ 66338, Cable: TAMVILLE Honiara. Forty-five km. west of Honiara by the scenic coastal road. Tambea features 24 Melanesian-style bungalows, with private toilet facilities. A large dining hall and pleasant bar serve meals and drinks. All kinds of water sports are available, as are hiking, horseback riding, and beachcombing. Scuba and snorkel gear can be hired. Special feast and dancing on Saturday nights. $40 double.

Tavanipupu Island Resort. Box 205, Honiara; telephone 22907 (office), 22410 (home). Two fully furnished South Seas style cottages 104 km. east of Honiara in Marau Sound. Accessible by air or island trading boats. Each cottage contains four beds with toilets and cooking facilities. Recreations include swimming, fishing and shelling. Cottages are about $220/week with a $40 deposit.

Malaita

Auki Lodge. Box 9, Auki, Malaita Province. Located on the island of Malaita in the Langa Langa Lagoon area. Accesible by boat (6 hrs.) or daily Solair flights (½ hr.) from Honiara. White-sand beach nearby and cool, clear rivers for swimming. Transportation available for tours around Malaita, which is a center for custom crafts and, to the south, music. Six twin rooms and dining facilities. Double: $30.

Malu'u Rest House. C/o Mr. Isamel Ilabinia, North Malaita, Malaita Province. An 80-km. drive from Auki, situated on a ridge overlooking the port area. Booking by advance only. Rate is $10 per person per night.

In addition to the hotels and resorts listed here, there are Provincial Resthouses in many of the provincial centers, including Kira Kira (Makira Province); Ilata (Temotu Province); Tulagi (Central Province); Gizo (Western Province); and two in Buara (Isabel Province). Prices are about $12 per person per night, and there is often a small restaurant on the premises.

Munda

Munda Rest House. C/o Mrs. Agnes Kera, Box 9, Munda, Western Province. A comfortable hotel in secluded Munda. A restaurant serves meals and drinks;

some interesting handicrafts are for sale. Motor-powered canoes may be hired for excursions to Gizo, Seghe and nearby lagoons and coral reefs. Double: $30–$36.

Uepi Island Resort. Via Seghe, Marovo Lagoon, Western Province (book through Tambea Tours, Box 506, Honiara). The Seghe area is gaining a reputation as the finest dive spot in the Solomon Islands. This may not be the only hotel there by the time you read this book. There is a local dive shop in Seghe where gear may be hired and tours arranged. The resort itself is in the Marovo Lagoon, a short motorboat ride from Seghe itself. It has several modern houses with bathrooms and refrigerators. Each can accommodate one family or a number of guests. There are also two guestrooms with three beds each in the manager's residence. Each house is $88 a night. Guest rooms are $66. Inquire about family rates. Meals are $25 per day. Transport to and from Seghe is available for about $15/adult, $8/child.

RESTAURANTS. Aside from the restaurants serving the hotels, Honiara contains a number of good quality and reasonably priced eating establishments. Check for availability of ingredients before ordering, or you may end up with pot-luck.

The Lantern. Chinese, European, and Asian dinners. Near the public market. Phone 22549.

The Mandarin. Good Chinese food; in Chinatown. Telephone 22832.

Nippon. Downtown Honiara. Japanese and Asian food. Telephone 23178.

Sea King. Chinese and Asian dishes. Near the Solair office.

Triffid's. Mixed international cuisine. Very innovative. In the NPF building. Telephone 22069.

All of the local restaurants are moderately priced; a satisfying dinner with a couple of beers will run about $15 per person, slightly less for lunch (the Lantern has good lunch specials). There are also a number of smaller restaurants and other fast-food shops around the downtown area.

HOW TO GET AROUND. Transportation from Honiara's Henderson Airstrip to the hotels in town is available by the *Solair* hotel bus (SBD $3) or by taxi (SBD $10–$15). Once in town, taxis are plentiful and cheap. There are no meters, so you must decide on the fare in advance. Solomon Island taxi drivers are generally very fair-minded people, and will not try to overcharge you. Don't haggle; if a price seems unfair, try another cab.

For day-trips to WWII sites and other points of interest, there are several options. Once again, a taxi may be hired. The prices seem to vary; expect to pay anywhere between SBD $50 and $80 for a full day's hire, gas included. Some drivers may ask for SBD $1 per kilometer, which is ridiculous. Find another cab.

Car rental is available through *Budget* and *Avis*. Check at the hotels and/or travel agencies. $3/gallon.

The Solair office in downtown Honiara will arrange bookings for visits to almost all of the outlying islands, with daily service to many of them. Most of their aircraft are small twin-props seating 6–12 passengers, so book as far in advance as possible.

TOURS. *Seltour,* Box 114, Heniara. Telephone 20071. Office in the Hotel Mendana. Can arrange for groups and individuals. Accommodations, diving tours, and snorkeling tours and all other sightseeing arranged. Make reservations well in advance.

The following are tours most popular with visitors to the Solomons and most can be arranged after arrival; however, it is usually wise to make reservations well in advance if possible. Prices below are approximate.

Town Tour: (1½ hours) Visit Honiara Market, Chinatown, Vavaya Ridge, Botanical Gardens and Kakabona Village. Approx. $US12. *Honiara and Environs:* (4 hours) Visit Solomon Islands National Museum, Botanical Gardens, Point Cruz, Holy Cross Cathedral, Skyline Ridge. Approx. $US25. *Tambea Village Resort:* (full day) Coastal drive along the West Guadalcanal shore, through villages and coconut plantations, visiting Vilu Village enroute. Bungalow facilities available at Cape Esperance. Swimming, shell-collecting, and lunch. Approx. $US25. *Battlefields of WWII and Betikama Carving Centre:* (4 hours) Visit underground hospital, Bloody Ridge, Red Beach, battlefields and Swiss Memorial. Lunch included. Approx. $US15. *East Guadalcanal:* (6 hours) Tours of oil palm, rice and cattle projects, Henderson Field, Bloody Ridge, Red Beach and Henderson Field. Approx. $US25.

West Guadalcanal: (6 hours) Tour west coastline and plantations, tropical gardens, WWII relics. Picnic lunch included. Approx. $US25. *Alite Village, Manmade Island, Langalanga Lagoon, Malaita:* (Full day) *Solair* flight over Iron Bottom Sound, Indispensible Strait, old capital Tulagi, Taiyo factory, transfer by war canoe, stone age factory, Malaita shell money. Approx. $US80. *Western Solomons:* (3 days) Departs Honiara Sunday for Gizo, calling at 10 intermediate ports en route. Twin berth-cabin, passengers provide own meals. Arrive Gizo at 6 P.M. Monday; overnight in a/c Kasolo Hotel. Return flight Tuesday.

Hunts of the Pacific Ltd., Box 104, Honiara, S.I. Visit the battle grounds of WWII, and many primitive islands. Special bird watching, photographic, or skin diving tours arranged for groups. Most all other travel services also available.

Solair. Box 23, Honiara, S.I. Will arrange for scheduled and charter service throughout the Solomons. Agents for services are Air Nauru and Air Niugini, Air Pacific.

Melan-Chine Shipping Co. Ltd., Box 71, Honiara, Solomons. Operates freighter/passenger services throughout the Solomons. Room for 40 passengers but cabin facilities for only four; others have deck space. Not recommended for the comfort seeking. There are ships on the line that carry up to 70 passengers with different facilities and schedules.

Valor Tours, 10 Liberty Ship Way, Sausalito, CA 94965. World War II battle zone specialists with organized programs for units that served in both the Pacific and European Theaters. With the help and cooperation of national and civic leaders of the host countries, plans are underway for a series of reunions for a number of units who served in the Pacific. Visits: Australia, New Zealand, Papua New Guinea, Solomon Islands, Marianas (Saipan), Micronesia (Truk), New Caledonia, Vanuatu, Japan, Korea, Hong Kong, Singapore and Malaysia. Valor Tours will also arrange any individual tour—just tell them where you want to go, for how long, the approximate number of persons traveling together and when you would like to travel. They will plan your itinerary and provide a cost estimate.

Shipping. Local companies operate scheduled services to a number of islands and several other companies provide non-scheduled services. The Government Marine Department runs scheduled and non-scheduled services and like the commercial operators mentioned can carry a limited number of passengers. The most regular services run from Honiara to the Western Solomons and Malaita. (Refer to Inter-Island Ships in Planning Your Trip section.)

Special tours of sunken WWII wrecks are available for divers through *Island Dive Services.* See Sports.

SPORTS. Honiara has a number of facilities for land sports such as tennis and squash; the locals love to play soccer, and if that's your interest you can probably find a casual match going and join in. The number for the Golf Club is 30181, and the Squash Court is 22230. For the most part, though, the Solomon Islands are famous for their water sports, such as fishing, sailing, canoeing and especially snorkeling and scuba diving.

There are a number of diveshops in Honiara, but the best is *Island Dive Services,* with three separate locations. The central office is in the Mendana Hotel (telephone 22103; Telex HQ66315), and dives to a variety of interesting wrecks are made several times weekly. They also operate out of Anuha Island Resort and Tambea Village Resort. All equipment, including camera gear, is available on a rental basis, and IDS also offers one-day E-6 slide processing for SBD $15. Single dives cost $45 per person (one tank) and $57 (two tanks). The cost includes tank, backpack, weight belt, and choice of a wreck or reef dive. Other gear rental is extra. Full scuba diving courses leading to international certification are available from professional instructors for SBD $275 per person; an introductory dive can be made for $55, all equipment included. Snorkeling trips are $15 per person.

In the Western Province, *Adventure Sports* in Gizo (radiophone 60199 or c/o Gizo Hotel) is a smaller operation which offers dive trips to some truly spectacular reefs, walls, and wrecks. All equipment is available for rental; dive trips cost $30, and include tank, weights, backpack, guide and/or instructor. If you love to dive and want to do a lot of it, good-natured manager/instructor Dan Kennedy might encourage your enthusiasm with a discount. Full open-water certification course is $250; an introductory dive is $50, all equipment included. Highly recommended are the dives to the Toa Maru (a torpedoed Japanese transport lying in 40–135 feet of water) and Wrasse Reef, where you'll see many sharks.

Swimming is possible off most of the islands' beaches, but be careful of sharp reefs and strong currents before going out. Reports of sharks around the Solomons are true, but the danger has been greatly exaggerated.

Other water sports are available at nearly all the island resorts mentioned in the Accommodations section.

SHOPPING. Duty-free shopping is extremely limited, with a few items available at The Trading Company and Quan Hong. All duty-free items must be purchased at least 24 hours before leaving the country.

Shop hours are generally 8 A.M.–12 noon and 1:30 to 5 P.M., although banks and government offices have more limited schedules. It is nearly impossible to do business during the lunch hour unless you have made arrangements in advance.

Woodcarvings, local handicrafts, and traditional jewelry, including shell money necklaces, may be found at the following shops: *B.J.S. Agencies,* phone 22393. *The National Museum,* 22309. *Solomon Islands Handicraft Centre* (in the new Plaza shopping arcade). *Betikama Carvings,* 30223. *Mendana Hotel Gift Shop,* 20071.

Books about the Solomon Islands and South Pacific, as well as cards, maps, magazines, and general fiction, are available at the following downtown bookshops: *Aruligo Book Centre,* Kingsley Arcade, 23174. *The Bookshop,* next to Solair, 21239.

In addition, the Honiara Branch of the University of the South Pacific (USP) carries a number of fascinating books by local authors such as Julian Maka'a, Jully Sipolo, Sam Alasia and Celo Kulugoe. These books provide unique insights into the mind and spirit of the Solomon Islands.

There is a public library in Honiara, and a National Archive with interesting records of the Islands' history. The Solomon Islands Broadcasting Corporation ("Radio Happy Isles") records and sells cassettes of local music, from panpipes to rock n' roll; ask the taxi driver to take you to SIBC.

There are several good supermarkets in Honiara, including the Honiara Consumers Co-op and Joy Supermarket. You will find a vast variety of shops selling souvenir T-shirts and "lavalavas," the traditional wrap-around garment.

HONIARA NIGHTLIFE. Honiara is quiet at night. The two movie theaters do a roaring trade but there are no nightclubs or discos. Residents make their own fun. Visitors not content with an after-dinner drink at their hotel on a balmy tropical evening are welcome at the two well-run clubs close to the town center. The *Guadalcanal Club* and the *Point Cruz Yacht Club* frequently have evening entertainment.

DEPARTURE TAX. SBD$20.

PAPUA NEW GUINEA

Adventurous, Exciting, and Exotic

by
LOIS K. BRETT

Papua New Guinea is one of the most exciting destinations in the world. It takes the visitor back to a people and a way of life still closely related to the Stone Age. No matter where you travel here, you will encounter bits and pieces of that long-ago period.

The natives who live along the coasts still travel by boats similar to those used by their ancestors. The people no longer practice cannibalism or headhunting, but they retain many of the ceremonies of their heritage and culture. Papua New Guinea is very much alive with adventure and mystery and is an anthropologist's dream. Scientists are still trying to capture the flavor of these people and still trying to explain how and why they missed the industrial revolution.

The country is a series of exciting destinations from border to border—each uniquely different from the others. Almost all the tribal communities have only just recently stepped into the twentieth century. In a few places, some people have had little or no exposure to the western world or white people.

The more advanced communities are those along the coasts because of their meetings with traders or missionaries in the end of the nineteenth century. Those inland had no opportunity of exchange until just before or during World War II.

The People

In the past, and in some instances even today, each tribe in Papua New Guinea was a unit unto itself—that is, it had almost no contact with other tribes. Each developed a distinct character due to the very diverseness of the land. Distances between tribes were great and still are. In the past, one tribe might have been able to trade with the tribe immediately next to it, but that was it—nothing beyond. With some 700 tribes and so little communication, each tribe developed its own language. Today English is the official language of Papua New Guinea along with Motu and Pidgin English, but many still converse only in their own tribal language.

The unusual mixture of cultures in Papua New Guinea has puzzled anthropologists for years. A widely accepted theory is that the original inhabitants were Negritoes, a small people with Negroid features and hair who migrated down from southeast Asia at the end of the last ice age, 20,000 to 25,000 years ago. Most also agree that later migrations from Micronesia and Polynesia probably forced the Negritoes into pockets in the mountains. The newcomers populated the islands of Melanesia, as far as Fiji, and the coasts of Papua New Guinea.

The last migrations brought many of the Polynesian people who settled in the Trobriand Islands. They came in their great canoes, probably through the Philippines, between 1000 and 2000 B.C. The Micronesian people landed in the Northwest Islands, which lie west and north of Manus Island.

Geography

Papua New Guinea is only half of an island that lies in the middle of a long chain of islands stretching from the Asian mainland into the South Pacific. It forms the eastern half of the second largest noncontinental island in the world (only Greenland is larger).

The country varies remarkably, from vast swampy plains to high, majestic mountains, broad upland valleys, volcanoes, and the rugged central mountain range. The mountains are the source of fast-flowing rivers that descend to the coastal plains to form some of the largest river systems in the world. The Sepik and the Fly are the largest and are navigable for about 500 miles. A line of active volcanoes stretches along the north coast of the mainland in an irregular line through the island of New Britain. Volcanoes and thermal pools are found in the southeastern part of the country and other islands.

Much of the country, except for the intensively farmed highland valleys, is covered by tropical rain forest, alive with orchids and brilliant butterflies and ancient mangrove swamps, where crocodiles are seen. The savannah grasslands teem with cassowaries, wild duck, wallabies, and deer. Most of the mainland and many of the large and small islands are protected by coral reefs and stretches of fine sand beaches. Many people think that the highly developed tourist packages to the highlands are all Papua New Guinea has to offer. Actually, the entire country is worth exploring though not all areas are geared to tourism. Each area is so distinct from the others that many people going from one to another wonder if they are in the same country.

Papua New Guinea is 100 miles north of Australia and lies wholly within the tropics. In the west, it shares a land border with Irian Jaya, a province of Indonesia, and in the east it takes in the islands of Bougainville in the Solomon Islands group.

Because of the mountainous regions, there are no continuous overland routes. All long-distance travel is by air. There are some very good roads around the major cities of Port Moresby and Lae. Otherwise, the roads are from good to very bad, depending on the industry and settlement in the surrounding areas. In the outlying areas, travel is mostly by four-wheel drive.

Because you must travel by air inland, and since there is only one international airport, most flights are by small plane into small airports—some with very short runways. You must book your seats well ahead of time, since space is at a premium, and you should book your travel through a reliable tour operator who can take care of all the details for you. (Because of the expense, it's best to book your PNG air travel in conjunction with your international ticket. To book once you arrive can be very expensive and time consuming because of the limited seating.) This is one country where booking your air travel or exploring far afield on your own is not generally recommended—unless you are the very adventurous type and have lots of time to spare. A list of competent operators offering a variety of tours is listed in the Tours section in Practical Information.

Port Moresby and the Central District

Because it has the only international airport, most everyone enters the country through the capital city of Port Moresby. Port Moresby was first sighted in 1873 by English Captain John Moresby, who named the city after himself, Fairfax Harbour after his father, Sir Fairfax Moresby, and the entrance to the harbor, Basilisk Passage, after his ship, H.M.S. *Basilisk*.

The major settlement in the area at that time was at Hanuabada—a large and busy coastal village, where the people had built their homes high on stilts over the water. Today, Hanuabada is a short and leisurely coastal drive from Port Moresby; you can still see some of the same style stilt houses—most now with tin roofs instead of thatch.

Missionaries were the first Europeans to settle in the country, and the London Missionary Society was first established at Hanuabada. British, Spanish, Portuguese, and German traders soon followed.

Port Moresby was proclaimed a British protectorate in 1884, became the responsibility of Australia, and grew into a small but typically colonial city.

Japanese forces landed on the mainland of New Guinea in 1942, and Port Moresby was heavily bombed. The city was a major objective and the stepping-stone from which the Japanese expected to take Australia. However, they were defeated on the Kokada Trail, only 20 miles from their goal, after fierce battles with Australian troops. When the Allies landed, General MacArthur, American allied commander in the southwest Pacific, made the city his headquarters. Reconstruction after the war was slow, but much of the old town, canoe village, and Koki market are still there. Today you can visit the trail and the war memorial here by taking Serpentine Sogeri Road, once the supply route. Vairata National Park is nearby.

Port Moresby sits on a hilly promontory, Paga Point. From there you can see the coastline and nearby islands and the National Capital District, with its modern, new National Parliament, National Museum and Art Gallery, National Library, and Supreme Court.

It is a sprawling city with the old town near the harbor and the new government center in another section of the city, making it not quite as easy to get around as tourists may like. The best way to see the city is to take one of the many available tours.

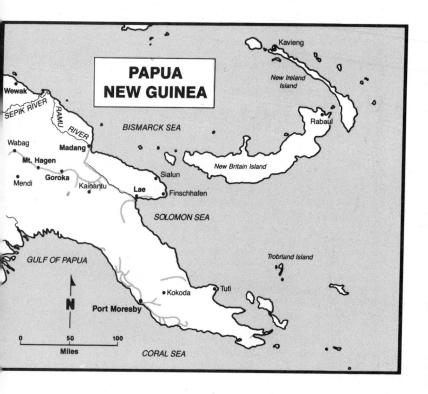

Port Moresby has a number of good international and standard-class hotels. The city is proud of its sports—from skin diving to parachute jumping—and its facilities—an international stadium and Olympic pool. Football, softball, boxing, cricket, and canoe racing are among the spectator sports that draw weekly crowds in season. Other attractions: two golf courses, tennis, bowls, horse riding and racing, rifle shooting, bush walking, swimming, yachting, and motor sports.

Out of Port Moresby

It is possible to take a flight to Tapini, Yule Island, or any of the jungle airstrips along the Kokoda Trail.

A short plane trip from Moresby, Tapini is tucked high in the Owen Stanley Ranges. Several trails welcome bush walkers. Tapini is also accessible to four-wheel-drive vehicles. A small resort hotel and a group of holiday cabins provide accommodation.

To see the city come to life visit Koki Market, especially on Saturdays. Fresh vegetables, fruit, fish, wildlife, and more are sold.

Rigo Road, near the airport, takes you through rolling savannah country. It will take you to the government-owned artifacts retailer Village Arts, the cliffs of Varirata Plateau on one side of the road, Bootless Bay on the other. A ferry can take you across the bay to Loloata Island Resort, for swimming, diving, and boating.

Brown River Road, heading north and west from Moresby, takes travelers through a teak forest, mangrove swamps, cattle ranches, and copra plantations. At Kairuku, you can look across the bay to Yule Island, site of the first Catholic mission in Papua, a hundred years ago. You can reach Yule Island by road, about 80 miles, following the coast through picturesque coconut plantations.

Lae and Morobe Province

An hour's flying time from Port Moresby on the north coast, Lae is the country's second city and an important commercial center and seaport. It is also the terminal for two major road systems—the Highlands Highway to the west, which passes through the Markham Valley and the Kassam Pass to the valleys and plateaus of the Highlands, and the Wau-Bulolo Road, which runs south through timberlands to the site of gold fields at Bulol and Wau. There is a great deal of civic pride in this beautiful little garden town, as well as in the whole of the Morobe Province.

From Nadzab Airport you travel along the Highlands Highway to the busy port city of Lae, gateway to the Highlands, through beautiful coffee, cocoa, and tea plantations. This is an exciting area worth spending several weeks exploring.

Fifty years ago Lae was a little mission station with an air strip developed by the Guinea Gold Company so that freight could be taken into the gold fields. The gold strike of the 1920s and '30s brought gold diggers from around the world to nearby Wau, Edie Creek, and Bulolo. During this time Guinea Airways created air history by flying in dredging equipment in what has been called the greatest airlift the world has ever known.

German missionaries first settled in Finschhafen, a pretty little coast town east of Lae. Germany made the region a colonial territory, and Germans established themselves throughout the Morobe Province. The Tami Islands are easily accessible by boat from town. You can rent boats for game fishing or sightseeing.

The Japanese occupied Finschhafen during World War II, but the Americans drove them out. The area is now occupied by many Australians who moved into the Bulolo Valley after the war. Because the city was never bombed, many of the old German-style buildings remain. Allied soldiers are buried in the beautiful Botanical Gardens complex, 130 acres of parkland within walking distance of the town center. The gardens contain an extensive collection of orchids and are one of the most beautiful spots in the country.

At Mount Lunaman is another war memorial—once a lookout point for the Germans, who named it Fortress Hill. The Japanese army used it for the same purpose, constructing a network of subterranean tunnels within it.

Sialum, not far from Finschhafen, is on a picturesque section of the coast known for its coral terraces. The Paradise Springs Holiday Inn is the focal point of development. Here charter boats are for hire for game fishing.

Wagan or Malhang Beach is five miles from Lae, near the Ampo Mission on Busu Road. The black-sand beach was used as an entry point for the 51st Japanese division in 1943. The remains of the landing barge

Myoko Mari are still visible. Permission to enter the beach should be obtained from the Wagan villagers.

Ampo Lutheran Mission was the site of the Japanese camp during the war; it is two miles north of the town on Busu Road. Japanese shrines have been erected near the mission by returning servicemen. The church, built in 1933, was used as a field hospital during the war and is one of the few prewar buildings left in Lae.

The Highlands

This area, one of the major reasons people come to Papua New Guinea, is the largest tourist destination. It is a fascinating step back into history. The majority of the country's population live in the highlands; yet this was the last section colonized by Europeans. In fact, the people of the highlands saw their first white man, their first steel tool, and the first wheel in 1937. Civilization here is just one step from the ancients.

The five highland provinces are extremely diverse, both in scenery and in the people—from low plateau country, sparsely populated, in the south, to high mountain country in the north.

Until a short time ago, there were some 700 tribal regions and 700 languages. Only recently have the people of one region known about the people of another, except for their nearest neighbors—whom they were usually battling. Today these same people dress in their fabulous and decorative finery, portray their battle dress, and perform in the famous "singsings". Instead of war, they compete for the best costume and best performance each year. Each province is different from the next in almost every respect.

The Simbu and Eastern Highlands

Some believe that people living in this region some 30,000 years ago had a culture totally different from those who live there today. No one in the outside world knew of the people until 1930, when two Australians, M. J. Leahy and M. I. Dwyer, who were prospecting for gold, explored the eastern fringe of the Goroka Valley.

Shortly after, the Australian government stepped in and established a station at Ramu (now Kundiawa); the station at Goroka was set up a few years later. The Goroka air strip was built by the RAAF during World War II.

As was usually the case in Papua New Guinea, once a region had been discovered, missionaries would move in. The people of the area then called Chimbu were warlike and engaged in many tribal battles and other clan demonstrations. In the 1930s some missionaries were killed and the area was closed to Europeans. Today the tribes are successful farmers and businesspeople with a strong commercial sense for development. However, not until the 1950s did development really begin. Today this area, with the adjoining western highlands, produces most of the high-grade coffee that is Papua New Guinea's second agricultural export.

The last to be developed, this region today is one of the country's major tourist spots. The Eastern Highlands Province, surrounded by Simbu, Madang, Morobe, and the Gulf provinces, is steep, rugged country with fertile river valleys, including the Asaro Valley, home of the world-famous mudmen. The land ranges from lush and dense rain forest on the mountains to light scrub and grass of the rolling foothills. The province is noted for its pleasant climate and its wildflowers. More than 200 acres around Mt. Wilhelm has been set aside as a national parkland, with walking tracks and rest-house facilities for the adventure seeker. The people of this area are a colorful and picturesque group who hold many fascinating singsings.

You can travel by car from Lae on the coast road through the Markham Valley and the Kassam Pass to the eastern highlands, through the center of the extensive coffee plantations and processing factories of the upland plateau. Coconuts, papaw peanuts, sugar cane, and pineapple all flourish in the area. Travel time is five hours to the town of Kainantu, through these plantations and villages. Kainantu has one hotel. Goroka has a number of international- and standard-class hotels.

Asaro is the home of the world-famous mudmen, who perform traditional chants while daubed in gray mud and wearing great helmet masks of mud and fiber. Their costume came about years ago when a tribe they were battling forced them to retreat to the river. When the Asaro tribe climbed out of the river and returned to battle, they were covered with the gray mud, which made them look so fearsome that their frightened enemies fled for their lives.

The J. K. McCarthy Museum features highland masks, weapons, and instruments.

Also in the area are a wool-weaving center, the Lufa Cave paintings, a trout farm, and the Ramu hydroelectric plant. Yonki Township was built to house employees of the Ramu Hydro Electric Scheme, which supplies power to most of the mainland.

All the tribes and clans of the eastern highlands have colorful tribal traditions, and each year groups alternate between Goroka and Mt. Hagen for the Highlands Singsing. The shows are held in August and September of each year and alternate between regions. Up to 10,000 members of clans gather, many walking for days from throughout the highlands for the chance to parade and dance in their magnificent costumes. Many more clan members come from near and far just to watch and enjoy the festivities. The best way for a tourist to guarantee seeing this spectacular event is to take a prepackaged tour.

In the Simbu Province each November, the people hold a festival in celebration of the pig with a series of singsings in several villages. You can drive to see the pig-kill festival by following the highway from Goroka through the eastern highlands, or you can take a scheduled tour from Goroka.

Sporting activities available to the tourist in the eastern highlands include: golf, bowling, swimming, and a sports club in Goroka. Visitors are welcome at the local clubs and can use the facilities. Arrangements can be made on arrival.

Western Highlands Province

From Simbu, the highway enters the western highlands. Mt. Hagen is the provincial capital, in the Wahgi Valley amid coffee and tea plantations. The people of this valley are less westernized than those of Goroka.

The region was discovered in 1896 by a German botanist, Dr. Carl Lautebach, who found it while exploring the Sepik River. The valley he saw is now called Wahgi and the highest peak, Mt. Hagen, he named after the acting administrator of German New Guinea at the time. The botanist did not, however, explore by foot. Consequently, it was to the amazement of the world that in 1933, three Australian patrol leaders wrote that they had "discovered evidence of a fertile soil and teeming populations. A continuous patchwork of gardens—laid off in neat squares like checker boards, with oblong grass houses in groups of four or five, dotted thickly over the landscape. Except for the grass houses, the view below us resembled the patchwork fields of Belgium as seen from the air. Certainly the 50 to 60 thousand new people we had found on the upper Purari were as nothing compared to the population that must live in the valley."

They had discovered a civilization dating back at least 8,000 years, and their findings made news around the world. These clans had a language, culture, and agricultural system unknown to the outside world, including a unique tribal battle system. Missionaries and other Europeans arrived shortly thereafter. The first coffee plantation was established in 1935 and a government patrol post in 1938. During World War II, Mount Hagen served as a staging point and a recreational center for American troops. All through the war a skeletal staff composed of an Australian government officer and a native police officer ran the government from there. After the war the European population began to grow with the coming of regular air service.

The people of the highlands were quite different from those in the coastal plains. Instead of carving, painting masks, or making pottery, they decorated themselves. Decorated shells were money; the other item of value was the ceremonial ax carried by the men during their cult festivals. One type of exchange for a bride then, and even today, is with pigs. Money or other goods are also used in acquiring a mate.

In the early 1960s the Australian administration decided to stage a great annual singsing so ancient traditional enemies could come together on neutral ground. These spectacular shows were a hit from the start and have grown in size ever since. Thousands of warriors perform, glistening with pig grease and charcoal, heads decked with feathers from birds of paradise. Their show has become a major tourist attraction. Besides the major shows at Goroka and Mt. Hagen, smaller singsings are held by many local villages.

One of the best ways to see the highlands, if you are not on a prepackaged tour, is to base yourself in one of the many excellent hotels in the region and travel from town to town by air or road. Activities available to tourists include horseback riding, climbing, trout fishing, golf, bushwalking, and village visiting.

The Baiyer River and Nondugl wildlife sanctuaries offer opportunities to see birds of paradise. Many drives provide the chance to see people in their traditional dress, especially on Sunday.

If you don't have time to stay overnight in the area, it is possible to take a regular daily flight into the region from Port Moresby or Lae to either Goroka or Mt. Hagen.

The Southern Highlands

The first Europeans penetrated the southern highlands in 1935, and a patrol post was set up in 1937 at Lake Kutubu. During the prewar years patrols explored the Tari basin, but it was not until 1949 that the government patrols decide to put in an air strip at Mendi. Until the air strip was built all supplies were sent in by airdrop. Between 1954 and 1957 roads were built and the first cars were hauled in from Mt. Hagen. The country of the southern highlands area varies from high mountain ranges to great grasslands. This area has had little contact with westerners, making this an exciting destination for the tourist.

Wewak and the Sepik River

For the adventurous and those interested in primitive art and culture, the Sepik probably has more to offer than any other part of the country. Some of the finest primitive woodcarvings and pottery are here. The towering *haus tambarans* (spirit houses) are the center of the villages, and their huge decorated gables and richly carved pillars are fine examples of the unique talents of the people. Living in river villages, the people travel from place to place in canoes carved from single tree trunks, rowed masterfully using spade-shaped oars. One of the delightful sights is to watch the children, dressed in spanking-clean European clothes, standing in these narrow canoes, paddling their way to school in the early morning.

The great Sepik River, a mile wide at its mouth and navigable for about 500 miles of its 700-mile length, is a reservoir of animal, reptile, insect, and bird life. The center of the east Sepik region is Wewak, set on white-sand beaches and connected by road to Maprik and Pagwi, on the Sepik River.

In Wewak you'll see the markets, the prime minister's house, and the cultural center. A drive along the north coast will take you to Cape Wom. Wewak was a center of Japanese activity during the war, and in 1960 the Japanese placed a large granite memorial on Mission Hill in commemoration of their war dead.

The road following the coast from Wewak and ending at Aat Dagua brings you through scenic plantation country and villages set on beaches.

The Sepik River, largest in the country, is the main highway of the people; most of them live in villages on the banks of the river. The main direction of the river is west to east, but its course is serpentine. Within the river you'll find lagoons, dead ends, small lakes, and floating islands—land torn from the banks during heavy rains.

The Sepik has been the natural trade route since the Stone Age. The primitive art work of these people is now known throughout the art world. Some of the people and their lives have been lovingly described in the work of anthropologist Margaret Mead.

The West Sepik region, which borders on Irian Jaya, is undeveloped and largely inaccessible to tourists. The provincial capital is Vanimo, near Aitape, known for its abundance of World War II relics and its fine beaches.

Many tourists fly in from Mt. Hagen, join a river craft, and travel downstream to the famous Karawari Lodge, which is outside Wewak on the Karawari River, a tributary of the Sepik. The lodge overlooks the jungle-fringed water.

Madang Province

Madang is a picturesque town in the heart of a group of tiny islands with sand beaches and lots of palm trees. Its resorts are known for their international standards and their quiet and unspoiled atmosphere. The site of one of the early German settlements, Madang has flowered streets lined with great shade trees, some of which survived the bombing during the Japanese occupation.

Madang sits on a coral hill in Astrolabe Bay overlooking a magnificent harbor and protected by more than a hundred nearby tropical islands. It is a town of waterways, lagoons, rivers, and bays—all easy to explore on your own. You can picnic on your own private beach or go bush walking or trekking. From here it's even possible to climb Mt. Wilhelm, the highest peak in the country, as well as three other ranges all with established tracks used for centuries by the local people.

Madang Market is colorful and busy. The best time to visit is Saturday. Handicrafts, artifacts, and shell jewelry can be purchased.

There is a small museum with items from the German colonial days to the present time, including small canoes and boats—the only means of transportation before the Germans built roads. The museum is near Smugglers Inn. Open: Mon. to Fri. 8 A.M. to noon and 1 to 4 P.M. A donation is expected.

A harbor cruise or ferry ride will give you your chance to see one of the most beautiful harbors in the country, loaded with colorful coral and many sunken Japanese landing craft. Swimming and snorkeling are available; masks and equipment provided.

The most popular beaches in the area are Lion's Reserve Beach, north of Smugglers Inn, Siar Island; Kranket Lagoon; Pig Island; and Wongat Island. Gear for snorkeling and diving at nearby islands is available at the Madang Resort Hotel and the Dive Centre.

You can take a short flight over Papua New Guinea's highest mountain, Mt. Wilhelm, now a national park teeming with exotic birds. Another air tour takes you over the four active offshore volcanoes, one submerged and three on densely populated islands. You can also get there by boat.

The town is renowned the world over for spectacular diving opportunities—from untouched coral reefs to the relics and wrecks of ships and planes of World War II.

Since Madang is almost on the equator, the climate is ideal, and there is always a pleasant sea breeze to temper the sun's heat.

Four types of people live in the regions: island dwellers, coastal people, riverbottom settlers, and mountaineers, including the Simbai pygmies who inhabit the foothills of the central highlands. All the people of these regions look similar, except for some Simbai tribes, who number only a few hundred and are tucked away in the southwest corner, off the beaten track; many Madang people hardly know that these people exist. Some live in cool thatched houses on short stilts; others live in high stilt houses at the river's edge. Mountaineers live in dwellings that are almost completely enclosed by their roofs.

Interesting to see are the many women who still wear their sago-leaf skirts or narrow stringy skirts; the men wear a meshy net apron in front and a cluster of leaves on their backsides.

The crocodiles that roam the rivers are protected by law. Specified sizes of the animal may be shot and skins exported only with government permit. Visit the crocodile farm in Madang for a close-up look.

Large marine turtles can be seen on the volcanic island of Long at breeding time. Wildlife is abundant.

Boating facilities are available for sailing, wind surfing, water skiing, and game fishing—for mackerel, marlin, barracuda, or shark. Madang is noted for deep-sea fishing. The Madang Hotel has boats for rent, as does the Madang Marine Center. The Madang Golf Course, which runs along the coast, has two tennis courts, a grass-bowling green, and a modern clubhouse with restaurant. Tourists are welcome to use all facilities of the club. You can also rent a car, boat, or bicycle in Madang. Tours can be arranged on land and sea, from a half-day tour on the harbor to a full week's cruise on the Sepik River. Tours take you along the oceanfront to Coastwatchers Memorial Lighthouse, erected by Australia in memory of the coastwatchers who lost their lives during World War II. You travel along pleasant roads by the lagoons, to the old German cemetery to Chinatown to Rotary Lookout, which commands a glorious view of Astrolable Bay. You can see the Rai Coast, pass the Japanese War Memorial, and visit Bilbil Village, where the women of Bilbil specialize in making distinctive pottery prized by tourists as souvenirs.

Other tours travel along the north-coast road past copra and cocoa plantations to Sia Village, which is situated on a peninsula surrounded by scenic waterways. Tour returns by way of Tusbab High School, known for its collection of birds. A singsing group from the school frequently performs at the hotels.

You can visit the vulcanology observatory on North Daughter slopes, along Tunnel Hill Road to Matupit Crater rim.

Milne Bay and The Trobriand Islands

Named after Denis Trobriand, an officer of the D'Entrecasteau Expedition, the islands became world-famous as a result of anthropologist Stanislav Malinowski's work on the people's courtship patterns.

The Milne Bay Province includes some 650 islands and atolls and extend well into the Solomons Sea. The most accessible to the tourist is the Trobriand group and its largest island of Kiriwina. The Trobriands are best known for the Kula Ringa—a ceremonial, traditional trade system operating throughout the islands involving the exchange of white armshells, shell necklaces, pottery, and yams. The Kula ritual is part magic, mythology, and tradition.

The people are also well known for their highly decorative Massim art style with its intricate designs on ebony, gables, yam houses, and war shields. Their canoes and carvings are decorated with cowrie shells.

Nearby Samarai Island, another picturesque island in the region, just off the tip of the mainland, is one of the most attractive islands in the Pacific. In the nineteenth century it was a boom town. In 1878 it became the chief missionary station for the London Missionary Society. Flattened in World War II by Japanese bombs, it has since been rebuilt.

The best way to see the islands is on an organized 3-day, 2-night or 6-day, 5-night tour from Port Moresby. Tours are for those who just want to be lazy and enjoy a South Pacific island experience. Accommodations are included, as are village trips, entertainment by a local band, and traditional dancing by young girls in short grass skirts.

Because of their early contact with Europeans, many people speak and understand English. But the people are special in that they have changed little from their ancestors in lifestyle, customs, and dress. They are subsistence farmers relying on yams and fish. Their wood carvings, known throughout the international art world, are used for local trade. (There, however, be wary—you may have to fight off the touts hawking the local tourist ware.)

Also of interest to visitors are the natural caves in the area and, in particular, the cave at Kalopa, where anthropologists found human remains in a mass burial ground.

Rabaul: New Britain

New Britain is the largest of Papua New Guinea's offshore islands and Rabaul is the beautiful prime attraction.

Archaeological finds of pottery in East New Britain date back to 600–500 B.C. Looking for spice, William Dampier on his 1700 voyage in the *Roebuck* sailed along the east coast of New Ireland and the south coast of New Britain, naming them both, but missed the strait separating them, which was discovered by Philip Carteret in 1767.

In the 1870s a thriving business existed in pearls, rare wood, copra, and *beche-de-mer,* and trading stations were established by British and Germans, mainly on the Duke of York Islands and on the east coast of the Gazelle Peninsula. In 1879, the Samoan "Queen Emma" Forsyth arrived, established a flourishing business in copra, made millions of dollars, and built one of the most beautiful mansions in the South Pacific. Queen Emma's family cemetery can still be seen off the main road in Kokopo.

During the 1870s missionaries made their first contact with the people of East New Britain, but many were killed by natives or died of disease.

The northeastern part of the mainland and the islands of the Bismarck Archipelago were proclaimed a German protectorate in 1884. One year later a charter was given to the New Guinea Kompagnie to administer a German colony in the area and in 1899 the German headquarters were moved to what is now called Kokopa. Rabaul became the administrative center in 1910 and remained so until the outbreak of World War I in 1914. The Germans left a heritage in the form of broad tree-lined avenues and the historical remains of the governor's house on Namanula Hill. There's not much left, but the view is outstanding; there are also orchid gardens here.

Thirty years of German control ended abruptly when an Australian naval force landed in Blanche Bay in September 1914, putting Rabaul under military occupation. In 1921 the League of Nations gave Australia a mandate for the civil administration of New Guinea, and Rabaul became the capital.

On January 23, 1942, a large Japanese naval force invaded Rabaul, and during the next three years, heavy bombing by Allied forces destroyed Rabaul completely. The Japanese were forced to build an elaborate system of tunnels and bunkers and virtually lived underground. You can still see the tunnels all along the Gazelle Peninsula. Other relics of the war lie scattered in the bush and on plantations. The town has been rebuilt and is considered one of the most beautiful in the country.

There is a large Chinese community in Rabaul. Exotic bargains are available at fairly low prices.

Rabaul is situated on the Gazelle Peninsula and is known for lush coconut, cocoa plantations, and beautiful scenery. The local Tolai people have had the longest contact with Europeans and are among the more sophisticated people of Papua New Guinea.

New Britain is the largest island in the Bismarck Archipelago, with a mountain range that runs down the center of the island from one end to the other. Because of this mountain range, the southern side receives much less rain than the north coast and gives Rabaul its pleasant tropical climate.

Tours go to the Baining Mountains where you can watch the Fire Walk, a fertility dance, where the performers dress in grotesque masks and dance on hot coals and flames.

Along the north-coast road to Keravat is an experimental farm, a copra drier, a cocoa fermentary, and the Bita Paka War Cemetery, Catholic Mission, and Kokopo—site of Queen Emma's residence; only the stone steps remain but the view is magnificent.

Gaulim is an easy drive from Rabaul; it's home of the Bainings people, whose huge and elaborate masks make excellent souvenirs. Nearby are many World War II relics, including Japanese tanks. The naval command bunker, where Admiral Yamamoto visited before his fatal flight to Bougainville, is now a war museum. At nearby Coastwatcher's Memorial Lookout, there are a Japanese zero fighter and antiaircraft guns. And on the shores of Blanche Bay, a floating crane is beached—captured by Japanese forces in Singapore and towed to Rabaul for their use.

Bougainville (North Solomons Province)

The Spanish explorer Torres in 1606 and later Louis Antoine de Bougainville in 1768 were the first Europeans to spot the area of the North Solomons. When the Catholic missionaries arrived shortly after, a European settlement was attempted but was not very successful. Both Buka and Bougainville were a part of the Solomon Islands group—a British possession. However, the British were not too interested in the islands and traded them to the Germans for the New Hebrides and Tonga.

In 1914 the Australians took back the islands from Germany and the German copra plantation owners, and the islands became British-mandated territory again, along with New Guinea.

Both Buka and Bougainville played important roles in World War II when two coastwatchers, Jack Read and Paul Mason, were able to supply the Allied forces with information about the Japanese and their plans to strike Guadalcanal. American troops landed in the area in 1943, followed by the Australians in 1944. The battles were costly to all sides, but it was a turning point for the Allies in the war in the Pacific.

After the war the islands returned to their sleepy-town status. In 1964 copper, silver, and gold were discovered at Panguna, and Bougainville became an international name again when it hit the world newspapers.

Buka is a small island just to the north of Bougainville; its basketware is noted throughout the art world for the fine quality of artisanship. Most of the work comes from Buin, near the southern coast of Bougainville.

Kieta is the main town and major port, with a small-town atmosphere. There are a few hotels, which cater to people doing business with the mines.

Gulf and Western Province

This area covers the whole of the western part of what was formerly the country of Papua. Most of the region is inaccessible. The Bensbach River runs westward through lowland forest and lush grassland to the Irian Jaya border of Indonesia. The wildlife in the region is fantastic in one of the most remote and unspoiled places in Papua New Guinea. Anyone wanting a rare and exciting opportunity to explore the outreaches of this lush and beautiful country should consider a stay here.

New Ireland

New Ireland is a long, skinny island north of New Britain. Europeans have known of the land as long as they have New Britain. Germans located here and built extensive copra plantations and an excellent road system. The island was captured by the Japanese in World War II, and Kavieng became a major Japanese base. A few Australian coastwatchers, in grave danger, stayed behind and did invaluable service for the Allies. The Allies did great damage to New Ireland, but the Japanese held the island until the final surrender. It has since been restored with productive copra, coffee, rubber, and timber plantations.

Kavieng is the type of town most people dream about when they think of the South Seas. It is a quiet, sleepy village where people wear comfortable south-sea-island dress. Most of the local people are very dark, have very blond, short, curly hair, and are quite friendly. They see few tourists, so they will be most interested in you. Be prepared for an audience wherever you go. As you drive along the road from Kavieng to Namatanai, people will wave. If you have a Polaroid camera, you might share some of your photos. Your hotel can arrange car rental, tours, and fishing trips.

Northern District

The Northern District is where the Kokoda Trail plays a very important role. For Australians, it is more famous than any other battle area in the South Pacific. On this trail the Japanese and the Australians battled it out. The Japanese intended to take Port Moresby, then move on to Australia.

The Australians held them 20 miles from Port Moresby on the Kokoda Trail.

The trail goes through heavy jungles, and neither the Japanese nor the Australians were prepared for the heat, the mosquitoes, or the rugged supply lanes that they had to keep open. Here the New Guinea natives (lovingly called fuzzy-wuzzy angels because of their bravery and strength) worked as carriers. Not only did they carry the ammunition, food, and medicine, but they also carried the wounded over treacherous trails and saved hundreds of Australians.

With 16,000 troops, the Japanese fought viciously to the bitter end. Only 700 survived the battle. The Americans joined the Australians at Oro Bay, which became a headquarters for shipping during the rest of the war. Day trips can be taken to the battlefields.

The Kokoda Trail, about 40 kilometers north of Port Moresby, is not a casual stroll, but a tough five-day hike. Fitness and preparedness are of vital importance. You can also fly to Kokoda from Port Moresby or Popondetta.

Coastal scenery in the Northern Province is spectacular, with deep fjord-type inlets. There is a small but delightful village guesthouse built of local materials at Tufi run by members of the Yariyari clan, who take visitors fishing and sightseeing in their outrigger canoes. You get to Tufi from the airport by canoe. There are lots of white-sand beaches. At Wanigela on Collingwood Bay, there is a plantation resort with a guesthouse.

Wuvulu Island

Wuvulu Island, with its Alaba Lodge, is a destination in itself. The lodge can entertain only 12 to 16 guests at a time. The island, owned by the residents, is idyllic. Jean-Michel Cousteau, James Michener, and William Holden have claimed Wuvulu to be one of the most remarkable areas and one of the finest diving spots, not only in the country, but in the world. The area offers deep, tropical reefs with an amazing variety of marine life. A colorful coral reef surrounds the island. One side is a placid lagoon, and the other side is like a cliff overlooking a chasm a half mile deep. There is also an underwater cave, complete with stalagmites and stalactites.

PRACTICAL INFORMATION FOR
PAPUA NEW GUINEA

HOW TO GET THERE. By air: Service from Honolulu on *Qantas* via Sydney and Cairns, Australia. Cheapest fare is through Cairns and then via *Air Niuguini* to Port Moresby. Connecting flights from Los Angeles and San Francisco, Brisbane, Cairns, Sydney. Other international destination connections: Christchurch, New Zealand; Honiara, Guadalcanal, Solomon Islands; Singapore, Manila, Vanuatu, and Jayapura, Indonesia.

CLIMATE. On the coast, the temperature rarely rises above 86°F by day or falls below 73°F at night. The sun is strong between 9 A.M. and 4 P.M.; consequently, it is wise to wear sun screen to match your type of skin during these hours. A wide-brimmed hat will protect your face, especially around noon. Coastal rainfall varies widely; the rainy season in most districts is between November and March. Most of the rain falls at night.

In the highlands areas, the days are warm but nights can be cool–77°F, falling to 57°F. Light woolen slacks and sweaters may be necessary. Because of the higher altitude, ultraviolet rays of the sun are accentuated, and fair skins should be protected.

Average Temperature (°Fahrenheit) and Humidity

	Jan	Feb	Mar	Apr	May	June	July	Aug	Sept	Oct	Nov	Dec
Average max. day temperature	97°	97°	95°	93°	92°	93°	92°	92°	94°	95°	97°	97°
Days of rain	16	18	18	15	8	7	6	7	7	7	8	14
Humidity, percent	77	81	80	82	79	78	77	74	73	69	68	73

HOW TO DRESS. Leave your tie and jacket at home. Summer dresses, slacks, skirts, and blouses for ladies. Women wear loose-fitting cool fabrics and rarely wear stockings. For men, T-shirts, shorts, and sandals are all that's required by day; slacks and short-sleeved shirts in the evening. Most people prefer drip-dry cottons.

Women should not wear shorts around town or when visiting villages, and *revealing* bikinis on a village beach may attract unwanted attention or, occasionally, even protest. Do not offend—dress modestly. Bring a light plastic raincoat or umbrella and comfortable shoes for walking.

CURRENCY. The Papua New Guinea currency is the *kina* and *toea* —pronounced "keener" and "toya." The currency circulated in K20, K10, K5, and K2 notes and the coin K1 with a hole in the center. The kina is divided into 100 toea, with coins of 1t, 2t, 5t, 10t, and 20t. At press time: 1 Kina = $U.S.1.06.

Banking hours: Mon. to Thurs. 9 A.M. to 2 P.M.; Fri. 9 A.M. to 5 P.M. No Saturday banking. Airport currency exchange service every day.

Traveler's checks are accepted by most shops and hotels in the major tourist centers. *American Express* and *Diners Club* are accepted by most hotels. *Visa* and *MasterCard* are new and just now being accepted.

ENTRY REQUIREMENTS. Passport and visa required. Stay limited to request. One photo; letter of guarantee from company for business applicants. Single-entry visas available to tourists only on arrival at Port Moresby airport for stays of 30 days or less. If you arrive by sea, you must have a visa beforehand. Ticket to leave and sufficient funds required.

HEALTH. High malaria and dengue-fever risk. Visitors should take anti-malaria tablets for 14 days before arrival, while in PNG, and for at least a month after leaving the country. See your doctor for actual types and dosages required. Since some people have had a reaction to Fansidar, have your physician check you out before taking it. Smallpox vaccination and cholera shot are required if coming from an infected area.

LANGUAGE. There are three national languages: English, Pidgin (pronounced pisin), and Motu. English is spoken in all shops, hotels, and restaurants. A Pidgin phrase book is handy in the highlands and coastal areas and can be bought in Port Moresby.

TIME. Papua New Guinea is 18 hours ahead of U.S. Pacific Standard Time, or GMT plus 10.

ELECTRICITY AND WATER. 240 volts mostly 50 Hz AC but DC in some areas. A three-pin plug is used. Water in most areas is safe; however, it is suggested that tourists use the water provided in hotel flasks.

TIPPING. Not customary and not encouraged. Please respect this custom.

COMMUNICATIONS. There is no home-delivery mail service in Papua New Guinea. Everyone has a post-office box and collects her or his mail daily. **Telegrams** are normally phoned through and then left for collection at the post office. **Tele-**

phones are limited to the main centers, but service is good and there is direct dialing to Australia. There are some pay phones in the country, but it is best to make calls from your hotel or at the post office. Local calls are 10 toea. If you want to guarantee hotel reservations, it may be wise to telephone, telex, or cable, since mail tends to be very slow.

When dialing direct to Papua New Guinea from the U.S., dial 011 (international access code) + 675 (country code). When transmitting telex messages from the U.S., the code 794 or 795 for Papua New Guinea must precede the telex number.

Postage rates. Letters within PNG 10t; aerograms 20t; airmail letters per 20gm to: Australia 20t; New Zealand 25t; Europe and North America 45t.

GENERAL HINTS. This is a fragile country—only a few years into tourism. Please remember that how you act toward local people in villages is sometimes their only introduction to western civilization. Treat people as kindly as you react to people at home.

Although most people do not mind being photographed, a polite request is always welcome. **Do not** assume that everyone speaks English or that instant service is a natural happening. In this exotic country, the tropical climate tends to put people and service at a leisurely pace.

Do not be afraid to bargain, especially when purchasing artifacts in villages.

Do not wander alone at night—*anywhere,* and in particular Port Moresby or nearby suburbs. Individuals are advised not to travel alone into rural areas.

Do drive carefully, especially on the country roads. If you are involved in an accident and someone is hurt, do not stay on the scene but drive directly to the nearest police station.

Do dress appropriately—especially women. Bathing suits and short shorts should not be worn when visiting towns or villages.

TOURIST INFORMATION. *Air Niugini* acts as the government tourist bureau in the United States. Contact their office for information: *Air Niugini,* Suite 3000, West Tower, 5000 Birch St., Newport Beach, CA 92660. In PNG write: Head Office Dept. of Tourism, Box 7144, Boroko, Papua New Guinea; tel 25–9447 or 25–1269; tlx 23472. Or write to the tour operators who handle tours in PNG. See section on *Tours* following.

You can obtain your visa from the following offices, or on arrival at Port Moresby.

United States: *PNG Embassy,* 1330 Connecticut Ave., N.W., Suite 350, Washington, DC 20036. Tel. (202) 659–0858. *PNG Permanent Mission to the UN,* 100 E. 42d St., Room 1005, New York, NY 10017. Tel (212) 682–6447.

United Kingdom: *PNG High Commission,* 14 Waterloo Pl., London SW1R 4AR.

ACCOMMODATIONS. Some of the hotels in the major tourist towns are deluxe and geared for the international tourist. However, the majority of the hotels are just the comfortable, standard motel-type accommodation. Many have refrigerators in rooms and coffee- and tea-making facilities. Not all have laundry service. Guests should not expect rapid service or the services of a deluxe hotel. Rather, realize that you are in an exotic destination where many of the hotel staff are just being trained in the tourism field and are a generation or less away from the Stone Age. Please take this into consideration when making demands on service. Also, since *everything* must be flown in, food and other amenities are usually expensive.

A few hotels, such as the Karawari, Ambua, Bensbach, or Wululu Lodges are destinations in themselves and are deluxe and unique—not only in furnishings and surroundings but in the structures themselves. Although the rates may be considered high, they include all meals, tours, and entertainment.

Several of the hotels in Port Moresby are in the deluxe international category with fine restaurants, entertainment, and other facilities. Some of the hotels near Port Moresby are popularly used by local people on weekends, as getaways; they are standard but very comfortable hotels with unique beaches and/or retreat facilities.

Hotels in the island communities of New Britain, New Ireland, and Trobriands are geared to international travelers seeking a pleasant South Seas Island adventure but not deluxe accommodations or services. These hotels are comfortable, usually in an ideal setting with a very relaxed atmosphere and service to match, but cannot be compared to those in Tahiti nor Hawaii. Some are steps into the world of Somerset Maugham, James Michener, or Robert Louis Stevenson and are popular with the expatriate community and knowing Australian and New Zealand tourists.

Hotel guide: *Expensive,* K70–K150 and up; *moderate,* K50–K70; *inexpensive,* K50 and below. See listings below.

Port Moresby

Islander Hotel. *Expensive.* Box 1981; tel. 25–5955; tlx 22288; cable ISLANDER. 90 a/c rooms. Near Waigani Government Center and near University. Handsome structure surrounded by pleasant gardens. Banquet facilities, restaurant, water sports, TV, swimming pool, tennis courts. Credit Cards: *American Express, Diners Club. Visa.*

Port Moresby TraveLodge. *Expensive.* Hunter and Douglas streets. Box 3661; tel. 21–2266; tlx 22248; cable: TRAVELODGE. 177 a/c rooms. Restaurant, coffee shop, cocktail lounge, bar, swimming pool, souvenir shop, meeting facilities, nightly entertainment. Accepts most credit cards. On prime hill site overlooking harbor, beaches, and town center.

Davara Hotel. *Moderate–Expensive.* Box 799, city center; tel. 21–2100; tlx 23236; cable DAVPOM. 65 a/c rooms. Restaurant, shops, swimming pool, room service, wind surfing, laundry service. Credit cards: *American Express, Diners Club, Visa.* Close to town center on Ela Beach Road High rise beach resort—one of best in city.

Gateway Hotel. *Moderate—Expensive.* Box 1215; tel. 25–3855; tlx 230821. Near airport. 35 a/c rooms, dining room, 5 bars, room service, disco, in-room refrigerators, laundry service, money exchange. Credit cards: *American Express, Diners Club.*

Huon Gulf Motel. *Moderate–Expensive.* Box 612, Lae; tel. 42–8844. 30 a/c rooms. On Markham Rd. near air strip and on high ground near botanical gardens. Motel style. Dining room, 2 bars, swimming pool, function room. Credit cards: *American Express, Diners Club.*

Lae Lodge. *Moderate–Expensive.* Box 2774, Lae; tel. 42–2000; tlx 427473. 89 rooms. Banquet facilities, 3 restaurants, swimming pool, tennis courts, TV. A new and an old wing are in a pleasant garden setting. Poolside barbecue, lunch on Sundays. Credit cards: *American Express, Diners Club.*

Melanesian Hotel. *Moderate–Expensive.* Box 756, Lae; tel. 42–3744; tlx. 44187. In the city center on 1st St., on high ground in commercial center near airport; nicely situated in pleasant garden surroundings. 89 a/c rooms. Meeting facilities, swimming pool, restaurant, cocktail lounge. Noted for its restaurant. Credit cards: *American Express, Diners Club.*

Pine Lodge Hotel. *Moderate–Expensive.* Box 90, Bulolo; tel. 445–220; tlx 44402. In residential area. 11 rooms. Restaurant, swimming pool, golf. Credit cards: *American Express, Diners Club.*

Owen Stanley Lodge. *Moderate.* Box 6036. 8 rooms. Restaurant, meeting facilities, laundry, travel service. Credit cards: *American Express, Diners Club.*

Papua Hotel. *Moderate.* Box 92; tel. 21–2622; tlx 22353. 56 a/c rooms. Restaurant, cocktail lounge, coffee shop, dining room, laundry service. In town center on Musgrave St., excellent restaurant popular with local people. Credit cards: *American Express, Diners Club.*

Tapini Hotel. *Moderate.* (Central District), Box 19; tel. 259–280; cable TAPINI HOTEL. 7 rooms; 3,000 feet up in the Owen Stanley Ranges. Small resort. Dining room, swimming pool, tennis courts, room service, kitchen facilities, video, coffee shop, cocktail lounge. A landing at the Tapini air strip is probably the most dramatic introduction possible to the gigantic mountain backbone of Papua New Guinea.

Boroko Hotel. *Inexpensive–Moderate.* Okari St., Box 1033; tel. 25–6677. 38 a/c rooms. In main suburban shopping center. 5 bars, room service, disco, in-room refrigerators, laundry service, money exchange. With 5 bars, the hotel can get a bit noisy. Credit cards: *American Express, Diners Club.*

Civic Guest House. *Inexpensive.* Box 1139, Boroko; tel. 25–5091. On Mairi Pl. near Angau Dr. in suburban Boroko. 20 rooms, share bath. This clean little guesthouse is popular with tourists.

Kokoda Trail Motel. *Inexpensive.* Box 5014; tel. 21–2266. 16 rooms; at Sogeri, 30 miles from Moresby in the Owen Stanley Range and less than a mile from the beginning of the trail. Built in 1965. Bush-style bungalows in riverside garden setting at cool, airy 1,700-foot elevation. Base for exploring wartime Kokoda Trail country and Variarata National Park. Good value for quiet stay. Fans, pool, licensed dining room.

Loloata Island Resort. *Inexpensive.* Box 5290; tel. 25–8590; tlx 23016. On the beach. 9 rooms, meeting facilities, laundry service, travel services, fishing. Credit cards: *American Express, Diners Club.*

Western Highlands

Plumes & Arrows Inn. *Expensive.* Box 86, Mt. Hagen; tel. 551–555; tlx 52088. Near the airport. 16 rooms. Dining room, bar, swimming pool, travel services, conference rooms, library, golf, shops. Credit cards: *American Express, Diners Club.*

Highlander Hotel. *Moderate–Expensive.* Box 34; Mt. Hagen; tel. 521–355; tlx 55108; cable HOTELS. 38 rooms. Barber and beauty shops, restaurant.

Hagen Park Motel. *Moderate.* Box 81, Mt. Hagen; tel. 521–388; tlx 52056; cable HAPARK. 30 rooms. Meeting facilities, restaurant, color TV, doctor on call, disco.

Tribal Tops Inn. *Moderate,* Box 13, Minj; tel. 565–538; tlx 52070. 12 rooms. Dining room, bar, swimming pool, golf course, gardens, travel services. Credit cards: *American Express, Diners Club.*

Baiyer River Sanctuary Lodge. *Inexpensive.* Box 490, Mt. Hagen; tel. 521–482. In national park. Hostel-type accommodations. 8 rooms, kitchen facilities, table tennis, hiking.

Kaiap Orchid Lodge. *Inexpensive.* Box 193, Wabag; tel. 522–087; cable KAIAP LODGE. In highlands. 12 rooms. Bar, gardens, parking. Lovely garden setting with lots of orchids. Credit cards: *American Express.*

Kimininga Lodge. *Inexpensive.* Box 408, Mt. Hagen; tel. 521–865; tlx 52008; cable KIMININGA LODGE. 37 rooms. Dining room, laundry, parking, video, swimming pool, shop, restaurant.

Wabag Lodge. *Inexpensive.* Box 2, Wabag; tel. 571–122. 12 rooms. Dining room, 2 bars, conference rooms, parking. Polynesian round house bures (cottages). In remote Enga Province. Good touring center by four-wheel-drive vehicles. Central *Haus Wind* restaurant features open fire for cool nights.

Eastern Highlands

Bird of Paradise Hotel. *Moderate.* Box 12, Goroka; tel. 721–144; tlx 72628. 39 a/c rooms. Banquet facilities, barbershop, 2 restaurants, shops, swimming pool, squash courts, video. On main street of town not far from airport. Saturday buffet luncheon. Hotel restaurants are popular with locals. Rooftop bar and lunch snack bar. Credit cards: *American Express, Visa, Diners Club, MasterCard.*

Chimbu Lodge-Kundiawa. *Moderate.* Box 191, Kundiawa; tel. 751–144; tlx 75651. Near business area. 22 rooms. Meeting facilities, restaurant, bank, tennis courts, laundry service, room service, color TV. Small country hotel with pretty garden, mountain scenery. Good base for exploring Simbu region. Small but good restaurant. Credit cards: *American Express, Diners Club.*

Kainantu Lodge. *Moderate.* Box 31, Kainantu; tel. 771–021; tlx 77632. 17 rooms. Restaurant, tennis court, laundry service, bars, video, color TV, in-room refrigerator. On hill above quiet town on Highlands Highway near Kassam Pass. Motel style. Credit cards: *American Express.*

Lantern Hotel. *Moderate.* Box 769, Goroka; tel. 72–1776; cable LANTERN. 8 rooms. Dining room bar, restaurant, travel services. Buffet lunch on Sundays. Restaurant offers European, Chinese, and Indian cuisine. In residential area. Well-run, pleasant hotel.

Minogere Lodge. *Moderate.* Box 450, Goroka; tel. 721–00; cable, GOROKAUNSIL. 57 rooms. Rate includes breakfast. Video. Town swimming pool, steps away, open 9 A.M. to 6 P.M. daily. Hostel-type accommodations run by city council. Short walk from town—central location with good views. Fair prices and good value.

Western Highlands

Ambua Lodge. *Expensive.* Tari. TransNiugini Tours, Box 371, Mt. Hagen; tel. 521–438; telex. NE 52012. Or: ATS/tourPacific, 1101 E. Broadway, Suite 201, Glendale, CA 91205. Credit cards: *American Express.* 12 bungalows. Large lounge, bar, and dining area with central fireplace. Built in the Karawari Lodge-style with a highland flavor. You stay in luxury circular accommodation units with private facilities. This new lodge is a destination in itself in the southern highlands. The lodge is at 7,000 feet and overlooks the Tari Basin, home of the "wig men" and birds of paradise. Stay includes visits to villages and cultural events where you are allowed a rare opportunity to study the Huli people, whose lives are still governed by their belief in the ancestral spirits and sorcery. Only since 1951 has a government station been established in the region.

You travel to Ambua Lodge by road from Mt. Hagen. Bird watching (10 species of birds of paradise are found in this region), high-altitude orchids, and bush walks are part of the daily activities. Lodge management is another quality performance by the operator of Karawari and Bensbach and Wuvlulu lodges. An outstanding opportunity to live among the birds of paradise and to see them up close daily. A real adventure and one of the newest offerings in the country.

Southern Highlands

Mendi Hotel. *Inexpensive–Moderate.* Box 108, Mendi; tel. 591–188; tlx 590. 14 rooms. Meeting facilities, squash court, TV, Restaurant. In garden setting of valley overlooking small, quiet outpost town. Close to airport. Comfortable motel style. Good restaurant.

Wewak and the Sepik River

Karawari Lodge. *Expensive.* Write: TransNiugini Tours, Box 371, Mt. Hagen; tel. 52–1438; tlx NE 52012. Or in the United States: ATS/tourPacific, 1101 E. Broadway, Suite 201, Glendale, CA 91205. Hotel overlooks river and has fantastic view of the mountain regions beyond. 20 rooms, cooled by overhead fans. Sleep under mosquito nets in grand setting. Dining room, bar, swimming pool, shops. Credit cards: *American Express.* Includes meals, entertainment, tours.

The lodge is attractively situated. Each cottage is a self-contained duplex and features extensive use of native building materials. They are clustered alongside the main lodge and built on the style of a traditional *haus tamboran,* or spirit house. Atmosphere is more on the grand-lodge style. As part of the package guests travel from the lodge on river trucks—aluminum river boats, powered by outboard motors. They see reenactments of traditional native ceremonies and observe the day-to-day activities in the villages along the river banks. There are opportunities to explore the extraordinary variety of plant, bird, and animal life. The region is safe. It is difficult to get to—but worth the effort! This is a quality operation. The owners have captured the spirit of the country and have been able to pass this feeling on to their guests.

Wewak Hotel. *Moderate–Expensive.* Box 20, Wewak; tel. 86–2155. Cable HOTEL WEWAK. 35 a/c and ceiling-fan rooms. On a hill overlooking the sea. Banquet and meeting facilities, restaurant and cocktail lounge, video. Credit cards: *American Express, Diners Club.* Good base for road trip to middle Sepik area.

Sepik International Beach Resort. *Moderate–Expensive.* Box 152, Wewak; tel. 862–388; tlx 86119; cable SEPK. On the beach. 20 rooms. Popular restaurant and bar. Fishing arranged. Good traditional open-style restaurant; nice bar.

Sepik Motel. *Moderate–Expensive.* Box 51, Wewak; tel. 86–2422; tlx 86143. 14 a/c rooms. Dining room, cocktail lounge, swimming pool, room service, conference room, banquet facilities. Travel services. Credit cards: *American Express, Diners Club.*

Angoram Hotel. *Moderate.* Box 35, Angoram; tel. 88–3011; tlx 86134; cable AR-SHAK. 14 a/c rooms. Garden hotel with bars, dining room, restaurant, TV room. Excellent touring base for the middle Sepik area; canoe trips, visits to local artifact-rich villages.

Madang

Masurina Lodge. *Expensive.* Box 5, Alotau; tel. 611–212; tlx 61107; cable MA-SURINA. In residential area. 29 a/c and fan rooms. Dining room, bar. Diving trips and local tours arranged. Credit cards: *American Express.*

Madang Resort. *Inexpensive–Expensive.* Coastwatchers Ave. Box 111, Madang; tel. 822–655; tlx 82707. Situated along the harbor and Yamilon Bay opposite Kranket Island at the entrance to the harbor. Set in 5 acres of landscaped gardens among thousands of native orchids. 60 a/c rooms. Banquet facilities, barbershop, beauty shop, restaurant, swimming pool. More expensive rooms have sea view. Credit cards: *American Express, Diners Club.* The Melanesian Explorer Marina is here for its Sepik Cruise.

Jais Aben Resort. *Moderate–Expensive.* Box 105; tel. 82–3311; tlx NE 82716. 16 rooms. New resort with self-contained units, half with kitchens. Swimming pool and restaurant. Boats for hire and all water sports. Near the beach within a coconut plantation overlooking lovely Nagada Harbor, 12kms from town off the main road on the waterfront. Deluxe rooms along oceanfront—all with screened patio area adjacent to small coral beaches. Dive shop.

Smugglers Inn. *Moderate–Expensive.* Box 303; tel. 82–2744; tlx 82722; cable SMUGLER. 45 a/c rooms. Banquet facilities, barbershop, beauty shop, restaurant, swimming pool. Excellent location. Open-air restaurant has view and sea breezes. Lions Reserve Beach is nearby. Credit cards: *American Express, Diners Club.*

Coastwatchers Motel. *Moderate.* Coralita St., Box 324; tel. 82–2684; cable COWAMO. Rates include breakfast. 14 a/c rooms. Dining room, bar, swimming pool, golf course, travel services, boating, video. In beautiful gardens opposite the Coastwatchers Memorial with view over the golf course and Astrolobe Bay. Credit cards: *American Express, Diners Club.*

Kirwina Lodge. *Inexpensive—Moderate.* Box 2, Losuia. Near the lagoon. 16 rooms. Air conditioned by sea breezes. The lodge is very popular with weekenders from Port Moresby. Can arrange tours and transportation.

New Britain

Hamamas Hotel. *Moderate–Expensive.* Box 139, PN139, Rabaul; tel. 92–1999; tlx 92959; cable HAMAAMAS. In city center. 56 a/c rooms. TV, conference room, restaurant, two bars, Western and Chinese food.

Kaivuna Resort Hotel. *Moderate–Expensive.* Mango Ave., Box 395, Rabaul; tel. 92–1766; tlx 92982. In city center. 56 a/c rooms. Restaurants, swimming pool, scuba diving. Open-air bar. Credit cards: *American Express, Diners Club.*

Palm Lodge. *Moderate.* Box 32., Kimbe; tel. 935–001; tlx 93114; cable PALO. Near beach. 20 a/c rooms. Restaurant, swimming pool, TV, travel services. Credit cards: *American Express, Diners Club.*

TraveLodge Rabaul. *Moderate.* On the corner of Mango Ave. and Namaula St., Box 449, Rabaul; 92–2111; tlx 92975. Overlooks harbor. 40 a/c rooms. Queen Emma Dining Room, bar, swimming pool, shops, laundry, beauty shop, minibar. Room service. Most credit cards accepted.

Kulau Lodge. *Inexpensive–Moderate.* Box 359, Rabaul; tel. 92–2115; tlx 92930; cable KULAU LODGE. Six units built like local Kunai huts with all conveniences, including refrigerator and room service. Banquet and meeting facilities, restaurant, shops, fishing, snorkeling, boating, laundry service. In pleasant garden setting overlooking ocean, a few kilometers out of town on the North Coast Rd. Credit cards: *American Express.*

Kieta

Bensbach Lodge. *Expensive.* Book through Trans Niugini Tours. Like Kawawari Lodge, Bensbach is built entirely from local materials and blends right in with the landscape. Here you become a part of the landscape with its spectacular wildlife. The lodge is comfortable and rooms are spacious and cool, with ceiling fans and refrigerators. Covered verandas link the accommodation wings to the main building, which has dining room, bar, and lounge. Food is excellent, and much care is put into the meals—venison, duck, freshly caught barramundi, and other fresh seafood. Rates include all meals, tours, and sports equipment. Deer, wallaby, and bird life are abundant. Bensbach is a fisher's paradise, and arrangements can be made with local fishers to accompany you to some very special fishing spots. Bensbach Lodge is a destination in itself and is another quality operation by the owners of Kawawari Lodge. (See *Wewak* section on Karawari Lodge.)

Arvo Holiday Island Resort. *Moderate–Expensive.* (Out of town) Box 44, Arvo Island; tel. 95–1855; tlx 95867; cable ARVO ISLAND. The resort is a short ferry ride from the Kieta Yacht Club. 16 rooms. Kept cool by sea breezes. Pleasant little resort with banquet and meeting facilities, restaurant, tennis courts, scuba diving, fishing, snorkeling, wind surfing. Perhaps the best accommodations in the area.

Davara Hotel. *Moderate–Expensive.* Box 241, Kieta; tel. 956–175; tlx 95852. Cable DAVARA KIETA. Near the sea on Toniva Beach. 46 a/c rooms. Bar, restaurant, radio, TV, laundry service, meeting facilities. Swimming pool. Credit cards: *American Express* and *Diners Club.*

Kieta Hotel. *Moderate–Expensive.* Box 228, Kieta; tel. 95–6277; tlx 95843; cable KIETOL. Located near the shopping area. 24 a/c rooms. Restaurant, cocktail lounge, TV lounge, laundry service, in-room refrigerator, room service, tea-coffee-making facilities in rooms.

Buka Luman Sopho. *Moderate.* Buka Passage, Bougainville, Sohano; tel. 966–057; tlx 50014; cable BUKALUMA. 4 rooms. Rates include meals. Bar, video, meeting facilities.

New Ireland

Kavieng Hotel. *Moderate.* Box 4, Kavieng; tel. 942–199; tlx 94904; cable HOTEL. In the center of this capital town. 24 a/c rooms, some with private bath. There are also a few fan-cooled rooms without private bath. Dining room, restaurant, laundry service, bar, parking, color TV, tennis. Relaxing atmosphere and what you'd expect if you've read many stories of the old days in the South Pacific. Credit cards: *American Express, Diners Club.*

Namatanai Hotel. *Inexpensive–Moderate.* Box 48, Namatanai; tel. 25; cable HOTEL NAMATANAI. 6 rooms. On the waterfront. Fans and private bath, radio. Meals available.

Kavieng Club. *Inexpensive.* Box 4, Kavieng, tel. 942–199; tlx 94904. Cable HOTEL. 8 rooms, some with fans, some a/c. Club atmosphere and delightful place to meet local people.

Northern District

Lamington Hotel. *Moderate—Expensive.* Box 27, Popondetta; tel. 297–065; cable LAMHOTEL. 18 a/c rooms. Dining room, laundry service, parking, bar, in-room movies, cocktail lounge. Popular with returning Australian veterans.

Mirigina Lodge. *Inexpensive.* c/o post office or district officer, Tufi. 7 double rooms. Rates include meals. Fishing, diving, and sightseeing trips can be arranged. This small lodge is on scenic Cape Nelson. Cabins are of native materials. Situated above the fjord waters at Tufi Station.

Waijuga Park Guest House. *Inexpensive.* c/o Post Office Wanigela. 14 rooms. Rates include meals. Canoe trips and glass-bottom-boat trips arranged. Other tours arranged.

Kofure Village Guest House. *Very Inexpensive.* c/o post office or district officer, Tufi. About 1km from airport via outrigger canoe. 18 double rooms. Rates include all meals and entertainment—and fishing.

Wuvulu Island

Alaba Lodge. *Expensive.* Wuvulu Island. For rates and information contact Air Niugini or Trans Niugini Tours. Box 371, Mt. Hagen; tel. 52–1438; tlx 52012. In the U.S.: ATS/tourPacific, 1101 E. Broadway, Suite 201, Glendale, CA 91205. Rates include food, lodging, laundry, land transport, all diving and snorkeling equipment (not regulators), and scuba and fishing boats with guides. This charge also includes air for two dives per day with bottles provided. Booking must be made well in advance.

RESTAURANTS. Hotel food is international; Chinese food is very popular. Most tourist hotels have dining rooms; some have coffee shops or snack bars. A few hotels serve barbecue meals at noon on Saturday and/or Sunday.

The prices of meals are not expensive anywhere, except at the best restaurants in the deluxe hotels in Port Moresby. Most meals are included in the prepackaged tours. Meals average breakfast, K3; lunch, K5; dinner, K10 but will vary depending on whether you are eating in a regular restaurant, a café, or an international hotel.

HOW TO GET AROUND. Papua New Guinea's rugged terrain has prevented the establishment of a cross-country road network, but all main centers are connected by frequent air service. In addition, the *Highlands Highway* connects Lae with the major highlands centers of Goroka, Kundiawa, Mt. Hagen, and Mendi. There is also a seasonal road between Lae and Madang.

By air: Offices of the airlines dealing with air travel within Papua New Guinea: *Air Niugini,* Box 7186, Boroka, Papua New Guinea; tel. 25900. In the U.S., write: 5000 Birch St., Suite 3000 West Tower, Newport Beach, CA 92660. Tel. (714) 752–5440.

Aviation Developments PNG Pty. Ltd., Box 1975, Boroko. Tel. 259–655; tlx 22241. Scheduled air tours.

Douglas Airways, Box 1179. Tel. 253–499; tlx 22145; cable AIRTOURS. Five- to 18-passenger charters. Also offers aerial safaris.

Talair, Box 5350, Port Moresby. Tel. 255–799. Scheduled and air charters throughout the country.

Bougair–Bougainville Air offers extensive service from Kieta around the North Solomons to the neighboring islands of Buin, Torokina, Nakunai, and Buka.

Because the small planes used in travel throughout the country have limited seating space, it is imperative that all bookings from November through February be booked well in advance; it is wise to book in advance in any period.

Internal air fares within the country are quite high. Major airports with daily flights are: Lae, Rabaul, Kieta, Goroka, Madang, Wewak. Because of the distances involved, there are both large and small airports throughout the country.

By car: Renting is not a problem in major centers. *Avis-Nationwide, Budget Hire Car,* and *Hertz* are represented in Port Moresby, Lae, Rabaul, Mt. Hagen, Madang, Wewak, and Kieta.

By bus: Bus services operate in major towns, including Madang (cost 25 toea; pay when you get off; depot at market; you can also travel out of town), and Port Moresby (for the adventurous only) and the Highlands. Buslines provide a service between Lae and Mt. Hagen.

By sea: For inter-island shipping see also *Planning Your Trip.* The Lutheran Shipping Co. (tel. 82–2577) has weekly service from Lae or Wewak to the islands on Milne Bay. Takes 24 hours; costs K14–K214. Not the most comfortable, but a great way to see the islands. *Melanesian Tourist Services Pty Ltd.,* Box 707, Madang, Papua New Guinea, offers 5-night cruises aboard the *Melanesian Explorer* along the Sepik River, stopping off at various villages between Angoram, Ambunti, and Pagwi. Good accommodation and food. Excellent opportunity to experience river culture, purchase artifacts. Much used by tour groups. Also operates 4-wheel overland expeditions through the highlands and coastal regions. Tel. 82–2766; tlx 82707. See *Tours* below.

TOURS. A number of major tour operators deal with all-inclusive package tours to specific areas in the country. Bookings should be made with your travel agent. A number of local tour operators can arrange local sightseeing after you arrive. However, the safe bet is to book through a major operator before arrival in order to guarantee hotel and air reservations. The number of hotel rooms is limited in certain areas, and plane capacity is also limited. You should confirm your reservations well in advance.

Listed below are tour operators who handle packaged tours to the most popular destinations within Papua New Guinea. You can also usually arrange tours through your hotel.

The three largest operators, whose trips are highly recommended:

Trans Niugini Tours, c/o Greg Stathakis, 408 Islay, Santa Barbara, CA 90131; (805) 569–0558. Offers 2- to 15-day package tours throughout the country. Exciting

188   THE SOUTH PACIFIC

four-wheel-drive trips into remote areas. Special-interest tours; also excursions to Baiyer River Bird of Paradise Wildlife Sanctuary and village cultural tours.

TransNiugini also arranges trips to the famous Kawari and Bensbach lodges. Or call toll free ATS/tourPacific in California (800) 232–2121; U.S. (800) 423–2880; Los Angeles or Canada, call collect: (805) 569–0558.

Travel Plans International, Box 3875, Oak Brook, IL 60521 (800) 323–7600; Illinois (312) 655–5678. Fascinating natural-history and anthropology special-interest tours of the country, as well as special helicopter expeditions—a new way of seeing remote areas that cannot be reached otherwise. Travel Plans International is a creative group operator that handles group and individual tours and provides escorted national and local tours working with TransNiugini Tours, Melanesian Tours, and Pacific Expeditions (the helicopter operator). They will work with any individual or group wanting to go anywhere in Papua New Guinea.

Melanesian Tourists Services Pty. Ltd., Box 707, Madang. Tel 822; tlx 82707. Unirep, Melanesian Tourist Services, 850 Colorado Blvd, #105, Los Angeles, CA 90041; (213) 256–1991; (800) 521–7242. Interesting *Melanesian Explorer* cruises of Sepik River, the Trobriand Islands, and highlands expeditions. Full- and half-day tours. For individuals or groups.

Air Carriers. *Bougair Air Services Pty. Ltd.,* Box 986, Arawa, Kieta, Bougainville. Arranges flights to government and mission stations throughout Bougainville. Scenic flights of the copper mine at Panguna and Mt. Bagana. Scheduled service between: Kieta and Buin and between Kieta, Torokina, and Kieta, with Tonu–Boku–Wakunai as options, and from Kieta to Torokina. Scheduled flights to Buka via Wakunai, Unus, and Sabah. Write for rates.

Talair Tourist Airlines of Niugini, Box 108, Goroka. Operates 60 aircraft serving major centers and outstations with scheduled service to all provinces.

Douglas Airways, Box 1179, Boroko, Port Moresby. Operates 19 aircraft in Gulf, Central, Western and Sepik provinces. Aerial safaris are available. Rates are by size of aircraft and by the hour.

The following tour operators also arrange trips to and within Papua New Guinea. Your may write or call for details, then ask your travel agent to do the rest.

Abercrombie & Kent International, Inc., 1420 Kensington Rd., Suite 103, Oak Brook, IL 60521; (312) 954–2944; (800) 323–7308. Escorted deluxe tours and South Pacific options.

ATS/tourPacific, 1101 E. Broadway, Suite 201, Glendale, CA 91205; (800) 232–2121 (CA) or (800) 423–2880. Individual travel throughout Papua New Guinea.

Wilderness Travel, 1760 Solano Ave., Berkeley, CA 94707; (415) 524–5111; tlx 677 022. Individual and group tours off the beaten track. Trekking and island exploration.

Brendan Tours, 15137 Califa St., Van Nuys, CA 91401; (800) 421–8446; tlx 215 393.

Burns Philp Travel, Box 87, Rabaul; 92–2645 or 2798; for tours in Rabaul area.

Hemphill/Harris Travel Corp., 16000 Ventura Blvd, Suite 200, Encino, CA 91436; (213) 906–9086; (800) 421–0454. Escorted deluxe tours as part of their South Pacific tours.

Lindblad Tours, Box 912, Westport, CT 06880; (203) 226–8531; (800) 243–5657. Escorted tours in conjunction with South Pacific tours.

Mountain Travel, 1398 Solano Ave., Albany, CA 94706; (415) 527–8100; (800) 227–2384. Emphasis on adventure among peoples, throughout the country. 20 days escorted.

Nature Expeditions, Box 11496, Eugene, OR 97440; (503) 484–6529. Escorted adventure tours throughout the country. Emphasis on culture, with lectures by professionals.

Olson-Travelworld, 5855 Green Valley Circle, #300, Culver City, CA 90230; (213) 670–7100; (800) 421–2255. Deluxe escorted tours as part of South Pacific tour.

Pacific Dateline Tours, Box 1755, Newport Beach, CA 92663; (714) 675–7620; (800) 854–0543. Individual tours covering entire country.

Pacific Expeditions, Box 132, Port Moresby; 25–7803; tlx NE 22292; for tours within PNG.

RTC World Travel, Box 221, Rabaul; 92–2826 or 2849, for tours around Rabaul.

Sobek Expeditions, Box 1089, Angels Camp, CA 95222; (209) 736–2661. Adventure tours with emphasis on white-water rafting and trekking.

See and Sea Travel, 680 Beach St., #340, San Francisco, CA 94109; Tel (415) 771–0077. Scuba-diving tours.

Society Expeditions, 3131 Elliott Ave., Suite 700, Seattle, WA 98121; (206) 285–9400; (800) 426–7794. Land and sea tours of Papua New Guinea using the World Discoverer and Society Explorer.

Travcoa, 4000 MacArthur Blvd., Newport Beach, CA 92660; (800) 992–2003. Escorted deluxe tours as part of South Pacific tours with in-depth emphasis on Papua New Guinea.

Valor Tours, 10 Liberty Ship Way, Sausalito, CA 94965; (415) 332–7850. Emphasis on war-veteran tours to Papua New Guinea and throughout the Pacific.

SEASONAL EVENTS. Papua New Guinea's annual singsings in the highland towns of Mt. Hagen and Goroka have become world famous. They are held alternating years in each province during August and September. But if you can't make these, you may be able to attend other singsings and cultural activities that mark national and local holidays. The following is a guide to scheduled special events held throughout the country. Dates may vary year to year.

End January/early February: *Chinese New Year.* Chinese community in major centers stages festivities with fireworks and traditional dragon dances.

April through June: *Yam Festival.* Held in Kiriwina, a subprovince of Papua. This annual event of the Trobriand Islands is to celebrate the harvest of yams, a staple crop of the area. Singsings, of course, and ceremonial gift exchanges are held.

May. *Frangipani Festival,* Rabaul. Three days of celebration including a parade, Mardi Gras, Frangipani Ball, and beauty contest.

June 7: *Marborasa Festival in Madang.*

June: *Queen's Birthday Weekend.* Port Moresby: National Capital Show, cultural, agricultural, and industrial displays. Madang: Maborasa Festival, weekend of cultural events, including music festival, dance and drama performances, and art show.

September 16–18. *National Day.* Celebrated throughout the country, marked by yacht races, singsings, cultural performances, art and craft displays. Hiri Moale (Port Moresby): Festival to mark the early voyages of the Motu people, who traveled along the Papuan coast. Weekend event has canoe races, beauty contast, and singsings. *Papua New Guinea Festival* (Port Moresby): Month-long event with guest performers from other third-world countries participating in traditional- and contemporary-arts program.

September–October: *Tolaii–Warwagira, Kavieng–Malag Festival.* Traditional performances for two weeks. Exciting festival held at East New Britain province's major center. Weekend firework displays, singsings, fire dancers, string-band competition, and performances by choral groups. *Morobe Show* (Lae): Weekend of cultural and agricultural displays. Major singsing is staged on Sunday. Many highland groups travel great distances to participate in the event.

October: *Morobe Festival* in Lae.

November: *Pig Kill Season.* From the beginning of November until Christmas, the Simbu people, near Kundiawa, stage traditional feasts within their village communities. Hundreds of pigs may be killed for one such event. A movable feast marked by singsings moves from village to village. *Pearl Festival* (Samarai Milne Bay Province): Weekend-long festival celebrated by beauty contests, art and craft displays, canoe races, and junior sports events.

December: *Tolai Warwagira, Rabaul,* East New Britain. An annual festival including string-band competitions, yacht races, and performances by drama and choir groups. A major singsing is held near Rabaul during which a *duk duk* dance is performed to represent all *Tubuan* (secret) societies.

SPORTS AND BEACHES. All water sports are extremely popular, snorkeling and diving included. See also Accommodations for resorts that offer sporting activities. *Ela Beach,* 5 minutes from Port Moresby's center, is a popular sunbathing beach. The **Kokoda Trail,** about 40km from Port Moresby, where Australians fought Japanese during World War II, makes an interesting hike. The trail to Owers Corner, where the war memorial is situated, is an easy hike; after this it gets tougher.

Follow the **Sogeri Road,** with its magnificent views, including Rouna Falls, through many rubber plantations. Visitors make it a day outing with a picnic or lunch at the Kokoda Trail Motel (38km from city) where the most popular dish is barbecued crocodile. *Royal Papua Yacht Club* membership includes water skiers, power-boat devotees, big-game fishers, dinghy sailors, and keel boaters, both racing and cruising. Situated on Port Moresby Harbour. Provides extensive amenities and has a dining room serving light meals. Visiting tourists welcome. Phone: 21–4454. You can also contact *Tropical Diving Adventures,* Box 1644, Port Moresby; 25–7429.

In the **eastern highlands,** you'll find golf, bowling, swimming, and a sports club in Goroke that welcomes visitors.

In **Madang Province** scuba diving among coral reefs and wartime wrecks in Hansa Bay can be fascinating. Boating is available; Madang is known for deep-sea fishing. Tourists are welcome at the Madang Golf Course.

In **Milne Bay,** you can rent boats from the Madang Hotel and the Madang Marine Center. The Madang Hotel and the Dive Center (82–2766) can arrange for snorkeling and diving trips. The Dive Center also offers lessons.

The most popular beaches in the area are Lion's Reserve, north off Smuggler's Inn; Siar Island; Kranket Lagoon; Pig Island; and Wangat Island.

In **New Britain,** the Rabaul Yacht Club. Box 106, Rabaul, welcomes visitors, even non-yachtsman. Good place to have a cool drink and a smorgasbord luncheon while enjoying the sights of Rabaul's Harbor. The three golf clubs on the island, each with its unique setting, welcome visitors to use the courses or the clubs. There are a number of other social and sporting clubs in Rabaul that welcome overseas visitors (golf, aquatic, squash, tennis, snorkeling and sports club). Check with the local tourist office on Park St., 92–1823, or at your hotel for information on local events, festivals, singsings. Tour operators in town can arrange for fishing, sailing and underwater exploration.

Wuvulu Island offers some of the finest diving in the world.

OTHER THINGS TO SEE. Just seeing the country is a fascinating experience in itself. Here we list some particular sites of historic and cultural interest.

Port Moresby

National Parliament. The new Parliament House at Waigaini was opened in August 1984 by Prince Charles, heir to the British throne, before a gathering of commonwealth leaders. It is built in *haus tambaran* (spirit house) style. More than 100 members in the national parliament conduct their proceedings in three languages: English, Motu, and Pidgin. If parliament is in session, a visit to the public gallery is recommended. Visitor's gallery open Mon. to Fri. 8 A.M. to noon and 1 to 4 P.M.

National Museum. Opened in 1977 as a gift from the Australian government on independence. The museum, an interesting example of modern architecture, is in the suburb of Waigani, close to the government-office complex. It features excellent displays of pottery and birds of paradise from all the provinces and has a fine collection of Melanesian artifacts. Art is attractively presented; the museum is well worth a visit. Open Tues. and Thurs. from 8:30 A.M. to 3:30 P.M.; Sun. 1 to 5 P.M. No admission charge. Bookshop open Mon. to Fri. 8 A.M. to noon; 1 to 3:30 P.M.; Sundays from 1 to 5 P.M.

National Arts School and Design Center. Good place to watch a painting or sculpture being created by a student or village carvers, or preview the *National Theatre Company* in rehearsal of a play or a dance. Students play ancient Sepik flutes and other native instruments and combine their music into modern folk-rock. The artists live and work together and the work done by the students is on sale to the public. Close to the National Library and the Supreme Court. Open Mon. to Fri. during school hours.

University of Papua New Guinea and the National Botanic Gardens. This modern university has some 3,000 students. Follow the signs to the gardens of one of the world's great orchid collections. More than two-thirds of the world's known species can be seen here. Hybrid double and treble bougainvilleas were developed here. *Botanical Gardens:* Open 8 A.M. to 4 P.M. except Saturdays.

Bomana War Cemetery. Resting place of some 4,000 men from Papua New Guinea and Australia who died fighting for their countries during World War II. Beautifully maintained. About 16km from Port Moresby.

Vairata National Park. On the Sogeri Road about 40km from Port Moresby. This visit can be combined with a trip to the Kokoda Trail (see Sports). During the early-morning hours you can occasionally see the famous and beautiful birds of paradise. In this lush rain forest and nature sanctuary there are a number of hiking trails. From Lookout Point on a clear day you can see all the way to Port Moresby. Picnic facilities are available, and it's possible to camp on Sogeri Plateau.

Moitake Crocodile Farm. Only a few miles from town, behind Jackson's Airport. Crocodiles are bred in captivity, and you can watch their feeding on Friday afternoons.

Lae

Botanical Gardens. The gardens were established in 1949 and occupy 130 acres of parkland within walking distance of the town center. Adjacent to the gardens is the War Memorial and resting place for some 3,000 Allied soldiers. Gardens are also a sanctuary for small animals and birds. Extensive collection of orchids and one of the most beautiful spots in the country.

University of Technology. 11km from Lae on Butibum Road. Note the sharp contrast of the university's modern buildings with the Sepik-style coffee shop and restaurant.

SHOPPING. Papua New Guinea art is known throughout the world. Masks and other creative objects carved in the Sepik region are only a sampling of what to look for. There is also a wide range of crafts made by the people in wood, copper, pottery, shell, and basketwork. Look for the work from the Trobriands or Buka. Artifact shops can be found in every center, or they can be bought from the missions or directly from village craftspeople. *Village Arts,* outside Port Moresby, has a few artifact bargains.

There is stringent control on the export of artifacts of national, historic, or cultural significance, so care should be taken when purchasing articles directly from villagers. A visit to the town market in each center is an experience that should not be overlooked. *Koki Market* in Port Moresby is perhaps the best known. There are two markets at Lae: the *Main Market,* south of the air strip, where Morobe and Highlands people sell their produce and handicrafts, and the *Butibum Market,* on Butibum Road, decorated with traditional murals.

Do not expect local people or small shops to cash traveler's checks; plan on having enough currency to get you through each day. If you plan on bargaining with the local people, make certain you have plenty of smaller-denomination currency.

AIRPORT TAX. There is a 10K international departure tax.

Index

General Information

Geographical and Practical Information

Fodor's Travel Guides

U.S. Guides

Alaska
American Cities
The American South
Arizona
Atlantic City & the
  New Jersey Shore
Boston
California
Cape Cod
Carolinas & the
  Georgia Coast
Chesapeake
Chicago
Colorado
Dallas & Fort Worth
Disney World & the
  Orlando Area

The Far West
Florida
Greater Miami,
  Fort Lauderdale,
  Palm Beach
Hawaii
Hawaii *(Great Travel
  Values)*
Houston & Galveston
I-10: California to
  Florida
I-55: Chicago to New
  Orleans
I-75: Michigan to
  Florida
I-80: San Francisco to
  New York

I-95: Maine to Miami
Las Vegas
Los Angeles, Orange
  County, Palm Springs
Maui
New England
New Mexico
New Orleans
New Orleans *(Pocket
  Guide)*
New York City
New York City *(Pocket
  Guide)*
New York State
Pacific North Coast
Philadelphia
Puerto Rico *(Fun in)*

Rockies
San Diego
San Francisco
San Francisco *(Pocket
  Guide)*
Texas
United States of
  America
Virgin Islands
  (U.S. & British)
Virginia
Waikiki
Washington, DC
Williamsburg,
  Jamestown &
  Yorktown

Foreign Guides

Acapulco
Amsterdam
Australia, New Zealand
  & the South Pacific
Austria
The Bahamas
The Bahamas *(Pocket
  Guide)*
Barbados *(Fun in)*
Beijing, Guangzhou &
  Shanghai
Belgium & Luxembourg
Bermuda
Brazil
Britain *(Great Travel
  Values)*
Canada
Canada *(Great Travel
  Values)*
Canada's Maritime
  Provinces
Cancún, Cozumel,
  Mérida, The
  Yucatán
Caribbean
Caribbean *(Great
  Travel Values)*

Central America
Copenhagen,
  Stockholm, Oslo,
  Helsinki, Reykjavik
Eastern Europe
Egypt
Europe
Europe *(Budget)*
Florence & Venice
France
France *(Great Travel
  Values)*
Germany
Germany *(Great Travel
  Values)*
Great Britain
Greece
Holland
Hong Kong & Macau
Hungary
India
Ireland
Israel
Italy
Italy *(Great Travel
  Values)*
Jamaica *(Fun in)*

Japan
Japan *(Great Travel
  Values)*
Jordan & the Holy Land
Kenya
Korea
Lisbon
Loire Valley
London
London *(Pocket Guide)*
London *(Great Travel
  Values)*
Madrid
Mexico
Mexico *(Great Travel
  Values)*
Mexico City & Acapulco
Mexico's Baja & Puerto
  Vallarta, Mazatlán,
  Manzanillo, Copper
  Canyon
Montreal
Munich
New Zealand
North Africa
Paris
Paris *(Pocket Guide)*

People's Republic of
  China
Portugal
Province of Quebec
Rio de Janeiro
The Riviera *(Fun on)*
Rome
St. Martin/St. Maarten
Scandinavia
Scotland
Singapore
South America
South Pacific
Southeast Asia
Soviet Union
Spain
Spain *(Great Travel
  Values)*
Sweden
Switzerland
Sydney
Tokyo
Toronto
Turkey
Vienna
Yugoslavia

Special-Interest Guides

Bed & Breakfast
  Guide: North America
1936…On the
  Continent

Royalty Watching
Selected Hotels of
  Europe

Selected Resorts
  and Hotels of the U.S.
Ski Resorts of North
  America

Views to Dine by
  around the World